PRAISE FOR *THE FIRST TO KNOW*

'Used to hopping between Paris and London, Lida Hujić manages the impossible by delivering a precise study of the cool and *branché* these last twenty years. Fly-on-the-wall observations are finely compiled in this well researched study. Fashion, music, trends, attitudes, brands, consumerism… *The First to Know* dissects all with great attention to detail and convincing analysis at hand. A labour of love sure to become a reference in years to come.'

Jerry Bouthier, DJ (Vivienne Westwood, Kitsuné, Ponystep/BoomBox)

'Usually, historic overviews talking about the changes in human behaviour, activities and beliefs span over long periods of time. This book is different… It talks about the last twenty years: twenty years of desire for new and better; twenty years of establishment denial. Elegantly written by someone who was a participant, a witness and a trailblazer. Highly recommended.'

Sasha Savic, Executive Vice President – Global Managing Director Starcom/MediaVest Group

THE FIRST TO KNOW

How Hipsters and Mavericks
Shape the Zeitgeist

Lida Hujić

To Giles
Many happy returns
Lida
27/2/2014

First published in Great Britain in 2010 by Bubble Publishing
www.bubble-publishing.co.uk

A catalogue record for this book is available from the British Library.

ISBN 978-0-9566258-0-9

Typeset by Liz Dalby Editorial Services
www.lizdalby.co.uk

Printed in Great Britain by MPG Biddles

www.thefirsttoknow.info

To my parents, with love and gratitude

CONTENTS

PART THREE:
THE NOUGHTIES

Acknowledgements

I feel blessed to have had the opportunity in life to be around wonderful people, who have inspired me to write this book and who have also inspired others through their work, perhaps even you the reader. As the story spans over two decades, it would be an impossible challenge to credit everyone I met along the way. You will also notice that some people I talk about in the story are missing from this acknowledgement. For most part, that is simply because I know them well and/or have worked with them on the particular experience I describe. That I acknowledge them in the book is a measure of my admiration.

As for those I equally admire but did probe, I am grateful for their valuable thoughts, observations and for letting me hang out with them. At times, we talked for hours and then I still had follow-up questions and every time, they obliged.

Starting with the Londoners: Alex Carlé, Alexia Somerville, Andrea Gorgerino, Antoni Burakowski, Carri Munden (Mundane), Francesca Forcolini, Gareth Skewis, Garfield Hackett, Hamish Menzies, Harriet Vine, Jerry Bouthier, Lauren Cochrane, Lulu Kennedy, Mandi Lennard, Marjan Pejoski, Mei Hui Liu, Michael Oliveira-Salac, Namalee Bolle, Neil Boorman, Orsola de Castro, Philip Normal, Piers Atkinson, F. K. Ranx, Richard Mortimer, Robb Young, Rosie Wolfenden, Saško (Sasha) Bežovski, Steve Slocombe.

The Parisians and non-Parisians interviewed in Paris: Claude Sabbah, Diane Pernet, Ed (Edouard) Rostand, Gildas Loaëc, Guillaume Le Goff, Guillaume Salmon, Jacques Shu, Karim Ben Geloun, Mr and Mrs KIND, Lio (Lionel) Bensemoun, Maxime Souverain, Michaël (Mika) Huard, Nic Jones, Pierre Hermé, Pirjo Suhonen, Rafael Jiminez, Yan Ceh.

The Bosnians and those who have been involved with Bosnia and Herzegovina in some capacity: Ado (Adnan) Hadžić, Amel Baftić (Bafta), Anthea Norman-Taylor, Boris Šiber (Šibi), Boro Kontić, Brano Jakubović, David Wilson, Dino Mustafić, Dunja Mijatović, Elvir Čelebičić, Gaša, Haris Kulenović, Jasmin Duraković, Martin Bell, Nataša Drakulić, Neven Kulenović, Irma Osim, Samra

Lučkin, Senad Zaimović, Zoran Ćatić and the VIZA talent and production team (with special thanks to Dave Austin).

The following people interviewed are/were affiliated to the brands or institutions cited: Anna Orsini, Antonio Fiengo, Kim (Kimberly) Caroll, Sarah Mower (British Fashion Council), Nick Hughes (Kuoni), Edson Matsuo (Melissa), Brent Hansen, John Dunton-Downer, Jonathan Lewis, Justin Eade, Simon Guild (MTV), Acyde (Nike).

Whether that is help with bits of research, facilitating production or simply chatting to me when I needed to clarify a point, the following people have been generous with their time: Alexandra Derouin, Amanda Johansson, Callum Turner, James Mannox, Jeffrey Reed, Lucile Troquet, Lee McCormack, Masha Mombelli, Matthew Stone, Dr Nada Zečević, Naoki Kameda, Pip Dann-Hansen, Rose (Rosemary) Turner, Tomoko Oishi, Valentina Tiurbini, Zamir Antonio. Dr Glenn Adamson from the V&A gave me feedback on the first draft of the book's proposal.

Thank you to Dunja Mijatović for her input on select sections; Saša Savić for all his useful thoughts; Dr Maria Pini for feedback on the manuscript. Big up to my editorial team: Chris Brocklebank for the first copy edit and Liz Dalby, for her invaluable support, competence, expertise and guidance.

For any unintentional omissions and mistakes in spite of their help, I take responsibility.

On February the 11th 2010, just as I was ready to submit the manuscript for reviews, I got a message saying that Alexander McQueen had passed away. Nothing on the news, confused I texted Leo [Belicha] who immediately texted back with a "what????". Leo hadn't heard. I then tried Michael ('from Blow'), who soon responded "honey yes it's true", by which time the BBC reported it too. McQueen's influence on the community of Hoxtonites is huge. I decided not to change any references to McQueen in the book and to pay him tribute here at the outset. R.I.P. Lee, your legacy lives on.

On April the 8th, the sad news that Malcolm McLaren had lost his battle with cancer was announced. Too fast to live, too young to die, the 'one minute of mayhem' was respected on the day he was put to rest in Highgate Cemetery.

I am enormously grateful to my parents, Mersa and Braco Hujić for all their love and support. Words can never be enough. To them, I dedicate this book.

Photo Acknowledgements

An image speaks a thousand words. This book would not have been the same without photographs. I truly believe that they tell the story as powerfully as the words. Each image is timely. It represents a testament of the events as they unfolded or a stage in the life of the person it portrays. In most cases, the photographers are part of the scene. Thanks to all who helped me collect the pics. Photo credits go as follows:

Omladinski Program poster © Darko Skert
MTV logo and VJ Pip Dann © MTV Networks Europe
MTV/East German Border Guards © Michiel Bakker
Kashpoint Battle of the Boutiques © Jonathan Pearson
Kashpoint Grace Brothers © Paul Morgan
        (photo)/Dominic Harris (montage/graphics)
La Johnson © La Johnson
La Compilation du Baron; André/Vitamin water © colette
Kokon To Zai magazine spread © *Hooligan* magazine
Kokon To Zai backstage © Mila Nesterova
Tatty Devine © Tatty Devine
KIND back stabber © Mr and Mrs KIND
Mandi Lennard © Alistair Allen
Michael Oliveira-Salac © Fats Shariff/Lida Hujić
Blow Off-Schedule Guide © Blow
Superblow and Super Super © Steve Slocombe
Namalee Bolle © Simian Coates
Carri Munden (Mundane) © Tim & Barry
BoomBox © Billa Baldwin
colette inside store and limited edition collaborations © colette
PURE magazine cover © Iko Ouro-Preto
Pierre Hermé boutique and Ispahan © Pierre Hermé
Third Floor Barcelona © Paul Reynolds
All other images © Lida Hujić

Andrew Denton: 'What is it you actually do for a living?'

Malcolm McLaren: '[…] I think, somehow or another, I remain permanently cool.'

Enough Rope, 10th July 2006

Malcolm McLaren (1946–2010)

THE FIRST
TO KNOW

Introduction

SHOREDITCH, APRIL 2009

It was a bright cold day in April, and the clocks were striking nineteen. My chin nuzzled into my breast in an effort to escape the breeze; I am stood by Christ Church Spitalfields waiting for my friend Leo Belicha, stylist extraordinaire and top party promoter.

We're going to a special exhibition by Jean-Charles de Castelbajac, an eminent fashion designer who shows his collections on the most prestigious catwalk: Paris Fashion Week. In this east London 'hood, however, he is known simply as JCDC. He was given this nickname by a faction of the local underground scene who were fascinated by his street art and cartoon-inspired fashion. JCDC found kindred spirits on the scene, and remains a staunch endorser of cutting-edge innovation, despite his status among the fashion elite.

Tonight, 2 April, is the opening night of JCDC's art exhibition ('Triumph of the Sign') staged in an east London warehouse, deliberately off the fashionable track (the aftershow party will be even further off-track, deep in the council-estate land of Dalston, an area on the brink of generating the interest of the cool hunters who follow the arty crowds). The event itself will be low key, but will draw all the significant people solely through word of mouth. The press too will be select, consisting of authentic scene journalists, or so it would appear. All this I am to discover later. Meanwhile, I wait for Leo.

Across the road from me is Spitalfields Market, which has become one of London's 'cool' tourist attractions following the old market's redevelopment in the mid-noughties. At one end is a street sign that reads: 'Tourist information

300m'. To my left is a popular hangout, judging by the number of trendy people congregating around the entrance. It is called Public Life but I cannot remember if that was its name at the turn of the noughties, when my friends and I used to frequent it. We referred to it as 'The Toilet' then because the space really had been a public toilet before being converted into a bar. We went there not because it was à la mode but because it was conveniently located a few steps from a friend's house and was one of the few bars in what was then a dead zone.

This friend lived at 1 Fournier Street, one of the small streets just up the side of Christ Church Spitalfields leading on to the now very fashionable Brick Lane. The old Ten Bells pub is still serving at the corner of Fournier and Commercial Streets but the friend had to move out about six or seven years ago when the property wave struck these shores, resulting in an upsurge in real estate prices. Incidentally, the friend had been doing rather well financially. He was an executive in one of the most successful dotcom companies, for that was the time of the dotcom boom. Financial security was not to last in this sector (the bubble burst shortly after) and it certainly ended before my friend had a chance to seriously think of investments, preferring instead to live life for the moment.

Short-lived though his prosperity had been, it had allowed for a comfortable and exciting lifestyle shaped by innovators and artisans from various creative strands. This part of east London in the early noughties was a self-contained microcosm where you could buy anything – from the most amazing outfits by a new breed of designers to groceries directly from the farmers and producers. The denizens of Shoreditch all lived on the margins of the City, London's financial district, without ever crossing paths with the bankers and lawyers who worked there. In fact, the beginning of this area's gentrification was prompted by the City workers' colossal investments in anything dotcom-related, which was all the rage in venture-capital land at the turn of the millennium.

As I'm lost down Memory Lane, I start taking notes. Before long, a young woman from the crowd outside Public Life approaches me. Nowadays, if you're spotted with a camera in the vicinity of Brick Lane (or apparently even a notebook and pen) you won't be alone for long. Hordes of wannabes sporting up-to-the-minute styles are on the lookout for an opportunity to get snapped by street style scouts, the shots of which are then posted on blogs. A photographer with a professional-looking camera around his neck and accompanied by a crew was stopped four times during the short walk from his parking spot to the boutique where a shoot was taking place. The hopefuls did not know the purpose of his trip but he looked the part and so they desperately wanted to be in the frame. They want to be looked at, indiscriminately. The objective is to get their picture seen anywhere.

This latest wave of street style scouting was inspired by Shoreditch's creative community. It started as a way of capturing its alternative dress sense (looks that were antithetical to homogenised high street and high-fashion styles). Blogging (from 2006) allowed shots to be posted in real time. As with any trend initiated by a handful of mavericks, street style scouting would later become so widespread that there were ultimately more people with cameras on Brick Lane than actual trendies worth snapping. Brick Lane became synonymous with this hip pursuit.

I have a chat with my new acquaintance, Tracy. I talk about the good times I had at 1 Fournier Street. I also moan about how the area has changed so much in such a short time. From a small underground community of 'arty' types and non-conformist entrepreneurs, it has become one of London's most commercialised neighbourhoods. Independent stores, street market stalls and rented homes were snapped up by developers, who saw them as prime real estate. Tracy appears fascinated by the short lesson in this area's recent history (though it feels like ancient history to me as the area is unrecognisable). She sympathises with the plight of the independents. 'Find me on Facebook,' she said, jotting down her contact details, before returning to her friends.

Today, 1 Fournier Street is occupied by Timberland, 'the Boot Company'. The company's card, which I pick up in the store, boasts about the way it combines 'the best of modern innovation' with 'earlier ideals of craftsmanship' as well as the way it creates bespoke retail environments ('a unique fusion of heritage, craftsmanship and regeneration'). From what I can gather, the store has indeed retained the old floorboards and some wood panelling from my friend's former home. There is also some antique cobblers' equipment on display in the window. The problem is that the shop assistant is absolutely clueless. When I enquire about the items on display and their heritage (was it Timberland's own, I wonder), he looks bemused (unlike Tracy, who immediately understood my grievance). He neither knows what the items represent nor what they are called (they turn out to be old shoe lasts). He has no knowledge whatsoever of the craft of shoemaking, either. And that's the difference between the independent designers who revived the mainstream market's interest in crafts (being craftsmen themselves), and 'cool' brands such as Timberland who later adopted them in their advertising communications and shop design. By this time it was all about the look ('bespoke retail environment', trendy-looking shop assistant), no longer about substance.

However, the case of brands such as Timberland that opened shops in Shoreditch (a trend that began significantly in the latter part of the decade), will come at the end of my story. That brands moved into a fashionable area to be fashionable is the inevitable consequence of a decade of an underground movement crossing over into the mainstream. This book will not be a critique of brands shamming authenticity and passing off their creative cues as 'unique fusions of heritage, craftsmanship and regeneration'. My focus will rather be on how and why crafts became hip. Crafts (the revival of which will be symbolised by knitting in this story) were the naffest thing you could possibly imagine in a world of Timberland-wearing punters and a competitive landscape involving brands like Nike. Timberland was one of the staple brands of hip hop fashion. It was 'ghetto fabulous'. This certainly didn't involve crafts (which were 'granny fabulous'), but as 'ghetto fabulous' was wearing out, a new story was needed to revive the brand. The word on the street was that 'craft' was cool.

How does the initiation (or revival) of a trend on a specific underground scene progress to becoming all the rage in the corporate boardroom? And why is it that only select scenes have the power to influence such decision-making processes? For my purposes, London's Shoreditch provides one of the richest ponds for cool fishing, so much so that it became a byword for the wave of hip that defined the noughties. I won't be chasing fads in this tale. I am interested in the processes that trigger transformation: from 'ghetto fabulous' to 'crafts chic' in the case of Timberland, though Timberland is just one among the early-adopter brands that shifted from 'ghetto' to 'crafts' to create a new story that influenced mainstream retail thinking. In turn, mainstream retail is just one industry among others that also adopted crafts thinking in their own ways. This book is not about cool hunting, though. It is about the big picture.

In order to talk about hip in the noughties, I shall begin my story at the turn of the 1990s, when other neighbourhoods were drawing in an earlier wave of underground communities that inspired their contemporary new entrepreneurs. Having found myself in the right place at the right time at three seminal moments in the history of popular culture, I'll take you on three journeys from the underground to the mainstream: the rock 'n' roll movement that brought communism down in the former Yugoslavia; the rise of MTV Europe from a five-person start-up into the greatest empire of 1990s cool; and the spectacular development of London's Shoreditch neighbourhood from a perilous urban dead zone to an ultra-fashionable area initiating global trends in the noughties. I'll use this as a backdrop to describe two decades of European history as seen through the lens of hip, since the dismantling of the Berlin Wall in 1989. By contrasting the 1990s and the noughties, I'll look at how the notion of hip has evolved cyclically to cause a paradigm shift in each decade.

This is the tale of how underground scenes and the maverick businesses that shared their ideals and aesthetic sensibilities together shaped the zeitgeist. My interest is in success stories: the businesses that made a quantum leap (and changed established professional mindsets) as well as the subcultures that inevitably sold out. By using the simple model of crossing over and selling out, I shall explore the trajectory of leading-edge subcultures from underground incubation into the mainstream and their impact on driving societal change (through their adoption by maverick businesses). I shall look at their role as a resource for innovation in brand-led economies and as a positive force in shaping identity politics in an age where consumerism and citizenship have become blurred. (Here, new communication technologies act as catalysts.) Hip cultures are therefore a paradox: they are at the frontier of independent thinking and innovation but, as such, they are also the lifeblood of consumer societies.

As an alternative to the mainstream, hip ideologies have both commercial and social implications. Be prepared for a radical challenge to the marketing mantra that the youth market alone is an indicator of early trends. This book taps directly into a global web of what marketing professionals categorise as 'the notoriously difficult-to-reach' hipsters. Influential but invisible for the most part, they are the ones who opinion leaders listen to, the ones who dictate the trends that mainstream brands get their cool cues from, and the ones who initiate the fashions that mainstream consumers will eventually buy into. Could it be that for the first time in (marketing) history, we have a case of parents being cooler than the kids?

Brace yourself for a fresh critique of the 'celebrity' culture represented by *Big Brother* and driven by crass materialism. (Top marks to readers who spotted my homage to George Orwell's *Nineteen Eighty-Four* at the outset.) More than a mere dismissal, I shall concern myself with the way that vacuous 'celebrity culture' promoted by the likes of *Big Brother* has eroded merit-based values in favour of complacent ignorance in greed-led economic climates. This trend is even more pronounced in former communist countries where *Big Brother* is not just an entertainment format but also – I would argue – a new form of censorship. Could it be that Orwell's totalitarian scenario is becoming a 21st-century reality?

Welcome to the world of the first to know. I hope you enjoy the ride.

PART ONE: HIP

SETTING THE HIP SCENE AND FRAMEWORK

'To be hip is to believe in the possibility of reinvention – to understand oneself as between states, neither one nor the other, without original sin, forever on the road [...] to see, to open one's eyes.'

John Leland, *Hip: The History*

SARAJEVO, FEBRUARY 1987

The communist officials in charge of Radio Sarajevo 2 have finally succumbed to Boro Kontić's proposal to allocate some of this station's dormant airwaves to a new youth-radio concept. Boro, a leading-edge broadcaster on Radio Sarajevo 2, who has a cult Saturday morning show called *Primus*, has been trying to extend the basic premise of his show into something bigger for a couple of years now...

It had been in vain, even though technically there was plenty of airtime available. There was no particular reason why there was a barrier between him and the establishment other than the usual inertia so engrained in a political system that was almost worn out. Radio Sarajevo 2 was the frequency covering the then Yugoslav Republic of Bosnia and Herzegovina. Radio Sarajevo 1 was the only other Bosnian 'republic' broadcaster. The rest were local radio stations (for the city of Sarajevo it was a network called Sarajevo 202). The most important, as far as the communists were concerned, was Radio Sarajevo 1, as it catered for what they considered to be a diversity of subjects and thus there was no need for more. In communist parlance, 'diversity' actually implied conformity. Each of the six former Yugoslav republics had a similar set-up of two national and a series of local radio stations, but it was always the first station that would transmit the shared national broadcasts, including news distributed from a central hub (a local equivalent of news agencies such as Reuters, called Tanjug). By maintaining this structure, the government could control the output of international news as well as spoon-feed its citizens with the 'brotherhood and unity' diets on which the idea of Yugoslavia had been raised.

This is not to say that brotherhood and unity was purely propaganda, which is what most of the world must have thought given the bloody consequences of Yugoslavia's break-up that dominated the news headlines for the first half of the 1990s. There actually *was* a sentiment of national belonging and pride. It is just that there were two different strands: one strand fitted the self-serving communist vision and would eventually result in the formation of the bigoted nationalistic parties that led the country into bloodshed. The other was a truly cosmopolitan vision. Omladinski Program (meaning 'youth programme' or 'youth radio'; the names were used interchangeably), Boro Kontić's new venture that would fill four hours on weekday afternoons (later six hours, plus Saturdays) on Radio Sarajevo 2, was a leading exponent of the latter.

Omladinski Program went live on air on 9 April 1987. Boro Kontić was its visionary editor-in-chief who handpicked a team of reporters that today is often referred to as 'the legendary generation of radio broadcasting'. Omladinski forged connections with other 'youth' radio stations (Radio Študent in Ljubljana, Radio 101 in Zagreb and Radio B92 in Belgrade) that formed Yugoslavia's alternative movement, but it was the voice of Omladinski that was the loudest – simply because it had the largest reach. Its regular listeners were not just in Bosnia and Herzegovina but also in the neighbouring former Yugoslav republics. Omladinski Program was not a Bosnian radio station as such. Its team was multi-ethnic for sure, but that no one was tainted by nationalistic colours was a given. Omladinski was simply a cosmopolitan radio station, and the whole network of youth stations would prove to be the greatest challenge to the communist system that the regime had seen since it came to power after World War Two. It would also form the strongest anti-war movement following the break-up of Yugoslavia.

The battle between Omladinski Program and Radio Sarajevo 2's establishment reflected the dynamic between the alternative and the mainstream in Yugoslavia. The mainstream consisted of the rural population and the semi-urbanites. Urban identity was, above all, defined against that of the semi-urbanites and, though in the minority, urbanites were nevertheless considered the cultural elite. The culture of the semi-urbanites was called *novokomponovana kultura* ('neofolk culture'). This referred to a newly composed hybrid culture that derived from Yugoslavia's authentic and diverse folk tradition (*narodna muzika*), which had mostly been nurtured and preserved by urbanites.

Semi-urbanites began to populate larger Yugoslav cities following the massive migration from villages that occurred post 1945. Despite the move, the semi-urbanites never made any concessions to city life, and maintained close connections to their rural roots. Activities such as going to the theatre, visiting art galleries or even the cinema that are so much a part of city living were virtually non-existent for them. Most frustratingly for city folk, even basic urban rules, such as respecting a code of conduct when using public transport or when in communal buildings, were not just ignored but often deliberately violated. Urbanites felt that their cities were literally colonised by hordes of vulgar semi-urbanites. They derogatorily referred to them as *primitivci* (from the word 'primitive') or *seljaci* ('peasants') – used as a defiant reaction to those infringing upon city life.

Uncultured behaviour was coupled with a narrow-minded, and in most cases bigoted, outlook on life. Semi-urbanites and peasants alike had no interest in cultures other than their own. They also nurtured mythologies by glorifying the historical achievements of their ancestors; this was particularly prominent in Serbia's rural parts. In terms of their media consumption, semi-urbanites and peasants rarely watched television programmes beyond those about their immediate environment. Only occasionally would they watch dramas, humour series or films that were produced for the whole of Yugoslavia.[1] Anything foreign had no relevance.

That type of mentality was also engrained among a significant portion of Yugoslav workers who were 'on a temporary work spell abroad' (known as *gastarbajteri* – from the German word for 'guest worker'). About a million people left Yugoslavia when Comrade Tito decided to open the country's borders in 1962. *Gastarbajteri* represented the wealthier section of the neofolk population. They cared very little for the cultures of the Western countries where they lived. Instead, they concentrated on acquiring material possessions, which often necessitated a lot of day-to-day denial in terms of lifestyle in the guest country. *Gastarbajteri* lived for their annual-leave trips back to Yugoslavia. Showing off cars, flaunting golden chains and 'label' clothes was typical behaviour. Often, they saved money to build a house where they would eventually return to live, thus adding a nouveau-riche flavour to Yugoslav cities. A favoured business was opening up establishments – usually snack bars that also served alcohol (often called *birtija* or *kafana*) – where neofolk ruled.

This lack of interest in the other came to symbolise all that was wrong with communism. The bulk of regime officials – particularly those in the mid-range echelons – were considered *seljaci* by the urbanites. An unscrupulous bunch who still lived in 'communist time', they hindered progress and, by extension, served the interests of the ruling class. The concept of 'communist time' was a general system for maintaining the status quo, which made all the communist countries backward in terms of access to trends, and consequently isolated them from progress. Some pop-culture tendencies arrived late, others never. By the time anything to do with style had travelled from the capitalist world, past the Iron Curtain and into the East, it would often be devoid of its original meaning and past its sell-by date. This is why unsuspecting Westerners – an exotic breed in short supply in Yugoslavia – would often get an overwhelming amount of attention from the indigenous population. Effectively, a foreigner provided a much-cherished and immediate link to the outside world.

Though an open country, Yugoslavia too was infected by the communist-time syndrome. Few people spoke foreign languages and even fewer felt the need to travel abroad. Even among the elite – those working in high-ranking positions for the government or as company directors – there was rarely a desire for that worldly connection. Only a select few and their families from the elite circle were interested in going abroad – even though foreign travel was, in theory, not just the preserve of the wealthy. It was, rather, the cultural realm of those who felt the need to broaden their horizons and who would often sacrifice material possessions in order to travel, especially in the 1980s when inflation was spiralling and devaluing the local currency on a daily basis. Some people could never afford it, but nevertheless had the *desire* to feel that connection. Spiritually at least, they were part of this cosmopolitan segment. For this cosmopolitan minority, *Zapad* (the West, the antithesis of communist Eastern Europe) was the dream, and the right to belong to it had been 'stolen' by the regime, as one-time Czechoslovakian dissident writer Milan Kundera eloquently put it.[2] That open-minded faction was Yugoslavia's urbanite population.

In contrast to neofolk culture, the urbanites aspired to *Zapad* or *Evropa* (Europe), which had the same connotation as *Zapad*. Keeping up with Europe was the greatest sign of emancipation in Yugoslavia and communist countries in general. The West was seen as everything that the East was not. In contrast to the mind-numbing regime of technocratic inefficiency, the West was streamlined and efficient. In contrast to dogmatic thinking, the West had freedom and democracy. In contrast to utilitarianism, the West was about cultural excellence and trend leadership (though the latter served as much as a source of styles to ape for the *gastarbajteri* as it did as a source of inspiration for the local avant-garde).

The urbanites and semi-urbanites were, above all, publicly differentiated by musical tastes. Semi-urbanites were drawn to *novokomponovana* (neofolk) music, which was a hybrid, somewhere between a bastardised version of traditional folk and pop music. Neofolk was by far the top-selling music genre. The rest, who defined themselves against neofolk, enjoyed a very diverse music scene ranging from classical to jazz, a rich variety of folk traditions, and various genres of popular music. In a country of 22 million people with a decent-sized music industry, 'the rest' could manage to live well from selling records and playing live.

The soundtrack to urban life however, was rock 'n' roll, and this had the biggest ideological impact. Rock 'n' roll represented an international culture that defined itself against the parochialism of neofolk. Semi-urbanites and peasants associated the explicitly English-language code of rock culture with the new, the unknown, the different and the alien. For this reason, rock culture provoked openly antagonistic reactions among its neofolk opponents, especially the younger peasants. A move to the city for the purposes of education could change their tastes over time in that they would become slightly more accustomed to rock sensibilities. But even so, this would be in favour of the most mainstream local rock, not international acts.[3]

Unlike in the Eastern Bloc countries, where rock was truly an insurgent movement, Yugoslavia had a vibrant mainstream rock scene, accompanied by various sub-genres. Bands came from cities from all over Yugoslavia, with Belgrade (the capital of Yugoslavia) and Zagreb (the second-largest city) being the central hubs in terms of the concentration of music production and media. Even so, Yugoslavia's most successful rock band, Bijelo Dugme (White Button), was actually from Sarajevo. This band was part of the 1970s wave of Yugoslav rockers influenced by their Anglo-American contemporaries. These rockers were born in the 1950s and provided the generational bridge between the baby boomers – whose rites of urban passage involved the sounds of San Remo and Elvis before upgrading their *omladina* status to 'adult', meaning that they got jobs, started families and stopped 'rebelling', just as The Beatles and The Rolling Stones were emerging – and their offspring, the Omladinski Program Generation (those who could see through the hypocrisy of communist leaders and more importantly rebel against such a system).[4]

At the end of 1984, Bijelo Dugme released a groundbreaking album that fused elements of folk with rock ('Kosovka Djevojka'). This partly explained why they crossed over so significantly into the 1980s mainstream. Those folk elements made rock more palatable to the young peasants. At the same time, this fusion would kickstart the trend of local rock musicians' fascination with Yugoslavia's diverse folk tradition. From rock albums, the frontman of Bijelo Dugme, Goran Bregović, would start composing folk-influenced music for films. Romany (or 'gypsy') music was his particular fascination, something that would launch his future international and critically acclaimed musical career as a composer of a genre that is often called 'Balkan beat'. The first unveiling of Bregović's 'sound' to the world would be via Emir Kusturica's film *Time of the Gypsies* (1988). An iconic scene from the film features *Đurđevdan* (*Erdelezi* in Romany), both a Slavic Christian and Romany holiday, reworked as a soundtrack for Emir's film as well as a rock anthem fusing folk elements, as a track from Bijelo Dugme's album 'Ćiribiribela' (1988).

Other than being the home city of Bijelo Dugme, Sarajevo also experienced a period of cultural renaissance. Building on the positive energy of the 1984 Winter Olympic Games – a result of Sarajevo's own multicultural spirit as much as the great, albeit ephemeral, experience of being at the epicentre of the world – the city grew into a hub of cultural excellence. In the early 1980s, a whole new scene developed there, influenced by punk's DIY attitude. This would grow organically and create a movement that would not just cross over into Yugoslavia's mainstream, but would also produce internationally revered artefacts. This movement came to be known as the 'New Primitivs'. It was a local version of a subculture with its own set of ideals and aesthetics. It was rock 'n' roll in attitude and cosmopolitan in orientation. By that time, the spirit of rock was encapsulated in punk and new wave, and had not bypassed Yugoslavia. Most notable were the Belgrade and Zagreb scenes, whose identities were not Serbian or Croatian but rather defined by their new sounds, just as people would later refer to 'Manchester' or the 'Bristol Sound' in the UK. In fact, the British music paper *New Musical Express* once praised Akademija – the focal Belgrade venue for the new wave of alternative culture in the early 1980s – as being on a par with any hip UK venue.[5]

It was no coincidence that the largest organic subcultural movement came out of cosmopolitan Sarajevo. The New Primitivs built on a European tradition where another type of *kafana* (coffee house), different to the ones opened up by the *gastarbajteri*, had been central to the fostering of new thinking. As the story goes, the first-ever *kafana* in Europe (before even Paris or Vienna) opened in Sarajevo in 1534.[6] From then on, the coffee-house environment acted as a place for exchanging ideas and meeting the similar-minded. Fast-forward a few centuries to the 1970s, and the first license was issued for a new type of *kafana*, now called a *kafić* (officially listed in administrative books as 'caffe bar'). Up until then, the main night-time hangouts had been either *bife* (from the word 'buffet' – but it came to mean any venue with music) or disco clubs. The *kafić* became a symbol of urban culture and the urban population's orientation towards Western values. It was a venue that opened at night (but it could also work by day) with select rock music played on the latest technological equipment and with attention to interior design. Each element distinguished it from the uniform communist venues. The *kafić* was elitist, attracting a select crowd, or *krema* (from the French *crème de la crème*).

One of Sarajevo's first iconic *kafić* venues was Davor, opened in 1977. It was owned by the late Davorin Popović Pimpek, another legend from Sarajevo's baby-boomer rock scene and the lead singer of the band Indeksi. Davor was famously decorated by the designer of Bijelo Dugme's 1970s record sleeves (I stress the era because in the 1980s, Dugme's sleeves would be designed by a gifted young Sarajevan graphic studio at the heart of the New Primitivs called Trio), who created wallpaper made out of the band's fan letters. Over that, paintings by the famous Bosnian painter Mersad Berber were hung. The choice of music was exquisite. It attracted the avant-garde. The culture of going to the *kafić* extended into the 1980s, when select venues acted as subcultural hubs for the next wave. They harboured Sarajevo's 1980s underground scene, which took shape as the New Primitivs. The *kafić* concept also spread across the former Yugoslavia and covered all music genres. (Still, a rock fan would never go to a neofolk *kafić* and vice versa. That was simply inconceivable.)

The New Primitivs formed a network of interconnected scenes that fully matured in the period 1984–1986. First, there was a group of comics calling themselves *Top Lista Nadrealista* (Hit List of Surrealists), who were Yugoslavia's answer to the Monty Python gang, and every bit as sharp. They had their first break on Boro Kontić's *Primus* show. They went on to do a number of TV series and became hugely popular across Yugoslavia as well as the Yugoslav diaspora. Second, there were a number of bands, most notably Zabranjeno Pušenje (No

Smoking) and Plavi Orkestar (Blue Orchestra). The latter emerged from the New Primitivs but went on to become a phenomenon in their own right. With their distinct soft-rock sound, they were the only rock band that managed to achieve mega-success on a scale that previously only Bijelo Dugme had managed in terms of record sales, stadium gigs and merchandising. Finally, Sarajevo's Academy for Film [and Theatre] Studies, Akademija, produced an exceptionally talented generation of actors and directors. A spoof performance of an audition for actors called *Audicija* (The Audition), which started in the basement of Akademija and grew into a hugely successful play (and popular VHS release), catapulted a class of students and their teacher – who was 'auditioning' them – to cult fame. As for film and theatre directors from this era (who were teachers rather than students at Akademija), they notably included Ademir Kenović, Miroslav Ćiro Mandić, Haris Pašović and, last but not least, Emir Kusturica whose Palme d'Or in 1985 (for the film *When Father was Away on Business*) confirmed what Sarajevo's scene intuitively felt: it was indeed on a par with any international equivalent.

And then along came Omladinski Program. Essentially pirate radio broadcast on national airwaves, Omladinski broke down all boundaries of broadcasting known thus far to become a trend-leader and the voice of a new generation. The first rule broken was over how Boro recruited his team. During communism, it had gone without saying that the children of the elite had a privileged position: a place at a chosen university, an automatic qualification for a grant, a secure job afterwards, a flat (allocated by the State – workers could wait a lifetime to get one, or anything else for that matter). Favouritism was so engrained in the system that it was accepted that, should you want to improve your lot in life, you needed a connection rather than relying on merit. This level of privilege was encapsulated in the term *štela*.

Shockingly, to join Omladinski, you did not need *štela*. Instead, Boro scouted for people who had passion and attitude, as he felt that there must be a new generation of young people out there of 'exceptional quality'. 'Back in those days, to be a journalist was a vocation. You couldn't be a journalist unless you wanted to do something good, to change things,' he later said. Curiosity and rock 'n' roll were the basic common denominators. Candidates also needed to have a good general knowledge coupled with a specialised area of interest, preferably bordering on obsession. Some people were fanatic about sports or politics (having almost encyclopaedic knowledge) while others were into rockabilly or river-water fishing, or else they knew everything that there was to know as well as everything that needn't necessarily be known about lead guitarists in rock bands. On the basis of what stood out at auditions, the programming strategy took shape over time and so did the core team.

A lot of Western literature documenting the anti-communist movements that led to the system's demise refers to them in terms of underground resistance, with the main focus being political activism. It was not quite like that, at least not for the Omladinski Program Generation in Yugoslavia. To begin with, Omladinski was an alternative network within the system rather than underground. But part of what Omladinski represented was indeed political challenge. Politics was the battle arena where Omladinski hit the communist hierarchy really hard, because that was the only language that the officials understood. The engrained belief was that by controlling political information (which was synonymous with news output) the government controlled the masses and protected their interests.

Omladinski was a national pioneer of free speech. It openly criticised the system, which was unprecedented, and denounced all its deficiencies by introducing the concept of critical journalism. It also opened up its airwaves to listeners. 'Calling in' became one of its trademarks. Listeners wholeheartedly embraced the possibility of voicing their opinions and participating in debate on any subject, not just overtly political ones. Specifically, there was a daily topical show called *Pitanje Dana* (question of the day) consisting solely of a 30-minute edit of uncensored listener-talk. The authorities did not quite know how to deal with this other than to regularly summon the 'man in charge' (ie Boro) *na raport*, which meant to 'report back' to the disciplinary commission and explain why such-and-such a presenter had behaved in a defamatory fashion, as well as offering repentance and apologies. If anything was deemed particularly outrageous, the perpetrator (the presenter) would be suspended for a period. Boro went *na raport* almost on a daily basis to the point of ridicule.

But politics was just one strand of Omladinski. Its appeal was its innovative format and attitude. It went out live, with pre-recorded reports never exceeding three or four minutes. The programming scheme was regularly refreshed, but for most of Omladinski's duration, the schedule ran something like this: the first couple of hours of the day were the main weekly topical slots comprising sports, society, politics, Europe (connection with the West) and offbeat stuff; the next hour was split between the imposed 30-minute news and *Pitanje Dana*; the 5pm slot was the hour reserved for the most prominent characters that entertained the nation with their breed of silliness; and the latter parts of the airtime were split between contact programmes and music playlists, such as the rockabilly show (with Edo Kukavica) or the show dedicated to guitar heroes (with the Lubovac brothers).

Omladinski produced a generation of talent, who all made a mark in their own fields once it ceased to exist. Those who still live in Sarajevo today are market leaders. They include Senad Hadžifejzović, the first presenter on Omladinski, now Bosnia's most respected TV news anchor. Senad Pećanin is the voice of the independent press and owns the magazines *Dani* and *Gracija*. Senad Zaimović, who experimented with the first notions of advertising and marketing in communism, now owns an award-winning communication agency (co-owned with two out of the three graphic designers from the aforementioned Trio). Internationally, Saša Savić, in spite of years of spreading propaganda for his Fishing Democratic Party, whose anthem included industrial (Laibach) and hip hop (Tone Loc) beats, sadly never became Fishing Minister. He had to settle for being a big fish in the corporate pond. He is an executive vice-president global managing director within the Starcom MediaVest Group in New York, part of Publicis Groupe. Aleksandar (Saša) Hemon is a critically acclaimed novelist, now also based in the States. And that is just the Senads and the Sašas.

I joined Omladinski Program in June 1987, the summer before I started university at the tender age of 17. My USP was my unconventional upbringing. I grew up in Montmartre in Paris but unlike other children of *gastarbajteri*, I was raised in a part Bohemian, part populist milieu. My father left Yugoslavia to study journalism at the Sorbonne while also earning money as an artist. My childhood reference points were icons ranging from Muhammad Ali to Salvador Dalí, whom Dad had the privilege of socialising with. From Dad, I acquired a go-getting attitude. From Mum, I got my sense of individual style, something that made me stand out in Yugoslavia for all the 'communist time' reasons. This sense of individual style continues to exert a strong influence on people's perceptions of me to this day. I spoke fluent French and regularly travelled to Paris once we moved back to Yugoslavia in the 1980s. My parents were keener to invest in me keeping up my Parisian accent than in material goods. All of this meant that I had the most immediate connection with the West. Boro thought I should host *Evropa*, which became the Thursday topical show. He also thought that I was bonkers, so I was given the 5pm slot. I created a contact programme for women only where we shared relationship-related issues. Occasionally, it was plain silly, introducing risqué topics but always handled in an elegant fashion ('I caught my boyfriend with my dog. Who should I leave, the boyfriend or the dog?'). This show was called *Sandy* and it was the highest rated programme on Radio Sarajevo 2.

The ambivalent tone of *Sandy* echoed the overall attitude of Omladinski Program. We all had an ironic sense of humour. Listeners never knew for sure whether we were serious or joking and we made no attempt to differentiate between what was real and what was satire. Occasionally, it got us into trouble. We were also often accused of being arrogant. In hindsight, we probably were, but Omladinski would not have been the same without the authentic belief in our cause that came with it. For example, the offbeat Friday team – Zrinka Bralo, one of the most committed presenters whom we all fondly called *Majka* (Mother), together with Savić, Hemon and co. – once fabricated a story about a young boy brought up in the mountains by wolves. The show was pre-recorded but it was played out as if it were live so that no one suspected anything. As usual, there followed random callers reacting to the story as well as 'eyewitness testimonials' – all of them actors. It was just for a laugh but to our astonishment as well as amusement, an established weekly magazine picked up on it. They wanted an exclusive. Delighted to oblige, the team gave them further 'insight' and let them publish a large spread of complete nonsense only to then admit live on air that the whole incident was phony. The journalists were outraged and demanded disciplinary action. The team was suspended for a while. Needless to say, this only boosted their kudos.

Another time, there was an incident following a scoop acquired by the two most high-profile political journalists, Mladen Bilić (who went on to work for the BBC in London) and Neven Anđelić (also based in London, and who continues to work in the international political arena). They hyped an exclusive interview in the run-up to the presidential elections in Yugoslavia with the two candidates for the top job. The guests gave their honest answers to all the questions that were put to them about their views on the future of the country. It is just that they were not the real election candidates whom everyone had expected and had no reason to doubt: they were simply two namesake pensioners from the phone book, who went along with the joke.

What linked all the diverse programmes on Omladinski into a seamless flow was the station's strong sense of identity. The programme came before the individual, even though the individual personalities were what made the programme. Omladinski Program also became the first branded station in Yugoslavia. We paid meticulous attention to jingles, both in the way they were produced and their timing live on air. For example, the 30-minute show about guitar heroes took all night to produce because all the jingles were synchronised with the guitar riffs. And because every week there was a different guitar hero, the Lubovac brothers created different jingles. They were two main types of jingles: those that promoted Omladinski Program, and the jingles created from vox pops. These were snippets of listeners who had called in, cut from their original context and edited into the live broadcast by the sound engineers as replicas of presenter-talk. That was very funny. One listener, in particular, provided a rich source of catchphrases. Apparently he became a bit of a star among his peer group; his friends even started to call him 'Jingle'.

Last but not least, there was the music. Though focused on talk, all the shows had a strong musical identity. The main sound was rock 'n' roll and it had to be in English. However, we strived to promote new sounds, which meant a focus on emerging music genres, such as house, rap, indie rock and some local alternative musicians. We never played Michael Jackson nor did we play local mainstream rock. For a while, I was dating Saša Losić, the frontman of Plavi Orkestar, but I never played any of their music (even though they were hugely successful) for it did not fit my playlist. *Evropa* was (obviously!) about Western music. I was keen to promote alternative music that was not just Anglo-American. For example, I pushed French independent music labels New Rose and Bondage Records really hard. I even befriended the latter's founder, Marsu, and we are still in touch. *Sandy* was very 'Motown'. Saša did not mind. If anything he found my dedication to Omladinski (read the extreme sense of elitism that the Omladinski team cultivated) amusing.

When Omladinski became 'big' and we finally came to terms with the fact that we weren't in a bubble, we started to collaborate with select 'mainstream' bands on tour, including Plavi Orkestar. In spite of these 'concessions', Omladinski remained loyal to its ambition of being part of a cosmopolitan community. Such was our dedication to bringing the best new sounds that our guys would drive all the way to Germany over the weekend to buy records and come back in time to play them fresh on Monday. The money for food and sleep, supplied by Radio Sarajevo 2, they spent on foreign booze and then had to beg their way back home by flashing their journalist passes.

Once Omladinski started to spread its message (purely by word of mouth as there was no concept of on-air cross-promotion or advertising – in fact, Omladinski would be the first to introduce advertising as a form of funding the network), there was no way of stopping the wave of change. Omladinski demonstrated the possibility of an alternative lifestyle, which felt real for the first time. This had less to do with its alternative political stance and more to do with everything else on the network that was not politics. Omladinski's mission was, above all, to broaden horizons and facilitate debate. I guess that could be called democracy but it was also about having gratuitous fun.

Omladinski was a counterculture. It promoted rock 'n' roll as a way of life and recruited fans who shared the same ideals. It harboured a cosmopolitan community of citizens whose set of values represented progress in contrast to the self-serving regime of compliant poltroons. And because all of that was 'outside' politics, it slipped through the net. Beyond political denouncement, the hierarchy within the radio station whose remit was to protect the status quo had no resources to deal with what they clearly perceived as the enemy within. In the end, they capitulated. If you can't beat 'em, join 'em. Boro even eventually became the controller of Radio Sarajevo 2. With the arrival of our new generation of broadcasters and the way we challenged the status quo, it looked like the long-suppressed dream of being connected to the West might become a reality. It proved not to be, but while it lasted, it was not just a dream; it was very real for all of us who made the programme and for the fans, who felt the programme was their own. Browsing through the blogs that still remember us fondly is quite humbling:

'They were the best FM station in the Balkans. It was impossible to imagine afternoons without Zoka's [Stevanović] hysterics on Mondays, Saša's [Savić] brainstorms [and] female issues with Lida [yours truly]…'

'From 1987 until the aggression on Bosnia and Herzegovina there was a team, led by Boro Kontić, rumoured to have made the best radio ever to be broadcast across the former Yugoslavia…'

'They were serious and playful at the same time. They had knowledge, they had ambition but, above all, they had guts…'

Omladinski Program will forever remain the soundtrack to a happy period in the lives of those for whom the abrupt silence on 98.9 MHz in April 1992 marked the end of an era.

LONDON, FEBRUARY 1987

A team of five are sharing a room in Conduit Street in central London. Two IBM desktop computers take up most of the tiny space. The walls are decorated with portraits of tribal chiefs posing pompously in their leopard skins. In one way, there's nothing strange about this, as we're in the High Commission of Sierra Leone – but the room is being rented by MTV (Music Television). Welcome to the headquarters of the new venture set up to bring one single channel to the European youth!

This set-up is a far cry from the grand Broadway offices of MTV USA in New York City. Launched in 1981 and already a triumph, MTV is being hailed as 'the third major breakthrough' in music broadcasting in the United States, the first being Billboard's Top 100 chart in 1955 and the second the advent of 'freeform' radio with rock and album-based playlists at KMPX, San Francisco, in 1967. A 'corporate innovation of major proportions and psychodemographic success', MTV USA established itself as a leading force in the American music and media landscape.[7] Whatever people's thoughts on MTV, few disputed its impact on popular culture. MTV was credited with resurrecting the struggling record industry after its 'great depression' in 1979, launching the careers of major acts from Duran Duran to Madonna, revolutionising the film, television and advertising industries and heavily influencing style and fashion.

Despite the success of MTV USA, MTV's debut in Europe was viewed sceptically. There were massive barriers to market entry. First, there was the issue of how to generate advertising revenue from across different markets. A handful of advertisers (Levi's, Coca-Cola) did sign up before MTV went on air, but that wasn't enough to get the network running.[8] The idea of MTV – a brand that would stand for 'youth, jeans and rock 'n' roll' – was sexy in theory. In practice, television advertising in Europe was exclusively national. Enter MTV, a channel instantly beamed across borders, wanting to convince potential advertisers that the future was all about developing economies of scale. This was easier said than done, as MTV's two-strong advertising sales team quickly realised.

The second barrier was distribution. Satellite television in Europe was in its infancy while cable television was unevenly distributed across the continent. Often, these technologies were used as a means of replacing TV aerials to capture terrestrial programmes rather than as a source of multi-channel TV. Satellite television was a novelty and MTV was part of this new wave. There was a lot of work to be done in conjunction with satellite and cable operators to get viewers to start subscribing. This involved changing mindsets. Television was a service, not a commodity. Why would people pay for more channels? And what *was* satellite television, anyway? One of the main issues that the new pay-TV operators were grappling with was how to explain to viewers what a TV decoder was. Back then, knowing how to operate a video recorder meant you were at the cutting edge of technology. For many, the TV decoder was akin to science fiction.

The final barrier was overcoming the challenge of creating a channel for a culturally and linguistically diverse market. The Eurovision Song Contest was the nearest thing Europeans had ever had to a mass live-music broadcast, but this was no model for MTV. Eurovision aside, all other attempts had failed: the competing pan-European television music channels (the music video programme on Rupert Murdoch's Sky and 10 hours of *Music Box* on Richard Branson's Super Channel) had both proved unsuccessful. The likelihood of a pan-European public service channel was equally remote, given the spectacular failure of the European Community's initial attempts with the Eurikon and Europa channels. Strangely enough, it took an American-owned network to finally achieve what 'Europe' could not. Not only did MTV invent a solution to the perennial problem of how to generate revenue on satellite/cable TV in Europe, it also became the most successful attempt at European unification since the Middle Ages, albeit virtual. MTV would not just change the music and television landscapes forever. Being at the frontier of cultural trends and, in its own way, even challenging identity politics, MTV became the voice of a generation who wholeheartedly embraced it.

After two failed launch dates, MTV Europe finally went live on 1 August 1987. Excitement among the team was tinged with a sense of relief. Elton John symbolically switched the channel on by igniting a stick of dynamite at the official launch party in Amsterdam. 'Money for Nothing' by Dire Straits (starting in falsetto with 'I want my MTV') was the first video played. Brent Hansen, then the news producer, collected as much footage of the launch as possible before flying directly back to London and entering an edit suite. While preparing the feature for broadcast the following day, Hansen pondered this frenetic schedule, later joking that he'd feared that staff might burn out and lead to MTV's premature demise.

The number of people who actually got to see these highlights will forever remain a mystery, as the first significant audience figures for MTV were not published until the end of the year. At the year's end, MTV was available in nine countries and just over two million homes. MTV's largest market was the Netherlands, with just over a million households tuning in. The smallest market was France, reaching just under 5,000 homes. No one could have anticipated at this stage that by 1995 – the golden year of MTV Europe – the channel would reach over 60 million homes in 37 countries. Nor could Brent Hansen – a New Zealander who applied for a job at MTV to support his trip to London – have imagined the brilliant career ahead of him: not only would he survive the challenges of fast-paced production at MTV but he would also live to become its head honcho. After a series of promotions, Hansen was appointed President and Chief Executive Officer at MTV Networks Europe (1996), the umbrella company of the multiple brand channels that MTV's network expanded into. In 2003, he became the President, Creative Director and Editor-in-Chief of MTV Networks International. He would hold this latter position until 2006 when he stepped down, leaving behind a multi-channel network that reached approximately 120 million viewers and employed approximately 1,200 people.

I first saw MTV around 1989, when a satellite dish illegally erected on our block of flats in Sarajevo brought foreign multi-channel television into my life. From the moment I saw it I was fascinated by MTV; it became the background to my life when I switched it on every single morning. I watched so devotedly that I sussed the playlist and can recall even today the broadcast sequence: MTV clock on the hour telling Central European time, followed by MTV News bulletin, followed by a couple of videos, followed by an advert break. I can still recite with equal zeal the lyrics to Madonna's 'Vogue' and the tagline for Vidal Sassoon's Wash & Go ('Take two bottles into the shower? Not me!'). Even if I had wanted to, I could not have bought that new brand of two-in-one shampoo and conditioner or any other Western product (bar Coke) in Yugoslavia. Instead, as someone involved in media myself, I enjoyed watching the visual standard of production of everything on MTV, including the ads. MTV was simply mesmerising.

MTV perfectly echoed the aspirations of young Eastern Europeans. By combining the two most powerful symbols of emancipation – the West and rock 'n' roll – into one, it effectively embodied everything that commanded our respect, including first-hand access to information about the latest trends. More importantly, we witnessed all of this in real time. The days of backward communist time were truly numbered. Unwittingly, MTV became our urban cultural reference library and the ultimate symbol of cool, a feeling that was even stronger in the Eastern Bloc countries than in Yugoslavia. We could travel freely, but the rest of our communist brethren were literally cut off from the world. Up until then, the only access to Western artefacts, including records, had been through bootleg markets.

Fashion and style were of particular interest to me. The chameleon-like styles of Madonna made her my ultimate style icon. Her look changed with every new video. The style of the female 'video jockeys' (or 'VJs', a term coined by MTV that later entered the Oxford English Dictionary) was also a barometer of cool. Daily I checked what VJs Kristiane, Rebecca or Pip were wearing. Pip's style was my favourite: she was a bleached blonde in a black-and-white houndstooth jacket, with brightly coloured lapels and matching pockets with little shells sewn on them – utterly fabulous! Later, Pip was to become one of my dearest friends and I would inherit the outfits I once coveted – including the houndstooth jacket, created by a Soho-based label called Idol. Alas, I never inherited Madonna's clothes, but in a twist of fate many years later, I became friends with a fashion designer called Ashish, and an enthusiastic wearer of his creations. Ashish went on to become one of the hottest names on London Fashion Week and Madonna began ordering custom-made clothes from him for her Confessions on the Dance Floor Tour in 2006. Having once devoured Madonna's videos on MTV as a style-hungry girl trapped behind the Iron Curtain, I ended up wearing clothes Madonna would later be seen in.

The key meeting that set me on my journey from backward communist time towards ahead-of-even-Madonna time was my television interview with MTV VJ Paul King. My success on Omladinski Program had opened the door to television on the newly launched TV station Sa3. Again, I hosted various shows but my speciality was to evoke the idea of a connection to the rest of Europe. This was a big hit because no one had ever interviewed foreigners on a regular basis before, let alone bona fide rock stars. In the dying days of communism, that foreign connection was still a big thing. A magazine had published a list a 57 high-profile people whose phones were bugged by the Ministry of Internal Affairs. My name was on that list. The rest were people of my parents' generation. I remember my mum being very edgy about that article, given that the Ministry never officially denied the existence of the list. I found out only recently who was behind that headline, having completely forgotten about the whole incident. I'll return to it the final chapter.

When I interviewed Paul, I had already established myself on radio and television as an interviewer of Westerners, but the buzz generated by Paul's visit among viewers and colleagues was unprecedented; kids waited outside the building to get his autograph after my live show. This hadn't happened with any other guest. My colleagues were as excited, organising a dinner and panicking when they found out that Paul was vegetarian. No one was vegetarian back in those communist days, so the restaurant prepared special food (look at us, we can do vegetarian, we can do anything like the rest of Europe!). Ivan Stojanović, the production director of Sa3, panicked too but for a different reason. He only recently told me that he lost sleep during Paul's visit to Sarajevo for fear of anything happening to him and us lacking insurance resources. Personal insurance just didn't exist as a concept. In short, Paul was our ultimate guest because he represented MTV.

Paul came, he saw and he conquered – or perhaps it was the other way around. We fell in love and that's how I ended up in London. I never had time, then, to consider the impact that this encounter had outside my private life; after I left home, I couldn't return because of the escalating conflict following the break-up of Yugoslavia. It was only after that horrendous episode that I realised how public my relationship had actually been. I was the local girl who conquered the heart of the boy from MTV. It was so big a deal that when I moved to London (and was obviously no longer on live TV or radio) a government minister called my mum to ask if the rumours were true. In retrospect, that fuss explained why so many people, including those who vaguely knew me, would drop my name in conversation. Every time I met someone from the former Yugoslavia, they would always send me regards from someone else (most of the time I was convinced I'd never met that 'someone else'). One guy, a make-up artist from Zagreb whom I briefly met in Sarajevo, sent his regards via a marketing manager from Austria who happened to work for a chewing gum brand that sponsored Paul's visit to Budapest, where I accompanied him. 'I believe we have a mutual friend,' said this complete stranger (the Austrian marketing manager). 'Do we?!' I was astounded, but when I eventually remembered whom she was talking about, then yes, I guessed we did.

That trip to Budapest in 1994 was in itself a testament to MTV's power in Eastern Europe at the time. This was, in fact, a highly publicised state visit where Paul and his first lady met the then Hungarian Minister of Culture, Fodor Gábor, and his first lady. Gábor had been in an anti-establishment punk band, equivalent to heresy under the regime. His appointment following the collapse of the communist system was a sign of progress, and MTV was inextricably connected to that trajectory. Once, rock had been seen as capitalist propaganda, corrupting youth. Now it was a sign that those times of oppression were truly over. It was the same story across Eastern Europe. I travelled with Paul to Poland, Russia and reunified Germany (many a time), where the same enthusiasm for MTV was replicated, not just among the ruling classes but also among the fans. In fact, on a Polish trip in 1991, the car Paul and I were being driven in was mobbed. Security was utterly unprepared for that kind of near-hysterical fan reaction and so were we. It was scary. I felt I was sat next to Paul McCartney circa 1964, not Paul King in the 1990s.

When I first met MTV's team in London, they were a compact community. MTV's production side was located in rented facilities in Hawley Crescent, Camden Town, known for its street markets. The production office was a friendly place where MTV staff and their friends and guests congregated on the sofa, either waiting to be interviewed or to go out. The studio was next door. I remember being surprised at how small and unsophisticated it was. It was roughly the same size as our studio at TV Sa3 – and we'd had had the smallest studio in the TV building. MTV's management was located in nearby Mandela Street, but there was little hierarchical division between the two (and what there was wasn't rigid, especially on the programming side). It didn't matter that Brent Hansen was Head of Programming – if he was a fan of a band that popped into MTV, he would interview them. MTV was about music, about breaking boundaries and about the cosmopolitan idea of a united Europe. That vision drove the network and everyone did their utmost to make the best programmes. It was the hub for cutting-edge creatives, underground scenes and musicians. It was open house. You could drop your demos and videos off and the right people would deal with them. There was little division between work and play. People at MTV worked and socialised together. We went to lots of gigs, parties and dinners.

It is difficult to pinpoint exactly when MTV slid towards becoming corporate. In reference to the burgeoning corporate climate at the company, Tom Freston, one of the early team at MTV USA, later president of entertainment at MTV Networks, said, 'We took the soul out of the channel.'[9] Freston was specifically referring to personnel changes (in 1987) resulting from Viacom's determination to recoup its heavy cost of acquiring MTV USA. It was in this process that Freston was appointed an executive. When MTV USA 'lost its soul', it was almost as if its maverick spirit flew over to Europe: MTV Europe was launched as a start-up in the same year as MTV USA definitively ceased to be. It was the turn of MTV Europe to grow and grow.

MTV's corporate transformation would not immediately kick in when Viacom extended its initial 25 per cent share into a full takeover (from media mogul Robert Maxwell holding 50 per cent and British Telecom holding 25 per cent) in 1991. MTV's financial future was still uncertain then – they were still experimenting with the concept of a pan-European music channel. The real impact of Viacom's ownership would not be properly felt until around 1993. Three major events that year triggered the change in professional mentality at MTV: they broke even, becoming Europe's fastest growing satellite channel; their first true competitor, VIVA, launched in Germany in December (its impact would be felt immediately and for the remaining duration of MTV's phase as a pan-European channel); and they moved premises.

This symbolic change involved MTV moving from the rented studio to the TV-am studio, a large professional space previously occupied by one of the UK's main terrestrial channels, just across the road in Hawley Crescent. The move signalled the end of an era and was accompanied by job losses, as at MTV USA years before. Those who had once been part of the core team were no longer wanted. People left with pay-offs, but disappointment still hit hard. For many, it was not about the money – MTV was more than just a job. Whatever happened to 'the family'? Some were secretly expecting a promotion rather than the boot, but instead, recruitment began of people with 'proper' TV experience, particularly at senior level. Whether you liked music or not didn't matter anymore.

The move to TV-am would mark MTV's coming of age. The period from 1994 to 1996 was the true Golden Era in corporate terms; its influence on the television, music and advertising industries would be huge. MTV became a brand leader and a pioneer of what in the 1990s, the era of irony, came to be known as 'cool marketing'. This trend reached its zenith in 1997 with the Cool Britannia phenomenon and New Labour's landslide election win, ushering in the belief in a 'new, youthful Britain'. This was also the year when MTV Europe – an idea that had actually died a good few years before – officially ceased to be. Digital compression technology finally allowed the network to split into four regional feeds under the umbrella of the MTV brand. The next phase in MTV's life would concentrate on the diversification of their portfolio into a series of channels and across different platforms (digital TV, Internet, mobile phones).

'Cool' soon became a big noise in corporate industries across the board, not just music and television. The Cool Brand Council was set up in the UK in 2001, later spreading internationally. This council sought to award 'cool' status to select brands via an independent panel of experts who would assess the merit of a brand according to a set of criteria cross-judged with consumer poll results. However, 'cool' as defined by industry experts and through quantitative consumer research is an oxymoron. Cool Britannia signalled the beginning of the 'corporate cool' era in marketing and the beginning of New Labour governance, but it was also the end of the 'real cool' – that which was once radical, shook the status quo and helped shape that new cool vision. It was time for hip to reinvent itself. The underground cool – that which would also ultimately be discovered by marketing, win 'cool brand' awards and fully flourish in 2007 – was indeed bubbling under elsewhere.

Let's head to Hoxton Square, Shoreditch – at that time a nondescript area of east London.

London, September 1997
The Rise of Cool Britannia

Three strangers are lost in Bethnal Green, east London. I am one of them. From a quick glance at one another, it's evident we're going to the same event, not least because there's nothing else remotely 'arty' in this area. We need to get to somewhere off Brick Lane, if only we could find this Brick Lane, so we join forces. This was years before Brick Lane (the nearest tube is *not* Bethnal Green, but we didn't realise!) assumed its 'edgy fashion' status.[10] It was also before Monica Ali's 2003 novel *Brick Lane* and subsequent film (directed by Sarah Gavron in 2007) contributed to this street's fame. Historically associated with crime, poverty and prostitution, this part of town had one of the highest crime rates in the country and its greatest claim to fame was Jack the Ripper. The area was also haunted by the spectre of right-wing extremism, stretching from the British Union of Fascists in the 1930s to the British National Front in the 1980s, whose headquarters used to be in the nearby Shoreditch High Street (in the 1990s it splintered, giving rise to the British National Party).

Eventually, we found our spot. The occasion was Jake and Dinos Chapman's housewarming party-cum-show, the first since Sensation, the pivotal exhibition that catapulted the duo to international fame. Sensation was inaugurated at London's Royal Academy of Arts in September 1997 and ran until December before travelling to Berlin in 1998 and New York in 1999. It showcased controversial art by relatively unknown artists, mostly from the private collection of advertising magnate Charles Saatchi. Young, energetic, sexy, cocky (and Cockney) were just some of the adjectives used to describe this collective. They were also labelled 'rebellious' – not in the traditional 'anti capitalist' way, but rather because they upset the establishment with their art, which orthodox critics considered 'scandalous'.[11]

It was precisely the unabashed commercialism of their language, combined with a conscious emphasis on media hype, that made them opportune. They slotted perfectly into the ironic *fin de siècle*. They revolutionised the arts as MTV had revolutionised youth television. They acknowledged that the boundaries between high and low culture (and by extension, art and commerce) were blurred. With this breed of artist, art became 'ironic'. Less an art movement per se – more a cool brand – from then on, the Chapman brothers and their contemporaries became known as the Young British Artists (YBAs). Echoing the hedonism of Generation X and the ironic language of recent DIY punk-inspired subcultures, they provided the art facet of Cool Britannia. With Sensation, they moved from obscurity into the spotlight.

The opening of the second White Cube Gallery in Hoxton Square in 2000, (which represented many of the artists featured in Sensation) marked the shift from the YBAs upsetting the establishment to becoming part of it, albeit its radical arm. In the noughties, this clique of East End artists would become highly sought-after. The works of a select few would fetch millions, notably those of Damian Hirst. A key figure among the YBAs, he conquered the barren market of the former Soviet Union, his works becoming trophies for ex-communist billionaires who began to spend colossal sums on art. It was fitting that the White Cube was located in Hoxton – the spiritual home of the YBAs. Long before they became a brand that shook up the art establishment, long before their 'bling art for oligarchs', this bunch were outsiders and unlikely contenders for living the Life of Riley. In his book *Lucky Kunst* Greg Muir documents the rise and fall of the YBAs, telling the story of their ascent from a once 'sleazy as hell neighbourhood' to their demise, symbolically marked by the 2004 warehouse fire that destroyed most of their notorious works.

Until the late 1990s, few had heard of the 'Shoreditch Triangle', an unmarked area between Shoreditch High Street, Old Street and Great Eastern Street. Why would they have? As Muir recalls, it was then an area where it was easier to buy drugs than a pint of milk. There was little there except disused factories, run-down warehouses and grotty council estates. There were corner shops and fruit and vegetable stalls (either selling traditional English or ethnic foods), but no chain mini-markets or other branded stores. From a commercial perspective, Shoreditch was like a ghost town. Shabby though it was, the group of artists later to become the YBAs called it home. Rents were cheap and life Bohemian.

Hoxton Square itself is just off Old Street, outside the triangle. Its importance in this story is reflected in the surfeit of defining cultural events that have occurred there. It was the late Joshua Compton's 'A Fête Worse than Death' in 1993–1994 which epitomised a generation that was, in the words of Muir, 'gripped by a profound sense of togetherness'. Speak to anyone who hung around Hoxton at that time and their faces will light up at the mention of the Fête, where Damian Hirst famously sold plates for a pound. Ask about when Alexander McQueen had a studio in Hoxton or when Tracey Emin and Sarah Lucas had a 'shop', or if they sipped beer with Jarvis Cocker at the local. Everyone will have a tale or two.

Of course, those soon-to-be-household-names were not the area's only residents. In order for them to succeed it 'required people from all walks of life, not just artists and dealers but also hangers on, musicians, barmaids, toffs, you name it'.[12] I found myself hanging out in this area simply because I studied at Goldsmiths College in the mid 1990s, where the legacy of 'Generation 88/89' (Hirst and his YBA contemporaries) continued strong.[13] Goldsmiths' profile was further raised by the fact that members of the band Blur also studied there at the same time. Blur became one of the key Britpop acts that defined the music of Cool Britannia.[14] When 'cool' reigned at the turn of the millennium, Goldsmiths College became the first (and for some time, only) educational institution to be awarded the 'cool brand' accolade by the newly formed Brands Council. Coupled with the Cool Brits, the alumni before them were definitely a factor in securing this title – Malcolm McLaren, Vivienne Westwood, Mary Quant and Bridget Riley to name but few.

Long before the terms 'Young British Artists' and 'Britpop' were coined and cool became a marketing tool, it was word of mouth that drew people to east London. A big attraction was the private parties in warehouses, artists' studios and illegal squats, which have assumed a somewhat mythical status today. According to Hackney Council, some 10,000 artists populated this area. Hoxton and Shoreditch are in the London Borough of Hackney, as is Dalston, now being hyped as the next hip neighbourhood. Ironically, Dalston was where I partied in between 1993 and 1996 before relocating to Shoreditch. A handful of my fellow students even bought dilapidated property there for a pittance, with no thought of investment – in what turned out to be a shrewd move.

Outside of the parties, there was only a handful of bars where this community congregated, but they were important hubs where ideas were exchanged. Mention of the Bass Clef in Hoxton Square, a music venue later renamed the Blue Note, brings fond memories to mind. Before 1997, the Bass Clef was the only 'cultural' reason to go to Hoxton Square. Then came Greg Muir's Lux Cinema, which brought intellectual panache (until it was converted into the Hoxton Bar and Kitchen). Around the corner now lies 333, previously The London Apprentice. The Bricklayer's Arms, The Barley Mow and The Golden Heart were the favoured pubs. The Vibe Bar, 93 Feet East, the Electricity Showrooms and the basement of the Great Eastern Dining Room were newer additions, all still around but now under new management. And that was pretty much it.

It was impossible to imagine that this area would become one of the most fashionable destinations for nightlife, just as it was impossible to envisage that the neighbourhood itself – a vision of urban decay – would become prime real estate. 'Shoreditch' and 'Hoxton' would be redefined as bywords for cool. Night and day, an international crowd now gathers in this part of London in search of the Shoreditch lifestyle. This sea change came about in just under a decade. In the early noughties, Hoxton (or Shoreditch – though technically adjacent areas they are used interchangeably) would become one of the most spectacular examples of urban redevelopment.

In *Hip: the History*, John Leland demonstrates how proto-hip convergences initially congregate in the dead zones of the real-estate market. Historically, when downtown neighbourhoods emptied during times of crisis, artists and other hipster types moved in, serving as 'the advance troops of the gentrification'. Shoreditch fits into this pattern, albeit with a time lag in the traditional gentrification cycle. The decline of Shoreditch and surrounding areas began at the end of the 19th century, when its textile and furniture industries disappeared and its enviable Victorian traditions of music hall and theatre died off. Shoreditch would never fully recover. It plunged into disrepute in the first half of the 20th century, was badly blitzed in World War Two and the post-war high-rise developments would bring more misery than prosperity. Then the hype of the late 1990s triggered a rejuvenation process of unprecedented velocity. Subsequently, Shoreditch's tourist-attraction potential grew, and with it the strange appeal of its sinister and villainous history. In fact, the elusive street that I was trying to locate when I went to the Chapmans' housewarming had been one of the Ripper's main preying spots. Wandering blindly around those streets, I was effectively tracing a route that has since become a ghoulish tourist trail called the 'Jack the Ripper Walk'.

While credit for the rebirth of Shoreditch is usually attributed wholesale to the Cool Britannia phenomenon, this actually spawned only the first phase, covering the period from 1997 to 2004. The second phase was a reaction against Cool Britannia. This occurred in parallel, underground, while the commercial world was still preoccupied with Cool Britannia, a phenomenon soon to run dry and create a space to accommodate the influence of this new wave. The new creative and entrepreneurial denizens would put their own stamp on the neighbourhood and turn it into the vibrant area it is today. It is ultimately their influence that extended the hip legacy of this neighbourhood, taking it from residential property boom, where artists acted as 'advance troops of gentrification', into a commercial development and tourist attraction.

Shoreditch Post Cool Britannia: Phase One
The first phase of Shoreditch's rebirth went hand in hand with the dotcom boom and the relationship between Shoreditch and cool marketing.

At the turn of the millennium, the bulk of London's dotcom industry was based in Shoreditch and adjacent areas. Initially, the movement boosted Shoreditch's cool reputation because its practitioners were seen as misunderstood innovators challenging traditional ways of doing business: they were hipster types seeking cheap rents and Bohemianism. And they loved to party. New media became a developing economy fast when venture capital began to pour in. From then on, this milieu made 'creative young professionals' out of what would formerly have been seen as 'webbies'. With money in their pockets, they could now buy warehouses and turn them into funky offices and homes, striving for coolness on both fronts. The dotcom crash would produce casualties but the sector would recover. When the bubble burst, what this episode proved above all was that 'an entire economy could soar without tangible profits, at least briefly, as long as it offers the promise of hip'.[15]

The second trend is tied to the relationship between hip and the needs of marketing communication. The legacy of Hoxton's warehouse underground parties and its spirited nightlife is relevant here. This was still a relatively closed community, miles away from popular West End hangouts both psychologically and physically. Talk of weird-looking people with strange haircuts who partied in the pits of east London began to spread. The first endemic hairstyle to replace the 'oxton skin 'ead was the Hoxton Mullet, which had little impact outside Hoxton at this early stage. A later signature hairstyle, the Hoxton Fin, would become a fad of epic proportions. The cut was also sported by local estate agents who helped sell outrageously priced lofts for those with more money than sense. Hearsay was accompanied by a growing number of press articles with the magic word in the headline: hip. This type of endorsement took the Fin global.

For those who knew Shoreditch when it was a hedonistic weekend hive, the beginning of the gentrification process marked the end of an era. As one of the old settlers eloquently put it, '"Cool Britannia" was the worst thing that could have happened to Shoreditch because those motherfuckers made it so that we couldn't have our parties anymore.' Commercially though, this was the dawn of a new era. One of the first micro-industries to develop in Shoreditch was the nightlife economy. Its rise went hand in hand with the marketing need to keep up with the latest trends, as 'cool hunting' was all the rage – especially in Shoreditch. Not only would clubs develop, representing a thriving mini-sector, but corporate brands seeking to build a youthful and hip image would start tapping into this industry, too. So Shoreditch became a new territory for hip associations via sponsorship, with plenty of scope for street marketing and guerrilla advertising. As the legacy of underground parties from the turn of the 1990s was turning into the cult of the mega club and the superstar DJ, Shoreditch started to provide a hip alternative to this mainstream trend. Still, one of the first casualties of co-optation was actually the Blue Note, taken out of its original home in Hoxton Square and transposed to a super club in the already-gentrified hip neighbourhood of Islington. Eventually, it was demolished to make way for a shopping mall.

The hunt then began for hip Hoxton promoters to facilitate the dialogue between the cool street punters and the brands, with their agenda of profiting from being cool. My friend Ranx, an original Hoxtonite, followed a route from underground to mainstream that was representative of how the first generation of Shoreditch party people – by their own admission – sold out. A 'blues party graduate', Ranx originates from the old school, when the DJ and the promoter were one, possessing records and a sound system (as opposed to becoming a DJ by getting a kit, practising and then looking for a promoter, as is now the case).

After twenty years in the industry, Ranx still fondly remembers his first toy-like Citronic party kit from the 1980s: a simple set-up of two turntables with a lid. His first DJ gig was at a function at Shoreditch Town Hall circa 1985, when he was still a teenager.

Ranx threw many a memorable warehouse party in Shoreditch between 1990 and 1998. His USP for partygoers was the gap he bridged between the seminal Detroit and Chicago scenes and the UK subcultures; other than being connected to those scenes through shared ideals, Ranx's technical savvy and degree in computer science equipped him with the knowledge to make free phone calls to the States. It may seem comical today when Skype is freely available to anyone, but back then, international calls were really expensive, especially if they were also intercontinental, so this ability to bypass the mainstream communication channels was truly advantageous. Punters knew the music would be great too, as one could expect live sets from the likes of Derek May, Underground Resistance and Tyree Cooper. Ranx was also a DJ at The London Apprentice (later 333). A straight man at an overtly gay night, his presence was happily accepted in the name of hedonism. In one way, this shows how music – the backbone of autonomous subcultures – acted as a diversity catalyst among the underground crowd who congregated in a notoriously intolerant 'overground'.

Around 1998, just after Cool Britannia had peaked, Ranx decided that it was time to call it a day. By changing his *modus operandi* from charging partygoers a small entrance fee to getting paid by corporate companies, Ranx became a leading purveyor of cool-for-profit. He organised events under the banner 'Transit' in car parks and empty warehouse spaces, filmed the punters and sold content to his commercial partners in the early days of developing online networks. Alternatively, he took sponsorship for product placement in party venues. This was also an inventive way of circumventing the law where brands had advertising restrictions (for example, cigarettes and alcohol). Because it was a funkier way of advertising, brands aiming for the youth demographic started to sponsor such 'street' events. Playstation have even converted Shoreditch warehouses into bars for game launches. At Transit, the likes of Jazzanova from Berlin, Lady Miss Kier (of Deee-lite fame) or Jarvis Cocker span their records at a time when it was still unusual to have someone who wasn't an accredited DJ on the decks. Transit was a watered-down version of the 'authentic' hedonistic parties Ranx used to host, but it retained the image of attracting the 'Hoxton trendies' that the brands were after.

The area also attracted new blood such as Neil Boorman. Like Ranx, Neil began to provide alternative outlets to what he called 'mega clubs and overpaid DJs' where brands could reach hipsters by acting as sponsors. He organised nights at the 333 club whose reputation had been boosted by wild nights at The London Apprentice. I got to know Neil a little in person but more so through his publishing work, and was charmed by his unique sense of humour, bordering on sarcasm. Popular local fanzine *The Shoreditch Twat* was one of Neil's ventures. This satirical publication featured social commentary on the negative impact of gentrification on the underground community. It lampooned wannabes buying into the Shoreditch lifestyle as a result of hip hype rather than a genuine interest in its potential to offer an alternative existence, itself on the wane because of rising property prices.

Ironically, *The Shoreditch Twat*, distributed in local outlets, provided a desirable guerrilla advertising medium. Exposure in this fanzine enabled brands to be at the cutting edge of youth culture and was a great testament to the power of cool marketing and the privileged place it held in the corporate boardroom. The zine openly ridiculed many brands. However, thanks to the use of irony, unconfident brand managers were often confused by what was cool and what wasn't. *The Shoreditch Twat* was published until around 2003. This experience would later lead Neil to the position of editor at the locally based iconic street-culture bible *Sleazenation*. This troubled magazine did not survive for long, folding in 2004, something I shall look into later.

In 2005, Neil's publications inspired terrestrial TV broadcaster Channel 4's sitcom *Nathan Barley*. This fictional Shoreditch character was a satirical swipe at people working in creative industries (marketing, advertising, film, design and dotcom) and attempted to bring some of the Shoreditch cool to a mass audience, but its humour never really caught on. *Nathan Barley* was thought to be timely but it actually missed the boat. It appeared to be set in the period of the Gold Rush to Shoreditch when Shoreditch was about dotcom, new bars in minimalist décor and the rise of the hip loft, which in turn attracted young professionals and wannabes, cool hunters and brands, all wanting their piece of the action. However, unlike *The Shoreditch Twat* fanzine – which had an immediacy about it, key to hipness – *Nathan Barley* on television a few years later seemed oddly irrelevant.

The case of *Nathan Barley* was symptomatic of something else: the type of cool hunting that characterised the post-Cool Britannia period was nearing its end. Corporations were investing significant resources into keeping up with the latest trends but by the time the findings had filtered up through the corporate echelons, the moment had passed. Had *Nathan Barley* been commissioned for a mainstream television youth slot a few years earlier, perhaps it would have been funnier. By the mid-noughties, it made no sense to parody Shoreditch, as the whole neighbourhood had become a hip brand. By then, Shoreditch was colonised by 'Postcode Plonkers' and 'Shop DJs' – stereotypes from Neil Boorman's illustrated guide to London clubbing, *Devil's Dandruff*.

These were just two examples of typical wannabe archetypes. The Shop DJ was the embodiment of club culture gone overground. Resplendent in ostentatious mid-priced sportswear, he carried his DJ kit around in a set from a mid-range department store (a gift from his mum) and played in youth-oriented high street chainstores, dreaming of becoming a superstar DJ. The Postcode Plonker was 'healthy in bank balance but lacking in personality' with an eye on areas like Shoreditch, which promised hip loft living. The Postcode Plonker would complain to the council about the noise from the nearby block party immediately after he moved in. These were caricatures, but not far from reality; a perceptive eye could maybe identify the Postcode Plonker (usually via a fashion faux-pas) but it was often difficult to separate the authentically hip from the phony. For example, a Transit party was a really cool party. That Transit was a watered-down version of something even cooler mattered little to commercial brands and its punters; the vast majority knew no different.

However, the distinction between 'authentic and fake' or 'hipster and wannabe' is relevant on the scene. Often perceived as elitism by outsiders, this type of cultural distinction has always operated within alternative movements, and Hoxtonites are no different. In order to differentiate their world from the commercial pretender, hip events in Shoreditch stayed underground by avoiding club listings. Unless you were part of the inner circle ('authentic'), it was difficult to find out about such events.

Ranx's Hoxton Pimps was one such 'authentic' event. A non-stop party weekender 'from late until the cops come', Hoxton Pimps was held in secret venues – car parks, disused warehouses – and never in the same one twice. Unless you were a friend, you'd only know about the parties from bills posted around Hoxton and flyers distributed in select bars and record shops. The posters and flyers would indicate a number to be activated shortly before the party began (usually around midnight) which you'd call to get the address. The USP of

Hoxton Pimps was the exquisite selection of DJs and MCs: turntable pioneer and world champion J-Rocc of the Beat Junkies, ?uestlove from Philadelphian outfit The Roots, musician Santigold (then Santogold), DJ Gilles Peterson, DJ/ producer Andy Weatherall and many more of that calibre. There would often be artwork and performances too. Hoxton Pimps would pull in the local hipsters and would often act as a launch pad for new music talent. There was also a website, where a group of us were encouraged by Ranx to write about our experiences of living in the area. It was an early form of blogging (I wrote under the moniker 'The Pimpette').

As Hoxton Pimps grew, it inevitably got listed. Again, were you a Pimp virgin the change in atmosphere at the nights wouldn't register, but a veteran would no longer be there. Now discovered, Hoxton Pimps provided treasures for the cool hunter, not least for its 'street' credentials – a much-loved concept in corporate cool circles. Thus, warehouses, car parks, DJs and trendies in the latest cool brands and Hoxton Fins automatically equalled cool. However, this type of cool was already epitomised by the sell-outs from the rave scene that had given rise to mainstream dance culture. By 2004, dance culture had reached a crisis point, falling victim to its own success. Mega-club brands, which had diversified into an array of businesses, began to scale down or close down. This crisis coincided with the maturing of the Shoreditch underground scene, which did not have the particular 'street' feel that the corporate cool sought. It was now a universe in its own right, and its expanding network would become the Next Big Thing: Shoreditch Post Cool Britannia – Phase Two, to which the bulk of this book will be dedicated.

This new network would provide cues for a new breed of maverick businesses. Together they would do for the noughties what MTV and cool brands did for the 1990s. As with the previous hip cycle, the incubation period of this new scene was between 1997 and 2003 and it reached maturity between 2004 and 2006. This was the time when mainstream businesses began picking up on the 'new' trend, just as cool marketing in the mid 1990s had crossed over from cool companies into the boardrooms of corporate companies. The scene would peak in 2007, just like Cool Britannia a decade earlier. From then on, its influence on the mainstream style and communications industries would be ubiquitous.

The effect this new wave of cool wrought upon the gentrification of Shoreditch also took place in stages. During this scene's incubation, Shoreditch was outside the catchment areas of branded stores. The gentrification process had begun but it was predominantly about converting disused warehouses into luxury flats. The changes were on a scale unseen for a century, but as it turned out, this early phase of redevelopment was only a small beginning: during the latter part of the maturity phase, the first chain supermarkets, restaurants and hotels began to appear in the area. Daring commercial clothing brands moved in, including All Saints and American Apparel, and landmarks such as Spitalfields Market, which had been central to the development of the new scene, were redeveloped as major tourist attractions. From 2007, the status of Shoreditch as London's hippest neighbourhood was confirmed with the endorsement of cool brands: Nike, K-Swiss, Lee and Reebok outlets, members' club Shoreditch House and Terence Conran's delicatessen, café and converted Victorian warehouse hotel. Also, cool mainstream advertising agencies such as Mother and Wieden+Kennedy relocated to Shoreditch, as did new communication agencies. In 2009, the trend was going strong. In spite of the global recession, Shoreditch was still an operational building site.

A FRAMEWORK FOR HIP
Hip and the Haphazard

This is how I found myself three times at the birth of movements that became labelled hip. Yet I do not think of myself as being hip. John Leland posits the theory that 'hip' is a social movement whose parameters are defined by the people watching it: hip factions come about haphazardly as 'a collision of peoples and ideas, thrown together in unplanned social experiments'.[16] That certainly rings true: I was merely in the right place at the right time. However, looking back over the past two decades, it seems the haphazard had its own method of morphing ideas into networks. Seemingly disparate people – those labelled by others as hip – would eventually always flock together. This brings me to the six degrees of separation theory – that which says one person is never more than six connections from another. Malcolm Gladwell elaborates on this idea in his influential book *The Tipping Point*. According to this theory, as we associate with people who occupy the same physical spaces as us, a small number of people are inevitably linked. In my experience in the inner circles of a scene defined as hip by others, that separation tends to be reduced to one or two degrees. Kudos among non-conformists is accumulated through where you hang out and who you know. Being seen in places and name-dropping (and I do not mean this in a pejorative way) is a form of authentication. If you know so and so, it implies that you share a world-view.

I do not think of myself as being conceited. Yet hip is a form of self-conscious elitism and separatism. As with any identity construct, hip exists in relation to another identity. Someone is hip only because someone else is not. Hip operates within its own cultural distinctions, a thesis put forward by Sarah Thornton in *Club Cultures*, a seminal text in cultural studies. Hip is a set of binary oppositions such as 'the diverse' and 'the homogenous', 'the radical' and 'the conformist' or 'the distinguished' and 'the common'. Within this framework, a particular crowd is defined as hip in relation to a perpetually absent and often denigrated mainstream. In other words, the mainstreamers are the wannabes against whom the hipsters 'protect' their territory. Though no one ever admits to be being a wannabe, it seems everybody wants to be a hipster.

This kind of elitism is not the preserve of self-consciously hip crowds. The British cultural theorist Raymond Williams set the precedent; his work provides the foundations of the discipline of cultural studies. In his conclusions about the dichotomy between mass culture (barbaric, for the common masses) and high art (enlightening, for the distinguished minority), which had been at the heart of cultural debate since the advent of mass media and spread of television, Williams famously conceded that, 'There are, in fact, no masses; there are only ways of seeing people as masses.'[17] By way of analogy, I would say that there are, in fact, no wannabes. There are only ways of seeing people as wannabes. Similarly, there are no hipsters – it is all a matter of perception.

The question then, is who 'decides' who the hipsters and wannabes are and from what vantage point? Not me. This book is not a directory of who's cool according to The Pimpette. Instead, I intend to locate the hipster and the wannabe within a specific framework.

Hip or cool? The words can be used interchangeably, and although 'hip' in this context has a longer history while 'cool' became fashionable in the 1990s with cool marketing, semantics do not much matter for my purposes here. In my story, I am scrutinising three movements that started small and went on to have a significant social impact. Small rock 'n' roll agitation – for which Omladinski Program became the loudest voice – was the main force for positive change under communism, subsequently becoming the strongest anti-war movement during the 1990s conflict in the former Yugoslavia. MTV is the best example of a 1990s cool marketing trend, which ultimately became the norm in the commercial sector and even redefined political marketing. The Hoxton story is that of a number of small trends that spawned various brands and a larger movement that redefined consumerism in the noughties. This will become apparent once I start my analysis and separate short-lived fads (such as the Hoxton Fin) from long-lasting effects (the general enduring legacy of Hoxton).

The process of a small group crossing over into a wider trend follows a specific trajectory. Here again, *The Tipping Point* is the most accomplished book on how small movements – ideas, trends or specific behaviours – become big trends: this moment Gladwell dubs the 'tipping point'. There is no need here to reinvent the wheel – just to recapitulate the gist of his argument. Gladwell uses the six degrees of separation theory as his starting point. In this context, he talks of mavens (the brokers of information), connectors (those who spread information, mainly via word of mouth) and salesmen (the persuaders) as the protagonists of processes that make the obscure visible.

To put an aspect of the separation theory into context, I can see from my own experience that it made sense for me, when I was an alternative youth broadcaster in Eastern Europe, to contact MTV and for them, as an aspiring pan-European youth channel, to reciprocate. We were on different sides of the Iron Curtain but our mindset was the same: our lingua franca was rock 'n' roll. Then there was the novelty of our physical space becoming reconfigured under new communication technologies. Being in the right place at the right time essentially meant that both of us turned a set of circumstances into an opportunity to act as 'connectors' – or the special few who constructed communities of interest – and did so ungoverned by rules of proximity.

Degrees of separation provide only a partial explanation for the tipping point that primarily accounts for the occurrence of fads (for example 'unfashionable' Hush Puppy shoes becoming fashionable again, a case study explored in *The Tipping Point*). However, I am interested in paradigm shifts. There must be a series of fads to create such a large movement. So let me bring the diffusion model into this bigger picture. This refers specifically to the challenge of innovation, about 'breaking' new ideas or products originating from a small group. In such a scenario there is the barrier of world-views: the smaller group of innovators and the early adopters of ideas are the partisans of change, whereas the majority of people would be sceptical. This is where mavens, connectors and salesmen play a central role, over time, in translating original ideas into a more universal language.

Transposed to an institutional situation (business or public sector), it becomes the chasm between risk-taking (making a quantum leap) and eliminating risk (building incremental market value or adhering to policies that hinder political change). New ideas challenge the status quo. I am interested in the transition process from risk to norm.

The diffusion model accounts for hip's trajectory from inception to wider trend. Once the nucleus is formed, hip spreads outwards in concentric circles until the outré becomes the ordinary, whereupon it retreats inward to seek out a new identity.[18] As hip begins to cross over, the inner circle's knowledge assumes importance outside the scene. The ideology and language that traditionally governed this transition process is rock 'n' roll – an attitude rather than a musical genre per se. It is about 'crossing over' (paying your dues by gradually developing your artistic skills and increasing your success and fan-base) and 'selling out' (bands who start as artistes but end up compromising their integrity by surrendering to commercial demands). The community of fans perceives the sell-out as a betrayal of roots. By extension, hip's hunger for authenticity – on which the affinity between the artist and the fan is founded – is lost.

The concept of diffusion provides a model for the crossover, but hip occurs as a result of the interplay of economic and cultural needs at a particular stage of technological development; these elements combine to create it. With the advent of satellite technology in the 1990s, the world became a smaller place. People could form communities unbound by rules of proximity, something that MTV also achieved when it created its 'nation of Europe' based on a shared language of rock 'n' roll. Fresh technologies helped this new interest extend its identity beyond nationality, borders and territory to become part of a wider rock 'n' roll community. Back then there were fax machines to speed up connections. Obsolete now, the fax was hugely important when the telephone alone would no longer do; if you were *au courant*, you faxed. The world shrank further still with the rise of the Internet in the 1990s and noughties. The deregulation of the airline industry made cheaper travel possible, helping virtual communities to materialise. The possibilities for communities of shared interests are now multiple. In this context, it is economic and cultural factors that determine which communities of interest become prominent. Hip operates in relation to those needs, filling both a gap in the market (need for innovation) and a vacant cultural space (need for diversity).

Hip and Commerce

The connection between hip and commerce has always been a touchy subject, not least among hipsters. Hip is intuitive, natural. Being hip is not something you can acquire – it is effortless. You either have it or you don't. This is certainly the belief within inner circles of hip communities. If hip's authentic, surely you can't buy it, right? Wrong. Some 50 years of marketing history has been predicated on packaging and selling cool. Here, the rock 'n' roll trajectory can be rewritten in terms of a continuum: innovators, early adopters, early majority, late majority – the opinion former (maven-connector-salesman) being somewhere between the innovator and early adopter. In my story the innovator is the alpha trendsetter, the originator of the idea. The early adopter is the first to buy into the idea because he or she relates to it. Next comes the wannabe, part of the early majority who buy into the hype after the original idea has filtered through and been diluted. Finally, the late majority come on board.

Hip is therefore a paradox. It is a constant interplay between authenticity and co-optation with the lines between the two being both positively blurred (to the mainstream, the hip and the phony who passes for hip are indistinguishable) and unmistakably clear (in underground circles, people intuitively know who's got it and who hasn't).

The tale of hip, then, is one of countercultural youth and their co-optation, or at least that's how the myth of authenticity goes. The marketers' fascination with youth culture began in the early 1960s, even though the teen market technically dates from the 1950s with the advent of the pop single and music charts. The standard explanation for this fascination is the size of the market. In the 1960s, the youth market was, by all accounts, massive. In the USA alone, around half the nation was under 25. From a commercial point of view, this demographic was regarded as a powerful force. They were attractive because of their numbers and their sizeable discretionary income and because of the way that the youthful had become arbiters of taste (this also meant that marketers could target parents through their children).

Thomas Frank, in his book *The Conquest of Cool*, the most astute chronicle of hip's paradox, argues that market size is only a partial explanation as to why the youth market was attractive to marketers. It is worth summarising its main arguments because it will provide a historical context for the 1990s cool marketing and a foundation from which to follow hip's journey into the noughties. Frank begins his book with the premise that the 1960s are the 'homeland of hip'. Being a decade of vast social and political changes, 'the sixties' is often used interchangeably with the term 'counterculture'. What makes Frank's account unusual, if not contentious, is that unlike the huge body of work dedicated to the study of countercultures, his is a study of co-optation – that is, 'the forces and logic that made rebel youth cultures attractive to corporate decision-makers.'[19] What Frank does remarkably well in this exercise is avoid what he calls the 'co-optation theory', which he sums up as 'faith in the revolutionary potential of "authentic" counterculture combined with the notion that business mimics and mass-produces fake counterculture in order to cash in on a particular demographic and to subvert the great threat that "real" counterculture represents.'[20] This co-optation theory pervades not only much academic literature, but also draws many sympathisers because it sides with the underdog as symbolised by the image of the untainted rebel.

Rather than maintaining that hipness and business are irreconcilable, Frank demonstrates that, far from oppressing the cultural changes of the 1960s, the business revolution did in fact *parallel* and in some cases actually *anticipate* the impulses and new values associated with counterculture. By focusing on menswear and advertising – two industries that were deeply affected by the corporate and cultural changes which defined the 1960s – Frank shows how these industries were at the cutting edge of the shift in corporate practice and by doing so became the leading lights of co-optation. For it has become widely accepted that from the very beginning business dogged the counterculture with fakery, but in actuality, it remained difficult to distinguish between authentic and fake counterculture precisely because the counterculture was triggered at least as much by developments in mass culture (for example the success of The Beatles from 1963) as by grassroots-level changes.

What also happened in the 1960s was a revolution in marketing practice, management thinking and creative ideas – all of which were as far-reaching in their own right as were the revolutions in manners, music, art and taste-making. Just as 1960s youth counterculture came to be perceived as a symbol of liberation from the conformity of 1950s mass consumerism, new management thinkers went through their own version of the mass society critique. Against the stultifying regime of technocratic efficiency, they embraced a new individualism-promoting, bureaucracy-smashing and anti-hierarchical business practice. For these entrepreneurs, the fascination with youth was not about the size of the market, which is the universally accepted marketing position. If this had been the case, advertising would have neither ignored the young people who did not partake in the counterculture, ie the silent majority (which it did) nor applied symbols of rebel youth to all sorts of products, not just those aimed at youth (which it also did).

While the creative industries appreciated the demographic bonanza that baby boomers represented, their fascination with counterculture was characterised by the way it provided them with an array of symbols with which to express their new consuming vision: to think young meant to think creatively; to embrace difference and non-conformity. On the one hand, counterculture reflected their values and how they positioned themselves against the established business structure. On the other, counterculture became an ideal voice through which to express their business ideology. Through its hostility towards the establishment, the counterculture seemed to rebel against whatever they had once taken to heart. This attitude was the ideal vehicle for constant creation of new demand by making the previous craze obsolete. As such, hip didn't just drive youth culture but was also the lifeblood of consumer society. What Frank's study implies is that, paradoxically, rebellion became the language of the system youth sought to rebel against. The attraction of youth was therefore the countercultural attitude of its rebellious faction, not demographics per se. And this is the single most neglected fundamental factor in the bulk of existing literature on countercultures. Frank dexterously identifies this paradox in the context of the 1960s but argues that it is also relevant for our understanding of the 1990s hip consumerism.

My premise is that the 1960s provided the blueprint for 1990s hip consumerism as well as for how hip migrated to the noughties. It took a couple of decades to re-establish the connection between the 1960s and the 1990s because there was a historical discontinuity: the 1970s put an abrupt end to 1960s prosperity, which was preceded by that of the post-war 1950s boom. As recession replaced growth, experimentation and risk-taking were no longer on the corporate agenda. Brands that had once been partisans of change became arbiters of tradition. The 1980s was a conservative decade symbolised by yuppies and money obsession. During this period, hip consumerism was on the retreat, before returning with a vengeance in the 1990s, which is where we effectively pick up the story.

This will be the story of revolution in marketing practice from the 1990s onwards. I will look at how maverick businesses adopted the idioms of the countercultural equivalents to express their new consuming vision in the 1990s and noughties. As in the 1960s, the new consuming visions of these two decades

– initially the preserve of mavericks and market-leader brands – would eventually find approval in the corporate boardrooms of mainstream businesses. I am interested in these paradigm shifts in business models. At the same time, the new consuming ideologies expressed through a set of aesthetics would provide the cues that would influence the mainstream style and communication industries. In the 1960s, the 'peacock revolution' changed the menswear industry, which sought to imitate the style pioneered by hip young people, while the creative revolution changed advertising when Madison Avenue advertising executives embraced countercultural imagery and rock music in ad-making. As part of this process, the rebellious Madison Avenue coterie also shed their grey flannel suits in favour of flares and beads to express their non-conformist business vision. By way of analogy, the countercultures that went on to be co-opted in the 1990s and noughties would feed the mainstream style and communication industries with a vast collection of symbols. However, the commercial potential of the underground culture is just one facet of hip. The other is related to identity politics.

Hip and Identity Politics

With the publication of the hugely influential book *Subculture: the Meaning of Style* in 1979, Dick Hebdige made a seminal contribution to youth cultural studies. This text is still the key framework for any discussion of urban youth and resistance in Britain and beyond. Hebdige's work chronicles the evolution of British working class youth movements, starting with the hipsters and beats, working through teds, mods, skinheads, rude boys, Rastafarians, hippies, glam rockers, Bowie freaks and finally concentrating on punk's emergence in 1976. The central tenet of the book is that style is used by young people to negotiate a sense of oppositional identity to the dominant relations of power, by using an approach that combines semiotics, social anthropology and Marxism. Much has evolved since Hebdige introduced the notion of subcultures. However, the way he uses 'style' to refer to the distinct types of music, clothing, gestures, jargon and overall mannerisms used to form a sense of group identity, remains relevant. The principle of combining a dress code with a soundtrack to create a sub-group will resonate throughout my story. On the one hand, and somewhat ironically, this combination – historically a sign of 'resistance' – has become the dream scenario for trend-spotters. It is a great tool for creating consumer fads. On the other, there is urban myth, for British subcultural legacy has unconsciously strengthened the perception of the eccentric Brit and of London as the capital of 'street style'. In the early 1990s, the hip reputation of Camden Town (stemming from its hordes of punks, goths and unique street markets) attracted maverick companies such as MTV, just as Shoreditch – as fashioned by Bohemians – later attracted the creative industries. Subcultural legacy would also resonate when international fashion taste-makers rediscovered London as the ultimate source of edgy fashion in the second half of the noughties.

What changed was the command of resistance. This ideological shift coincided with the coming of age of Generation X, the one 'documented' in Douglas Coupland's novel of the same name in 1991. I say 'the one' because there is no official agreement as to which cohort Generation X represents (look at trenchant academic studies or robust marketing segmentations – they won't nail it. Even the definition of Generation X by those who coined the term in 1965, Charles Hamblett and Jane Deverson, does not fit with that of Coupland's because their Generation X is older). Coupland's version is the most relevant for us simply because it coincides with the coming of age of the leading-edge faction of a population whose underground lifestyle went on to influence the mainstream. That is my generation and I'm talkin' 'bout it. Age-wise, for Coupland, Generation X is roughly those born between the early 1960s and late 1970s, which suits my purpose. When it became a buzz term in the 1990s, the idea of Generation X as co-opted by marketing managers most commonly started to refer to those born between 1965 and 1978. Though outside the marketers' area of interest to begin with, for Eastern Europe, the equivalent were those born between 1960 and 1972; the collapse of communism being a generational milestone. The next demographic category was designated Generation Y – those born between 1979 and 1995. That is our demographic distinction.

With his book, Coupland sought to acknowledge the coming of age of the post-baby boomers, a generation of adults who thought differently from their parents and lived in different circumstances. This realisation is another reason why Coupland's version is relevant. What matters more than demographics is the shared mindset that defined Generation X. That mindset (or set of ideals, if you wish) will be a key variable in this book whether I am talking subculture, marketing or politics, but this is also the point at which I shall part with Coupland. The mindset shared among our Generation X would prove to be different from Coupland's vision. The success of his novel nevertheless created much hullabaloo about this new generation, not least because marketing was ripe for something new.

Rather than there being a chasm between generations, there were fundamental similarities between the two that were being ignored. Members of Generation X in the 1990s, like the baby boomers in the 1960s, were rebellious and cynical: they just expressed their attitude to mainstream politics and commerce in a different way. But being different did not necessarily comply with the way that Generation X came to be stereotyped. That is, as somewhat careless and less engaged than their parents, condemned to McJobs. This latter term was also popularised by Coupland's novel, which explains the connection between fiction (the main character in the book has a low-paid, unrewarding, no-future, no-prospect job) and its echoes in reality. The ideas of Generation X were ironic indeed but to equate it with apathy was erroneous.

When it came to politics, the cynicism for which Generation X became notorious reflected reality. Perhaps we understood that 'smoking dope and hanging Che's picture' was no more a commitment than 'drinking milk and collecting postage stamps', unless a revolution actually happened, and it did not.[21] Capitalism was resilient, for as Generation X reached adulthood, it emerged victorious when the Eastern Bloc fell apart and hailed capitalism as its saviour and path to freedom and progress. Generation X was Reagan's Progeny, Thatcher's Children or a new breed of *omladina*. A product of recession and political crisis, we became the last bastion of 'grand' political causes and the first to embrace a new form of consciousness and political activism.

This was a different kind of politics, attuned to a new sense of individualism. Though the rhetoric of the underground cultures at the vanguard of Generation X *was* rebellious, it was no longer about politics of resistance through style, but about the stylisation of politics – revolution through lifestyle, with politics being one element of that lifestyle. Acts of citizenship became activism based around temporary issues. This could be politics proper (for example the anti-war movement in the former Yugoslavia) or a cause of any kind (such as the fight for the right to party: the British ravers' cause which led to the creation of the Criminal Justice Act of 1994, the first subcultural youth gathering prohibited by law).[22]

In his book *The Time of the Tribes*, the French philosopher Michel Maffesoli provided an interesting interpretation for lifestyle cultures and their link to identity politics at a time when traditional values were being reassessed. It was published in France in 1985 when postmodern theory became the first intellectual movement to address the perceived clash between reality (traditional life) and hyper-reality (mediated life). Events such as Live Aid (also 1985) were cause for questioning established norms: Was this a one-off? What if it wasn't? After all, satellite broadcasting was soon to become an everyday item.

Maffesoli contends that life is lived through fragmented tribal groupings, organised around the catchphrases, brand names and soundbites of consumer culture. These microgroupings who share common interests in metropolitan areas are effectively 'urban tribes'. This concept offered a possible answer to the fragmentation of society where acts of solidarity in the form of social activism take place in the midst of fashion fads. Whether called an 'urban tribe' or something else, this new generation of young adults did not care less than their parents about mainstream politics, but rather were disillusioned by them. There was an institution called the nation-state but both the concept of space and the idea of belonging were being reconfigured under the impact of new communications technologies. The real problem was the inability of mainstream politics to capture the imagination of its citizens in a meaningful way – particularly the young – as opposed to a malady within Generation X. This lack of interest in mainstream political parties would only intensify with Generation Y or the post-MTV generation, for whom politics proper is notable only in its absence from their world-views.

The cynicism of Generation X was also reflected in their attitude to commerce. In the 1980s, the DIY ethos – a direct legacy of punk – really bloomed. To clarify, the post-punk subcultures in question and of interest for my story are those that became mainstream in the 1990s. These are hip hop (an umbrella term encompassing rap, breakdancing and graffiti art) and dance cultures (an umbrella term for what emerged from acid house and rave). They would fuse (in fact, the underground was never quite divided – this categorisation was a marketing construct) and splinter to give birth to even more subgroups, but the ideological shift that marked Generation X – as expressed through an ironic outlook on life – is primarily a product of these two subcultures. The mindset of this faction would set the tone for challenging the status quo in the 1990s.

For these guys, heroes were not political figures such as Che Guevara but radical young entrepreneurs. Once again, it was about reality. These subcultures were not about 'revolution' – trying to abolish the system as in the 1960s – but a 'revolution through lifestyle rather than politics'.[23] For the next generation, being rebellious was about turning the existing social order to one's own advantage. Far from being resigned to McJobs, the forerunners of Generation X were particularly skilful at finding ways to operate within the system. Mavericks of this generation often turned social disadvantage into an opportunity by applying DIY ethics to start record or fashion labels and clubs, thus bypassing the entertainment conglomerates. This mixture of work and play was often equated with hedonism. Fair enough. 'Work hard, play hard' became a generational motto, an ironic twist on being the product of a conservative era.

Another prominent characteristic of Generation X became the refusal to grow up. Procrastination of 'social ageing' gave way to the phenomenon of 'never marrieds' in the noughties. This idea is based on the first-hand experience of one Ethan Watters, single well into his thirties. His book *Urban Tribes* is a testimony to his own quest to understand why this was the case, only to realise that his situation was indeed a generational phenomenon. Watters' is an American story, but it resonates strongly in Europe and various demographic statistics back up this trend. *Urban Tribes* represented a reaction to the widespread interpretation of Coupland's Generation X, where the idea of not getting married in one's twenties was an implicit warning sign. What Watters' story shows instead, is that people can live a fulfilled life with a 'family' of friends; tight-knit groups who party together and also provide a support network, thereby replacing the (often absent) family in modern urban landscapes as well as redesigning the fabric of the latter in this process. Popular television series from the 1990s such as *Friends* and (to some extent) *Sex and the City* reflected this lifestyle. Helen Fielding's Bridget Jones, 'still' single in her thirties yet cushioned by her council of friends, whom she consults before making any decision – no matter how big or small – is another humorous take on this generational characteristic. Though not necessarily participating in conventional civic duties like their parents' generation, individuals in urban tribes can be generous, compassionate and reliable. On a micro-level, these small acts of kindness mirror their wider attitude to society, echoing Maffesoli's idea of an urban tribe, where acts of solidarity take place through temporary but meaningful causes.

Inspired by the post-punk subcultures, attributes such as refusal to grow up, hedonism, entrepreneurialism, self-reliance, anti-conventionalism, being apolitical (but into causes!) and even being vegetarian (as a defiance statement rather than a religious one) defined the mindset of Generation X. Such activities became alternatives to the mainstreaming of hip. Rather than subverting dominant cultures in the manner attributed to the counterculture, the post-punk subcultures effectively offered an alternative to the dominant social order and established cultural hierarchies. That hip would be co-opted was inevitable – that lesson had been learned from the counterculture. However, this did not mean that operating in the margins before the inevitable co-optation was futile – the creation of diversity was not to be abandoned simply because co-optation increasingly became the logical conclusion. In the 1960s, hip's chief characteristic became the 'agnostic cult of style worship', where the main concern became 'staying one step ahead of the consuming crowd'.[24] This way of cultivating difference was revived with the 1980s DIY post-punk subcultures. Their essence was not the product, but its ideals and aesthetic sensibilities. These ideals were not so much opposed to the mainstream as they were simply a market cycle ahead of them.[25]

And this is exactly how hip was redefined by cool marketing in the 1990s: from countercultural resistance to being the first to know. And this is exactly how 1990s cool brands began to operate. Calvin Klein, Nike and Diesel all invented their own sensibilities, but MTV remains the example par excellence from this era, being the forerunner of the first-to-know trade. By turning underground ideologies into business acumen, MTV cracked the formula of making cool lucrative. Being perpetually at the cutting edge meant that nothing was constant on MTV except change, which became the engine that fuelled hip consumerism. As the cool brand model proved to be profitable, creative industries invested heavily in cool hunting in order to stay a step ahead. With competition intensified, the degree of risk within cool companies was gradually reduced by measures (including various types of market research and cool hunting itself) being put into place to eliminate risk. In this context, cool hunting was no longer about creative risks but about reproducing a safe formula to build incremental value. This is fine, but the risk associated with the safe formula is not entirely without hazards. There could be something newer, something more cutting-edge and, by extension, a step ahead of them in hip's concentric circles – and this is indeed what happened. A new generation of underground scenes and maverick businesses sharing their values would begin to challenge the status quo established by the cool brand industry and ultimately steal the cool crown. Hip would reinvent itself in the noughties by making 1990s cool marketing obsolete.

Methodology, Hypothesis and Design

Haphazardness is a key element in this book. Had I not been in some of the right places at the right times, I doubt I'd have a story to tell. But my presence is not itself enough to justify a book. There needs to be some order mapped on to the apparent randomness of the situations – and a killer hook. I have always been a curious person, though I never saw that as an asset – it was simply part of my upbringing. I grew up bilingual, speaking Serbo-Croat at home and French outside, with a heavy dose of French culture instilled into my psyche while cultivating elements of Yugoslav culture. I spent the 1980s living in Yugoslavia, this time cultivating my French connection via annual trips to Paris and occasionally to the French coast during school holidays. I moved to London in 1991 and felt part of a new country while losing another, as Yugoslavia fell apart a year later. This ability to see the same thing from different perspectives would prove useful in my postgraduate education and subsequent professional life as a marketer.

When I applied to do a doctoral thesis in the early 1990s, Goldsmiths College was the only establishment that accepted me. In hindsight, I had neither the right theoretical foundation nor the right command of the English language to do a doctorate. I was at a disadvantage compared to my fellow research students, many of whom held masters degrees from prestigious universities such as Oxbridge or Goldsmiths itself. So I was lucky that (Doctor, later promoted to Professor) David Morley accepted me. With great effort on my part and great commitment on his, we pulled it off. Professor Morley even listed my thesis in his biography under works supervised ('The Cultural Significance of MTV Europe': that'd be me!). Another reason for my initial slew of rejections was that I wanted to do a PhD on MTV. Only Goldsmiths was interested.

This is where the degrees of connection and the not-so-haphazard-after-all nature of events become significant. One of the founding tutors of the Media and Communications Department at Goldsmiths where I was enrolled was none other than Dick Hebdige. Although he had already emigrated to the States by the time I was there, I had the pleasure of meeting him and attending a lecture he gave at Goldsmiths during one of his visits to London. This was a once-in-a-lifetime experience, and the main amphitheatre got so packed that people sat on the stairs and any inch of available floor space in order to experience his charisma. Hebdige, like my supervisor David Morley and a number of tutors who taught me including Angela McRobbie, Paul Gilroy and last but not least, Stuart Hall (who guest-lectured), are a group of mavericks, all part of the intellectual movement known as the Birmingham School. This was located at the Centre for Contemporary Cultural Studies in Birmingham where the academic discipline of cultural studies was born in the 1960s.

This field considers popular culture and media as subjects worthy of analysis and encompasses a combination of academic specialisms dedicated to understanding how audiences construct meanings. Here, various research methods are allowed, including observation *in situ*, or ethnography, something that I would become relatively well versed in. The common thread between the different subjects under scrutiny was the study of how the interplay between a dominant power and empowerment of the individual worked. Originally, cultural studies were about class, race and gender. Over time, it developed into the study of forms of resistance to globalisation. It was no wonder that my otherwise wacky idea to study MTV was appealing to this academic circle. The Birmingham School was also underpinned by left-wing beliefs. My thesis and now this book were written with a commitment to cosmopolitanism. The prolific works of these scholars about the relationship between popular culture, media, and the politics of identity shaped my thinking.

I completed my thesis in the late 1990s at the same time as the emergence of Cool Britannia. Anything related to youth culture was highly prized in the marketing sector and so I was tagged a 'futurologist'. This implied that I was in touch with youth culture and brands – indicators of future consumer patterns. It was also synonymous with cool. This was the time when cool advertising agencies such as St Luke's were emerging, while established players were opening up specialist youth divisions, such as McCann Erickson's Magic Hat. When I first became acquainted with Magic Hat, there were only two people in the London office – it is now an international network. Though my work is associated with leading-edge trends, I'm not in advertising. I work on the strategic side of brand development, a branch of the brand industry that particularly developed at the turn of the millennium. The role is essentially about innovation – coming up with new products or services and new ideas for brands in need of a facelift. So I am at the cutting edge of the industry.

In order to be able to project brands into the future, as a consultant I need to be able to anticipate that future or, as it would prove in my case, already live in it. In the mid-noughties, it was becoming increasingly apparent to me that my brand of marketing was taking little inspiration from contemporary youth culture. There was much more exciting stuff happening in my private life. The people I was hanging out with were more forward-thinking. Mixing my play with work in the margins (doing PR and events for friends, which were not part of my proper job) corresponded to the labels of maven and connector. I did not recognise these as worthy skills (they just seemed normal) until I read *The*

Tipping Point, but that certainly made me realise that connecting people has been my vocation ever since I joined Omladinski Program. And I know many in my circle of friends who do the same. That is how new projects come about. I started to involve my 'forward-thinking' network of 'underground' friends (and related people – often 'one-degree separations') in my corporate work, essentially replacing the role of cool hunting with something else for the purpose of future strategy. Fortunately, I had colleagues and clients who were open to fresh ideas; it's not easy in the corporate world to introduce unconventional methods. As it happened, my intuition was right. This underground network would do for the noughties what cool brands did for the 1990s.

An inadvertent catalyst for this book's hypothesis was the Hoxton Pimps. Around the time the Hoxton Pimps ceased to be (mid-noughties), I met up with the founder of a cool brand innovation agency from the late 1990s business revolution, which had eventually been taken over by a communication conglomerate. This agency produced an annual youth tracking report which aimed to show potential clients that they were in touch with the latest trends – implicitly equating youth culture with emerging trends. Two pillars of coolness ruled. The first involved new media and technology (my colleague appeared to be fixated on the online community Second Life). The other was the corporate understanding of street culture (warehouse, graffiti, that sort of thing). Ironically, they cited Hoxton Pimps as an example of cool street culture, but from the period when it had gone overground. (If their cool hunter had really been cool – truly the first to know – they would have discovered the Pimps about three, if not four, years earlier. I also had no heart to tell him that I was, in fact, The Pimpette.) This late discovery of trends was becoming typical of corporate cool hunters. Instead of being a step ahead, they were lagging behind. Many findings were no longer based on first-hand experience. Furthermore, Ranx and his friends, including The Pimpette, were no longer youths – we were all on the wrong side of 30. Some of the core team were in their twenties, but others were in their forties and fifties. The point is that age did not matter really; attitude was the thing.

Hoxton Pimps was one little clique that fitted the street aesthetic but there was a lot of stuff going on underground that did not fit into that canon and, if anything, was a reaction against it. An emblematic movement from this period was Cast Off: the Knitting Club, something I was closely involved with. When I mentioned this venture to my fellow brand consultant, he looked blank; he simply did not get it. For sure, knitting was not traditionally cool, far from it – but things changed. The man appeared to be oblivious to the potential of hip radically reinventing itself, in spite of my attempts to try to convince him to think outside the box. I suggested that youth culture was not the sole indicator of future trends and that there was a whole universe outside Second Life. He thought I was near the edge; I thought his ideas were dated. Years later, in 2007, I came across an article about the imminent publication of the aforementioned youth tracking monitor. They'd changed their tune. There was now a backlash against social networking, we were told. My colleague was quoted saying that young people could not keep on top of Second Life and the like, and that they were reverting to knitting! Just for the record, Cast Off, which triggered the new knitting hype – and by extension, craft movement – began in 2000. If their intention was to be the first to know, then frankly, they'd missed the boat. Or else youth culture really *isn't* setting all the trends.

Our conflicting interpretations of what constituted the leading edge led me to formulate the hypothesis of this book (or my killer hook). Could it be that for the first time in (marketing) history we have a case of parents being cooler than their kids? Could it be that the next non-conformist generation that rebelled against 1990s hip is Generation X – older still? Could it be that the Shoreditch phenomenon – developed off the back of the decade that peaked with Cool Britannia – inaugurated the post-youth-culture era? If in the 1980s 'video killed the radio star' to become the new cool that defined the 1990s, in the noughties, knitting became the new rock 'n' roll. If that's the case – and this book shall provide much evidence for it – then this movement is cooler than cool. In other words, it is a cycle ahead of the corporate cool. Call it über cool. If so, what are the implications for the marketing industry and wider society?

In order to address this issue, I shall use the same hip framework for each decade. Essentially, it is my favourite type of futurology: anticipating the future by looking at the past. I shall take hip's 1960s framework and map it onto the 1990s and then use that same method for the noughties. In each decade, it will be about subcultures and maverick businesses coming together to challenge the status quo, spur on change in established business models and ultimately influence the mainstream style and communication industries. It will also be about a contribution to identity politics. With every subcultural coming-of-age moment, there will be a step towards positive change in the guise of facilitating liberties.

In my framework and by extension, book design, hipness is about:
- Risk-taking (maverick businesses that challenge the status quo and in this process identify a new market: the early adopter).
- The kinship between mavericks and underground ideologies and aesthetic sensibilities, as well as the role of maverick businesses as chasm translators (using the diffusion model).
- The crossover process and influence on style and communication industries (translating underground language for the mainstream).
- Last but not least, cosmopolitanism: openness to diversity and the right to be alternative. The sell-out occurs when diversity is diluted and becomes used as a marketing tool favouring homogenisation and consumption patterns.

The crossover timeline also follows the same pattern for each decade: incubation phase (1987–1993), maturation period (1994–1996) and the peak (1997) from which follows the commercial phase. Once the trend hits the mainstream, something new bubbles up (1997–2003), reaches maturity (2004–2006) and peaks (2007). This timeline applies to both the advent of maverick businesses and subcultures. I am interested in the moments that triggered the beginnings of the underground co-optation rather than their actual inceptions. There appears to be a historical pattern when it comes to the year of incubation: 1967, the summer of love; 1977, release of 'God Save the Queen' by the Sex Pistols; 1987, the new summer of love with rave and the commercial explosion of rap (although hip hop had first developed alongside punk in the late 1970s); 1997, the arrival of the second-generation Hoxtonites, and 2007, the peak of the new underground trend associated with Shoreditch post Cool Britannia and potential new beginnings. This is an interesting way to view such phenomena, but there are, and will be, exceptions. Who knows what 2017 will bring?

But let us now return to 1987. 'Ladies and gentlemen – I give you rock 'n' roll!'[26]

PART TWO: THE 1990s

THE RISE AND FALL OF MTV EUROPE

1. Risk Taking

*'These guys are about to take showbiz down the tubes. They have the ugliest
fucking logo behind the stupidest idea you have ever seen.'*

Account Executive, Ogilvy & Mather, on the subject of MTV[1]

BARCELONA, NOVEMBER 2002
From the moment I disembark at Barcelona airport, it's impossible not to notice
that MTV is in town. The terminal building is plastered with posters of Robbie
Williams, announcing that he'll be in Barcelona for the 2002 MTV Awards.
The airport's arrival zone, right by customs, is occupied by MTV greeting desks,
buzzing with young staff running around with clipboards and walkie-talkies,
looking self-important. Their role is to meet the VIPs – albeit those who travel on
public planes rather than private jets – and transfer them to their respective hotels.
Around 700 accredited international journalists and about 100 photographers are
also expected.

Held in a different European city each year since their 1994 inception in
Berlin, the European Video Music Awards became MTV's 'tent pole' event and
one of the most high-profile annual happenings on the European entertainment
calendar. During the few days surrounding the awards ceremony, all notions
of reality seem to collapse in the microcosm of the inner circle. The host city

becomes a Mecca for glitz where egos are as plentiful as the complementary alcohol. Outwardly jolly and tipsy, this glamorous world is in fact ruled by the tyranny of access and VIP passes, which themselves have a hierarchy: an invite to the televised awards ceremony (the only part of the experience for which a limited number of tickets go on public sale); an invitation to MTV's afterparty; access to VIP areas within the afterparty; invitation to private parties (word of mouth only); and access to hotel lobby and bar (an exclusion zone where a select few crash until dawn). The colour of your wristband denotes your place in the pecking order. Anyone attempting to climb above their allocated station will be gently reminded of their place by gorilla-sized bouncers stationed on the door of every party venue.

As with any state, this one has its chief. If you do not know what Brent Hansen looks like, watch out for the guy whose 'access all areas' MTV staff accreditation bears the legend 'El Presidente'. The inner circle is then divided into castes from VIPs down to competition winners. Outside this circle, native residents hang around the venues and hotels hoping to catch a glimpse of their favourite star. This broader circle also includes tourists for whom the awards are an added holiday attraction, like the Scandinavian couple I observed while sipping latte on the Ramblas. They determinedly embarked upon a complicated mission of peeling an MTV poster off a lamppost. Equipped with a ladder and a mop-stick borrowed from their nearby hotel, the man was obstinately jumping up and down, trying to stretch high enough to reach this prized memento. Soon, a small crowd of amused onlookers formed. Eventually, our man succeeded. Everyone clapped and cheered.

Privileges in Ga Ga Land are mainly enjoyed by the A-listers, their entourages (some absurdly sized) and the well connected, such as yours truly and the rest of Brent's hangers on. More usually a pejorative term, being a 'hanger on' during the MTV Awards has its perks. Some of my most cherished memories survive from the events surrounding the awards, where surprises came thick and fast: from an impromptu piano session performed by Sasha Baron Cohen and his brother in a hotel lobby at the Frankfurt-held awards in 2001, to a private Iggy Pop gig in a tiny venue in Dublin in 1999 for barely 200 people. As if Iggy himself wasn't enough of a treat, Bono joined him during the encore, sliding down from the balcony above the stage Tarzan-style, via a heavy velvet curtain, leaving Mick Jagger at the table the two had been sharing. Marilyn Manson then jumped from the mosh pit on to the stage where he head-banged with The Offspring (of 'Pretty Fly for a White Guy' fame) and picked up a guitar. En masse, they engaged in an acoustic jam, Bono leading a rendition of 'Gloria' – 'G.L.O.R.I.A!' we sang along. It was exhilarating. And out of tune.

Another year, another ceremony: Edinburgh 2003, in the exclusion zone of the hotel lobby bar. The tabloids' view of these places is salacious. The truth is more a case of Pink having a quiet drink opposite me rather than misdemeanours galore. Mind you, if one is looking for the latter, it does help being around the Jackass collective, they of MTV's notorious daredevil series. I had a new best mate in Mike Liddle, 'the camera dude' of the Jackass team. Back then, I was already toying with the idea of writing an MTV-themed book, so Mike volunteered to be my 'research assistant' for the night and feed me with anecdotes. They were really funny but as they mostly involved huge stars in compromising situations, I'm unable to reveal any, lest I attract a mob of flash LA lawyers desperate to sue me. (Though I can reveal hearing about the Jackass member who 'accidentally' mistook the sink behind the bar at this exclusive Edinburgh hotel for another type of bowl you find in bathrooms – and it was not the bidet.) But what did actually happen, earlier that evening during the ceremony, was that Jackass's Chris Pontius managed to seriously upset The White Stripes by announcing them as winners in a particular category, before retracting this and declaring that in fact, the real winners were Coldplay. Truly, this is the kind of trivia that 700 or so journalists were fishing for.

Following that night, I went to sleep at the time I would normally get up. Already the morning papers had Beyoncé or Justin Timberlake on their front covers. The breakfast programme, GMTV, was showing highlights of the awards, including Pink's performance (which seemed surreal as she was still in the bar I'd just left). The top story on BBC News Scotland was the MTV Awards, which were being hailed as 'the biggest event that Scotland has ever seen'. MTV was praised for its positive contribution to Scottish tourism with all the concerts and festivities staged around town and the majority of hotels reaching full capacity. The euphoria surrounding MTV in the Scottish media, both in terms of amount of coverage and the priority status in the news, could not have been further from the attitude of the British media and music industries towards MTV in the early 1990s, when it was sneered at.

Let's rewind.

THE EUROPEAN MEDIA LANDSCAPE AND THE CRISIS IN
YOUTH BROADCASTING

The prospect of pan-national, multi-channel television in Europe – or 'satellite television' as it was popularly known – became a reality following the change in regulatory principles that took place in the 1980s. This 'deregulation' marked the shift from the public-service era of broadcasting towards an era driven by entrepreneurial imperatives. Up until then, television broadcasting – and by extension the notion of identity – had been a national affair. Now, there really was potential for imagining identities beyond those geographic boundaries. It was both exciting and daunting. Even though there was then no formula as to how a pan-national sense of identity might be fostered, there was one dominant reference that politicians (as guardians of national identity) and marketers (as shapers of new communities formed around common logos, brands, stars, music, advertising slogans and that sort of thing) shared: the idea of 'European' identity. Whatever their respective spin on what being European actually meant (and the political and marketing interpretations were indeed different) Europhilia was in the air. In the period preceding 1992 – the year of the official unification of the first twelve Western nation-states into a single European market – the political elite of the European Community (the EC, later to become the European Union or EU) showed much enthusiasm for a common European identity. This was intensified by the unforeseen collapse of communism, symbolically marked by the fall of the Berlin Wall in 1989. It was not just Western European politicians who were thrilled by this new chapter in European history; the Russian President Mikhail Gorbachev hailed this new era with reforms in the guises of *glasnost* (openness) and *perestroika* (political and economic restructuring). He, like Western European politicians, talked of a 'common European home'.

President Gorbachev's quote highlights how our senses of place and space were being reconfigured under the impact of the new communications technologies that respected no established national frontiers. In this context, 'space' (or 'home') could be defined as both a symbolic boundary (through the talk of a shared European culture) and a physical boundary (through the aspiration to develop new markets across geographical borders). Conceptions of national identities, once fixed, were now 'threatened' by the idea of satellite television, which ignored and undermined national boundaries and built new loyalties. The focus of the political rhetoric became cultural but the real issue was economic. At stake was not the cultural threat but the growing tension between national governments and the rising economic and political power of transnational corporations. Since the question of identity is always related to a particular stage of technological development, it is no wonder that the audiovisual arena became the main battlefield between states and corporations, as they all vied for the same space that was simultaneously 'virtual' and 'real'. The battle of citizenship against consumerism thus commenced.

In the 'citizenship' arena, the prospect of satellite television brought fears among the European cultural elite about the erosion of their respective cultures. Their assumption was that the increase in the number of channels would inevitably lead to an increase in the number of cheap American programmes on their grids. This, in turn, was influenced by the dominance of American programmes in international televisual exchange. Fresh out of the 1980s, the spectre of the American serial *Dallas* and its phenomenal international success was only too vivid. Debates about 'American cultural imperialism' that surrounded *Dallas* had barely been put to rest when this argument was resurrected. European civilisation was once again under threat from cheap American imports that would begin a process of erosion of European cultural values, we were told.

If we were to believe the proponents of this thesis, then the arrival of MTV in Europe was a serious danger. Its 'crass, three-minute culture' was another example of 'Yank cultural imperialism'.[2] MTV in Europe, we were warned, would feature American artists at the expense of European ones, playing 'native artists' only if they 'parrot[ed] Western genres of rock'.[3] On top of that, MTV would also increase the clout of major transnational record companies by largely limiting its playlist to artists affiliated with these labels, thus undercutting 'regional' and 'local' record companies unable to promote their acts on MTV.[4] Such assumptions and allegations were unfounded, as we shall see, but they hoodwinked many critics and they certainly chimed with the anti-American political climate.

Unless something was done to prevent this, it was said, satellite television would lead to the dreadful scenario whereby we ('civilised' Europeans) would be watching 'American images on Japanese screens', as the late François Mitterand, then president of France, vividly conveyed. Good job we had European politicians to save us from this dreaded prospect. Unfortunately for these crusaders, though, European media legislation had been drafted by a group of technocrats with no business acumen and a lack of foresight. Its resultant audiovisual policy was gibberish, concerned above all with implementing protectionist measures to safeguard European visual production (a nonexistent concept) from global conglomerates. This policy was highly influenced by the French politicians, who were the loudest to express their anti-American sentiment as a means of defending their own sense of national identity. This anti-Americanism was not widely shared across Europe nor was it representative of everyone's feeling in France. The British elite was sympathetic to the French view but the Germans had no such concerns. Nevertheless, protectionism was on the European agenda. The 1989 European Directive 'Television without Frontiers' stipulated 'quota' requirements to protect European production.

Ironically, these European quotas achieved precisely what they sought to avoid. 'Quotas' were prescribed for what were called 'generalist channels' in the document. This referred to the traditional model of public service television that offered a mixed programming stream. Assuming that 'television without frontiers' would be a supra-national version of public service television, the legislators ignored all the evidence that suggested this model was dying (their ignorance possibly stemming from a lack of insight). Thematic channels, then new, signalled a departure from mixed programming towards a focus on a dominant theme, such as round-the-clock news, sports or music. As such, they were either exempt from quotas on the basis of their content (news, sports) or fell into the category of 'European quotas where applicable', as in the case of MTV. Essentially, that meant that MTV could be broadcast in Europe, including France, where it had to sign a special agreement with the French media regulator, in exactly the same format as it was produced in London. The coast was clear. Instead of Euro-citizens, the MTV Generation was born, sponsored by hungry advertisers.

The battle in the 'consumerist' arena was led by MTV. Let it be known that MTV, even without imposed quota obligations, became the channel with the most European content compared to any other. This was consistently supported by independent statistics throughout its phase as a pan-European channel. MTV's motivation might not have been altruistic (though MTV's staff genuinely espoused this idea during the channel's incubation phase) but it nevertheless offered a vision of European unification that became more meaningful than the political one, as we shall see. Even so, the question of European identity from a corporate point of view was secondary if not almost irrelevant. Whether you addressed your audience as 'Europeans' or 'Dudes' was a matter of lingo. The point is that MTV found a lingua franca, which was not so much European as it was the language of rock 'n' roll.

The real challenge for any player in the audiovisual arena in the early 1990s was to devise a channel that would attract advertisers whilst at the same time striking a chord with a pan-national audience. MTV managed to do this not so much because it was 'European' but because it was cool. An ideological shift was then taking place, in which the worlds of commerce and culture were merging. At the crossroads was a new wave of creative thinking forged by a new breed of entrepreneurs who had a relaxed attitude to business, which had traditionally been reserved for the world of leisure. That mixing of work and play was a trait of Generation X, a particularly rebellious, hedonistic, Peter Pan generation into citizenship ideals on the one hand and consumerist values on the other. Instead of looking up to conventional businesses, they were learning their trade through a DIY approach. Their attitude was punk, their language rock 'n' roll, their culture rave and hip hop. MTV encapsulated that outlook and would gradually introduce it to the boardroom. By pioneering a creative new concept, MTV became not just an example of a successful global thematic channel, but also the thematic channel par excellence that revolutionised television. MTV was the model that the rest of the industry would follow: it was the blueprint for the new age.

MTV succeeded because it filled a vacant cultural and economic space, offering a two-in-one solution that pandered to both audiences and advertisers. For viewers in general, the thematic channel – with its varied diet of niche programming – answered a call for innovation at a time when studies across Europe revealed that there was a great dissatisfaction with public service broadcasting. In France, for example, opinion polls consistently showed that its output was considered 'stultifying and unimaginative'.[5] In Germany, the defection of viewers to the new commercial operators offering new programmes led to an unprecedented fall in ratings and revenues for the public sector in the first half of the 1990s.[6] For advertisers, the thematic channel provided a sorely needed advertising medium, as the relaxation in regulation meant that the new satellite television operators did not have to comply with the legislation that stipulated the advertising restrictions on terrestrial TV.

Specifically, the key to MTV's success was that it cracked the formula of how to gain the youth audience – the holy grail of marketing – at a time when advertisers were desperate to snare this demographic. In the late 1980s and early 1990s, the greatest warning sign that public service television was losing its appeal came from the European youth broadcasting sector. There was a genuine crisis in youth broadcasting. Perhaps most alarmingly, this crisis was seriously affecting the UK, the only European country that could match America for international dominance of youth culture. In the eyes of Europeans, Britain was the only other country they could look to seriously for new trends in music and style, while Britain itself seemingly looked to the USA, the birthplace of rock 'n' roll.

In the UK, TV viewing figures from this period were catastrophic. They indicated that almost half of what constituted the 'young' population was outside the broadcasters' reach, while television viewing time among those within the statistics was ten hours below the average weekly viewing figure. On the basis of such evidence, youth music programmes that were once considered flagship – Channel 4's *The Tube* and the BBC's *The Old Grey Whistle Test* – were axed.[7] The state-sponsored BBC Radio 1 had a major problem with cool youngsters defecting to pirate radio stations. To make things worse, the prospect of being banned from Radio 1's playlist was actually desirable, as it commanded underground respect.[8] Last but not least, traditional bastions of independent music such as the *New Musical Express* (*NME*) and John Peel's Radio 1 show were haemorrhaging readership and listeners respectively.[9] The youth broadcasting sector was in serious need of rejuvenation. Enter MTV.

The ascendancy of MTV Europe should be seen as a result of the failure of traditional broadcasters to reach a young audience. As in the USA previously, MTV in Europe came to life on the basis that it would deliver to the advertisers this elusive yet desirable audience segment that could only be reached imperfectly or wastefully by traditional broadcasters. Though the music video is the lifeblood of music television, it is to television itself that we must turn our attention first.

A NEW KIND OF TELEVISION
The Big M

Justin Eade was 19 when he left school in 1990 to seek employment, joining a recruitment agency to increase his chances. His USP was knowledge of computer software, and graphics packages in particular, then in their infancy and only relevant in niche industries. Finding that first job would have been a struggle, were it not for a peculiar opening. 'Have you heard of a channel called MTV?' asked the recruitment agent. A question that may well sound like lunacy nowadays, it was perfectly appropriate to assume that one would not have heard of MTV in 1990, let alone seen it. The satellite TV uptake in the UK was still relatively low (around 1, 418, 299 homes connected at the end of 1990), hence knowledge of MTV was specialist.[10] Happily, Justin was one of the initiated.

MTV's logo, or 'the big M' as Justin refers to it, had made an indelible impression on him. Passion for the visual medium ran in his blood; his paternal grandfather had produced pioneering advertisements while his father was interested in the concept of 'a brand' for his own business. In fact, Justin had just completed some 800 three-dimensional graphics for his father's *World Aid* report, including his pride and joy, a cover image of the Earth held by two hands. That was sophisticated back in the day, but nothing compared to MTV's logo, which had inspired it. Being a visual aficionado, Justin was particularly interested in the concept of the music video and the synergy between sound and vision. Unfortunately, there were very few outlets where music videos were played. 'You were lucky if you'd see three a week on television,' Justin recalls, which is why the discovery of MTV was so exciting. However, in terms of creative potential, 'the big M' was more than just music videos. Up until then, no television channel had had a 'personality'. MTV was about to change everything. Television was entering a new era and 'the big M' was its symbol. Had Justin heard of MTV indeed…

Armed with his 3D portfolio, Justin went for his interview. There was a job in 'traffic', which entailed scheduling MTV's own short promotional films between videos and advertising breaks. Traffic would later become media planning, a global media industry in its own right. Back then, traffic was part of MTV's advertising sales department (ad sales for short), which was in turn part of the finance department. Those were simpler days when anything to do with money (essentially a few people in ad sales and accounts) fell into this bracket. The rest counted as 'creative'. Even though technically Justin had the right skills for the job because he knew how to use the software, what tipped it for him was the moment when the interviewer from finance showed Justin MTV's playlist. No matter what the position was, a passion for music was (at that time) a prerequisite for a job at MTV. Justin's face lit up when he spotted post-punks Red Lorry Yellow Lorry on the list. You couldn't hear that kind of music on mainstream radio. It also happened to be one of the interviewer's favourite bands: 'Congratulations Justin, you got the job.' The three years that followed were, in Justin's own words, 'the best days in the most creative environment a young lad could work in with a passion'. He added that he felt like 'part of music video history'.

What would indeed be a significant part of music and television history was the way MTV merged traffic scheduling (essentially the mechanical side of the job) with the creative side; a department within MTV that came to be known as 'on air'. The on-air department comprised just one person at its inception: Peter

Dougherty, who would go on to become MTV's most senior executive in charge of the channel's branding, from 1990 to 2001. The gist of Peter's job was to turn music television (a generic format) into MTV (the brand that would go on to become the undisputed leader in European music television as it already was in the USA). Peter was in charge of commissioning the various short films that promoted all aspects of MTV. This was in turn part of MTV's broader creative vision, which would become more strategic over time; 'on air' would later become the creative services department.

Justin effectively implemented that vision, mixing together short MTV films with video content. This was no longer a mechanical job, but involved a certain savoir-faire. It was about seamlessly blending the short films with music videos by synchronising the visuals from the film with those of the video. Looked at another way, it was about that little, elusive beat: what a joy for Justin when the last note of a video could be in tune with the first of MTV's short film! Imagine, then, the lucky animation student who would pop into the MTV office to drop off his short film in the hope it might be played. You could do that in those days. There was no security, just one receptionist and a couple of affable ladies, Caroline and Tracy, who managed MTV's production office upstairs (it was a lesser hurdle for European fans to get into MTV than it was for them to understand Caroline's broad Ulster accent and Tracy's Scouse vernacular). Justin was passing that day and noticed the animation student because he had 'full-on dreadlocks and crusty, pre-grunge clothes'. Justin identified with him – he was a raver, also on the scruffy side. The student's short film was entitled *Attack of the Killer Tea Bag*. It was just what Justin needed. He had been exasperated by a gap between the music video for the Butthole Surfers' cover of 'Hurdy Gurdy Man', played on MTV's alternative music show *120 Minutes*, and the advertising break. Bingo! *Attack of the Killer Tea Bag* fitted perfectly. Justin's attention to detail bordered on the obsessive. He embraced his role with zeal, until his skill became redundant sometime towards the end of 1993, when output became automated. This change was all part of MTV's maturation. Losing that human touch was just one of the many inevitable aspects of turning corporate, but at least there had been many happy and creative times before that shift.

A Banal Idea That Was Genius

When it came to its own promotional films, MTV created real art. No expense was spared. There were two main types of short promotional films and MTV actively sought the most cutting-edge filmmakers to make them. MTV 'promos' were 30-second or so spots used to advertise MTV's own programmes. MTV 'idents' (short for 'channel identifications') were used to promote MTV as a brand. Among those idents were spots that raised awareness about causes that MTV felt strongly about, such as environmental campaigns. In terms of numbers, to give a sense of scale, MTV (or effectively, Justin) placed around ten to 12 different promos, each scheduled to go out between four and eight times a day. That amounted to around 60 promo placings per day or 420 per week. On top of this, MTV scheduled about 80 to 100 idents per day, which amounted to around 700 per week. The sheer volume of these lovingly crafted pieces of film is what gave MTV its wow factor.

MTV's trademark zany image is where this channel made its greatest impact. For a generation of twenty-somethings who grew up with MTV, it might be difficult to grasp just how groundbreaking this channel once was. Today, the notion of channel identity is the norm and all TV stations have their own 'creative services' departments to coordinate branding and scheduling. MTV provided the blueprint for this type of self-promotion. When MTV was beginning to carve out its place in the television landscapes in the USA and subsequently Europe, to think of a television channel in terms of a visual package (MTV even had their logo ever present in the corner of the screen) rather than as a series of programmes was nothing short of madness. The words of an account executive at Ogilvy & Mather (MTV USA's first advertising agency) sum up how the industry establishment felt about the concept when they first came across it: 'These guys are about to take showbiz down the tubes. They have the ugliest fucking logo behind the stupidest idea you have ever seen.' They did not get it. Similarly, in Europe, no one had cracked the formula either. MTV had a quasi-monopoly of the market for a full seven years before the first real competitor – the German music channel VIVA – emerged. MTV's idea had seemed banal – 24/7 music videos – but it proved a stroke of genius.

'The big M' was a big deal indeed. Its constant flow of visually sophisticated images stood out when compared to any other television channel. There was nothing like it. Whether an 'MTVphile' (like Justin, representative of MTV's fans – the MTV Generation) or an 'MTVphobe', the novelty symbolised by 'the big M' did not leave anyone indifferent. When it was launched in the USA, MTV had proved divisive. The moral panic surrounding it ranged from church leaders linking rock videos to drug usage and conservatives linking the channel to violence

(*Beavis and Butthead* would be held up as an example of resident evil) down to purist rock 'n' rollers for whom video really had killed the radio star. Europe was little different. In media-industry circles, MTV challenged the established norms. Its constant flow of images was seen as 'anti-television', which is why the industry was initially sceptical. Effectively it was television with no programmes. How daft! However, this was precisely why MTV would appeal to the vanguard of the creative industries. In academic circles, the reaction towards satellite/cable television was mixed. The negative consensus in Europe was expressed, as previously mentioned, as 'American cultural imperialism'. Alternatively, it was related to concerns about the commercial imperative of thematic channels that drove them away from diversity towards producing more of the same programmes, which Bruce Springsteen famously summed up in his song '57 Channels (And Nothin' On)'. However, even the fiercest critics acknowledged MTV as the 'one aesthetic novelty' to find its way on to cable.[11] A handful of scholars would fully understand MTV's potential, including Andrew Goodwin, Lawrence Grossberg, Simon Frith and Serge Denisoff, whose book *Inside MTV* tells how the channel came to life in the USA.

At the opposite end of the spectrum was postmodernism, an intellectual movement very much in vogue, crossing over from academic journals into popular media, and worthy of inclusion here. Nowhere was MTV more glorified for its visuals than in postmodern theory, which hailed the channel as its supreme incarnation. Postmodernists perceived MTV as a seamless transmission of self-referential images, a pastiche of tradition (because it appeared not to have discrete programmes) acting in a constant present, thus signalling a break with the past and an abandonment of convention. This theory was deeply flawed in every way, but MTV went along with the hype.[12] It even called its alternative rock show *PostModern* in the USA (later rebranded as *Alternative Nation* on MTV Europe) to give the channel a hint of intellectual panache. That fashionable reference was the only real connection MTV ever had with postmodernism, but it reflected MTV's ironic take on life ('We don't care much about postmodernism in our day-to-day, but it sounds cool, so why not name a show after it?'). Contrary to postmodern theory, however, MTV was not a mere 'pastiche' that represented a break with the past in terms of ideological references, nor did it represent a complete disconnection with conventional television.

It's Just a Little Bit of History Repeating: the 1960s and the 1990s

Far from signifying a break with the past, the similarities between MTV's company culture during its early development phase and that of the maverick Madison Avenue advertising executives of the 1960s are quite striking. Thomas Frank concludes his analysis of hip's co-optation in *The Conquest of Cool* by pointing out that the language of the 1960s business revolution made a 'triumphant return' in the 1990s.[13] Indeed, this decade came to be known as the cool marketing era, with MTV standing 'triumphant at the centre of the global teen phenomenon', as noted by Naomi Klein in her influential book *No Logo*.[14] Incidentally, the point that Klein was making was not that MTV had links to the tradition of 1960s maverick businesses. Rather, her intention was to emphasise MTV's role as a leading force in homogenising youth culture, which is how MTV and cool marketing came to be perceived. However, this stance is not helpful when attempting to explain how and why MTV became 'triumphant'. What afforded MTV its leader position was the fact that it took a risk, turned the media industry on its head and subsequently became a model for innovation. As such, MTV was both very much grounded in the past – specifically the 1960s framework of hip – and consciously designed to be a departure from the traditional TV norm.

To claim that MTV had to be innovative is not to sing its praises; it had to be innovative to survive. There was indeed an opportunity in the market, which had been prompted by the crisis in youth broadcasting, but there was still a mountain to hurdle. In pre pay-TV days, a 'peak time' programme could deliver anything between 30 per cent and 40 per cent of the total viewing share. It was in such a landscape and with a professional mentality embedded around 'prime time' that MTV decided to have its own share of the advertising cake. Only there was one 'tiny' problem: MTV could barely muster 1 per cent of the European viewing share – even when at its peak as a single pan-European channel! To go head to head with the terrestrial sector would have been like capitulating before even entering the ratings battlefield. Success was therefore dependent on changing advertisers' mindsets by persuading them to shift from national terrestrial advertising fixated on prime time, towards developing economies of scale and scope. If you were perceived as having 'the ugliest fucking logo' by your potential clients, perhaps you could change it, but what about the established advertising businesses' conviction that MTV was 'the stupidest idea [they'd] ever seen'? A revolutionary model of television was therefore the only chance of winning. This is where thematic channels – MTV being widely acknowledged as the greatest success story of this era – made a quantum leap.

The crucial task for MTV initially was to get advertisers on its side. This is where the 1960s model of segmentation came in handy. This is not to say that MTV's team went through the annals of advertising history to look for a suitable pattern, but the connection exists nevertheless, and helps elevate MTV's case beyond it being channel-specific. For readers less familiar with marketing jargon, segmentation – also known as 'lifestyle marketing' or 'psychographics', terms now commonplace in marketing – involves devising sophisticated systems for categorising population data to take into account the complexities of consumer behaviour and, more importantly, to predict tendencies according to identified profiles in order to anticipate demand for new trends. Just like the start of the 1990s, marked by a shift from a public service era towards an entrepreneurship-driven one, the 1960s were marked by a shift from a management culture of hierarchy and efficiency to a culture of creativity and individualism, as documented in *The Conquest of Cool*. Market segmentation came to maturation in the 1960s because it quite literally enabled marketers to start competing on the grounds of brand image and consumer identity, as opposed to 1950s advertising that had stressed the functionality of products and the importance of conformity. Instead of 'keeping up with the Joneses' (an expression that sums up the 1950s), the new wave of 1960s advertising was all about diversity and appealing to consumer subjectivities, targeting not just who people were but who they might aspire to be.

The most famous example from this period is what is known in marketing history as the Cola Wars. Coca-Cola was all things to all people and the undisputed market leader until Pepsi came up with the 'Pepsi Generation', a construct of marketers that became a force to be reckoned with. Pepsi was all about youth, a great conceptual position based on an attitude to consumption and more generally, lifestyle, which anyone could aspire to. Overnight, youth culture – a marketing staple because of the still unformed tastes of youth and the perception of the young as trend leaders – monopolised advertising. The young became the voice of the decade as well as arbiters of taste and a gateway to their parents' pockets, as advertisers saw an opportunity to target them via their children. This perception would prevail in coming decades.

However, the 1960s, the very decade most commonly cited as the time when marketing became fascinated by 'youth', is the decade when marketers actually ceased to be interested in the demographic aspect. *The Conquest of Cool* adeptly reveals this paradox. The fascination among the 1960s non-conformist business community with youth idioms derived as much from its kinship to the new understanding of consumer culture embodied in their own creative revolution as it did from the demographic appeal of 'youth'. They approved of the new values and anti-establishment sensibilities that were developed by the young revolutionaries. For marketers, 'youth' had a meaning that extended far beyond the youth market proper. 'Youth' was constructed as a marketing segment with a common outlook, rather than a demographic; youth was anti-materialist and rejected conformity. Marketers were, above all, interested in the minority culture-rebel youth – rather than the majority conformist youth – thus privileging the hip over the square. In this context, Frank quotes an advertising executive from a 1966 edition of the trade magazine *Advertising Age*, explaining how for them, the youth market encompassed not just teens, but people up to 35 and in some cases, beyond.[15]

Thus the 1960s effectively redefined youth (or youthfulness) as hip. Hip was a state of mind that embraced innovative thinking and non-conformism, whose tones were expressed by using countercultural idioms. At the vanguard of this trend were the style and communication industries, which equated style (the peacock revolution in menswear symbolised by garments such as Pierre Cardin two-button jackets and narrow flared trousers) and communication campaigns (using the countercultural symbols of mods and hippies, 'flower power' and rock music) with rebellion. This is how hip became synonymous with rock 'n' roll. It was an attitude. In the offices, where this trend was marketed, the ad execs shed their grey flannel suits in favour of flares, loud colours, beads and long hair, for they were hip too. Hip became a matter of consumption, namely 'staying one step ahead of the consuming crowd'.[16] But the 1970s recession put an abrupt end to this creative insurgency. Experimentation gave way to a no-risk approach. Even Pepsi jettisoned their 'Pepsi Generation' tag in favour of promoting the beverage's more obvious attributes (ie that it tasted different from Coke). The hip bug subsequently lay dormant for a couple of conservative decades and returned with a vengeance in the 1990s. Like the 1960s reaction to 1950s conformity, lifestyle marketing in the 1990s became a reaction to the overly materialistic 1980s yuppie era symbolised by power suits and lunches. It was premised on two basic concepts at work: the move to market segmentation and an emphasis on design and visual communication.[17]

Segmentation and the Youth(ful) Market

What came to be known as cool marketing became the main manifestation of the new trend, with MTV being one of the brands to pioneer it. Like advertising executives from the 1960s, MTV became fascinated with subcultural idioms, a kinship that will become even more explicit in the section that looks at 'ideologies'. For now though, MTV had to convince select advertisers that it was the right medium for them. That MTV, unlike terrestrial broadcasters, could deliver the elusive target they were after – the beloved youth market that supposedly did not watch television. It is in this context that MTV resorted to the 1960s model of market segmentation. MTV reinvented its target audience by offering a cultural definition of youth. In marketing practice, this was a matter of extracting a specific viewing segment from the mass TV market. In MTV's account, an audience did not simply consist of particular viewers attracted to particular programmes, but was more about viewing behaviour that could be described as youthful. The basic premise was that the youthful viewer had a busy lifestyle in which TV viewing was only one activity competing for his or her time.

On MTV, being young was not so much about age as an attitude to life. Just as the 1960s Pepsi Generation had signified, it was a consuming position that anyone who exhibited a similar mindset could aspire to. The MTV Generation may have been a marketing construct but, at the same time, a cultural shift had genuinely occurred, which the marketing industry turned into an opportunity. The Italian scholar Alberto Melucci, most famous for his theories on social movements, wrote of traditional adolescent attributes (uncertainty, mobility, transience, openness to change) transcending age limits. Similarly, renowned British historian Eric Hobsbawm wrote of a late 20th-century cultural revolution characterised by the triumph of individualism. In this new paradigm, being young did not just constitute a 'separate social stratum' with purchasing power, but equally constituted a group who had in common their 'internationalism, jeans and rock music', a shared language and the rejection of moral restraints. Hip consumerism was not just a figment of the marketer's imagination but rather a response to this new individualism. Marketing was a step ahead.

'Freedom of choice' became the central motive in the advertising campaigns for the emerging thematic television channels. It was summed up by the slogan 'You can watch what you want, when you want.' If you were a news aficionado, you could tune in to a 24/7 news channel. Ditto if you were a sports enthusiast or a music fan. The French television channel Canal Plus is an even better example than MTV for demonstrating how these marketing campaigns pandered to the new individualism, because 90 per cent of its revenues came from the subscription fee (for MTV, it was the reverse until 1995 when the channel was encrypted) and therefore the focus was directly on convincing viewers to pay for the service. Canal Plus is another maverick success story from this era that started as a national pay-TV channel (albeit it on terrestrial television, owing to the peculiarities of the French audiovisual landscape at the time) and grew into a global group. In terms of being thematic, Canal Plus's selling point was its movie premieres, which appeared way ahead of other terrestrial television channels. It also screened live concerts, and added a few flagship cutting-edge programmes to complete its hip image.

To communicate its 'edge' to the viewer, Canal Plus developed its promotional strategy with a message along the lines of being one big family. This was groundbreaking at the time and it took a while to convince viewers to buy into this culture. In my interviews with Canal Plus staff in the early 1990s, they talked directly of having to educate viewers about TV decoders and the idea of paying for television. To this end, they set up telephone lines (this was years before customer service lines and call centres became commonplace) and all sorts of other mechanisms to support the consumer and make them feel like 'family', by always being a step ahead of their viewers' needs. The price of the subscription to Canal Plus was high (possibly the highest subscription fee in Europe for a single channel at the time) but their attention to detail eventually paid off. Canal Plus became the must-have reference among early adopters in France, and the rest of the market gradually followed. Essentially, here, MTV and Canal Plus shared the same leading-edge audience in France, who were willing to spend on new technologies as part of their lifestyle. This segment went beyond mere youth. So, while there was indeed some evidence that satellite channels across Europe were heavily patronised by young viewers who would nudge their parents to get a subscription so they could access MTV, there was equally a group of viewers who were into technology because it was a gateway to diversity.[18] These were the early adopters. Canal Plus subscribers were easier to convert to cable-TV subscribers than were pay-TV virgins, which helped MTV's work with cable operators in France in their mutual attempt to recruit subscribers.

More specifically, on MTV, the central appeal of youthfulness was freedom from necessities (for example 'adult' overheads such as mortgages), which enabled people who fitted this segment to spend their discretionary income on self-indulgence. Advertisers referred to this under the heading 'the 3Cs': CDs (or anything to do with music), cafés (or anything to do with going out) and clothes (or anything to do with style). However, this does not mean that an adult with a mortgage couldn't be self-indulgent or interested in 'youthful' trappings and therefore have that same willingness to spend on products that fitted their lifestyle – they could and they did. It was just that traditionally, the two had been separated by a demographic divide. Through MTV, their common interests united them. In commercial terms, the concept of youth was now effectively 'stretched' to encompass an older audience and create a segment bound by a similar spending attitude. This entailed redirecting pop programming from an audience of 12- to 24-year-olds to an audience of 18- to 34-year-olds. The former were 'youth' as traditionally defined by the music industry, whereas the latter had significant disposable income and were therefore more interesting from the point of view of the new commercial services.[19] In practical terms, MTV's audience originally encompassed targets even beyond 34.

This is a fundamental point in my story because what we have here is a combination of different concentric circles of protagonists in the hip trajectory, all under the umbrella of the 'youth market'. On the one hand, there is the demographically young, the key to generating revenue from advertisers seeking to reach the youth market – essentially the early majority (often denigrated as 'wannabes' by the self-consciously hip). Segmentation helped MTV deliver them to advertisers and generate revenue. On the other hand, there are the early adopters, that even more elusive segment interested primarily in innovation. This is the key segment one requires for hip kudos. This is the leading-edge faction of the population across the demographic spectrum, which includes youth but also anyone of that 'youthful' mindset. MTV was cool because it tapped into this market. Its audience included the opinion formers as well as the trendsetters (and they are the ones worth an advertising premium). MTV's approach to these guys was based more on intuition than research, because the channel initially had an unusual degree of creative freedom for a corporate company. MTV had a market monopoly in Europe during its risk-taking phase when it could experiment with what pan-European music television might be.

This meant they could take a degree of creative risk without fear of alienating less edgy audiences.

In the USA, MTV's access to alpha trendsetters and early adopters was almost accidental.[20] MTV's team was always adamant that they also wanted to reach an older and more intellectual *Saturday Night Live* audience with their rock-TV narrowcast (as opposed to broadcast) format. However, the blessing in disguise that made MTV edgy in its formative years (1981–1983) was the *lack* of rock music videos to fill the 24 hours. Instead of rock around the clock, as MTV professed to be, they had to resort to whatever music they could get their hands on that was accompanied by a video clip. What they found were British new romantic bands (also known as new wave or new pop in the USA) – the music video was part of their aesthetic. New romantics cultivated a strong look and a synthetic sound, which was completely alien to American mainstream audiences; thus it became synonymous with innovation. Suddenly, radio stations in cabled areas that carried MTV were getting requests to play Culture Club or Duran Duran, both unknown at that time in the States. The record industry was becoming intrigued and started to believe that MTV could indeed sell records. It appeared that MTV's own self-promoting motto, 'MTV: you hear it first', had genuine resonance.

MTV would enjoy that same trend-leader position in Europe. Let me use an example from Europe to further illustrate how MTV tapped into the leading edge market, rather than the concept of music television being youth television per se. When I said that MTV had no competition in Europe (prior to Germany's VIVA), it was not technically correct: there was a French music television channel called MCM. But no one bothered with it. MCM, like MTV, was a channel that played music videos. Also like MTV, MCM aimed to be pan-European, and if anything should have had the advantage, being truly European (albeit with a strong French flavour) as opposed to MTV, which was accused of being American. So what were the problems?

To begin with, it had three names: MCM (Ma Chaîne Musicale), MCM Euro-musique and MCM (Monte Carlo Musique), which was very confusing for advertisers and viewers alike. What's in a name? In an era that was going to be marked by visual culture, MCM had no tangible identity. Another barrier that this channel would face was the wretched 'quotas'. Being a French channel, it had to comply with playing a large percentage of French music (55 per cent of its playlist) but French music failed to translate to non-

French and non-francophones. 'Quotas' also stipulated that if a French act did not sing in French (for example Mano Negra, a multiracial French band who often sang in Spanish) it didn't count as French music so they too would be squeezed into the remaining 45 per cent. And yet, that band appealed to niche audiences across Europe. Last but not least, there had not yet been a coordinated pan-European record release. Each country had it own chart and the French chart was the slowest in Europe. Whereas on MTV 'you hear it first', on MCM, you heard it last. MCM's fate would change for the better in 1994, when Canal Plus purchased a share in their channel. MCM would then learn from both the Canal expertise and MTV about the importance of visual culture (in fact MCM poached an MTV executive for this endeavour). Until then, MTV was cool and MCM was not. Consequently, French fans, like the rest of their European counterparts, watched MTV (around 4.4 per cent audience share for MTV compared to just 0.3 per cent for MCM in the early 1990s).[21]

Focus on Visuals

The second 1990s trend that went hand in hand with the rediscovery of segmentation was the focus on design and visual communication. MTV's good looks were related to its commercial imperative rather than being some kind of postmodern visual crusade. MTV became the first television channel to promote itself as a brand: the domain at the intersection of the economic imperative of new satellite/cable channels to construct audience segments to attract advertisers, and 'cultural' necessity to produce innovative programming to attract the audience. MTV's 'environment' is where the two merged. Essentially, MTV was designed to accommodate youthful viewing behaviour: the channel fitted into your lifestyle, not the other way around. In contrast to conventional (and dated) youth programmes that simulated a youth group on the screen where we, as viewers, could place ourselves, MTV was set up as a community of consumption, or an 'environment', that you entered through mood.[22] Viewers could dip in and out when they fancied, without fear of missing the plot, as if it were a programme that ran 24 hours a day. You no longer had to work around the television schedule because MTV was constant. The pleasure of viewing TV was therefore described in terms of the experience of watching MTV (the channel as a whole). This does not mean that people did not tune in for specific programmes. On the contrary, the core MTV fans totally did, but the novelty principle was the format, not the individual content. This idea of non-stop 24/7 music television was an important distinction because it enabled MTV to sell itself not only as the right environment for advertisers, but also as a genuinely innovative channel with an identity distinctively different from terrestrial TV.

Having understood from the outset that MTV was a narrowcaster that could not compete with a broadcaster, the channel sold itself as a complementary choice to terrestrial television. MTV accepted that it was a default channel: when there was nothing on terrestrial, you'd switch to MTV. It was like a continuous option for short bursts of viewer attention. This short MTV viewing span did not exceed around 18 minutes. MTV was also conceived with the realisation that its viewers were zappers who flicked through channels, a trend that was set to grow with the increase in the number of available channels. A zapper was not a loyal viewer. This infidelity of its viewers raised the issue of TV reception not in terms of consumption of programmes, but in terms of the viewer's relation to them. Being able to switch on and off at any time was what rendered the routine of watching television tolerable for the easily bored, unfaithful viewer. However, this option of fast programme selection at any time ultimately worked to the narrowcaster's advantage because it turned the apparent infidelity towards a specific programme into an overall loyalty towards the channel. In numbers, that roughly translated to 20 per cent of viewers accounting for 90 per cent of ratings. This equated to a small group of people flicking to MTV when there was nothing better on – but it was worth an advertising premium.

Ensuring viewer loyalty became a matter of creating a shared culture between that viewer and the channel. It was all about establishing a connection by hitting the right emotional notes. Instead of stressing the functional side of products and their competitiveness, consumers saw the return of the 1960s language that promoted product awareness using emotional messages. Colour, shape and sound became the things that marked out individuality. It was all about self-expression, stylistic self-consciousness and associations with products through mood. Complicity with the viewer was fostered creatively through a strong visual culture, which in turn directly pandered to the emerging subcultural ideologies with which MTV would associate itself (more of which later). This is where the 'on air' role came into play.

Investing in the creation of a strong channel identity was a significant departure from the traditional method of allocating television budgets. Instead of programmes – the bulk of which, on MTV, were effectively music videos paid for by record companies – MTV focused on its own self-promotion by using its idents and promos. Prior to MTV making these spots de rigueur, they had been insignificant for broadcasters. While writing my thesis on MTV, my supervisor (David *Morley*) dug out an obscure paper for me about idents and promos by a scholar called David *Morey*. It dated from 1981 and there had been nothing else written about them since, which showed just how little-regarded these shorts were. Morey used the term 'continuity sequences' to describe these 'spaces between the programmes', for back then they did not even have a proper name. 'Continuity sequences' were not quite the same thing as 'interstitials', which were used to fill in airtime if a programme finished early. What struck me about this paper was its amazing foresight. Morey's point was that the television industry ignored the 'continuity sequences' because of their 'indistinct status' of 'unprogramme' at its own peril. With a bit of attention, they could actually play a central role in creating a relationship with the audience to maximum advantage for the channel. This is because they could function as what is called, in semiotics, a system of codes. They were a pool of signs, expressed through sounds, words or visuals. As such, you could fashion them to avoid any viewer alienation or puzzling by naturalising them with your own system of practices and house style. That is exactly what MTV sussed over a decade later, and it would change the industry.

MTV realised that these short, self-promotional films were not peripheral to the experience of watching television. They could play a key role if you jazzed them up; so they did just that. Previously marginal ephemera, MTV put them in the spotlight. 'MTV promo' became a euphemism for packaging the same music video according to MTV's judgement of its current worth. Typically, the same video would be promoted differently depending on its rotation on MTV's playlist, its genre and its chart position. For example, if a rock music clip were a new release, it would be categorised by MTV as 'fresh' (or even 'premiere'), 'alternative' (thus labelled it could be played in MTV's indie and alternative rock – but not metal! – shows) and 'European'. As such it would chart in MTV's European Top 20, 'the one and only European chart show', which was in itself, a non-event. But if you heard it in the background enough times, you might find, some 15 years later, that you still remember the jingle. In fact, I can tell you that the show was sponsored by Braun. Each time, the same clip would be presented in a new light, the promos ensuring that it appeared constantly interesting.

Idents promoted MTV as a brand. Sometimes, they emulated art, for example the pastiche on Magritte's '*Ceci n'est pas une pipe*', which MTV turned into '*Ceci n'est pas une télévision'*. Sometimes, idents were playful and self-mocking, such as the one with the solemn voice intoning 'MTV: the whole world is watching', followed by an image of a herd of cows idly chewing the cud. There were also a number of idents dedicated to various causes, such as ecology, or AIDS awareness. Idents created MTV's 'environment', setting it apart from other (music) television channels. If you were flicking through channels, MTV would appear as a seamless flow of images. But if you were the target audience, you knew exactly what the programmes were, who the VJs were and what time they were on. MTV also managed to prove that it was not just a source of the latest music, but was truly 'lifestyle' television. Examples illustrating its diversity include MTV *Sports* (featuring the minority 'crazy' sports of snowboarding and skateboarding); MTV *Pulse* (fashion and style); *Beavis and Butthead* (outrageous cartoon); *Unplugged* (live acoustic music); *The Real World* (the first 'youth' reality TV, whose impact was relatively insignificant compared to what this format would achieve a decade later) and *Most Wanted* (live phone-in programme, more of which in the 'European identity' section).

By virtue of being fresh and youthful, MTV became synonymous with youth television. MTV was perfectly aware that the 'cool' and 'youthful' talk was just hype, but it benefited from the fuss nonetheless. Jonathan Lewis, MTV's Head of Creative Strategy, (a position created during MTV's commercialisation phase) made this perfectly clear. Speaking to me in 1997, he said: 'MTV has an aesthetic, and a flair and tone which makes it feel that it is a young people's channel, but [BBC soap opera] *Eastenders* is an amazing young people's programme. It attracts more young people than any other channel. It just doesn't look like a young person's programme ...so you need to make a distinction between channels which look like they're for young people and channels which really appeal to young people.'

Stripped of its looks, it transpired that MTV was not so much original as it was clever. Even in its novel heyday, MTV was, in fact, conventional in many respects. It used the classic audience-building techniques of broadcast media schedules: day-parting (dividing the day into blocks of programmes to efficiently target different audience sections) and scheduling (screening the same programme at the same time of the day on a given day). MTV also employed 'thematisation', another tried and tested method of soliciting viewers' attention. Thematisation entails organising unconnected features into a preferred reading so that their divergent realities become linked through the overarching frame of the programme.[23] Many conventional television programmes had been using the same tactic for years, but unbranded. On MTV, however, everything was made to look cool and desirable; something as banal as thematising videos into different music-genre-based programmes became sexy because the idents and promos did their job so well.

MTV (and its big M) is a brand that produced nothing but changed everything. From the business of producing programmes, television turned to the business of packaging and selling. Everything was up-to-the-minute in MTV's universe. The principle of the channel was that everything was cool on MTV but that MTV itself was the cool*est*, the leader of the pack. By watching MTV you too could be cool by association. If you wanted to be the first to know, you knew which channel to tune into. It was indeed difficult not to admire 'MTV's cynical brilliance', as Professor Goodwin put it when he wrote about MTV in *Dancing in the Distraction Factory*. Whatever you think of MTV, this is the channel that found an answer to the perennial problem of cable (how to generate revenue) while at the same time being really fun to watch. It defined a generation and a whole decade, as everything from kids' TV to politics went cool.

From Street to Boardroom

I first heard the word 'strategy' at MTV when I did an interview with Simon Guild in 1994, shortly after his appointment at the end of 1993, the year of change at MTV. As noted earlier, this shift in corporate practice was symbolically marked by a series of events including MTV's breaking even financially, moving to a proper television studio and gaining a rival in VIVA. Simon called himself the 'corporate paranoiac' and defined 'strategy' as worrying about what might go wrong. He was admittedly the only person worried about this. Simon would become MTV's CEO and even the top dog for a short period when Brent stepped down as president in 2006 (Guild, too, left MTV in January 2007). What struck me when I first met Simon was that he wore a striped shirt, the kind you buy at TM Lewin of Regent Street. He was the first person I'd met at MTV who dressed like he had a proper job. Until then, all MTV's executives, including Bill Roedy, who was above even Brent, were trendy. Brent himself fitted the 1960s hip business archetype down to the shaggy haircut, funky clothes and trainers. (It was the look that came to define 'cool executives' in the cool-marketing 1990s. Think also Richard Branson.)

When MTV left its experimental phase and entered its maturation phase (1994–1996), it partnered up with other mavericks to begin the creation of the corporate-cool powerhouse that would eventually influence every aspect of society. Out with old hierarchies, in with the new entrepreneurial businesses – this was a new ideas-led economy run by young Generation X executives and friendly non-suited CEOs. Cool marketing (targeting youth) thus spread into 'new marketing' (targeting everyone else).[24] The phenomenon of Cool Britannia in 1997 was the pinnacle of this trend. Britain led the way as mavericks touched upon every sector of society: cool art (YBAs), cool music (Britpop), cool fashion (Alexander McQueen), cool brand-communication agencies (maverick advertising agencies such as St Luke's, media agencies such as Naked Communications and Michaelides & Bednash, brand development agencies such as Headlight Vision and the now-defunct Happy Dog), even cool education (Goldsmiths College) and cool politics (New Labour).

IKEA inaugurated this era in the mainstream with the 'Chuck Out Your Chintz' campaign, produced by the then new-cool advertising agency, St Luke's. I befriended one of its founding members, John Grant, through an MTV conference, so I remember first-hand that IKEA was the agency's first account. What they and MTV had in common was their rebellious and non-conformist attitude. They questioned everything. Nowadays IKEA is ubiquitous but back then modern furniture was not popular in the UK. Surveys showed that two thirds of people preferred 'traditional' English style. IKEA's task was to develop a campaign that would literally start changing the tastes in home décor. That was how 'Chuck Out Your Chintz' was born. In true 1990s cool marketing style, the advert had an ironic tone. It featured housewives chucking out their doilies and floral prints in favour of a sleek, modern look. The advert never actually said anything about IKEA. Instead, it invited you to enter the world of IKEA, just as MTV invited viewers to dip into its environment and become cool by association. The case of IKEA and other brands is fully recounted in John's book *The New Marketing Manifesto*, which is a great testament to this period. Minimalism would come to define cool design for the next decade, reaching its zenith with the loft-style aesthetic.

In the period post Cool Britannia, the segmentation that helped define MTV's audience became the norm. It was not just the television industry that addressed its viewers as fragments bound by interest. The brand industry, more generally, came to think of the public in terms of consumption patterns and market trends rather than simply demographic classifications. Mass-marketing strategy thus moved towards category management, whereby the same marketing

THE FIRST TO KNOW

manager would look after a portfolio of related products (rather than individual products or brands). These mini-groupings or product categories were run as a 'business unit', as the marketing parlance goes. Category management entailed forging partnerships with distributors and retailers, as a result of which retail environments were designed by 'categories', rather than organised by products or brands. For example, in a supermarket all the dairy products would be in one space, whether they were Danone or Kraft.

Innovation in the corporate sector became a marketing boardroom decision, which is a different matter from creation in the scientific laboratory. Marketing strategy underpinned with robust consumer and market research would lead new product or service development (in other words, whether your butter was low-fat or with added Omega 3). There are of course brands that manage to combine groundbreaking product invention with alluring design (Apple springs to mind). However, even then, some type of strategic element would underpin the brand positioning, simply because competition is fierce. Agencies with creative approaches towards unearthing unfulfilled consumer needs in increasingly saturated markets would come to be highly prized by clients, because they could combine the ability to come up with innovative products while managing risk. Consequently, we consumers were blessed with dozens of options when choosing cornflakes and as many different varieties of strawberry jam. This trend flourished in the first half of the noughties until we reached what Barry Schwartz described as the 'paradox of choice'. Here, a new opportunity began to take root. (Hold this thought for noughties' mavericks, later on.)

However, for all the success of cool marketing in promoting a consumerist vision of life, we must not forget that cool's original appeal is that it struck a chord with consumers: MTV spoke to its viewers not because they were a well-defined advertising segment, but because MTV was genuinely relevant to them. Viewers did not want any old music television. They wanted their MTV.[25]

2. Underground Ideology and Aesthetic Sensibilities

THE RECONCILIATION OF ROCK AND TV

The Displacement of Rock

In theory, the concept of music television should have been a failure. Traditionally, the relationship between rock and television was rather cool (ie cold), even hostile. Rock 'n' roll TV (rock being synonymous with hip) was a contradiction in terms. This predicament could have seriously affected MTV's credibility and prospects, and to some extent explains the music industry's initial scepticism towards it. Rock's antagonism to the medium was partly due to the low technological quality of sound and vision and partly due to television's inability to address youth beyond a domestic context. In contrast, rock was about rebelling against anything parental. Live music (the guitar, the voice, the drums), as well as the event of the gig itself and an anti-establishment attitude, was central to the authentic experience of being part of the rock community. Rock 'n' rollers shared such currency among their peer group, but not with outsiders and certainly not with the mainstream, which included television. Rock fans were not pop fans – full stop. Pop was another word for disco in the late 1970s (the decade preceding MTV), which crossed over from the gay and black underground into the mainstream. Then, a rock fan would never have confessed to any partiality to disco. A macho hetero guy who admitted to liking disco – the antithesis of cock rock – would have been committing social suicide. Equally, the idea of a gay rock star was inconceivable for mainstream rock fans (even with a band called Queen). Nowadays, it is perfectly acceptable – even desirable – to have eclectic musical tastes; a legacy of the 1990s, and we shall trace how that shift occurred.

Rock's self-conscious elitism, cultivated through the notion of 'authenticity', was still very much engrained among fans and the music industry when MTV began.[26] What MTV managed to do on both sides of the Atlantic, albeit under different sets of circumstances, was to adopt elements of the traditional rock credo in order to set it apart from the established TV norms, as well as associate with new subcultures to embrace a fresh ideology that gave the channel its hip kudos. MTV became relevant to fans not just because it responded to demographic shifts in music consumption, but also because it responded to the ideological shift that had occurred throughout the 1980s, which would redefine hip as something separate from rock. Ultimately, MTV Europe would displace the rock ideology. This is how it goes.

The 1980s signalled the rise of a new youth culture that was not centred on music. Instead, it was centred on a culture that foregrounded the visual.[27] The young responded in new and ever more ironic ways to these new visual forms; visual-based culture spoke to them in place of rock and at times even against rock. One medium that spoke to the young generation in the way that rock might have previously was cinema – specifically, a wave of 1980s films that focused on ordinary youths (rather than 'rebels') and deployed musical soundtracks. This in itself was not new, but what was new was the way these films essentially used rock videos to promote themselves. The first such film was *War Games* (directed by John Badham, 1983), followed later that same year by *Flashdance* (directed by Adrian Lyne), the following year by *Footloose* (directed by Herbert Ross) and culminating with the enormous success of *Dirty Dancing* (directed by Emile Ardolino) in 1987, which sold well over eight million soundtrack albums at the time of release. Such films provided a condition for the music video to become a means of origination and promotion of music.

The other 'visual formation' was the music video itself. Initially rejected by the music industry as a fad, this format eventually became the answer to the industry's crisis in profitability (sales of records had dropped significantly in the late 1970s and it was becoming evident that lengthy rock tours were no longer viable as a promotional tool). It was only in the early 1980s, when reports came through about records selling in cabled areas with MTV access, that record companies began to look upon music videos positively. However, there was an ideological aspect to the music video, which had appealed to audiences before the industry warmed to it. This ideological appeal stemmed from two major post-punk developments: the extensive use of music-making technology and the shift in artists' attitudes to music and commerce, as they began to develop self-conscious marketing hype.[28] The first musical artists in the post-punk era to employ the music video as more than a promotional tool were the British new romantics. The video was part of their aesthetic, which involved the synergy of music, image and business. These bands were not material for the traditional rock press such as the *NME*. Rather, they were in tune with the new style press, most notably, newly launched independent magazines like *The Face* and *i-D* that reflected the new pop order (which had given MTV USA its initial edge) and commanded street kudos.

In the mid-1980s rock would return with a vengeance with the likes of Bruce Springsteen. However, the seeds of change were already sown and there was no return to the old dogmas. On the one hand, the release of an album called *Thriller* would make an enormous impact on the music industry (hold this thought). On the other, the tide was set for a second wave of dance-oriented pop, which would enjoy chart success alongside traditional rock bands. The Pet Shop Boys, Depeche Mode and ABC were among the most internationally successful. (American success was – and still is – a badge of honour for British bands.) Like the new romantics before them, acts like the Pet Shop Boys came from a tradition of synthetic, electronic, European music (notably the German band Kraftwerk) and disco (notably the German-based Italo-Austrian producer Giorgio Moroder). What the Pet Shop Boys also did with their first hit, 'West End Girls' in 1986, was to tap into house and rap, both of which were still alternative genres at that time. This bridging of music divides created quite a stir. Their reaching number one in the charts both in the UK and the USA was a landmark moment in pop history. Years later Neil Tennant, one half of the duo, recalled how they'd doubted the song would get airplay, let alone become a huge hit. Moreover, the Pet Shop Boys adopted an ironic attitude in their performances, standing still and detached on stage – the antithesis of orgasmically writhing sweaty rock stars – and often appeared in disguise during live TV appearances (wearing dark sunglasses and a hood). All of these strategies were anti-rockist. Consequently, the Pet Shop Boys and their ilk generally received belated critical recognition, unlike their rock contemporaries. The 1980s music industry, whether the record labels or the credible music press, was still very much grounded in rock's hegemony. However, the two subsequent waves of dance music opened the door for a third wave of synthetic sounds, under the onslaught of which rock would ultimately capitulate.

The Rise of Irony

The late 1980s saw the ascendancy of house music with 1987 being the landmark year of the 'new [British] summer of love'. I shall use the expression 'dance cultures' as a generic term for the subcultural strand of the 1980s that crossed over into the mainstream and subsequently defined the style and communication industries of the 1990s.[29] As we are following the co-optation of the subculture rather than its essence, 'dance cultures' is an appropriate term. Matthew Collin explains how dance cultures came to be the accepted terminology: 'What was first called "acid house" and then the "rave scene" in the late '80s had turned into a multi-million-pound leisure industry known as "dance culture"; a far less mutinous and outlandish phenomenon [than the underground rave parties].'[30] Dance cultures is therefore the umbrella term for the various rave subcultures, building on punk's DIY legacy both as a subcultural phenomenon and a globally co-opted music genre.

Parallel to dance cultures, there was hip hop. As a subculture, hip hop dates back to the late 1970s, like punk. Unlike punk, it did not fully cross over into the mainstream until the late 1980s, arguably because of racism embedded in the music industry and society as a whole. As with house, the landmark year that kickstarted the global conquest of rap music was 1987, with the help of MTV Europe, as I shall shortly discuss. The division between dance cultures and hip hop is not as clear-cut as it may appear. Though I didn't personally experience the British summer of love in 1987 or any of the underground rave parties of the late 1980s, it is clear from speaking to friends who were there and from reading books that myriad music genres was played at the same rave, including (acid) house, techno, garage, rare grooves and electro (essentially the precursor of what would be called rap). Certainly, with the Hoxton underground parties of the 1990s (pre Cool Britannia), this was the case. This openness to exploration across genres in select underground clubs would be a prerequisite for their future cross-fusion.

One of the most important lessons of punk, which rebelled against both the political establishment and bloated rock-star elitism, was that anyone could have a go. You could make your own music without having to be a great artiste. You could make your own clothes without being a designer; creativity was flying in the face of haute couture. You could have your own distribution network to sell your stuff and fanzines to promote it, both of which represented giving two fingers to the established channels. This entrepreneurial attitude was embraced wholeheartedly. By the late 1980s, the barriers to entry to the creative industries were even lower than when punk emerged. Technologies in music-making and developments such as desktop publishing further democratised production. The new subcultures rebelled against the establishment, but not necessarily by subverting the dominant culture. Instead, they positioned themselves as an alternative to the mainstream. The two main strategies in maintaining an underground sensibility were a focus on the visual (reinforced with technology) and the use of irony. Adopting an ironic tone (parodying, ridiculing, self-mocking) became the means by which this alternative identity was expressed and asserted against rock's ideology of authenticity.

Specifically in the context of dance cultures, videos were considered the appropriate visual accompaniment to recorded music.[31] Dance cultures were driven by the belief that the use of animated or computer-generated graphics protected the 'authentic' aura of the artist, who refused to make a personal appearance. The cult of the (superstar) DJ would come later, once the scene had sold out. Originally, dance music was impersonal, an antithesis to the pop or rock star and guitar hero. To make a music video was desirable because its stylistic practices were valued as a means by which music could be televised while preserving autonomy, whereas music shows with live audiences were no longer acceptable. If you had to appear on mainstream television, then there were two basic strategies for preserving an underground sensibility: one was disguise (again, a hood, and sunglasses maybe) and the other was being ironic. Through mocking your own appearance on TV, you were effectively immunising yourself against the show's naffness. This is why cool young people across Europe deserted traditional 'youth' television programmes in favour of those with high video content, of which there were few. This is what Justin from MTV – pretty much on behalf of Generation X – was talking about when quoted earlier.

As for seeing the music video as a partner in the creation and dissemination of rap music, its significance became paramount because rap was frozen out of mainstream television and radio. Its association with poor, black, inner-city youth meant that advertiser-funded services refused to play it. Bear in mind that back in the 1980s, rap was above all perceived as the voice of the young black male. As such, it represented a vivid, contentious cultural symbol. In this context of alienation, parody was a creative means of expression. The use of parody provided a means of retaliation against the demeaning stereotype that young black men had grown up with. It often defined the self as sexually insatiable but, as *New York Times* writer Jon Pareles observed, '...not all rap machismo should be taken entirely at face value. Like other black literary and oral traditions, rap lyrics also involve double-entendre, allegory and parody. Some rap machismo can be a metaphor for pride or political empowerment; it can be a shared joke.'[32] Sexual conquest was not the only subject of the satirical rap of this era. Ghetto conditions, drugs and the pain of daily life were also often stressed with humorous candour, especially by Biz Markie, arguably the greatest comedy rapper to date. It gave people a voice in a system that otherwise did not want to know. Here again, MTV became the first 'virtual' home of rap, and fans could not get enough of it.

In *Hip: the History*, John Leland rightly says that the 1980s subcultures did not so much oppose mass culture as commandeer its resources by using brand logos to build their own alternative networks. Through manipulating mass culture and its imagery by removing it from its original context and holding it up for ridicule, they could establish their own place in the world. Ironically, it was their rejection of mass culture that pandered to the new wave of entrepreneurs, not least MTV, just as the rebellious idioms of the 1960s counterculture had pandered to the newly anti-conformist Madison Avenue crowd. Leland goes on to argue that the essence of the post-punk DIY cultures was not the product, but their aesthetic sensibilities. Right on! This sums up MTV perfectly, which did not produce anything either. All MTV needed to do was to adopt the subcultural mentality to establish itself as a business at the vanguard. By speaking the language of anti-rockist subcultures, MTV could build its fan-base by positioning itself as a member of the peer group, as one of us, against them – the invisible mainstream (for MTV, the mainstream actually *was* rock). Consequently, MTV's environment would become the epitome of cool.

The displacement of rock's ideology of authenticity (which occurred organically among subcultures) spearheaded by MTV Europe happened gradually, not least because rock's elitism was a potent form of identification. With a nod to tradition, MTV sported a rock *attitude* to set itself against conventional television. Its central imperative was not just to be hip, but to be seen to be hip in constantly new ways – an ideology drawn directly from rock culture. MTV broke a lot of unspoken broadcasting rules by developing a non-cerebral approach to programming that relied on mood. In the studio, wobbly camera-work, bad lighting and anything else that would not normally be tolerated on television was okay on MTV. To charm its viewers and incite loyalty, MTV introduced ideas such as competitions to meet the stars or have a peep 'behind the scenes', or getting stars to record drop-ins ('Hi! I'm such-and-such and you're watching MTV!'), all of which was groundbreaking at the time and contributed to MTV's wacky image.

In true rock style, MTV VJs were encouraged to cultivate a casual attitude. MTV appeared unscripted. Fluffed lines and mistakes were not edited out. VJ links were recorded as if they were live, which further emphasised the sense of intimacy for the viewer. Ideologically, VJs were not stars (though following MTV's success, some VJs would start exhibiting a bit of diva-like off-screen behaviour) but rather the boy or girl next door. The only difference between them and the 'ordinary' viewer was that they were peer leaders, recruited for their street kudos. VJs from all over Europe often came from pirate radio or would have some other authentic differentiator. A lot of VJs from the first half of the noughties were aspiring musicians (being a musician was still held in higher regard than VJing within subcultural ideologies) who saw MTV as a stepping-stone. The next generation would use it as a way to achieve stardom. A far cry from the days when MTV itself was the star, this mentality would continue to gain ground and culminate in the rise of celebrity culture in the noughties. Back in the day, however, VJ Paul King was MTV's only exception to this no-star policy – he received no preferential treatment, though he'd fronted the chart-topping 1980s band King before becoming a VJ. His move from musician to VJ was sneered at in the UK (especially by the rock press), but not on the continent where MTV was itself cool. Interestingly, Paul was encouraged to join MTV by his manager Perry Haines, a man with a flair for capturing the zeitgeist. A graduate of Central Saint Martins, Haines had coined the term 'new romantic', was one of the first writers for *i-D* and also Duran Duran's first stylist. By the early 1990s, he was co-managing Neneh Cherry and the newly formed Massive Attack, who would become one of the most critically acclaimed bands of the 1990s, associated with what came to be known as the Bristol Sound. Haines sensed early on that MTV would be a good move for Paul (albeit one potentially perceived as 'downgrading'). It was a risk that paid off. As for MTV, they were happy to have at least one recognisable name at a time when the channel was struggling to be taken seriously by the British music industry.

In order to be hip for the new age, MTV also needed to distinguish itself from rock. The plan was to overcome the barrier of rock's ideology of authenticity with an equally powerful alternative form of authenticity for the new generation. This was not about the death of rock but the possibility turning it into something new; it came in the guise of 'ironic inauthenticity'. This concept was introduced by the distinguished American professor of popular culture, Lawrence (Larry) Grossberg. I find his work to be the most prolific on this subject and shall draw from it to convey the feel of the emerging ideology which became the new rock 'n' roll. Here, and in the professor's words, '…the only possible claim to authenticity is derived from the knowledge and admission of your own inauthenticity… Authentic inauthenticity says that authenticity is itself a construction, an image, which is no better or worse than any other.'[33] In other words, the honest admission of your own inauthenticity (self-mockery) made you authentic.

What MTV did was to redirect rock's powerful structure of affect into a new affective logic – what Professor Grossberg calls 'ironic elitism'. The use of irony became MTV's weapon with which video (visual formation) killed the radio star (sound formation). If you understood the principle of ironic inauthenticity, then there was no better medium than music television to express it. At the heart was the following realisation: while rock empowered its fans by placing them into a particular affective alliance, which marked their difference (anti-popism being the base on which rock's elitism was built), television was indifferent to difference (everything was equally viable and potentially valuable as a televisual image, which renders difference not insignificant but ineffective). MTV's environment was the unification of the medium (television) and the content (music videos and the rest) within a specific structure of elitism built on a particular form of irony. Ironic elitism became the new self-conscious elitism that replaced traditional rock elitism to foster hip identity and cultivate peer culture in the age of rising individualism. Remember, an MTV viewer's relationship to the brand was not defined through specific programmes but through their positioning on the channel, so that fans could enter the environment when in the mood for it; the environment was cool regardless of the content. In other words, anything packaged on MTV became cool by virtue of association.

Here, we see the perfect synergy between subculture and maverick business. As Leland put it: 'If corporate brands produced marketing that acted like culture, the new underground produced culture that acted like marketing.'[34] The 1980s entrepreneurial subcultures acted like businesses, by turning play into work (setting up independent networks of production and distribution, organising parties – even selling drugs). MTV aped subcultures by incorporating an underground attitude into its business. Initially, MTV was sufficiently narrowcast to be credible among hip audiences. At the same time, it genuinely had a connection with alpha trendsetters. As such, it became a chasm translator – turning the vernacular of the emerging subcultures into a language that was palatable for the mainstream – in the crossover trajectory of dance and hip hop cultures towards the mainstream and their conquest of the 1990s. Their ideology, expressed through irony, became a cool-marketing tool.

The next section looks at how this translation process occurred. The displacement of the rock ideology was seen as a metaphor for this crossover process. First, MTV challenged the status quo (during its incubation phase up to the end of 1993) but the period of maturation (1994–1996) finally displaced rock ideology. In 1997, the trend peaked and dominated the mainstream style and communication industries. From there, it spread into the mass market, ultimately becoming the mainstream itself.

3. Diffusion Platforms

ROCK 'N' ROLL IS THE EUROPEAN LINGUA FRANCA
French Rock Is Like English Cooking

Let me begin with a short recapitulation of what we have established so far about the ideological shift. When MTV launched in Europe, its audience was made up of rock fans whose identity was moulded by a particular ideology overlain by a particular sense of geography (whereby the USA and the UK constituted one entity). The rock ideology was a value-system full of contradictions but nevertheless had become a powerful schema for organising the way audiences, musicians and record companies thought about music. Founded upon the belief that Anglo-American rock and soul is the most authentic sound and therefore superior, it became the principal ideology that governed a whole generation of fans and music-industry practices, and the reason behind the international dominance of Anglo-American music. This state of affairs meant that major record companies (or 'the majors') organised what they called their 'priority' policies around the production and promotion of Anglo-American acts at the expense of local repertoire. As far as the majors were concerned, Anglo-American acts had the biggest crossover potential from niche to mainstream markets on a global scale, and therefore commanded the greatest resources.[35]

This policy has often been criticised for not giving equal treatment to local acts, but the truth was that rock fans *believed* in the superiority of Anglo-American artists; anything else was second-rate and historically, 'local acts' rarely made it internationally. Take Johnny Hallyday. Despite his megastar-status and enduring career in France, Hallyday, 'the French Elvis', never made it beyond francophone markets. Even Cliff Richard (once dubbed 'the English Elvis') a native English-speaker (and therefore 'authentic') never succeeded in matching his international fame with that of the King himself. Elvis was cool. Cliff Richard... less so. Singing in English never helped non-Anglo-American artists, either. This trend, beginning in the 1950s, continued well into the early 1990s until MTV set about breaking the mould.

Closely related to the belief in authenticity was another powerful legend: the idea that a feel for a certain kind of musical tradition was culture-bound, which is best summed up by the saying 'French rock is like English cooking.' Laugh you might, but I've heard this one many times in interviews with some of the most influential people in the music industry, in their attempt to explain why local European audiences did not like their neighbour's music. Whether that was French *variété*, German *Schlager* or an Italian San Remo-style ballad, it rarely sold beyond markets that shared a language. These genres were also ridiculed for being 'cheesy' by local rock fans. The few successful exceptions to album-oriented rock (AOR) at the turn of the 1990s included U2 (Irish), The Scorpions (German) and Roxette and Europe (both Swedish); most European fans simply failed to realise these groups were not American.

MTV in this period was often accused of 'American cultural imperialism', which was incorrect. The combination of ideologies and music practices had already moulded music tastes among fans. I mentioned earlier that Omladinski Program (the Yugoslavian radio station where I was a host) played only select rock music (in English, *obviously*), subscribing to the British independent music press to be in touch with new bands. In our search for an alternative identity, we did not play Bruce Springsteen because the mainstream media did. Similarly, cool French radio stations of this era only played rock at the expense of French music, much to the despair of regulators, obsessed with their beloved quotas. For example, Skyrock, one of the most popular French radio stations, played up to 95 per cent English-speaking music. The clue was in their name, of course (they did later change their policy, favouring French rap and R&B, but in the early 1990s, the French rap scene was barely existent, save for MC Solaar).

English was not just the language of rock – it was the language of hip. In fact, MTV occasionally experimented with the use of local language. For example, they introduced a show with links in Flemish (prioritising Belgium was simply a matter of cable penetration rather than any national favouritism – it was among the highest-cabled countries in Europe at the time). This was, alas, in vain – MTV fans in Belgium didn't like it. Part of MTV's appeal was the use of English as the channel's first language. VJs from a European country were cool because they were on MTV and spoke English. If Marcel Vanthilt, a Belgian VJ from the first generation of MTV Europe presenters, had spoken Belgian lingo, he would have been the 'token Belgian'. That he spoke English made him a cool ambassador for Belgium. On MTV, Belgium thus became cool in the eyes of the viewer; surely there were other cool Belgians like Marcel? With the next generation of VJs, it was taken for granted that English was the common language, but these were the kinds of battles fought when the idea of European youth first became a reality. This was not a matter of imperialism. English was the language of rock 'n' roll because rock was a genuine expression of a shared culture among its fans.

In contrast, attempts at imposing a common language such as Esperanto had no meaning beyond books.

To assert its cool identity, MTV faced a great challenge. In search of a new sound with crossover potential, MTV began to experiment with its musical playlist. This, in turn, challenged rather than pandered to the majors' policies. Here again, MTV critics had quickly assumed – without evidence – that MTV Europe would automatically endorse the majors' policies and promote their priority acts, undercutting regional and local record companies. This did not make sense simply because, to establish its brand, MTV's commercial imperative was to assert itself as a leader in music. This meant that MTV needed a sound that was distinctively new (to shape the channel's 'alternative' identity); not Anglo-American (to give it a European feel); and full of crossover potential (so that it appealed to its culturally and linguistically diverse audience).

At first, MTV began to promote European artists who had had local chart success – especially francophone acts, partly due to Belgium (rather than France) being a highly cabled market. These included: Patrick Bruel, Etienne Daho, Mano Negra, Les Négresses Vertes, Mylène Farmer, Gypsy Kings, Khaled (*raï* artist of Maghreb origin), Lio, Les Rita Mitsouko, Niagara, Vanessa Paradis, rapper MC Solaar, one-hit wonder designer Jean Paul Gaultier, Sinclair, Alliance Ethnique and more. In some cases French artists had more exposure on MTV than on local rock-oriented radio. For example, the booking agent of Mano Negra at the time credited MTV for being more adventurous than French radio stations. The band scored their greatest export hit in 1990 ('Mala Vida') thanks to MTV. The channel was the first to play the accompanying video (back in 1988) before the band secured a major record deal. Similarly, Niagara's MTV-sponsored tour sold out venues in Scandinavia, Germany and Holland. In fact, Niagara somehow made it as far as Sarajevo where they were guests on one of my Omladinski Program shows, followed by a gig. However, in spite of MTV's efforts, none of these acts managed to establish an international career to match that of the Anglo-American acts. MTV experimented with other charts (Italian, German and Scandinavian) but the result was the same. Take the German megastar Herbert Grönemeyer and the French megastar Vanessa Paradis. Both were local 'priorities' in their respective countries and both recorded albums in English to boost their international careers. But despite their exposure on MTV, neither made a significant impact outside their native countries. In fact, Paradis's English album, produced by Lenny Kravitz, sold fewer copies in France than her previous ones recorded in French.[36] This lack of success was related to European audiences' tastes. Local artists within the AOR genre did not cross over – end of story.

One would expect that the possibility of immediate pan-European reach and MTV's endeavour to promote European artists beyond their local markets would be welcomed by the majors, but it wasn't so. The problem was the established music-industry system, whereby all key decisions about acquiring and marketing local acts had to be negotiated through the priorities and prejudices of executives in London and New York. The concept of coordinated pan-European releases for non Anglo-American acts did not exist as yet. What MTV was effectively doing was prioritising acts that were not the majors' priorities. At the same time, MTV was setting a promotional pace to suit its pan-European ambition, which was not compatible with the European market reality; music charts across Europe were not synchronised. They were very much a national affair. For example, records went in and out of the UK chart at a much quicker pace than the French *Top Cinquante*, where records appeared to be seeking asylum. Consequently, MTV was ahead of local promotional strategies. This was the case even with internationally successful acts, such as Bon Jovi or R.E.M. They would be releasing perhaps their third single in the UK, their first single in Germany and no single for months in either Italy or France. MTV was indeed helping artists by creating demand for their records, but it was often the case that their records were either not yet available in local stores or were never going to be because the majors had no plans to distribute the act in a particular territory. This lack of support from the artists' own divisional record companies was, in turn, related to their priorities. Different priorities created some tension between MTV and the majors. Add to this the ongoing battle between MTV and the majors over music-video broadcast rights, a saga that began with MTV in the USA, and we start painting a completely different picture to that of cultural imperialism or a happy-go-lucky relationship between the two corporate clans.

Another argument that made no sense was the sell-out. We can see from the experience of MTV (a corporate company with a maverick spirit) that without the support of major record companies, there was simply no way for bands to have a viable international career. For mainstream success (if that is what a band desires), selling out is actually a requirement. Promotion on MTV was not, in itself, enough. Bands could not fully benefit from this type of exposure unless there were coordinated networks of distribution and patterns of record releases across the markets where they were promoted. Even if those were in place, bands still needed crossover potential, which depended on the unpredictable factor of audience taste. As the majors opened European divisions, MTV began to work more directly with them on synchronised record releases and promotional campaigns.

Until that happened, MTV had no alternative but to look for alternatives. Perhaps that was a blessing in disguise. MTV could have been just radio with pictures, but what helped shape its hip image was the fact that it associated itself with emerging subcultures that challenged the dominance of rock 'n' roll. Their commercial potential stretched beyond selling records. If packaged correctly, they could be used to sell a whole lifestyle. Packaging is what MTV did best, so the initial risk (of going against the grain of the established music industry practices) paid off. It did marvels for the bottom line.

Going Underground

When looking for an alternative to mainstream rock, MTV stumbled on a goldmine of underground activity. It picked up on four musical genres beyond AOR: dance, rap, heavy metal and indie (independent) rock. Each genre represented a subculture. MTV produced specialist shows dedicated to each, which would in turn splinter into subgenres and fragment even further. Each specialist show was hosted by a connoisseur with a direct connection to the scene in question and independent labels. To help bands get on to MTV, the specialist show teams could always disburse some money from their allocated annual budgets to finance music videos for bands that sounded good but were too poor to produce their own video. Initially, knowledge of these specialist shows was spread by word of mouth among peers. From there, they reached wider audiences, more of which later. At this point in my narrative, none of these genres have reached beyond pirate radio while MTV is still sufficiently narrowcast to command underground respect.

Dance

MTV became the medium par excellence for dance-music exposure. Being a niche medium that combined visuals with technology, MTV was credible among hardcore dance fans.[37] From MTV's commercial perspective, this genre had a huge crossover potential. Dance music, or more precisely its Eurodance exponent, became the genre that replaced rock as the lingua franca that defined MTV's European identity. 'Eurodance' was the overarching term commonly used for this rootless and anonymous musical tradition, which did technically have geographic origins in Detroit techno, Chicago house and the sounds of NYC's Paradise Garage, but it did not draw on anything that could be obviously pinned down to a place of origin. With no lyrics beyond quasi-slogans, for example 'take me higher', and music videos designed to mask the artist, Eurodance was perfect for MTV.

When MTV picked up on it, house music was still excluded from mainstream airwaves across Europe, so that even the most mundane and derivative forms of European mass music were seen as club cult. Though Eurodance went on to become the cheesiest, most commercial music, its subsequent mainstream success should not undermine this genre's original merits. The producers who toyed with this genre were very imaginative, merging art, technology and commerce to create a new sound, and music videos to accompany it. They represented a rich pool of diverse influences and fusions of sound. Highlights from the USA included Deee-lite and C+C Music Factory. De La Soul pioneered a new rap sound that almost sounded like dance music, while PM Dawn rapped over Spandau Ballet, an emeritus band from the first generation of British synth music. Hits from European producers included 'Ride on Time' by Black Box (Italo house), 'Pump up the Jam' by Technotronic (new beat from Belgium) and 'The Power' by Snap! (German techno) to name but few. Beats International (a project that gave some of the early chart success to Norman Cook before he reinvented himself as Fatboy Slim), KLF, Adamski and Nomad were British acts. Even 'camp' acts such as Sweden's Army of Lovers were underground club hits in the late 1980s before they were picked up by MTV's chart and catapulted to international fame in the early 1990s. Their provocatively playful music videos expressed a type of gay identity that was not represented anywhere in the mainstream. Their flamboyant aesthetic was the antithesis of dress-down acid house. And if I remember correctly, some of their videos were deemed too debauched to play on MTV (or rather MTV played them but were ordered by the 'authorities' not to do so again, in case there was a fuss). While rock critics took a dim view of these acts, their views were later seen to have been narrow-minded. To critics at the time, Beats International was little more than cheesy European disco on MTV. Within the space of a few years however, the music industry would be all over Fatboy Slim.

By the mid 1990s, purely commercial acts were created specifically to milk the trend and the genre reached saturation point. Said acts included: 2 Unlimited, Captain Hollywood, Capella, Maxx, Culture Beat, Haddaway and dozens of others, mostly one-hit wonders. For the first time in history, music from the continent began to dictate the British chart via exposure on MTV. The ultimate example of this was the chart success of Whigfield, a Eurodance project (Danish singer, Italian producers). 'Saturday Night' went straight to number one in the British chart – thanks to exposure on MTV and clubs and some local radio stations picking up songs from MTV's charts – which was unheard of for a non Anglo-American act. What's more, it knocked Wet Wet Wet's cover of The Troggs' 'Love Is All Around' off the top spot. Not before time either, as this single, which was on the soundtrack for British box-office success *Four Weddings and a Funeral* (directed by Mike Newell, 1994), had been at number one for a record 15 weeks (4 June to 17 September when Whigfield stormed the chart).

Rap

The story of rap is even more spectacular. *Yo! MTV Raps* was the MTV specialist show that finally helped to bury the much trotted-out line about early MTV USA not playing black music. This rumour was still haunting the network years after the channel had changed its policy and began giving equal exposure to Afro-American artists. In its first few years, MTV USA *did* play overwhelmingly Caucasian artists, and their justification for the exclusion of Afro-American artists was the narrowcast format of the channel. It played rock, which was predominantly white. In this sense, MTV sadly fell in line with the music industry's historical practice of not rewarding Afro-American artists equally for their contribution and talent. However, with the release of Michael Jackson's *Thriller* in 1982, a historical precedent was set and policies began to change. *Thriller* broke MTV's 'exclusion' pattern following a dispute between the channel and Jackson's label, CBS. The label threatened to pull out all its acts unless MTV played Jackson's videos. The rest we know. *Thriller* would go on to become the biggest album of all time and make the now prematurely departed Jackson one of the greatest icons of the modern era. Much of his global success following *Thriller*, though, was down to MTV USA's support. *Thriller* also paved the way for new artists such as Prince and Whitney Houston, as well as the solo careers of Tina Turner and Lionel Richie, who all had huge 1980s hits.

One battle had been won but another conflict was simmering. MTV USA – nor any other network for that matter – did not play rap. Little did they know then that rap's commercial potential was as huge as *Thriller*'s. Rap was perceived at the time as the music of disenfranchised young black men. It was threatening.

There was no access for it on mainstream networks. Paradoxically, even the Black Entertainment Network (BET) did not play rap for fear of alienating their upwardly mobile audience. Just like MTV, they used the narrowcast format as an excuse. They aimed, above all, for middle-class Afro-Americans (as came to be represented by *The Cosby Show*) and that was their real reason for not playing the sound of inner city youth. The BET's audience lived in suburbia, had manicured lawns, and knew nothing of graffiti or breakdancing.

The first-ever music television programme entirely dedicated to rap music appeared on MTV Europe. *Yo! MTV Raps* was the brainchild of Sophie Bramly, who was of the first generation of MTV Europe's VJs. Sophie lived in New York in the early 1980s where she got involved with the hip hop scene. Upon returning to France, she began to work as a music journalist specialising in rap until she was hired by MTV for her expertise, and moved to London. And so a white woman from France, supposedly the most ardent anti-American European country, which stipulated quotas to protect its music, was to become instrumental in promoting black American music stereotypically perceived as misogynistic. It's easy to see the irony in that, but at this grassroots level, there was no racism. In contrast, in the industry, there was plenty (even if some of it was inadvertent). This is a great example of how stereotypes can hinder communication and cripple diversity (it's no coincidence that stereotypes are frowned on in post-colonial literature). This is a different matter from the humorous reference about French rock being like English cooking, which refers to how culture-bound influences shape tastes and consumer tendencies.[38] This is also why it is important to look at the incubation stages of maverick companies (and not just subcultures and how they get co-opted), because this is when companies are the least averse to risk-taking and therefore make the greatest impact in terms of innovation. MTV was actively looking for people like Sophie to host shows because of their first-hand knowledge of alternative scenes. Already, MTV USA was less willing to take that risk because its place was secured, hence it was playing it safe – there was no question of it playing rap.

Yo! MTV Raps was launched on MTV Europe in October 1987, but MTV USA initially refused to air it. The US team used the usual excuse that rap did not fit their narrowcast playlist. It took a lot of convincing to get them to air just a pilot episode. That is how *Yo! MTV Raps* was inaugurated on MTV USA in 1988… to unprecedented network ratings! This positive audience response would change the corporate mentality. In Europe, too, the rap show became enormously popular. So much so that it caught MTV's ad-sales staff off-guard. *Yo!* MTV *Raps* was among the main culprits behind the unexplained discrepancies between how many were aware of MTV and the channel's ratings. In the UK for example, awareness was at 81 per cent, but computer-registered viewing figures came in at 25 per cent. After commissioning some qualitative research to get to the bottom of this mystery, what transpired was that there was a black market of MTV videotapes (the video recorder, at that time, still being relatively cutting-edge technology that your parents struggled to operate) among students and schoolkids. Copies of *Yo!* MTV *Raps* commanded the highest bootleg prices in the playground black market. This explained why the people-meter got particularly excited when *Yo!* came on. People often gathered in the homes of friends who subscribed to cable or satellite, just to watch MTV (especially their genre-based programmes). *Yo!* MTV *Raps* also consistently registered as one of the most popular across Europe, and remained so throughout MTV's life as a pan-European channel.

Metal and Indie

In contrast to rap, heavy metal in Europe never made it big, but it was a hugely popular niche genre. Its specialist show on MTV was called *Headbangers Ball* [sic]. It was hosted in Europe by VJ Vanessa Warwick. The American version was the most popular show on MTV USA's network. In fact, heavy metal and rap (following the success of *Yo!*) became the dominant genres on MTV USA. However, in Europe heavy metal (with its many subgenres) only ever remained a niche taste, albeit with pockets of hardcore fans all across Europe. For them, *Headbangers Ball* was the prime outlet. Vanessa herself was almost deified among her fans.

In contrast, the indie specialist show, *120 Minutes*, proved prolific. Essentially, this alternative music programme showcased many acts that would later come under the banner of Britpop. Bands from the 'Manchester' scene (The Stone Roses, Happy Mondays) were played on here, as were Oasis before they were signed to a major. At the same time, *120 Minutes* in the USA was promoting its alternative rock and passing it on to Europe. So, the European *120 Minutes* was the first port of call for viewers who wished to see Nirvana and other bands that led to the mainstream triumph of grunge. The two versions of the show complemented each other.

120 Minutes in Europe also deserves credit for giving exposure to non-Anglo-American indie bands with distinctive sounds. This was quite a bold step because indie was still very much grounded in the rock ideology of authenticity. Indie artists might have been different from hair metallers and stadium rockers (then on their last legs) but they were still rock 'n' roll and they certainly did not have a phony accent when they spoke English. For example, this show was the first to feature the Icelandic band The Sugarcubes, thereby revealing Björk to the world. There was a whole industrial music scene regularly featured on the show, with acts ranging from the Belgian Young Gods to Laibach of the former Yugoslavia. The show's diversity was second to none. As with anything grassroots, it helped to have a personal connection. The host of *120 Minutes* was my then boyfriend, Paul King. Hence, bands from Yugoslavia got some special attention, including Laibach, Disciplina Kičme (later anglicised as Spinal Discipline) and Psihomodo Pop. My friend Marsu, of the Parisian Bondage Records, whom I met when I was scouting for alternative music for Omladinski Program, also benefited from this connection, as a number of his acts – largely ignored by French radio – were played on *120 Minutes*.

Whether that was Laibach (who got signed by Mute) from Ljubljana or the Washington Dead Cats (on Bondage Records) from Paris, these bands would have been played even without personal favouritism because *120 Minutes* was an experimental show in the truest sense of the word. Bands were played for being interesting. A real boon for many, given that they'd had little or no airplay on mainstream radio in their own countries. *120 Minutes* might have been only two hours a week (with repeats) but it combined the huge resources of MTV's network and brand with a genuine independent spirit that attracted similarly minded fans who knew exactly when to tune in. The point is that all of MTV's specialist shows had grassroots connections. Owing to its direct rapport with the indie scenes, MTV was the first-hand source for underground music. MTV, via these shows, was also a great partner for indie labels because it provided invaluable international exposure. How else would you find out about an Icelandic band in an age where industry practices and fan ideologies were organised around the single currency of Anglo-American music? Slowly, MTV began to break this pattern.

Crossing Over

MTV's specialist shows became talent pools for major labels to fish in. Ironically, new acts on MTV were developed the authentic rock 'n' roll way – by paying their dues (or rather by following MTV's version of the trajectory from underground obscurity to mainstream success). The starting points were the organic culture(s) from which bands emanated and the small live gig circuit or clubs. With unsigned bands, the contact with MTV's specialist shows was direct, but more often communication happened via pluggers. Typically, bands would be featured in one of MTV's four *specialist* shows first. If they had the all-important crossover potential, they would then cross over into MTV's *thematic* shows, which were marketing labels for new genres.

Exceptionally, there was no thematic show for dance music. There was no need for an intermediary stage because Eurodance was MTV's preferred commercial style for the build-up of its European image. A Eurodance video went straight into the main playlist rotation. The various alternative dance genres were too hardcore for the mainstream and were featured in the specialist dance show. The thematic show *Rock Block* was the umbrella for hard rock (but not metal, as MTV's promo was keen to stress) with grunge being a major component. *PostModern* (later *Alternative Nation*) was the commercial exponent of indie, which eventually became Britpop in the mainstream. Following the spectacular launch of *Yo! MTV Raps*, this programme continued to be aired on MTV Europe but MTV USA took over production. This meant it focused on American rappers, but it did not make it any less popular among fans. The thematic offshoot show was called *The Soul of MTV*. It was launched on MTV Europe in 1992 to accommodate a plethora of commercial genres derived from rap, classified under the umbrella of R&B (or contemporary R&B to give it its full title), a term previously only applied to blues, rock 'n' roll and soul. This was a new commercial definition, but if you are 20 now, that is the only definition you would be aware of (unless you are an original rock and soul aficionado).

From thematic shows, videos went into playlist rotation, which essentially involved patterns of a different number of plays per week. MTV's main playlist consisted of around 80 videos and it changed weekly. Approximately one quarter of the playlist was dedicated to new talent because MTV was keen to refine its image as a trend leader. Another criterion was what people want to hear, which essentially involved looking at national charts and weighing the findings against the level of MTV's distribution in a given territory. The most influential charts were where MTV's distribution was the highest: Germany, Benelux and Scandinavia. The British chart was inevitably consulted, even though cable and satellite distribution in the UK was still relatively low compared to these other markets, because the UK has always been the most credible musical market and the first for new releases. British sales charts were indicators of Anglo-American hits, whereas European charts dictated the velocity of MTV's playlist, ie the number of plays per week.

MTV's initial investment in risk-taking was, unsurprisingly, proportionately reduced with the channel's growth. Eventually, the specialist shows were dropped because they were too niche. The thematic shows had done their job, successfully identifying and catapulting acts with crossover potential from the underground into the mainstream. That is simply the commercial reality. The crossover principle on MTV or any other music medium remains the same in terms of how you break new bands, but it ultimately means there's less diversity to choose from. However, this should not undermine the fact that during its formative years, MTV provided a valuable platform for alternative music and helped break many new acts. They also played a significant role in displacing the rock ideology of authenticity and, by doing so, began a change in record-industry practices, particularly when it came to the dominance of the US in the international music exchange.

MTV also made an important contribution towards combating the engrained racist mentality that governed the music industry. *Yo! MTV Raps* was a landmark. From then on, the music industry's practice of building up white artists making black music to make a black genre more palatable for the mainstream would largely cease (though of course there are still white rappers). MTV's thematic show (by definition more commercial than a specialist show) *The Soul of MTV* also had a catalyst role. Hosted by Lisa I'Anson, a scenester poached from London's pirate radio station Kiss FM, this show built up a loyal fan-base across Europe. It was particularly popular among British kids from Afro-Caribbean backgrounds, according to Trevor Nelson, another MTV recruit from Kiss FM (from the platform of MTV, Nelson would become one of the most influential music broadcasters in Britain). Speaking about this issue at a big music conference in London in 1997, Nelson said that for these kids, 'Lisa and *The Soul of MTV* was God.'[39] In reality, 'black music' was popular among many ethnicities, from Caucasian to Asian (Sasha Baron Cohen parodied a British Asian kid in the character of Ali G who saw being black as the ultimate cool). 'Black music' was not a minority interest. In spite of that fact, however, producers of mainstream youth television programmes in the UK were still reluctant to commission programmes based around black music. They were stuck in their rock 'n' roll mentality, unequipped to deal with modern R&B beyond ghettoisation and tokenism. In 1995, three years after the launch of *The Soul of MTV*, the British

Phonographic Industry finally gave R&B a separate sales chart, acknowledging the place of this genre in mainstream sales.

In its maverick phase, MTV became the ultimate trendsetter: the first to know and synonymous with hip. Its position as such was widely acknowledged across Europe. MTV was the channel that trend-leaders watched – be they magazine editors, staff at rival TV channels, filmmakers or musicians. During its pan-European phase (especially the incubation years), MTV was the ultimate cultural reference. In the UK, the channel's credibility was measured by the British media's attempts to constantly undermine or ignore it. Surely it could not be that an American channel playing 'cheesy' European music was dictating the trends in Europe's supreme rock 'n' roll market? And yet it was. The crisis in youth broadcasting went some way to reminding the industry how out of touch they were – a huge blow to any rock 'n' roll ego.

The paranoia about MTV among the British rock establishment was such that, for example, Radio 1 had an internal policy of not mentioning MTV on air. Coming to terms with their own crisis in the first half of the 1990s, Radio 1 eventually poached MTV VJs Trevor Nelson and Lisa I'Anson to bring some cool on board. In fact the vast majority of new talent on UK mainstream television, too, was sourced from MTV. Once they established their names on there, they'd move on. Similarly in this period, the British indie press took every opportunity to criticise MTV and especially to play down the role of *120 Minutes* and the thematic rock shows on the grounds that they were all about 'selling out'. The truth is that there was not one musician who refused the chance of exposure on MTV (and there were few who refused to sign a deal with a major and take their careers to greater heights). When VJ Paul King moved to MTV's newly launched sister network VH-1 in 1994, a vacancy emerged for the host of *120 Minutes*. The vast majority of candidates who came to audition for this position were the aforementioned indie journalists.

4. Influence on Mainstream Style and Communication Industries

LOOK CASUAL AND BE IRONIC

The sell-out is less a betrayal of hip legacy, more a natural outcome. As MTV began to reign supreme in corporate cool, its position in the UK market was cemented; it was no longer an outcast. But in terms of hip's crossover, we need to look beyond the music charts. The greatest role that MTV played was as chasm translator between subcultures and mainstream business. The real impact was the ideological shift from rock's ideology of authenticity into another form of elitism expressed through irony. MTV opened up opportunities for the dance, hip hop and indie cultures, but each had its life outside MTV. There were, of course, other chasm translators contributing to their crossover and, ultimately, the displacement of rock's hegemony. This influence would not just be felt in the music industry but more generally in the way subcultural idioms translated into the mainstream style and communication industries.

By 1994, rap was among the greatest trading commodities, and hip hop would turn into a global lifestyle enterprise. Being an intrinsically entrepreneurial subculture, dormitory-room hustlers or small-time dealers from the 'hood would go on to become proper businessmen. Russell Simmons, one of the founders of Def Jam recordings (with Rick Rubin) whose signings included iconic acts like Public Enemy and the Beastie Boys, would branch into fashion in 1992. The label Phat Farm, from the hip hop jargon for 'hot' (as in looking good), was launched as hip hop style for the masses. In 1999, a worldwide licensing agreement was signed to exploit the brand to the maximum. Def Jam itself was sold off to majors, through a series of stake purchases of the company until a complete takeover occurred. Diversification became the norm. Examples ranged from Roc-A-Fella Records launching Roccawear Fashion, through to hip hop outfits such as Wu Tang Clan producing records *and* clothing lines. Similarly, dance culture would exert its influence on the mainstream music industry as well as on style, with a series of clothing labels reflecting what ravers were wearing. Like hip hop, this was another casual style, giving rise to the mainstream look dubbed 'combat' (sported by pop bands such as All Saints).

What is important to stress is that the categories of music genres were a means of commercialising the music, but that these divisions were somewhat artificial. The 1990s was the era when eclecticism took centre stage. A seminal moment marking this blending of genres and, more importantly, subcultural ideologies occurred when the British band The Shamen released their single 'Move Any Mountain' in 1991. The Shamen were considered indie. They were therefore a guitar-driven live-music band that fitted the criteria for MTV's *120 Minutes*. However, 'Move Any Mountain' sounded unmistakably like a dance track. Up until then, (acid) house had been a club experience and was certainly not live music. Live music was traditionally the territory of rock bands – but the mentality was changing. Other indie bands such as the Happy Mondays and Primal Scream (who released their landmark album 'Screamadelica' in 1991) were exploring the potential synergy between dance and indie rock. Translated into fashion, this meant that the combat style (from rave clothing) would also encompass what the indie bands were wearing.

Similarly, Def Jam was as much about American punk rock as it was about hip hop. Here, the Beastie Boys were a seminal band that brought a sound to the rest of the world and a look that was known only among a core punk crowd in New York. They became the spokesmen for an urban generation defined by music, skateboarding and graffiti art. Their global hit '(You Gotta) Fight for Your Right (To Party)' became an anthem for a generation. Originally it paid homage to DIY subcultures (or subcultural entrepreneurialism) and the right to operate in the margins. As for clothing, brands such as Stüssy and Burton, originally the uniforms of surfers and snowboarders respectively, were referential in the context of subcultures that defined the street style. The company Gimme 5 was among the first to distribute these brands in the UK and Europe and, by extension, to disseminate the ethos of these cultures. All of these acted as little chasm translators, each contributing in a small way to the crossover of 'street' into the mainstream.

Equally instrumental in promoting this culture in the mainstream was the discovery of a group of outsider artists, who came to be known as the Beautiful Losers. This was a collective of street artists in the US who came together in the early 1990s. Their art was a sideline to the other dominant interests of teens in suburban neighbourhoods: skateboarding, drugs and sex. It mainly took the form of graffiti as well as signs or tags on public places such as trains. Aaron Rose made a documentary about the collective in 2008 (*Beautiful Losers*), which tells the story of how they became commercially successful against all odds. (By the way, if you haven't experienced the 1990s first-hand and want to understand the ironic attitude of Generation X, this film is a great place to start.) The culture of the Beautiful Losers spawned similar cliques around the world.

For example, in France, the main exponents of this new wave were the seminal dance outfit Daft Punk. At last, MTV – albeit towards the end of its pan-European phase – had discovered the much-sought-after French sound with crossover potential. Predictably, that champion of indie, the now defunct *Melody Maker*, negatively reviewed the support-slot performance of the duo (before they were called Daft Punk), describing their music as 'a kind of daft punk'. Taking that as their name, their first single ('Da Funk') was an immediate success, earning them a deal with a major in 1996 and leading to the release of their first album, *Homework*, in 1997. It appeared that French rock was no longer like English cooking. Then again, just as Daft Punk was changing perceptions of French music, there was a commotion across the Channel that would contribute to a vast change in the perception of English cooking: a young chef, Heston Blumenthal, opened a restaurant in a village in Berkshire, in London's commuter belt. A non-event when it happened in 1995, this restaurant would be dubbed 'the best in the world' within a decade. But let us leave both Daft Punk and Blumenthal for now. They will reappear later in my story.

In 1997 a series of events and incidents would symbolically mark the sell-out of the post-punk DIY scene. It would also be the beginning of the full commercialisation of said trend. This was the year when an exhibition in a disused gallery in New York on 31 October presented the art of the Beautiful Losers under one roof. Soon, they would be in demand by corporate brands. This year also saw the premature death of rapper Notorious B.I.G., which cast a shadow over hip hop. No longer the voice of disenfranchised youth, it was now all about money, and also guns, which were never far from reach. This was also the year of Cool Britannia, when the Sensation exhibition presented a group of British artists who would create a storm, when Britpop dominated the charts, and when the world's fashion elite hailed London as the most creative source of talent. Last but not least, New Labour were elected.

'Street' became synonymous with cool and was fully exploited commercially in post-Cool Britannia until it reached overkill in around 2004. This is the period when the DIY subcultures became a major influence on the mainstream style and communication industries. 'Street culture' broadly encompassed music (rap-meets-punk-meets-house), graffiti art, skateboarding (or snowboarding) and some kind of rave experience. 'Streetwear' became a generic term for the cool 1990s dress code that would fully cross over in the first half of the noughties. Cool communication industries also went street. Cool hunting, street marketing and guerrilla advertising became all the rage in the corporate world. A lot of money was spent on 'cool hunters' who were fluent in street lingo, to act as interpreters and connect the street with the corporate boardroom. Protagonists from underground cultures became the main purveyors of cool in terms of executing communication. For example, graphic work by the Beautiful Losers would come to be highly prized. The right to party would also become commoditised, as dance culture triggered the 'economics of pleasure' and clubbing became an industry controlled by business interests.[40] While this was going on in the mainstream, something was bubbling up in the underground, but before we move on in search of the hip for the noughties, we need to look at the final element of 1990s hip, which was its cosmopolitan aspect. I shall explore that by looking at MTV's contribution to identity politics.

5. Diversity versus Homogenisation

THE BATTLE BETWEEN CITIZENS AND CONSUMERS
The Homogenisation Thesis

Marketing of cool is often dismissed in social studies literature as one-dimensional, a mere tactic used to exploit and homogenise the youth market, thought to be the most amenable to treating the idea of identity (defined as nationality and culture) as a fashion accessory. In *No Logo*, Naomi Klein said 'Standing triumphant at the centre of the global teen phenomenon is MTV... and the more viewers there are to absorb MTV's vision of a tribe of culture-swapping global teen nomads, the more homogenous a market its advertisers have in which to sell their products.'[41] Klein's view is widespread. Brilliant in many ways (hats off to the way it exposes child labour), *No Logo* falters on a couple of counts. First, by the time MTV 'stood triumphant' it was already a sell-out. To criticise a corporation at this stage for doing what they are in the business of doing, no matter how altruistic the intention, is facile. Another common oversight of Klein's is her use of quantitative data (primarily aimed at advertisers) to support the cultural homogenisation claim. For advertisers, this type of research shows that MTV viewers are more likely to purchase their product than non-viewers. In this respect, it is indeed true that the purchase patterns of Mars Bars are getting more homogenised, but to confuse economic motivation with a cultural effect is also facile: it does not work like that. First, when MTV began its global conquest, the idea of a global market was not a given. National habits were engrained. Second, what made MTV successful initially was that it responded to – and even anticipated – the need for a new kind of identity politics. Rather than homogenising cultures, MTV actually fostered diversity.

In her book *Branded*, Alissa Quart goes even further to show how market research involving young people can be a deceitful method, where marketers cultivate fake friendships with young people in order to monitor them. As a marketer, this allegation makes me defensive, because any bona fide market research involving adolescents is done under a strict code of conduct and permission is required from a parent or guardian. Participants in that kind of research know it is for marketing purposes and they get paid. In fact, if you happen to invite young people to participate in a project for a cool brand, you usually get a very positive response. Unless there is parental consent, the marketer cannot proceed – *Branded* does not take that into account.

Another problem I have with Quart's book is that it positions itself almost as an anti-consumerist manifesto for Generation Y, but the alternative it offers for their predicament is 'adbusting', a movement that grew out of identity politics fought by Generation X. As with any countercultural currents from the turn of the 1990s, the idea of adbusting had been appropriated by cool brands to subvert their own advertising (brands too could be ironic). They were very good at the cool game. I am not so sure that Generation Y is as antagonistic to branding as *Branded* suggests – not because they are 'duped' into embracing consumerism but precisely because they're already branded: they are of the post-MTV Generation where a (Western) world without brands does not exist. Pockets of adbusters have not resulted in an impactful anti-consumerist movement beyond getting co-opted by brands (and ironically, this is how a lot of people know about subverting logos – they bought the T-shirt because it looked cool!).[42] My suspicion is that adbusting is to Generation Y what hanging Che's picture was to Generation X. It had its time, but times were a-changin'. I'll address that in my identity discussion for the noughties.

First, let me offer a different perspective on the identity politics battle of Generation X at the turn of the 1990s. In this context, I shall venture to say that MTV actually contributed to facilitating liberties. What I am saying is not at all radical. When MTV segmented the market, it inadvertently tapped into diverse types. Prior to that, they had been a homogenous entity in the mainstream. Once you identify your types (speaking as a marketer, here), you can quantify them and if the numbers are large enough, then yes, you would start homogenising the market (in plain language, this could be anything from the way you organise the distribution chain of products through to advertising communication). MTV and cool brands fragmented a homogenous market by responding to a genuine need for individualism before they homogenised the market again, incorporating the fault-lines of those fragments, if you see what I mean. (And then the next wave of hip will rebel against that fragmentation, as we shall see.) To understand MTV's ideological appeal and its role in fostering a sense of diversity, we therefore need to look at MTV in phases. MTV's pan-European phase will shed a different light on the notion of global identity and the complexities and layers that made it possible for MTV to 'stand triumphant'. In the early 1990s, MTV *was* the alternative. Its interpretation of European identity acted as a diverse force against the homogenising political vision of unity that effectively suppressed diversity. In the noughties, MTV became the mainstream. The new cool (the movement that actually facilitated the expression of diversity) became an alternative to MTV and ultimately took over its cool crown.

Fostering a Sense of Pan-National Identity in the 1990s

The cultural commentator Kobena Mercer rightly said 'Identity only becomes an issue when it is in crisis, when something assumed to be fixed, coherent and stable is displaced by the experience of doubt and uncertainty.'[43] And this is exactly what was going on between the corporations and the governments in their battle between citizens and consumers when satellite TV became a reality. At the heart of the European identity debate were two different interpretations of the idea of 'unity in diversity': a political one that sought to protect national interests and a corporate vision that sought to cross over frontiers – to make money, of course, but that drive made the corporations more hungry to succeed than the politicians.

The EC's Unity in Diversity

In the political arena, the resurgence of identity debates took on the form of cultural protectionism. 'Coca-Cola satellites', an expression coined by Jack Lang, then French Minister of Culture, embodied the European political rhetoric of the time. European (and ambiguously French) artistic integrity was supposedly under attack and in danger of homogenisation at the hands of outsiders. We (Europeans) were facing the prospect of watching wall-to-wall *Dallas* on Japanese screens, unless, of course, something was done to prevent this scenario. The issue was economic but it was conflated with culture, as if this were the same struggle.[44] By appealing to the national sentiment that denounced the evil 'other' (implicitly American), cultural defence sounded perfectly legitimate while at the same time it conveniently ignored another form of homogenisation from within (or suppression of diversity, if you prefer).[45] Far too often, the protectionist warnings about Coca-Cola satellites turned into speeches that called for a return to French 'essentialist' values. Calls to drink 'good French wine' instead of Coca-Cola often highlighted an uncomfortable link between anti-Americanism and a 'focus on a national identity that excludes not only *Dallas* but North Africans, Turks, Asians, Afro-Caribbeans [and] Europe's Other as it were.'[46] In the 1990s, support for the French right-wing party Le Front National, which could initially barely muster 1 per cent of the vote, rose to 12 per cent, then 15 per cent.[47] This trend culminated with the party's leader, Jean-Marie Le Pen, entering the final round of the presidential elections in 2002, which was unprecedented. Rising support for extreme right-wing parties was evident throughout the 1990s across Western Europe. In post-communist states, support for nationalist parties even led to all-out conflict.

Overlooking this identity crisis, the politicians adopted what Professor Philip Schlesinger dubbed the 'sensible layman's' view of culture, whose logic was that national cultures were static objects under assault.[48] This point of view did not recognise how the combined effects of migration and free-market capitalism disarticulated citizenship, nationality and culture. Politicians were indeed grappling with the reality that national citizenship was becoming increasingly less significant in terms of having and enjoying personal rights. However, they were unable to offer a viable alternative that would reflect the post-national citizenship era. Instead, the sensible layman's view of culture was simply transposed on to a pan-European level – and the European protectionist audiovisual policy that, ironically, made it possible for MTV to enter the market also reflected this attitude.

The EC's attempt to foster a sense of pan-national identity was doomed to fail from the outset because its pro-European rhetoric was an affirmation of an identity that did not exist. Historically, European national cultures were always in conflict or competition – or simply neglectful of one another.[49] The only European reference that politicians celebrated was 'Western civilization'. However, the West was an historical configuration of power whereby Westerners came to think of themselves in terms of their noblest achievements and of 'the rest' in terms of their deficiencies. Perhaps the most influential book that describes this tension-filled relationship of superior and subaltern identities is *Orientalism* by the late Professor Edward Said. Yet, despite the dubious origin of what came to constitute Western tradition, this assumed common tradition was attributed a pivotal role in the creation of European identity. 'Unity in Diversity' was an empty slogan reflecting a vision that effectively flattened diversity. Not surprisingly, it became meaningless for its citizens.

MTV's Celebration of Diversity

In contrast, MTV captured the sense of optimism reigning over Europe in a meaningful way for its niche audience. MTV Europe is the closest that we ever got to a single European identity since the birth of this idea in the Middle Ages, because for the first time in history, technology enabled the construction of an imagined pan-European community. Like the EC's 'Unity in Diversity', MTV used the slogan 'Celebration of Diversity' but, unlike the EC's model that flattened diversity, MTV achieved a sense of unity on the channel that no political initiative ever did. MTV's state-of-oneness was soundtracked by rock 'n' roll, which had genuine international appeal. MTV's was an identity constructed, above all, around common logos and a common taste in music. As the essence of hip is to be seen to be hip in constantly new ways, it was, for a while, cool to be European – and MTV reinforced this.

There is no denying that celebrating European diversity was the commercial flavour of the moment, but it was nevertheless a vision that was implicitly and unambiguously cosmopolitan in orientation. It was not about anti-Americanism. It was not about seeing cultures as 'other', but about being open to one another. It was about curiosity. It was about facilitating engagement among Europeans and all those other dudes within MTV's satellite footprint – all equal in the eyes of MTV – by de-territorialising the creation of communities and promoting multicultural collations. Every aspect of MTV had a European undertone: European VJs with odd accents, regular features from all across Europe, The European Top Twenty ('the one and only European chart show') and MTV News and film reviews. All were united as part of MTV's European rock 'n' roll fraternity. As such, perhaps even more by accident than by brilliant planning, MTV offered a totally egalitarian vision of European life.

Nowhere did MTV's fervent advocacy of European identity appear more strongly than on MTV's *Most Wanted*. Hosted by Ray Cokes every weeknight between 1992 and 1995, this show was beamed simultaneously across some 38 countries to around 60 million viewers. This was one of the first ZOO TV-style programmes to introduce what was to later become conventional in television production: frantic camera-work, the host fooling around with the crew, outlandish studio décor and outrageous competitions where viewers could join the fun by calling in. To win an MTV goody bag, the challenges set were clearly parodying traditional television quiz shows. Juvenile behaviour was de rigueur. Questions were intentionally dumb. Buzzers made barnyard animal noises. Rules about winning and losing were not respected. I remember reading an academic analysis of *Most Wanted*, which deconstructed its every element to provide a rigorous intellectual interpretation of how Ray coped with the tension between public access and professional control. The reality was far simpler. Most of the jokes were conceived in the local pub or Ray's living room, often under the influence of, let's say, an assortment of creative stimuli.

The community around MTV's *Most Wanted* grew organically from a call-in request show into MTV's flagship programme. Ray's profile rose proportionally. He became a big star across Europe and the exception to MTV's rule of promoting the brand rather than the cult of the personality. Ray's success lasted for as long as the European idea drove the network. His relationship with MTV would come to an end following a controversial incident during a live MTV broadcast from Germany in 1996. It was just as well. A happily united Europe had ceased to make sense a long time before. Commercially, MTV was feeling the pressure of the music station VIVA in Germany, its most lucrative market. MTV would have localised its network sooner, if only the technology had allowed it. Ideologically, the spectre of the conflict in the former Yugoslavia had tainted this ideal with blood. As for Ray, he moved to Paris to reinvent his TV career in France. The last I heard, he was in Berlin. Whatever his next move, Ray will forever be fondly remembered as the guy who fooled around every night on MTV with his crew and his adoring European fans while pioneering an innovative style of journalism that inspired a whole new generation of broadcasters.

Citizenship TV: War and Rock 'n' Roll

There was also a serious side to MTV's overarching stylised life. In his analysis of the development years of MTV USA, Professor Andrew Goodwin reclaimed this angle.[50] Parody-based humour, unlike pastiche, actually makes a point, he rightly observed. At times, MTV was even more explicit about its opinion on this subject. It felt it was responsible, socially conscious, vaguely liberal and vastly ignored for its contributions in this arena. The same can be said about MTV in Europe. Among the multiple means by which a sense of belonging to MTV's community was fashioned, the station had moments when it fostered a sense of citizenship. MTV regularly promoted awareness of issues and causes including racism, AIDS and ecology. Occasionally it tackled politics. The point is that citizenship was only one facet of identity and it was no longer the privileged one. What MTV did in this respect was quite groundbreaking. Essentially, politics was packaged like anything else on MTV. This meant that it used its innovative, fast-paced editing, underlined with an ironic tone, to address a cause. This treatment even extended to traditional politics, which had never been attempted before. This language spoke to viewers more effectively than any political rhetoric.

Perhaps the most famous example of effective political campaigning is MTV's Rock the Vote, which was created in the USA to encourage apolitical young people to vote. It resulted in an additional two and a half million young people going to the polls in 1992. When the Democrats entered the White House, Vice President Al Gore officially thanked MTV for its support. In Europe, Rock the Vote could not be applied as efficiently, not because MTV was the wrong medium but because European politics, as expressed through a series of treaties, had no real sympathisers. MTV did stage political debate forums but there was no warm sentiment towards a European political entity. A Scandinavian viewer said it all in a vox pop: 'MTV, yes. Maastricht, no.'

The greatest challenge for MTV in Europe became the conflict following the break-up of the former Yugoslavia. The European political strategy for Bosnia – or to be more precise, the lack of – was a shameful and, above all, tragic episode when Western 'civilisation' failed to take action in the face of human suffering of horrific proportions. In Bosnia, the main principle of Western civilisation – democracy – was betrayed. Feeling let down by the political community, the Bosnian rock fans caught up in the war zone turned to MTV and the rock fraternity for help. Torn between its marketing vision of a Europe united for profit and the reality of war, MTV took some drastic measures. In contrast to political inertia, the rock mobilisation proved to be a lifeline. Far from being careless, Generation X – or the first MTV Generation – responded to the plight of their peers. The rock involvement, initially hesitant, is best understood as a reaction to inadequate political strategy (ideally, it should not have come to that).

The Quickest Way to Heaven

It snowed in London in January 2003. It was the first time I had seen snow that didn't melt since moving to the city over a decade earlier. My warmest outfit was white from head to toe and I remember wondering if Martin Bell was also going to arrive in his white suit for our lunch meeting at his local Italian. Martin is one of Britain's foremost war correspondents, as famous for his fearless reporting from dangerous zones as he is for his trademark white suit. At least, news reporting *was* his vocation until Bosnia changed his life. Not even a frontline veteran like Martin had ever experienced such merciless targeting of a civilian population and a war of such ferocious scale so close to home, he recalled in his memoirs, *In Harm's Way*.

One of the characteristics of contemporary wars is that battles are fought not only on the frontlines, but also in the media. Increasingly, we confront our moral dilemmas through the screen.[51] The case of Bosnia fell into a tradition of Western news reporting whereby Western media arrogated themselves the right to represent all non-Western (non-white, non-European, non-Christian) others in a way that created a distance between the West and the Balkans. Bosnians were portrayed as akin to Barbarians; distant people, 'people not like us', who fought a civil war.[52] If they wanted to go on killing each other, there was nothing that we, the 'civilised' people, could do. There was so much pointless coverage of this conflict that it became a case of morbid voyeurism: the Bosnians are at war while you wait for the casserole to warm up and flip channels from the tennis to the news and back, keeping track of the score.[53] It was the mass execution in Srebrenica in 1995 that finally triggered the kind of involvement needed from the international community, and which led to lasting peace (The Dayton Peace Accord was by no means an ideal solution, but at least it achieved the end of fighting). And yet, a lot of suffering could have been avoided had there been a coherent strategy sooner. To anyone who was connected to Sarajevo, it was patently clear from the outset that what we were seeing on the news were selected images that did not reflect what was going on in this city, whose siege began in April 1992 and symbolically marked the start of the Bosnian chapter in the conflict. I wanted to put that to Martin.

The greatest sense of unease, Martin told me, came from the lack of influence of 'the most powerful medium, using the most extraordinary images from the first war in Europe' in generating enough public sentiment.[54] In retrospect, perhaps too much was expected of reporters. At least they did not run away in the face of genocide, as Martin rightly said. However, impartial reporting alone could not achieve the goal (stopping the war) without an accompanying political strategy. In the case of Bosnia, there was a sense of moral responsibility, and you had to be partial. The news networks could not be seen to side with victims; the politicians could but they chose not to. Avoiding the moral issue, they propagated the erroneous theory of 'ancient hatreds'. As Martin told me: 'It happened from time to time, but no more than the [way the] British have been killing each other for hundreds of years.' 'Ancient hatreds' was a convenient way of justifying political inertia and PR stunts in the form of token visits to Sarajevo.

It snowed in Sarajevo in January 1993. Even under normal circumstances, that winter would have counted as bitterly cold but in a city that was cut off from any supplies (water, electricity, gas, food), it is impossible to imagine how people (in my case, closest family and friends) survived. That is without taking into consideration the constant shelling (800,000 grenades since the beginning of the siege) and the use of innocent civilians as human targets for snipers. The international community's consensus was that the bloodshed had to stop. On 1 January the then Secretary General of the United Nations, Boutros Boutros-Ghali, paid a visit to Sarajevo. Tired, hungry, helpless and angry at political indecisiveness, the Sarajevans greeted him with protest banners stating 'May 1993 Be to You Like 1992 Was to Sarajevo'. Mr Boutros-Ghali's visit, like that of the previous officials who had graced the city with their presence, achieved nothing. After leaving Sarajevo, Mr Boutros-Ghali went on with business as usual. And so did Sarajevo. A random headline from 26 June 1993: 'Massacre. Seven died... All of them children.' A few days later, on 30 July: 'Fourteen civilians dead, another 76 wounded from grenade attacks.'[55] As death became a regular occurrence, individuals were reduced to statistics. Sarajevo remained under siege for 1,421 days.

Another high-profile visit to Sarajevo in 1993 was that of Danielle Mitterand in October. Madame Mitterand came in a humanitarian capacity as the President of France Libertés and not as France's First Lady. This role distinction was important because her husband, the late François Mitterand, had paid a sensational blitz visit to Sarajevo in June 1992, which made him unpopular among Sarajevans. His agenda resulted in delaying military intervention, which not only the locals but also a number of Western politicians felt was needed to lift the siege. Instead, President Mitterand pandered to the perpetrators of the siege. In the words of a famous Sarajevan journalist: 'Whenever we received a visit from a high official from France, we got fucked over... Mitterand's stay was short... but his contribution towards the destruction of Bosnia was immeasurable.'[56]

Madame Mitterand came to visit the French UNPROFOR troops stationed in Sarajevo (in my parents' neighbourhood). As they were francophone and Francophiles, the officers befriended my parents. That is how the honour fell upon my father to be Madame Mitterand's guide during her visit and for my mother to receive her at home. The whole of the neighbourhood, ordinarily a chummy community and further drawn together by misfortune, was very excited. Everyone did their utmost to make her feel welcome. They did the best they could with a paucity of resources so that she could sample local hospitality, including 'war' cuisine. The local schoolchildren learnt some French greetings. Somehow, someone even found flowers. My mother describes the whole episode in detail in her published war diary but here is just one snippet that vividly conveys the painful reality of life under siege:[57]

'It was time for coffee. Semka [a neighbour] served everything unobtrusively at the right time. Mr Merieux [Madame Mitterand's travel companion] took a sip but the coffee wasn't sweet enough. Semka immediately handed over the sugar dish that she had prepared just in case but was reluctant to give, thinking that the amount of sugar she had put in would be sufficient. Semka, who generously always shared everything with her guests, was now saving sugar without even noticing that she was doing so. I am sure that Mr Merieux didn't think about whether or not there was enough sugar, either. All he wanted was sweeter coffee. Her, unconsciously not serving extra. Him, unconsciously asking for more. That is one of the contrasts and truths about the senseless war in Sarajevo.'

Madame Mitterand appeared genuinely moved by her experience. She even shed a few tears. She promised to send humanitarian relief (clothes for children who'd outgrown their old ones, notebooks, chocolate – simple things that Sarajevans were deprived of). However, no relief ever arrived. On 9 November 1993, the primary school that Madame Mitterand had visited was hit by a grenade. It went straight into the classroom of six-year-olds who had greeted her with flowers and the message '*Soyez la bienvenue Madame la Présidente*' written on the blackboard. The grenade killed three children and their teacher on the spot. Some 30 or 40 more were wounded or in shock. Part ashamed by their First Lady's broken promise and part shaken by this senseless killing, the French troops went out of their way to supply an ambulance and enough petrol (which you couldn't otherwise find for love nor money) to transfer the wounded to hospital. Had it not been for that act of generosity, more children would have died. Utterly shattered by this horrific incident, my father wrote to Madame Mitterand to inform her of what had happened. Not a word back. He wrote again begging her to do anything in her power to stop the fact that living in Sarajevo offered the unwanted privilege of being the quickest way to heaven. Not a word. Strange protocol from the lady who left a book as a memento for my dad with the dedication: 'In witness of the kind hospitality that I shall never forget. With all my wishes for peace for which we hope so much.'

That was the tragedy and frustration that Sarajevo was enduring. This had nothing to do with ancient hatreds. This had nothing to do with equally bellicose and equally guilty sides fighting one another. How could a six-year-old schoolchild have been a threat to anyone? This was a systematically planned genocide against unsuspecting civilians. It was a bigoted assault on cosmopolitanism by the prejudiced semi-urban and rural segments of the population. The cosmopolitans were simply defending their right to live together in peace. The war was portrayed as a complicated set-up of different ethnic tribes at war (Serbs, Muslim, Croats) and even here they got it wrong because they did not include the Jews (part of the Bosnian make-up since the 1500s, perhaps smaller in numbers but equally relevant in cultural heritage) and those of mixed religious belonging (a trend encouraged under communism – 'brotherhood and unity', remember). So, yes, being multicultural was complex but it was also simple. It boiled down to rock culture versus neofolk culture.

Traditionally the main signifier of cultural distinction between neofolk and rock, musical taste, also became a sign of political orientation when the war escalated. In Serbia, under the regime of Slobodan Milošević, a new genre of neofolk emerged called 'turbo-folk'. Eric Gordy, a fellow PhD student whom I befriended on the international academic conference circuit and who is now a university lecturer, incisively documented its rise in his book *The Culture of Power in Serbia*. Eric describes how the state-controlled media used turbo-folk for its nationalistic war mobilisation. The main turbo-folk outlets were TV Palma (whose owner was a member of Milošević's political party) and TV Pink (whose owner enjoyed a close personal relationship with Mira Marković, Milošević's wife, as a member of her political party JUL). The union between the ruling politicians and turbo-folk reached its peak when the wedding of the queen of turbo-folk, Ceca Veličković, to the king of slaughterers and war profiteers, Željko Ražnatović Arkan, was televised in February 1995. This symbolic association between turbo-folk and war was so powerful that even Milošević officially ceased endorsing this musical genre when he changed direction and needed to be seen to support the 'Contact Group' peace plan (at the time when Milošević broke his support for the Bosnian Serb leader, Radovan Karadžić).

All of that time, Milošević's regime had also had a policy of systematic destruction of alternatives in Serbia. Rock fans and the opposition despised turbo-folk, regarding it as 'an intentional creation of the Serbian regime, a product of war hysteria and fundamentalism, and a sign of arrival to power of a new "uncivilised" and "primitive" semi-peasant/semi-urban class, generally considered to be made up of criminals.'[58] B92, the sister radio station of Omladinski Program, was among the most persecuted and so was the anti-war movement, *Otpor*.[59] Rock thus became the music of resistance not just in Serbia, but also across the former Yugoslavia and of course, Bosnia and Herzegovina. Someone had to do something to try to stop the carnage. And that is how the rock community got involved: partly in opposition to nationalistic regimes and partly as a reaction to the failure of the Western governments to act.

MTV, Not Bullets[60]

'I was woken by a mobile loudspeaker saying that all Muslims and Croats had to turn in their weapons or else… Standing on my balcony I wondered who these Muslims and Croats were and why had everyone become a Serb, a Muslim or a Croat overnight, given that no one had ever paid attention to such things before. Who were these people marching on the streets and what were they doing in my town? It was like a circus, like a joke, but three hours later, everything became inextricably real, with houses burning and the bizarre militia shooting at civilians.'[61]

That testimonial was written by an anonymous Sarajevan, but what they witnessed on the day of the siege and subsequently was every Sarajevan's experience. I'd say this was your typical Omladinski Program listener, who perhaps even tuned in to 98.9 FM to find out what was going on but instead of celebrating its fifth anniversary in April 1992, Omladinski Program went quiet. We – as much the Omladinski team as the wider rock community and the cosmopolitan citizens – were forcefully silenced. But not for long. After the initial shock, a spontaneous mobilisation of citizens began in defence of their own turf (armed militia began to forcefully enter properties to loot and commit all sorts of horrors) and their cosmopolitan identity. They were not armed; culture was their weapon.

The plight of the cosmopolitan resistance was unanimous: let the world know what's going on here. This was not your 'normal' war zone, even though you couldn't be blamed for thinking so if you watched the news. An exodus of peasants carrying all their material belongings in a bag was the most common image, because according to audience research, it conformed to viewer expectations; too much bloodshed was not palatable (unless it was fictional). In other words, exterminating civilians (the reality of genocide) was too gross but violence in films such as *The Terminator* was okay. Refugees did indeed represent one painful aspect of the war, but not the only one. As it happened, in Sarajevo, people did not need charity relief in the form of old clothes and teddy bears, at least not when it all began. Urbanites did not wear jeans unless they were original Levi's or trainers unless they were Converse, thank you very much. As it became increasingly and painfully evident that the world had turned a blind eye, the need to feel normal and connected to the rest of humanity assumed a status as important as biological survival. There were stories of people burying their record collections to save them from the shelling (while obviously putting their lives in danger by doing so), and of young people's graves covered with Guns N' Roses T-shirts instead of wreaths.

Where life had no value, to live it as decently and as respectfully as possible was the greatest sign of defiance. Senad Hadžifejzović from Omladinski carried out a heroic live news broadcast, which provided the cosmopolitan interpretation of unravelling events (documented in his book *War: Live on Air*). The theatre community staged plays where the people who came to watch brought their own candles so they could see in the dark. The Sarajevo Film Festival was born under siege. At the same time, Sarajevans had also developed an even darker sense of irony and sarcasm, for which Sarajevo was already famous, especially with the New Primitivs successfully exporting this brand of humour to the rest of Yugoslavia. ('What's the difference between Sarajevo and Auschwitz? At least they had gas in Auschwitz.')

Senad Zaimović, my friend from Omladinski and Sa3 TV, started a show called *Rat Art* (War Art) where he used all the fresh materials that I had filmed in London barely a month before. Even that close to the siege, none of us ever thought that Sarajevo would be the next conflict zone. Footage ranged from stuff where *the* Ray Cokes (at the height of his fame on MTV) agreed to be my co-host for some features through to interviews and drop-ins with the cast of the BBC sitcom *'Allo 'Allo!* (it was popular among the parents but we did some ironic 'idents' for the TV network with the actors in character, including 'Herr Flick'). It was surreal to have that sort of entertainment on Sarajevan TV while the rest were beaming hatred and inciting nationalistic propaganda. It was also surreal for Hare, the main cameraman from Sarajevo who had filmed my show in London. His next assignment would be on the frontline with Martin Bell. He later told me he'd worn his brand new cool boots from London, while what was going through my head was, 'You plonker, you survived! Is that not what you should have told me first?'

That was the spirit of Sarajevo. Another mad one came from Senad, during the siege, when we spoke on the phone: 'Lida you won't believe this. We're starving. They're shelling us like rats. But guess what we're going to do!? A beauty pageant! We're doing *Miss Besieged Sarajevo*.' That contest, where young women paraded with their naked breasts covered with banners proclaiming 'Don't Let Them Kill U' would serve as the inspiration for the song 'Miss Sarajevo' as performed by Bono and the late Luciano Pavarotti at Pavarotti's famed Modena concert (1995). In hindsight, that conversation between Senad and myself was the result of another conversation we had had earlier. That earlier conversation turned out to be the pivotal moment that triggered the start of the formation of an international rock-mobilisation network that would start raising a different kind of awareness about the conflict in Bosnia – that it was an aggression rather than a civil war. Miss Sarajevo became its anthem.

When the siege started, Senad spent a lot of time at the TV building for safety reasons (it was dangerous to walk home), though no one was quite safe anywhere. All communication with the city was cut off but there was a satellite phone in the TV building and that is how we communicated, on an almost daily basis. I was the 'middleman' between Sarajevo and the rest of the world. My London 'outpost' became a makeshift embassy for cosmopolitan Bosnia and Herzegovina. A lot of people from the media and from 'showbiz' (from all over Yugoslavia) had my number. One day, Senad introduced me to Bill Carter, an American aid worker in Sarajevo. Senad told him about our work before the conflict and my personal situation as Paul King's girlfriend. Could we use that connection in some way, he wondered, given that I was too young and too exotic to be taken seriously by mainstream news networks (I was getting nowhere with those attempts)? MTV had already been supportive. For example, for the Sarajevo Film Festival, all the VJs recorded special links and *MTV At The Movies* did features about it. MTV also vouched for my credentials so that we could get films on video for Sarajevo that had not yet been released in the UK. The late Bill Tribe, a former English lecturer at Sarajevo University and a great supporter of Bosnian students in exile, took all the materials to Sarajevo. He had a special permit to travel. In return, Sarajevans sent me a music video ('Help Bosnia Now'), which was recorded in the spirit of charity rock ('We Are the World'), where a lot of prominent local artists sang together. MTV played that too.

So that was the phone call that started it all. Out of the nucleus that was our ménage à trois (Senad, Bill Carter and myself), the idea was born to try to get U2 on board. They were on their Zooropa tour, a multimedia-screen extravaganza with a live connection to satellite television networks. Initially, our thinking was to hook me up from London's Wembley stadium via satellite with my parents in Sarajevo, whom I hadn't spoken to for months, other than through

Senad and Bill, who both visited them. At the end I decided not to do it (I don't know why) but the principle of hooking up live with Sarajevo under siege would remain the basic premise. Once again, in order to guarantee authenticity, MTV would ensure that I got all the direct contacts for U2 bar the request sent by fax from Sarajevo. U2 agreed. Bill went on to describe the whole story of U2's involvement in his autobiography *Fools Rush In*. The band, and Bono in particular, wholeheartedly embraced the Bosnian plight. To hear a different voice coming from Bosnia to the one on the news was immensely important for the cosmopolitan cause. U2's support then would develop into a long-lasting love affair between Bono and his family and Sarajevo, where he returned a few times after his first trip in 1995 (when the peace was still very shaky). He even holds an honorary Bosnian passport.

Another important network was the charity War Child. Its first project was 'mobile bakeries', which distributed 4,000 loaves of bread in Mostar, another cosmopolitan place that, like Sarajevo, was under merciless attack from bigoted nationalists. A defining moment for War Child's development came when Anthea Norman-Taylor heard David Wilson, one of the two founders of War Child, speaking on the radio. His vision for War Child was not just to provide humanitarian relief but also to have a more political agenda. Against the nationalistic divisions, the charity would promote tolerance, and music could be a great way of bridging gaps between people. Anthea was moved by the idea of using music and culture as weapons to fight what was, effectively, renewed fascism in Europe. She immediately donated a generous cheque and offered to help. Well placed, she was: she was Brian Eno's wife.

Brian also gave himself to the cause, especially the idea of extending War Child's humanitarian relief into leaving something more permanent, putting in place 'a sort of cultural infrastructure that would flower after the war had finished' in the words of the man himself. The one-degree separation theory within the right network began to operate in practice. Brian happened to be U2's producer. The band was back in the studio to record new material, having completed their Zooropa tour. One day, Bono was interrupted by a phone call in the middle of a recording session with Brian. 'It was that man Pavarotti,' Bono told Brian. 'He wants me to sing with him at Modena but it's not my scene.' This is when Brian intervened by introducing Bono to War Child. Already Bono had an affinity with the Bosnian cause, so he was easily swayed. He would go on to support War Child, though not as an official patron, unlike Brian. Together, they talked further about the idea of building something permanent. It was not long before Bono was back on the phone to Pavarotti, and not long before Pavarotti himself became a patron. His wife Nicoletta, like Anthea before her, became very personally involved. Pavarotti started performing fundraising concerts for War Child. The idea for the 'Miss Sarajevo' song was born in the midst of preparations for the Modena concert. Its proceeds would go to the cause. Meanwhile, Brian also recruited his long-time collaborator, David Bowie, to become a patron.

MTV was another important network of support, with the boss Brent Hansen becoming a War Child patron. He had a close friend from Bosnia (me) so he was genuinely interested in and knowledgeable about the situation over there. Irrespective of that personal angle, MTV's management had also discussed how the situation in the former Yugoslavia affected MTV's own ideology of a 'united Europe'. This was 'the first thing that came up where MTV had a responsibility... we're never going to stop the war but we'll keep people mindful of that,' said Brent. MTV decided to go ahead with unobtrusively making references to the human tragedy that had struck the rock fraternity. That meant constant references to the conflict on the channel in the form of idents, MTV News reports and occasional live studio debates, media coverage of any War Child concerts and initiatives, donating space for fundraising events and collecting CDs and other merchandise to supply Radio Zid, the resistance radio station in Sarajevo. Later, the Bosnia Landmine Victims' Organisation received MTV's prestigious 'Free Your Mind' award for their humanitarian achievements. MTV would also later award B92 and *Otpor* in Serbia with 'Free Your Mind' awards and support them both financially.

What became evident is that MTV managed to inspire solidarity among its fans and generate the kind of public sentiment that traditional news had failed to do. On MTV, the Bosnians were no longer presented as strange-looking peasants from distant lands, but as 'people like us' who were caught up in a terrible tragedy. It is very easy to be cynical about the sincerity of rock stars supporting charities, but having gone through hours of unedited MTV footage related to Bosnia, the general sentiment that emerged was one of people outraged by political apathy. (I am not even talking about War Child patrons, whose dedication to doing something good for humanity I have witnessed first-hand.) MTV almost routinely asked the stars they interviewed to record messages of support for the anti-war movement. They usually accepted. Some did it as a PR stunt but many were genuinely confused by what was going on and wanted to find out more, or were well informed and would get into an animated discussion about politics with MTV's producers while the camera was still rolling.

I felt the same about vox pops. For example, MTV's crew went to Lebanon to ask young people if they'd record a message for Bosnia. Dozens of young people sent messages of hope ('I never gave up hopes and dreams during the war in Lebanon. Guys in Bosnia, don't give up…'). Most of the time, people in the war zones couldn't hear them, but doing nothing was not an option. MTV could not stop the war but its intervention – a mass cultural mobilisation through the immense resources of rock music – created a temporary yet powerful emotive alliance. It motivated people to engage in acts of solidarity. It was an example of new politics building on the tradition of mediated global events, the precedent for which had been set by Live Aid. The affective alliance to stop the war lasted for as long as there was a cause. As soon as it was possible, the rock community physically went into Bosnia, having supported the charity relief in the war zone (in addition to raising awareness).

In September 1997, Bono kept his promise to Sarajevans to stage a U2 concert in Sarajevo. In a city of broken promises, the locals were initially sceptical, but when they saw the huge trucks arriving with equipment, tickets (at discounted prices) immediately sold out. U2 lost money on that gig, but it had not been about making a profit. People from all ethnic backgrounds (a big deal, fresh from the conflict) travelled from all over the former Yugoslavia to see the gig. It was triumphantly hailed as one of the greatest cultural events of that year. In December 1997, the dream of War Child became a reality. The Pavarotti Music Centre – which offered a haven for children with war traumas and used music to bridge national divisions – was inaugurated in Mostar in the presence of patrons, supporters and children.

Unfortunately, the centre did not live past the two years during which David Wilson was its director. The fall of the Pavarotti Centre is a story of corruption within War Child. This started the moment a couple of executive members took a personal gift of 40,000 DM (German currency at the time) when the foundations for the centre were laid in 1996. David Wilson was also offered money, but he refused it. An internal battle erupted between various factions of trustees. By then, War Child had expanded into an international network and brand. A corruption scandal hit the British news headlines in January 2001 with reports on *Channel 4 News* and in the *Guardian* newspaper stating evidence of figures that didn't add up. It resulted in people being fired from the charity and new trustees either claiming in their defence that the misuse of funds had occurred before their time or that the alleged missing money had been 'given back' (should it have been taken in the first place?). Without re-opening old wounds, as far as the closure of this story goes, all the patrons (Eno, Pavarotti, Hansen, Bowie and [Tom] Stoppard) stepped down. They felt that their contribution, in the words of Brian, 'wasn't received with any gratitude any longer'. The director of the Pavarotti Centre and founder of War Child, David Wilson, received a redundancy letter by post. It was a painful moment for all, especially for Eno and Pavarotti as well as the closest members of their entourage, who'd put their hearts into the project. Unfortunately their genius and generosity were sabotaged by a combination of greed and local nationalistic politics. As a result of such politics, Mostar has since become the new Berlin, a city divided between West (Bosnian Croats) and East (Bosnian Muslims). The 'rest' are not even featured and yet if you dig just a little bit into Bosnia and Herzegovina's history (Mostar is actually in Herzegovina), you will find that one of Mostar's greatest sons was the poet Aleksa Šantić, a Serb who wrote about his beautiful Muslim neighbour, Emina, in the early 1900s. These verses were turned into a song. Emina is considered to be one of the most exquisite examples of the Bosnian folk-music tradition called *sevdah*.

Both events in 1997 should have marked a new beginning, but this was in fact the peak of a trend that began a decade earlier – its sell-out, if you wish. We started the (former) Yugoslav rock story, and more specifically that of Bosnia and Herzegovina, in 1987 with the birth of Omladinski Program. This rock alternative to neofolk and the communist regime reached its maturation phase during the conflict. Instead of the scene becoming commercialised, which is what would normally happen, a heroic symbolic fight took place to save the cosmopolitan ideal of the right of different ethnic groups to live in harmony. The year 1997 – symbolised by U2's Sarajevo gig and the opening of the Pavarotti Centre – was the triumphant culmination of a decade-long journey. Rock 'n' roll won a moral victory; but events that developed over the next decade would prove that this was also the year when rock 'n' roll in Bosnia and Herzegovina died. I'll pick up on this in the final chapter.

Local versus Global

The success of MTV as a single channel for a pan-European audience should not be confused with an emergence of a European (global) identity, just as the homogenisation of consumption patterns should not be equated to a homogenisation of cultures. *Most Wanted* was an aberration, an exception to the rule. That rule, which MTV was aware of from the outset, was that domestic productions always got better ratings than international ones. For all the international success of *Dallas* in the 1980s, it was always second-best to local soaps, in spite of their lower production values. MTV used 'Europeanness' to give the channel a collective feeling, which worked because there was no competition at that time. MTV became our 'local' European channel by default. Even during the time of MTV's quasi-monopolistic position in Europe, their success in any country was not a given and it depended on three factors: distribution and access to satellite or cable television; programme options on terrestrial television; and something that can be qualified as strength of national feeling, as some countries were more insular than others.

For all the talk of alleged American cultural imperialism, Germany was in fact MTV's privileged market because it favourably ticked all those boxes. First, it was Europe's biggest cable market in terms of distribution and so was relatively cheap in terms of access. Second, the German advertising market was exceptionally lucrative because of advertising restrictions on terrestrial television and sponsorship only being introduced in 1992. Those restrictions did not apply to cable TV, and MTV benefited from this enormously. Third, the public services' 'wearing off' was significant. The young, in particular, were hungry for entertainment. So much so that MTV became *the* youth television in Germany. Last but not least, in terms of strength of national feeling, Germany never had protectionist policies like France; it has been open to American influences since the end of World War Two. Rock 'n' roll had had a liberating effect on the post-war generation because, as film director Wim Wenders once put it, 'it had nothing to do with fascism'. The next generation, who grew up in the 1970s, continued to feel the burden of the country's barbed-wire division. The Berlin Wall was a constant reminder of that. Rock 'n' roll provided a sense of escapism and a connection to the wider world.

That the counterculture had wrought a revolution through lifestyle rather than politics had real resonance in Europe when communism collapsed. The dismantling of the Berlin Wall was its greatest symbol. The aphorism 'When the mode of the music changes, the walls of the city will shake,' took on a literal meaning in Germany.[62] The correspondence between rock and freedom was real. The successful musical career of actor David Hasselhoff in Germany following the popularity of his song 'I've Been Looking For Freedom', performed at the site of the Berlin Wall after its collapse, is literal proof of that: 'The Hoff' had no hits anywhere else. Coincidentally, MTV's Big Boss, Bill Roedy also found himself in East Berlin for this epic event. He was there to give a speech about how East and West could work together, a spiel that captured the zeitgeist, no matter how corny it might sound today. These were turbulent times but they also offered the promise of a better world. Bill's condition for giving his speech had been that in return, all hotels in East Berlin would be connected to MTV. Bill later recalled how, logistically, this was exceptionally complicated. It had to meet with the approval of the infamous Politburo, the threat of which was still strong – or so it appeared. When Bill turned up at the Politburo office, expecting a tedious negotiation, there was no one to greet him; they had all resigned. The unthinkable had happened, and 48 hours later, the Wall came down. Bill and MTV's crew were physically present at the Wall to share that extraordinary moment. In the years when Germany was in a euphoric state following reunification, MTV's cosmopolitan vision of Europe captured the hearts of young Germans and articulated their feelings.

The moment the German music television competitor VIVA emerged, MTV knew it had had its day as a single pan-European channel. However, it continued to sport its Euro-image for another three years because the digital compression technology necessary to split the network into regions was lacking. Launched in December 1993 as a venture backed up by major labels, VIVA became MTV's first real competitor because it understood the principle of narrowcasting. Its launch added further strain to the already ambivalent relationship between MTV and the majors because of the politics of playlist priorities. Because Germany was MTV's most important market commercially, VIVA's arrival hit particularly hard. To add insult to injury, VIVA appointed Steve Blame, one of the original MTV VJs and the host of MTV News, as its Head of Programming. His abrupt defection caused a lot of aggravation at MTV, because he was considered part of the channel's 'family', which was disintegrating fast.

It would be wrong to confuse VIVA with a local channel. The channel had a more localised feel than MTV in that it used German language, local references and had a target of up to around 40 per cent German repertoire. In 1994, to hit back, MTV itself became very German. It concentrated a lot of resources on various events in Germany, sponsored two main music festivals, opened a German advertising arm and premiered the first MTV European Video Music Awards in Berlin. MTV also played as much as 22 per cent German acts compared to 32 per cent on VIVA – not a huge difference. But what constituted German repertoire? I randomly looked at VIVA's playlists in 1997, and out of the 15 artists per week classified as 'German', only three actually sang in German. The rest sang in English. So was the music German or English? This debate, popular both in the media and in academic circles, was actually pointless given that the national sentiment was fashioned by multinationals. The battle between giants continued until MTV finally acquired VIVA in 2004.

This was not so much about the dichotomy between local and global. It was rather about the possibility of forming new types of communities of interest. Like it or not, lifestyle marketing was the quickest to exploit the proliferation of individualities following the rise of social movements (feminism, gay rights, black civil rights). It was a response to the identity fragmentation that the social movements ignited. And herein lies the paradox in the rise of individualism – it created the radical consumer and it facilitated liberties at the same time. The former is the materialist explanation of the success of the likes of MTV while the latter provides a cultural dimension. A positive result of this marketing trend was that it highlighted that national identity (a homogenising combination of belonging and citizenship) was something that was constructed and controlled. It was indeed an 'imagined community' – Benedict Anderson's famous concept that defined a nation as a unity, which solidified with the advent of the print press. This technology enabled the nation-state to create a sense of belonging and support its own sovereignty. So powerful was this feeling that people were prepared to die to for it. National sentiment was later reinforced with public-service broadcasting. What became apparent in the era of satellite television and the beginnings of instantaneous global communication was that identity could be fashioned in alternative ways to imagine new types of communities. Hip consumerism became one alternative. Brand representations of life began to offer – more by accident than on purpose – a wide range of symbolic resources at a time when the public service sector failed to do so, thus leaving a cultural vacancy for corporations to fill.

Fostering a Sense of Global Identity in the Noughties: the Rise of 'Celebrity'

In the early noughties, the television landscape in general and that of music television in particular could not have been more different from that of a decade earlier, when MTV enjoyed a quasi-monopolistic position. There were by now around 60 music television channels in Europe. MTV Networks Europe (still part of the Viacom conglomerate) was the umbrella company for a number of music channels, resulting from their diversification strategy and expansion across digital, mobile and Web platforms. MTV remained the lead music television brand, but a series of competitors emerged across Europe, particularly in the UK, which was Europe's most developed digital television market at the time. Here, there were 16 different music channels and MTV's portfolio consisted of eight: MTV, MTV2, MTV Hits, MTV Base, MTV Dance, VH-1, VH-1 Classic and The Music Factory (the latter available on the digital terrestrial platform Freeview). The main competitor was Emap Performance, part of a group that owned music magazines and radio stations. Emap entered the music television market with the purchase of The Box and it extended its portfolio via turning magazine and radio brands into music television channels: Smash Hits, Q TV, Kerrang!, Kiss, Magic and The Hits (available on Freeview). The remainder was The Chart Show Channel, a free-to-view option on Sky Digital.

In spite of the continuing downward trend in the music industry, the music-television market remained lucrative, generating revenues from a range of streams including advertising sales, carriage fees, merchandising and programme syndication deals. This meant that even more players had announced their intention to launch music television channels in this period, though not all of them materialised. Those with an eye on this market included The Mean Fiddler Group, Vivendi Universal, Thomas Middelhoff (an ousted executive from the Bertelsmann group), Capital Radio, Ministry of Sound, Virgin Radio and BSkyB. The latter put their money where their mouth was by poaching a long-serving MTV executive to oversee the launch of three new music channels in the UK in 2003, only to dispose of them 18 months later. The market had simply reached saturation point and began to cannibalise itself.

For years, platform operators across Europe were willing to pay high fees (never disclosed) for the 'privilege' of having MTV, which was considered a main driver for pay-TV take-up. Essentially, MTV (or indeed another network) charges pence-per-subscriber-per-month fees for the right to carry the channel on the platform. With intense competition, MTV's bargaining position was weakened. Already, rumour had it that MTV had to reduce its carriage fee when renegotiating its deal with Telewest (the cable operator later taken over by Virgin Media) and the press were now speculating that the same might happen with the (digital) satellite platform operator when MTV's contract with BSkyB came up for renewal.

To reassert its position as market leader, MTV used the publicity surrounding the MTV Awards in Barcelona in 2002 to announce a new direction in its programming strategy. MTV would turn from music television, primarily competing in the narrowcasting music television market, into a youth entertainment channel. This meant that MTV would now be competing for the killer 10pm slot with terrestrial broadcasters like Channel 4 and satellite channel Sky One. The latter had also redesigned itself as a youth-oriented channel by entering bidding wars for the rights to premiere high-profile series normally shown on terrestrial television, such as *The Simpsons*. With this announcement, a years-old trend – whereby thematic music-channel brands (MTV, MCM in France, VIVA in Germany) were increasingly looking like broadcasters and broadcasters were increasingly using narrowcasters' self-promotion tactics as pioneered by MTV – was made official. They were all now competing for the same advertising revenue on the basis of delivering the youth segment, which was still considered the most desirable. By now, MTV had reverted to targeting a younger demographic (not least because there was VH-1 for the 'older' viewer) and so too did the rest of the corporate-cool media. This would prove to be a costly repositioning for MTV in terms of its hip currency. By cool hunting in the wrong place, as it were, and becoming the victim of its own 1990s hype, MTV would miss out on new leading-edge trends and ultimately lose its cool brand status. From its origins – investing in risk-taking and being the first to know – MTV turned into a risk-averse corporation only commissioning programmes that would bring incremental value.

MTV's trump card, though, was the series *The Osbournes*, which had proven successful on the MTV networks globally, as well as on the national channels to which it was syndicated. This series was among the highest (if not *the* highest) grossing MTV programme ever in terms of third-party broadcast sales. The concentration of resources on programmes such as *The Osbournes* marked the beginning of a new era for MTV and youth broadcasting in general. In this 'brave new world', the reality TV format would rule. This involved the private and often mundane lives of 'ordinary' people (later joined by 'celebrities' in need of a career boost) being made public. The world of 'reality' had come a long way since its quiet beginnings on MTV's *The Real World*.

The explanation for the rise of such programmes is located in the shifting economics of the broadcasting industry, and the challenges of having to search for a mass audience in a competitive landscape of hundreds of channels on multiple platforms. Falling shares of viewing based on mass audiences for terrestrial broadcasters, and pressures to maintain niche audiences for narrowcasters, all led to fierce competition for advertising revenues. Reality TV became a relatively cheap production solution.[63] Unlike 'real' stars, ordinary people or the long-forgotten stars who were enlisted to take part in reality shows didn't require pay or rehearsal, as they just went about their ordinary business or else carried out tasks set by the producers. Research wasn't required either, because 'naturalness' was the supposed appeal. That is until lawyers and publicists realised that there was money to be made in drafting contracts for two new kinds of client: the wannabe and the has-been.

Curiosity gave way to voyeurism. The symbolism that accompanied this format morphed into Red Carpet Culture and the display of all things materialistic, summed up best by the expression 'bling bling' (or simply 'bling'). The term originated in hip hop slang, and referred to the sound of diamonds knocking against each other. Typically, bling would include a 'rock' (ring), a trademark chain pendant and maybe even a stud on a tooth cap. Originally part of an iconic look that reflected the ideals of a subculture, bling lost its original meaning in the sell-out – it had previously commanded respect as a sign of having 'made it'. Instead, bling came to signify an ostentatious display of wealth, synonymous with flashing rocks (jewellery), ride or limo (car or limousine), crib (house), designer clothes and anything else that shone (including guns).

Whereas on MTV's *Most Wanted*, the goody bag had been a little token, containing items such as an MTV-branded T-shirt (rare and precious then!) or a CD, now the goody bag was a much larger enterprise. In 2007, I heard a Radio 1 bulletin on the MTV Awards in Munich. The reporter was shamelessly marvelling at MTV's goody bags for the stars, which contained about £10,000 worth of designer gear. Apparently, the contents took 14 months to compile and there was even something like a £20,000 watch in ceremony host Snoop Dogg's bag. It was curious to hear reports of the MTV Awards on Radio 1, who had once forbidden even the mention of the channel's name on air. The two were now seemingly partners in 'celebrity' worship: Red Carpet was the currency shared by these youth-oriented mainstream media platforms, on the basis of which they formed alliances with their viewers and listeners respectively. Being on the red carpet was the pinnacle of aspiration within the cultural hierarchy of this ideology (driven by the desire to be famous).

By then, I was no longer attending the MTV Awards, previously an annual pilgrimage for me. Brent had stepped down as president the year before, which was just as well. I'd had my fair share of good times, having attended them all bar the first. MTV in 2007 was a very different place from the MTV of 1987, sent to bring rock 'n' roll to us. From rock 'n' roll culture, MTV shifted towards nurturing Red Carpet Culture. From championing the underground, MTV began to revere the cult of celebrity. From being the home of hip, heavily inspired by the arts and all things innovative, it became the home of bling. From its roots in celebrating the hipster, MTV now celebrated the wannabe; it had become the antithesis of its original self (this, in turn, being the inevitable outcome of commercial success and the pressure of maintaining a brand leader position in a saturated market).

Towards the end of 2007, I received a call from a colleague working for a global quantitative research agency. I sometimes commissioned this agency when I needed to add numbers to the more qualitative approach to my equally global brand development briefs, so I knew it like I knew MTV. He asked me if I would sit on a panel of 'experts' on all things cool, the analysis from which would then inform the content of MTV's own regular publications on cool trends. Normally, I would be happy to do that sort of thing, not least because of my history with MTV. Every aspect of my life has been profoundly touched by that company (private, professional and academic). But on that occasion, I paused: as far as I was concerned, cool had left MTV's building a long time ago. I declined.

PART THREE: THE NOUGHTIES

THE ERA OF ÜBER COOL

1. (New) Underground Ideology and Aesthetic Sensibilities

'Of all the clothing crimes committed in the name of fashion in the early seventies, the tank top was arguably the most heinous. [...] Of course I wanted one, of course I'd already spent far too much money on clothes, and so my mum suggested that she would show her prowess with a pair of needles and knit me one. I rather liked the idea of a bespoke garment, so went along with this plan. Certainly it was a mistake.'

Robert Elms, *The Way We Wore*

SHOREDITCH, APRIL 2001

I was fascinated by Rachael Matthews before I even met her. I found out about her accidentally, on a long walk from home in Islington towards the Bethnal Green Road in London's East End. I was on my way to meet friends at the warehouse home-cum-office of the founders of the seminal but now defunct *P.U.R.E.* magazine. I followed Old Street where the road forks with Great Eastern Street, a nondescript stretch now marked for change: as I write, developers are awaiting approval to convert The Foundry, a venue that occupies a prominent position on the junction, into a hotel (submitted to residents as 'Project Art Hotel'). If successful, this urban landscape will inevitably change once more. Back in the day, unless you wanted a paper, kebab or minicab, there was little of interest around here – except for one small independent boutique.

Understated and looking more like a bedsit than a business, it would have been easy to pass it by. Often, there was no window display. This occasion was an exception: my attention was caught by an impressive collection of colourful bags, all the shape and actual size of electric guitars. They were hung from the ceiling by invisible strings, offering the illusion of between ten and fifteen guitars floating in the air. I stopped to admire them. It was like viewing a fabulous piece of art at an exhibition. But this was a shop, with merchandise. This distinction between art and fashion, outlet and gallery, had always appeared somewhat artificial to me and I would soon discover a whole emerging creative community that shared my view.

Instinctively, I walked in to enquire about the bags. I wondered what other quirky things they might have in there, too. The guitar bags had been handmade from reused fabrics by a local artist-cum-designer called Rachael Matthews, I was told. I chatted more to the friendly person running the store; she wasn't preoccupied with trying to sell me stuff, and was simply happy to talk to someone who appeared genuinely interested in the story behind the merchandise. Before leaving, I asked the price of a guitar bag. It was high, in the designer bracket, and although I wouldn't be making an impulse purchase, I thought it worth saving up for. Those bags were unique, like small pieces of art to be treasured. The design did not have a sell-by date, as it did not follow fashion's seasonality – unlike the designer 'It bags' that were becoming all the rage. As it turned out, Rachael's guitar bags caught the eyes of style scouts, who were beginning to circle this area. They were, unsurprisingly, unpopular in the underground, as their scouting often resulted in ideas being 'borrowed' from the originators who themselves saw no returns. And mass-produced versions of those guitar bags did indeed appear – mainly in gift-shop-type stores rather than any specific high street retailers – though strikingly similar bags also miraculously showed up in Stella McCartney's boutiques. It is almost impossible to copyright an idea, the only consolation for the originator being that the inner circle knows where they saw an item first.

As it happens, I was soon to meet Rachael, and we became friends and even partners (more of which later) – and I also became the proud owner of a bag from the original batch, a gift from Rachael herself. When I eventually arrived at the

P.U.R.E. office that day, I shared my discovery with the team, but they already knew about Rachael. They were always first in the know.

Next time I came across one of Rachael's pieces was at Victim Boutique, which was owned by a mutual friend called Mei Hui Liu. She had on display a series of ragdolls, like the kind my mum used to make for me. But Rachael's were no ordinary ragdolls. Their outfits were pastiches of contemporary fashion trends, or else the dolls themselves were replicas of people. For example, a fashion editorial in *Nova* magazine featured the specially made dolls, all dressed in mini DIY-versions of the latest catwalk gear from select designers. (*Nova* was originally published from 1965 to 1975 and relaunched briefly in 2000 in an attempt to provide an alternative to the draconian celebrity contracts that consumer magazine editors now had to comply with.) What impressed me even more than the dolls, though, were Rachael's quirky knitting patterns. Cast Off patterns came in kits complete with needles, the correct amount of wool, and knitting instructions on a card with an image on the reverse showing what it might look like once done. You could knit a fag ('look cool, stay healthy') or a 'deluxe' lipstick ('guaranteed to last forever'). I thought them fantastically offbeat.

An even quirkier experience soon followed. Our friend Ms Liu was into organising events and it was on one such occasion that I walked into the party room to find a bunch of trendies all sitting on what would normally be the dance floor… knitting! Wool and needles were scattered all around. At that moment, I realised that my granny was hip. She just did not know it.

Once I befriended Rachael, I found out more about this scene. It was called Cast Off, the Knitting Club for Boys and Girls, and was established in 2000. I got involved with Cast Off shortly after, when Rachael asked if I'd like to help her with developing the club, having already done some work with Mei Hui in a similar capacity. So our somewhat extraordinary journey began. At the beginning, Cast Off gatherings were mainly restricted to the local pub, The Golden Heart, and occasions such as 'Knitting on the Circle Line', which involved exactly that: taking over a carriage on the tube and knitting while drinking tea from Thermos flasks and travelling around in circles. The concentration of ultra-modern people *knitting* – a hobby previously considered naff and the preserve of geriatrics – did not pass unnoticed.

The interest in Cast Off grew exponentially with every event staged. The buzz about knitting spread wider than we could have anticipated. Over time, Cast Off amassed a large amount of international media coverage, from broadsheets and magazines to primetime television. As a result, the theme of knitting began to be used in music videos and advertising, while the self-consciously cool media began to talk of knitting as 'the new rock 'n' roll'. Cast Off is often credited for kickstarting a movement, the legacy of which continues today through the many knitting circles it had inspired around the world, all with their own creative strands. Its marketing clones have become a constituent of contemporary cool, for example teaching the masses to knit at music festivals ('Look at me – I am so cool, I knitted my own wristband!' – but usually this is as far as it goes).

The knitting bug even extended to the White House in Washington (well, almost); Mark J. Penn, Hillary Clinton's chief campaign adviser during the 2008 presidential race and former advisor to President Bill Clinton, listed knitting as one of the most influential as well as the hippest 'microtrends' in his book of the same name.

Why do a growing number of young people knit? Why has knitting become such a popular phenomenon, not just among young people, but across a wide range of demographics and lifestyles in both the US and the UK and around the globe? Last but not least, how on earth did knitting become hip? The rise of its popularity in the US coincided with the rise of a new crafts movement made up of a new generation of DIY crafters, who put a fresh spin on this age-old old-age pastime. Cast Off emerged organically on this side of the Atlantic around the same period. Grassroots connections between Cast Off and the web of USA crafters in general and knitters in particular would be formed early on, long before the knitting revival became identified as a microtrend.

Beyond knitting, Cast Off has had one of the biggest impacts of any of the microtrends to emerge from Hoxton, post Cool Britannia. Rather than perceiving Cast Off as being just about knitting, or looking at this phenomenon in isolation, it should instead be seen as one small movement among many others sharing the same ideals – as per Malcolm Gladwell's maxim that in order to spread a specific behaviour to create one large movement (or epidemic), there need to be many small movements first. Cast Off was one such small movement among a network of other grassroots movements. If the first generation of Hoxtonites was responsible for generating the hype about Hoxton – thus supporting the truism that artists act as advance troops of gentrification – it is, in fact, the second generation that was responsible for the 'tipping point'. It was by extending their *modus operandi* into other sectors (beyond art) that this second generation helped instigate new social dynamics that would create a paradigm shift in consumption and ultimately inspire the style and communication industries.

I begin hip's crossover story in the noughties by looking at how the nucleus of second-generation Hoxtonites was formed. First, I shall concentrate on Cast Off as an example in the context of other similar small movements. What underpinned all the movements were similar mindsets (second-generation Hoxtonites would bring about a new set of values that differed from the 1990s corporate cool, more akin to a new type of entrepreneurship) the unison of which would trigger new consumption patterns. I'll also look at the shift in subcultural ideology in this chapter, while its kinship with new businesses will be addressed through a look at the new mavericks. The influence of second-generation Hoxtonites on the style and communication industries and the subsequent redefining of cool marketing will also be examined. On our timeline, this new movement was born post Cool Britannia, kickstarting the new millennium with a series of scattered activities that would coalesce into a more coherent network by the mid-noughties. The scene would mature between 2004 and 2006, becoming commercial in 2007.

MANY SMALL MOVEMENTS
Cast Off: the Knitting Club from Shoreditch
We were often asked to define Cast Off, which at the time was not easy because we were in the middle of an experiment for which we were seeking a direction, making it up as we went along. I feel better equipped to account for its social impact in retrospect. Simply, Cast Off, the brainchild of Rachael Matthews, was a collective of similarly minded people who, through knitting – albeit with an edge – found a medium for creative expression.[1] By doing the knitting in public places, the club also provided a meeting platform. In more complex terms, Cast Off is much more than that – it was a multifaceted phenomenon that emerged at the right time and right place, making a significant impact on the art establishment as well as the style and communication industries.

Occasionally, Cast Off became politically engaged. Here I would highlight the revival of 'Knitting on the Circle Line' after London was hit by terrorist attacks in July 2005. In the aftermath of the 7/7 bombings, many Londoners were reluctant to take the tube. Liverpool Street station, Cast Off's local tube station, had been targeted. Cast Off went in as soon as the station re-opened, with the message 'We are not scared'. However, it would be wrong to suggest that Cast Off was an underground political resistance group. Cast Off's true heritage lay in DIY punk subcultures. Its politics were the politics of punk, which is about providing a self-made alternative to homogenised mainstream consumer culture. How can we explain this phenomenon? I suggest we do so by exploring three of the avenues that constituted Cast Off's journey: fashion, arts and communications.

Being very much embedded in the second-generation Hoxton scene, where there were many new fashion designers operating on the margins of the mainstream, it was only natural for Cast Off to start experimenting with this world. It even did a season at Off-Schedule London Fashion Week in 2003, which was a platform for an emerging new breed of designers. It showcased knitting patterns (as opposed to knitwear). Although unconventional to say the least, Cast Off's presentation began to generate the interest of fashion buyers. This included, notably, the British high street brand Top Shop, which was among the first to capitalise on the Hoxton trend. Top Shop was interested both in selling Cast Off-branded knitting kits and staging knitting events at London's flagship store on Oxford Street. Preliminary discussions made us realise that Cast Off was neither equipped nor willing to comply with the demands of Top Shop's production deadlines. In addition, the Cast Off collective decided that the association with a mainstream brand such as Top Shop would simply be wrong, as their speedy mass production and disposable fashion went against the ethos of the collective. As a result of being independent-minded, Cast Off's brief courtship with the fashion retail industry met a dead end; but we were learning. Instead of branded stores, we opted to forge connections with a limited number of emerging independent boutiques, including the new 'concept' stores (more of which in the 'new mavericks' chapter).

Predictably in the fickle world of fashion, chunky knitwear became the new black for a season or two. Cast Off knitting kits also provided the prototype for the commercial revival of knitting patterns by high street brands, mainly for easy-to-knit items such as scarves (Marks & Spencer sold such kits for a season), but Cast Off's influence was more relevant within haberdashery than ready-to-wear. Haberdashery in mainstream retail, which encompassed yarn sales, was dying. Department stores were literally closing down those sections, which was bad news for wool manufacturers. The knitting revival generated by Cast Off and the like reversed this downward trend. For example, the West End's flagship John Lewis store reported a 60 per cent year-on-year increase in sales of balls of wool in 2005. Hip haberdashery boutiques started to mushroom in upmarket neighbourhoods. For comparison, we also worked with the brand Bergère de France, a French family wool company, who sponsored a few of our events in Paris. For this brand, an association with Cast Off was the necessary trigger for their revival as well as rejuvenating an interest in knitting in France. Even though the volume of wool sales had been declining in France overall, the French consumer was nevertheless prepared to pay a higher price for funky yarns and innovative patterns as well as the enjoyment of the convivial experience of knitting (a trend attributed to the hip knitting phenomenon).[2]

Statistics about the growing popularity of knitting that were published in the press were often accompanied by publicity shots of 'celebrities' knitting. 'Celebrities' were not spinning wool but using the trend to spin their image by jumping on the bandwagon of a growing craze dubbed as cool. Let me give you one concrete example of how the bug spread from underground incubation into the mainstream. The American singer Kelis started to knit when it was hip to do so and was therefore effortlessly cool, if we were to believe the hype. It's possible that Kelis was genuinely intrigued by knitting, but the point of my story is that the origin of her interest can be traced to a genuinely enthusiastic knitter rather than being some first-hand 'authentic' discovery by the singer herself. The link can be established by connecting Kelis to a member of staff at BBC Radio 1 who was a keen knitter, regardless of whether it was fashionable. She found out about Cast Off and began to attend events. She also started to knit publicly at Radio 1 around the time knitting was being hailed as the new rock'n'roll. This led to other Radio 1 DJs dropping hints about knitting into their shows (in an ironic fashion, more often than not). Kelis spotted our keen knitter during a promotional visit to Radio 1, asked if she'd teach her how to do it – and she obliged. Subsequently Kelis even flew her 'knitting instructor' over to the States to attend her wedding to rapper Nas.

The knitting trend therefore originated at grassroots level and flourished under ongoing press coverage generated by the communities of DIY crafters, before being picked up by 'celebrities' (or their publicists) on the lookout for something cool. This meant that besides knitting, other crafts became funky, contributing to a general crafts revival. In fact, within Cast Off itself, among the products most favoured by emerging hip retail outlets were the embroidery kits for record sleeves. These kits followed the same format as the knitting kit, providing all the elements for a DIY project. This idea was later emulated by established brands and new designers tapping into the embroidery world. Between 2004 and 2006, when the DIY craft trend – with knitting at its heart – was reaching its peak, Cast Off had done a series of high-profile public events in a number of countries. This had included a hugely publicised knitting extravaganza evening at London's Victoria and Albert Museum in 2004, which set a 'hip' precedent for their monthly audience-participatory event, 'Late'.

This leads me neatly to the arts avenue. After a stint in fashion, Rachael realised that she was first and foremost an artist, albeit an unconventional one, who used knitting as a vehicle for artistic expression. As a pioneer of this medium, she became one of the leaders in this field when 'knitting' became recognised by the arts. The new knitting wave – which is how the arts world began referring to artists who challenged the established rules of needlecraft – became *the* welcome innovation in a sector seeking fresh blood. New craft artists started to blur the boundaries between art and craft. They used the traditional craft medium but extended it into art disciplines. For example, in the case of Cast Off events, the knowledge and skill-sharing that had been part of the knitters' community for centuries was now taken out of its original context of garment-making and into a new dimension; you knitted things other than clothes, and the act of knitting itself could become performance art. The arty knitters used unorthodox materials such as exotic yarns, plastic bags or even cassette tape (as in the case of Rachael's 'Analogue Amnesty' project in 2008). There is a large amount of debate and literature on the subject of how this new wave challenged established art norms, but I shall leave it here, as it is beyond the scope of this book.

The most relevant route in my story of being first in the know is the communications one. In this context, the Cast Off event was unwittingly vying for its own place in an established industry where event organising followed a set of standards. Claiming a legitimate position for Cast Off was a voyage of discovery. The world of corporate events was positively alien to us. A challenge that I regularly encountered when trying to communicate the idea of Cast Off outside the inner circle – be it to the owners of a venue, a brand (other than wool manufacturers) or their associated communication agency – was having to explain the concept, which didn't fit neatly into any established precedent. In the early days, it was all about breaking down boundaries: arts, crafts, fashion, event promotion and DJing had previously all been separate worlds, whereas

Cast Off merged them. At the same time, it was about changing ideological beliefs among brand managers, their agency account directors, museum curators and so on. Knitting was just not seen as cool. In the early noughties, a 'cool' party mainly involved a superstar DJ, a branded mega club and punters wearing the 'right' clothes and hairstyles while dancing in the shadows of sophisticated visuals created by a rising VJ. What I had to flog was a set of folk DJs with a 'magic lantern', in a museum, with a bunch of knitters wearing salvation-army chic. And yet, that's not quite how it was when you actually experienced Cast Off. Cast Off was, dare I say it, really cool.

To encapsulate the energy of Cast Off in a simple description was not easy. To see it was to believe it, which is why we needed the publicity. This was not about seeking fame. In fact, Rachael was notoriously difficult to pin down for interviews, while I categorically refused to do any. It was only when we both became comfortable that our cause would be properly promoted that we agreed to any. Also, from a personal point of view, I became conscious that there was a very thin line between being rebellious and being unprofessional, for Cast Off did not operate in a bubble. This realisation prompted me to cooperate fully with the media, as long as the publication or the television show felt right. In today's atmosphere of mindless pursuit of celebrity, not to want to be on television may be perceived as bizarre, but for me Cast Off was genuinely about the ethos of the collective and spreading the message. It was not about five minutes of fame. With journalists – brave ones to begin with – increasingly giving our movement the thumbs up, and prestigious venues opening their doors to us, things started to roll.

It is through the medium of the event that Cast Off was able to expand its influence. It was one of the many burgeoning small movements that were linked through a shared set of anti-establishment values. The event was the platform where these values could be exchanged and connections formed. Being part of an underground movement that had the potential to cross over is what made Cast Off broader than an arts movement and longer-lasting than a fashion fad; the event would turn out to be a crossover catalyst. From an underground party, it turned into something that had commercial value, though originally there had been no conscious effort to become a cool communication tool (which is essentially where it was headed). As with any scene formation, the network expanded organically. It was a matter of intuitively tapping into other networks with a similar mindset, and most of it was done through word of mouth. Hoxton was our base but we were not constrained by locality in any way. Looking further afield is how we discovered a Parisian network of similarly minded people, which would subsequently grow into a hip powerhouse. This link was one of the first connections in a network of scenesters (whom the style and communication industries would soon define as 'hipsters' and start pouring resources into for their own image-building purposes) between London and Paris, which went on to have a significant impact on the mainstream style and communication industries.

Connecting with Parisian Scenesters

This tale of two cities began once upon a time when a beautiful place called Palais de Tokyo was inaugurated in Paris in January 2002. When it opened, Palais de Tokyo caused controversy among the art establishment on the grounds that it pretended to be street but was really about commerce. And yet it was precisely the glorified-squat aesthetic of the space that made it relevant and appealing to its clientele. The architecture of Palais de Tokyo was austere and deliberately unfinished, with exposed pipework and unpainted concrete, juxtaposed with stylish interiors (bookshop, boutique and even gourmet restaurant). Palais de Tokyo *was* shabby chic. Every detail of the space felt right. I immediately fell in love with it; it reminded me of Hoxton. Hoxton was also decrepit, but with their little boutiques, cafés and galleries, its scenesters were lovingly creating tiny sparkly enclaves amid the urban decay.

I particularly liked the boutique called Black Block. It was a quirky mix of curios, obscure Japanese brands, radical fashion designers (including names that resonated with 'my' scene: Eley Kishimoto and Henrik Vibskov) and some art, or at least, Black Block's own definition of what might constitute art, which suited me fine. This art consisted of a range of selected artefacts with a premium price-tag, intended to evoke a reaction like mine among punters. I felt as if I was seeing Rachael's guitar bags all over again. I completely related to the mindset that believed a carefully chosen commercial artefact could be a piece of art, but I also could see why this might not be everyone's cup of tea. I liked the way disused freezers of the kind you'd find full of drinks in a newsagents' were given a new lease of life as display cabinets. I could definitely picture Cast Off knitting patterns there. Keen to develop a relationship, I asked for the person in charge. Someone pointed to a guy sitting in the restaurant, which was behind the boutique (you could see straight through owing to the lack of walls). His name was André. I introduced myself and explained my idea. He offered me some delicious artisan violet syrup. We clicked immediately.

André was charming and debonair, but then how could a man who declared his love by spray painting names on shop shutters (first for his mum's birthday and later for girlfriends) be anything but? I had no idea about André's background when I met him. He was known within the graffiti community, with some success and a considerable fan-base in Japan, but was still relatively unknown to wider audiences. Originally, his USP had been his character, Monsieur André, which he used instead of a pseudonym tag, and his 'love graffiti', a commissioned project organised in conjunction with a Parisian art gallery in the early noughties. Within the space of a few years, André would be crowned the hippest man in Paris and one of the greatest purveyors of hip on a global scale, courtesy of the multifaceted enterprise that he runs with his business partner, Lio (Lionel Bensemoun).

Lio and André met on the underground scene via Chloé, a mutual friend (and for a while, Madame André, who ran a Parisian boutique of the same name). Lio and André shared a particular affinity, especially when it came to good times. Originally, they organised parties for friends, as is often the case with scenesters whose play merges with work. Lio's inspiration for getting involved in nightlife had been the Belgian house music of the early 1990s, which had 'a proper rave scene, unlike France'. Lio embraced the rave ethos and started promoting parties in the South of France around 1993–1994. A bit like Justin from MTV's early days, Lio was particularly fascinated by visuals, which were an intrinsic part of this culture. He operated Mac computers very early on and used the software to produce graphics for flyers. He moved to Paris in 1996, just in time to capture the first wave of France's own belated but nonetheless innovative dance scene before its full commercialisation and proliferation following the global success of Daft Punk. Their success, partly brought on by MTV Europe, who had finally discovered that elusive crossover French Sound, would kickstart the first wave of what is known as 'La French Touch'. The commercialisation of that scene, in turn, turned out to be the Parisian equivalent of Cool Britannia in terms of underground impact, which occurred in the same year (1997). From then on, it was underground no longer.

Once the Cast Off connection had been made with the Parisians, it was time to react to the cult of the superstar DJ, which Daft Punk and the like had become. I did not have to struggle to explain to André what Cast Off was about. We agreed pretty much on the spot to do a knitting event at Black Block. In fact, I found it harder to convince Cast Off. I spoke to Rachael about the idea of doing an event in this wonderland where they used freezers as display cabinets, she spoke to about 20 others from the collective, and the word spread, Chinese whisper-style, that we were going to Paris to open a supermarket ('Are you sure Lida is getting us to do the right thing, Rachael?')! Before we organised the knitting at Black Block, André hooked me up with Mika (Michaël Huard), André's partner (Mika was to André what I was to Rachael).

Mika's background was in contemporary arts but, like most of the scenesters from the Hoxtonite network, he felt constrained by the way the arts world was compartmentalised. He began to experiment by organising multidisciplinary events with friends, for fun. These would merge video installations, dance performances, live music and anything else that felt right. This would ultimately trigger his future career. Within the space of a few years from when I met him, he would be orchestrating seven-digit-budget events for luxury clients. For now though, we were preparing the knitting club's debut in Paris. I suggested that Mika attend our impending knitting party at the Victoria and Albert Museum, which would be a great opportunity for him to experience Cast Off first-hand. He came over with his girlfriend Carine Charaire. Carine was a scenester who was stretching the boundaries of contemporary dance performance into other media, such as catwalk shows. She was working with the then emerging designer Gaspard Yurkievich, who later became one of the hippest names on the Parisian catwalk. Needless to say that Mika and Carine both enjoyed the knitting extravaganza in London. We were all excited about the forthcoming one in Paris.

Cast Off almost didn't make it to Paris, as we got arrested at the Eurostar terminal. We were carrying large, chunky, wooden needles over a metre long, which looked like spears. Security wouldn't let us through. Eventually, we reached a compromise. We would leave the needles for a security check with the arms squad, or whatever the division that checks oversized knitting needles is called. The needles would then be dispatched on a later train for us to collect in Paris. Phew! We staged the Cast Off event on 3 July 2004, which turned into my birthday at midnight (4 July). We closed off Palais de Tokyo for this private occasion and celebrated in the restaurant, where Eric, the owner, prepared a huge birthday cake and champagne cocktails. Staying on after closing time was not a problem. The first directors of Palais de Tokyo, Jérôme Sans and Nicolas Bourriaud, were easygoing. They connected with the rest of the scene because they listened to the same records and had the same penchant for quirky stuff. Degrees of connection acted as 'authenticators' – it transpired that one of the tiny French indie-label scenes from the late 1980s that I had identified with (New Rose) had also been part of their own identity-forging. They were sold on the idea of Cast Off with no problems. They were also not burdened by 'health and safety' concerns, an attitude that I would later miss at less relaxed institutions and events I subsequently curated at Black Block.

Cast Off at Black Block was a case of Hoxtonites effortlessly blending with their Parisian counterparts in a memorable experience. I only wish I had kept André's posters, which he graffed for every knitting 'atelier' that Cast Off prepared for the occasion: 'French Knitting with Fifi' (actually a tall and handsome heterosexual bearded guy called Gary), circle knitting, or even 'Arthur, The Human Needle'. It all sounds wacky but each participative experience for the audience had been devised by artists and had a back-story, making them all truly innovative and unique. Cast Off had even designed a knitting kit especially for the Parisian expedition ('Knit your Own Baguette Holder') in blue, white and red. André's one-off posters for Cast Off would have been great mementoes from that time – their value increasing proportionate to his fame – but then that is perhaps part of the magic of the underground experience; it is, by nature, ephemeral. You live it in the moment. Leaving little tangible evidence once an event over, it becomes an urban legend until it's documented in a book or simply forgotten.

'When a Thing is Current...'

Anyone can get a bunch of trendy-looking people, provide wool and needles and get the more accomplished to show the others how to knit. It is just that someone had to think of it first. Being the originator gave Cast Off its head start but what made Cast Off hip was not really the knitting. Cast Off was hip because of the number of alpha trendsetters who were attending its gatherings. Cast Off was a hothouse. This is where musician Patrick Wolf made his debut (Rachael's then-partner, Capitol K, released his first record). Fellow musician Bishi was also a keen supporter from the outset. Emerging design-duo Tatty Devine were regulars. These are just some of the Hoxton-based figures and when we crossed the Channel to Paris, we intuitively hooked up with the equivalent French network, which even had a name: La Johnson. André, Lio and Mika were all part of it. La Johnson was a party network, which was formed as a reaction to 'La bouteille [bottle] & VIP room' elitist culture of mainstream Parisian clubs, as

Lio describes it. Between 2000 and 2004, La Johnson regularly organised parties, mainly in private apartments, which were reserved for friends and promoted only via text message. They were experimenting with fusions of art and other media, just as the second-generation Hoxton scene was doing in London. By the nature of being alternative, these networks became hip. Ironically, parties under the patronage of Lio and André would eventually become super-elitist, but that is the inevitable effect of hip's hype. Before it reached that stage, these guys were taking risks and even losing money in their quest to stage feelgood events for friends. The first Cast Off event in Paris – a product of our union – was free and open to all. You just needed to be curious enough and open-minded enough to attend.

The innovative aspect of the event, combined with the edgy crowd it attracted, drew opinion formers – the necessary element to start creating hip currency. Marshall McLuhan famously said, 'When a thing is current, it creates currency,' which is quoted in just about any literature on the subject of hip. This book is no different, only that with Cast Off, I experienced the power of that currency first-hand. After Cast Off's first Parisian event, word of mouth spread. My phone went crazy with calls from the media. Paris went mad for knitting for about two years solid (2004–2006). This led to invitations to stage more events. Needless to say, knitting parties became guest-list only; following the hype, everyone wanted to knit, with many punters claiming that they had of course, knitted before it was cool. (Free booze only enhanced that newfound desire.)

On one such occasion, Cast Off was invited to be part of a knitting event (rather than the host), which our French sponsors' communication agency staged by emulating our event at Palais de Tokyo. They even invited 'celebrities' to act as a press hook, but then the word spread that Cast Off would be coming from London. I thus got a call from Mélinda Triana, a Paris-based television director who specialises in cutting-edge trends and fashion, requesting an interview in London. Mélinda came over with Tania Bruna-Rosso. I later found out that Tania is one of the hippest music journalists in France and a member of the DJ outfit Les Putafranges. She also co-hosted a music show on French cable TV with MTV's Ray Cokes, which goes some way to showing how tight connections were within this network. The Cast Off feature was broadcast on the prime time programme *Le Grand Journal* on Canal Plus, on which Tania was a panellist. Actress Carole Bouquet, best known for her role as a Bond girl and modelling for Chanel No. 5 perfume, was the studio guest. Ms Bouquet even attempted to join in the spirit of the report by knitting right there in the studio. Effectively, Cast Off stole the show – we generated the most worth in terms of PR currency without having to do anything. All we were was hip – according to the image projected by the press. Hip is just a label that someone else gives you (and it can easily be taken away).

Another commotion from this early period of Hoxton's spiritual rebirth that was dubbed hip and became massive is the air-guitar phenomenon. Like Cast Off, this started as a small local movement. At the turn of the millennium, one of the early manifestations of Hoxton's second coming was a club night at 333, which had recently been turned into a (mainly) straight club, having previously been gay (and known as The London Apprentice). The night was called Sonic Mook. A small crowd would seriously dress up and turn up to dance to the sounds of DJs Ben and Oli, who played 1980s hair metal. Ben and Oli always arrived in style, carrying their records in plastic bags (parodying the superstar DJs with their cabin-sized record cases on wheels). This earnt them the nickname the 'Plastic Bag DJs'. The message seemed to be that everyone could have a good time without DJs being paid a fortune to create the fun. Ben and Oli made a tiny fraction of the ever-growing fees the big guys were paid to spin a few records at corporate parties. Their hair metal night was part of the Sonic Mook Experiment, which was one of the early multifaceted events that the second generation would become known for. It was promoted by Sean McClusky, a well-respected figure on the underground scene.

One of the resident DJs at the Sonic Mook Experiment, in turn, was all-round music promoter and producer Jeffrey Reed, better known as Disastronaut. My connection to Jeffrey when he became an American in London was via *P.U.R.E.* magazine rather than 333. Jeff too played metal as part of his repertoire. Before he moved to London, he had been based in Brighton since the early 1990s. He came up with the concept of air guitar for one of his club nights, never suspecting that it would spread beyond the confines of the club, let alone become an international movement within a few years. The Air Guitar Championships, when still hosted by Jeff, were one of the most bonkers things I have had the privilege to experience. I only wish a camera had captured the sight of my jaw dropping when Jeffrey turned up on stage in a grotty Camden Town venue as compère for the evening, dressed in a bear 'suit' that had clearly come from a taxidermist's rather than a fancy dress shop. You could just about see his face through the bear's jaws as he announced Iron Muff, a lady competitor who arrived on stage in gear every bit as spectacular as Jeff's. I don't remember if Satan Whopper Cock performed that evening, but I hear that he is considered a virtuoso on the air-guitar circuit (and going strong to this day). It is now an international event with live championships, and there is even a game series version (Guitar Hero) on the Nintendo Wii, Playstation and XBox 360. The Institute of Contemporary Arts (ICA) in central London would later host Sonic Mook Experiment, until its demise in late 2003.

Sonic Mook ran its course, but Cast Off and the Air Guitar Championships went on to have greater commercial impact, which makes them examples of very successful 'fads' in their own right. Each was a little bubble, with many others that together formed the larger movement of the second-generation Hoxtonites. Next I shall look at how the nucleus of this movement was formed.

THE FORMATION OF THE NUCLEUS
The Rise of the Second-Generation Hoxtonites

The second generation of Hoxtonites began to populate the Shoreditch area in the period post Cool Britannia – around 1998 – inspired by the fully-fledged mythology surrounding the YBAs. They went on to put their own stamp on the area by resourcefully carving out their distinct niches. Equally instrumental were the cheap rents for large spaces, which allowed for studios and fostered connections among like-minded people; these spaces tended to be rented by creatives or maverick-business types.

Of the three-letter acronym – YBA – the second generation would retain just one: the letter 'Y' for 'young'. Analogous to 'YBAs', the expression 'young designers' began to be used among the outré circles to distinguish a growing number of radical fashion designers from the catwalk designers at London Fashion Week. 'Young designers' referred to the anti-establishment attitude of the emerging breed rather than to their age. This new wave had not only a distinctive approach to the creative process, but also a different understanding of the fashion business, particularly the promotional side. Commotion on the margins often turns out to be ephemeral, but this time the fashion establishment took notice.

The Britishness inherent in the widespread perception of the first generation – the YBAs – was no longer a prominent feature; it was time to drop the 'B'. Shoreditch became the spiritual home of an emerging network that was truly international both in the sense that many of the second-generation Hoxtonites were not British, and in the sense that pockets of this same movement were operating in other urban enclaves outside London, such as La Johnson in Paris.

Instead of locality, the second generation was primarily united by a set of values. The compartments of 'art' (YBAs), 'music' (Britpop) and 'fashion' ('eccentric Brits', notably Alexander McQueen) that had formed during Cool Britannia no longer applied to this new generation. I shall henceforth use the term 'Hoxtonites' to refer to this network, regardless of actual geography. In this story, Parisians are Hoxtonites too, as are any who share the same mindset.

For this reason, let's also drop the letter 'A' for artists. The second generation further blurred the distinction between art and commerce in a process set in motion by the first generation. The second generation was on the sidelines of art and commerce, flirting with both but never fully belonging to either. The types of questions that Rachael and I were asking ourselves in relation to Cast Off and Rachael's position within it (fashion designer, artist, party organiser, occasional DJ or knitting tutor?) were the sort that other individuals from this developing network were also asking. Everyone seemed to be crossing over between art, fashion, design, music production, performance, DJing, filmmaking, event hosting and promotion, writing and publishing... the list goes on. Think Palais de Tokyo in Paris as a place of pilgrimage, rather than White Cube on Hoxton Square (that was *so* first generation!). Each alpha individual seemed to have their own little universe; each was a tribal leader, with like-minded followers. Their love of fusion was something that created an instantaneous 'zap' between individuals within this embryonic network, but was seen as radical from the outside. Over time, as the influence of the second-generation Hoxtonites over the establishment grew, individuals would find their preferred niches within established sectors – but not before they had challenged convention through a refusal to be categorised.

The impact of the second generation is best understood by contextualising the movement within the subcultural tradition in general, and London's significant historical contribution to subcultures in particular. Building on the subcultures that directly preceded them, the second-generation Hoxtonites adopted the DIY mentality that had governed subcultures since punk. They had inherited the entrepreneurial streak of their predecessors. Being hip was about being a cycle ahead rather than being in opposition to commerce per se. In the post-MTV era, to imagine a world without brands was impossible. MTV was no longer relevant to this scene, but its legacy – particularly the way it had produced marketing that acted like culture – was indelible. The challenge was to move on from the 1990s framework of cool and find your own space within a branded world, with select, forward-looking brands as partners rather than foes.

However, unlike the peer-based subcultures that bloomed commercially in the 1990s, here it is more appropriate to talk of a network of distinct individuals. These individuals were drawn together by their non-conformist values, rather than by a sense of group identity expressed through 'style' – traditionally seen as the essence of subcultures. The second-generation Hoxtonites' scene in the first half of the noughties was collaborative; supportive of any kind of individual expression and keen to encourage each other's talent. Coming together was, above all, for the purpose of promoting your right to be different rather than for the purpose of building a group identity. Belonging to one fraternity did not exclude the right to participate in another. On the contrary, there were no exclusionary policies within the scene. Instigators and patrons of happenings knew each other and frequented each other's nights, even though they did not necessarily sport the same look, as it were.

Essentially it was about individuals from the network, each with their strong personal identities, forming ad-hoc affiliations. These were fluid, territorially dispersed (not everything was happening in east London) and temporary – the duration could range from a one-off occasion to longer-term partnerships. Some of these became frequent enough and large enough over time to form small movements. The agglomeration of small movements, in turn, resulted in the creation of the Hoxton or Shoreditch phenomenon – instalment two – though, as noted, the network was not confined to east London, or even the UK for that matter. Think of it in terms of creative bursts forming the first concentric circle in hip's crossover trajectory. Each burst was an early indicator of emerging trends. The second-generation Hoxtonites' network was constituted of prominent examples of alpha trendsetters, who are the first to know in hip's continuum and whose influence on the style and communication industries on a global scale will become increasingly evident as I develop the noughties' story.

An apparent lack of consistency at the inception of the network made the trend-spotter's job difficult. For a while, cool hunters did not quite get it. Certainly, with Cast Off, trend-spotters (including the press) expected a club that regularly met for *their* convenience, which was not how Cast Off operated. However, this lack of understanding actually helped the organic evolution of the scene from its grassroots beginnings. That these events were not promoted to the press or otherwise listed only increased their desirability among those in the business of being the first to know. Curiosity about the commotion on the fringes of the City gradually grew. Who the authentic scenesters were, what they did, what they wore, what they ate, where they went, how they decorated their homes, what music they listened to – it all became valuable currency exchanged by word of mouth and select media at first, then by opinion formers and copycats en route to the mainstream. In the incubation period, the Hoxton movements (of which Cast Off is an example) that became contagious were formed through a network of sociability that operated 24/7. In true subcultural fashion, the catalysts for the formation of the movements were street markets, which had always had a strong tradition in London, and clubs.

Markets by Day

By day, the place to be seen was Old Spitalfields Market, little-known at that time. As the Camden Markets and Portobello Market in Notting Hill were becoming increasingly commercialised, the word began to spread among the creative community about another market in east London, just opposite Brick Lane, called Spitalfields. Commercialisation has been the fate of many of London's street markets, especially over the past decade, as borough councils became fond of selling them to commercial developers for material gain. The granting of planning permission to 'rejuvenate' a site inevitably meant turning a perfectly happy community of independent traders with vital roles in the life of a neighbourhood into a version of an impersonal shopping mall. In this process, a whole web of small-trade and free-spirited tradition – difficult to quantify and yet valuable enough to bring in the developers seeking to cash in on it – would get destroyed. Once broken, it could not be fixed. The old way of life disappeared, to be replaced by a co-opted version.

Portobello Market, famous for its antiques but also its traditional fruit and veg stalls, was brought to mass attention by the global success of the film *Notting Hill* (directed by Roger Mitchell, 1999). This kickstarted a battle between the independents, trying to hold on to their livelihoods, and the hungry commercial developers. The Camden Markets, where alternative styles – from hippy to punk and glam to goth – had thrived since the 1970s, suffered (or benefited, depending on where you stand) from the 1990s cool hype. It was redeveloped from a flea market with an exquisite stock of vintage gear and innovative design into one of London's greatest tourist attractions. It is still a buzzing place, owing its unique character to its subcultural heritage – but the cutting-edge spirit that once graced the area has been subsumed by mass-produced tat.

It was precisely the intense commercialisation of Camden and Portobello markets that drove away the hipsters who would go on to form the nucleus of the second-generation Hoxtonites. Word spread about Spitalfields Market. As it happens, Spitalfields' lifespan as the 'old market' would be even shorter than that of any of London's other street markets; the property boom triggered by the Hoxton hype did not bypass this hip landmark. Nevertheless, for a brief period in the late 1990s and early noughties, when Spitalfields Market was off the developers' radar, it thrived as a creative hub. Away from the limelight, it became the rescue zone for alienated non-conformists.

Spitalfields was a cross between a flea market, a food market and the London-style street markets that had historically been subcultural hubs. Market day was Sunday (now it is every day). At just £20 per pitch for the (Sun)day in the late 1990s (compared to £75 or more after the redevelopment), it offered affordable stalls for young designers. Other than fashion designers, there were also interior designers, vintage traders, vinyl record-collectors, artists, bric-à-brac sellers and other curios. As for the food, it had been grown by small farmers and was often local and organic. There was also a range of other organic produce (from candles to skincare). The rise of Spitalfields thus coincided with, as well as contributed to, the growing popularity of farmers' markets in urban areas, more of which in the next chapter. For small producers, the market environment provided a direct route to the potential customer. At the same time, hanging around the market offered the chance for like-minded people to meet, form relevant connections and spontaneously come up with ideas for collaborations.

Street Boutiques

On non-market days, a new breed of street boutiques performed the community-fostering function. These boutiques represented an upgrade from a market stall – a natural progression. Street boutiques continued to operate in the market spirit – they were as much about dropping by to keep in the social loop (as most happenings were not officially listed) as they were about selling goods. At the same time, they had a gallery aspect to them in that you could browse and discover new things without the pressure to buy. Thus many of their first patrons were stylists, niche-magazine editors, DJs, artists, promoters and other opinion formers. What was also novel about these boutiques was their collaborative approach to innovation. Developing the brand of the designer-cum-proprietor was as key, but so was showcasing other new talent from the network. In some cases, the street boutique would not even make a profit (sales in other outlets internationally, combined with design commissions for other types of work would compensate) but 'young designers' still retained these ventures as promotional and networking platforms. The street boutique phenomenon also thrived outside the Hoxton postcode – be it in west London or Harajuku, or indeed Black Block at Palais de Tokyo in Paris.

Let's look at a case in point: Macedonian duo Saško Bežovski (anglicised as Sasha) and Marjan Pejoski, global style leaders and my fellow (former) Yugoslavs, opened their visionary boutique Kokon To Zai in 1996 in London's Soho (rather than east London). A mix of Eastern and Western traditions, folkloric art and hi-tech, subcultural and tribal heritage, fashion and music; there was nothing like Kokon To Zai. More like an art gallery than a retail outlet, it was evident from the eccentric window display that you had to be adventurous to enter. Inside, extreme artefacts such as jars of killer bees, clothes that you were not sure how to wear but were too afraid to ask about for fear of seeming silly and jewellery with skull motifs (radical at the time) were on display. If you dared look upwards, you would probably retract your gaze in shame (or shock): a painted Pinocchio with a huge erection far greater in size than his extended nose (must have been a big lie) adorned the custom-made ceiling. Kokon To Zai was not for the faint-hearted.

The boutique was a miniature temple to avant-garde fashion in the form of Marjan's own signature collections. A Central Saint Martins graduate, he is best known for his couture-style label Marjan Pejoski. A name known in outré circles, Pejoski may not ring a bell among a wider audience. However, the egg-laying giant swan dress that Björk – a personal friend of his – wore on the red carpet at the Oscars in 2001 is the stuff of Hollywood legend, regularly featuring on gossipy TV programmes about 'shocking' moments in fashion and showbusiness.[3] The shock-factor of this dress as perceived by the Hollywood establishment pretty much sums up the essence of Kokon To Zai. There was an aura about the place that was somewhere between thrilling and provocative. Around 2003, Marjan also started a diffusion line called KTZ which, in terms of style, was a precursor of the whole movement that would define third-generation Hoxtonites, more of which later. Other than Marjan's own creations, Kokon To Zai was among the first to stock the likes of Jeremy Scott (Los Angeles-based) and Bernhard Willhelm (Antwerp-based). Like Marjan, they may not be household names, but they are hugely credible among creative-industry professionals as alpha trendsetters. Part of the novelty of Kokon To Zai was as a source of Japanese curios, ranging from weird dolls to ancient cultural artefacts. It also stocked Japanese trainers that could not otherwise be found in Europe.

The role of the store as a trend indicator didn't end with fashion – it also included music. Originally, Sasha had been a DJ, and to reflect his own experience and musical tastes, Kokon To Zai stocked a cutting-edge music collection. The shop became one of the places where musical opinion formers' tastes were shaped. At first, it was patronised only by the initiated, as it was not a conventional record store. You needed to think outside the box to be there – not something the mainstream music industry was known for. At first, word of mouth spread by cutting-edge DJs and promoters as well as the independent label-pluggers, who all scouted at Kokon To Zai. The shop's aural identity was mainly associated with the sounds of the now-defunct club Body Rockers, which essentially became the soundtrack of the second-generation Hoxtonites. Today, there are two Kokon To Zai boutiques in London and one in Paris. With over a decade of business under its belt, Kokon To Zai is no longer the best-kept secret, but the concept remains influential and is now recognised by the fashion establishment.

Another boutique from the early days of the scene was Mei Hui Liu's enterprise, Victim, located in Fashion Street just off Brick Lane in east London. The quintessential second-generation Hoxtonite, Mei Hui epitomised this new movement. Taiwanese-born, she settled in east London in the late 1990s having been attracted by the amount of underground street creativity, which the fashion capital cities of Paris and Milan lacked by comparison. Mei Hui employed an unconventional approach to tailoring that involved cut-and-paste techniques (as opposed to pattern-cutting based ones) because she had no formal training in dressmaking. Turning this disadvantage into a virtue in homage to the punk DIY tradition (and particularly Vivienne Westwood, one of Mei Hui's heroes), she customised old frocks and gave them a new lease of life by embellishing them with her trademark Victorian-period lace. Victim dresses were 'clothes for heroes' indeed. To wear one was to make a statement, as they were unique. A playful reference to fashion victimhood, Victim the label was in fact completely anti-fashion. With its new aesthetic (perhaps one that was too ahead of its time for the mass market), Victim did not pass unnoticed by the fashion business.

One of the early big fads that emerged from the second-generation Hoxtonite clique was the customisation trend. This cut-and-paste fashion was responsible for the original scruffy look associated with Hoxton. Mei Hui was among the most innovative practitioners of the trend (not *everything* customised was actually any good). Noki was another visionary designer in this vein. Some insiders would say that he was the first to start tearing up sportswear and sewing it back together – making striking, unique garments that were sold at Kokon To Zai. Another label that encapsulated this vogue at its best was Junky Styling. It would later kickstart a major eco-fashion movement together with other pioneering labels like From Somewhere and pioneering eco-fashion veteran Katherine Hamnett. (There will be more about eco fashion when I look at the influence of this scene on the style industry.) As for the customisation trend, this was soon picked up by the mainstream fashion industry. For example, trainer brands (Puma, Nike) began to produce 'personalised' footwear. Then high street chainstores picked up on it. For example, Jigsaw commissioned From Somewhere to produce customised collections for them.

Like most Hoxtonite designers from the turn of the millennium (ie 'young designers'), Mei Hui started out on a market stall. With her unique personality and striking look, she began to attract stylists and magazine editors in search of cool at Portobello Market (Mei Hui was among the first designers to move from Portobello to Spitalfields). From the market stall, she upgraded by opening her first boutique in Fashion Street in 2001. The Victim boutique became one of the key hangouts for second-generation Hoxtonite hipsters. Resembling a tea-house more than a shop, you would pop in for a cuppa (there was a kettle) and find out what the latest word on the street was. People would also spontaneously stage little block parties in the street (featuring egg and spoon races and the like), as neither the office spaces nor the Instituto Marangoni (Marangoni fashion school) were yet there. Bar a handful of tiny Bangladeshi stores, there was nothing. Our friend Philip Normal, a fashion student at Westminster College at the time, who would later become one of the foremost third-generation Hoxtonites, couldn't have put it better when he said, 'Mei Hui was one of the most important pubs.'

Clubs by Night

By night, the social network went underground. There had been a shift away from hedonistic warehouse parties (which had once defined Shoreditch's underground before being co-opted post Cool Britannia) towards a new kind of event. In the beginning, these events were more an excuse to bring the similarly minded together rather than money-making ventures. This was in contrast to the overground Shoreditch Saturday-night parties that passed for cool but were frequented by wannabes. Not that these commercial parties weren't offering an alternative to the mega club. They were, but it was not the leading-edge cool. The underground parties were a world apart. This underground incarnation was governed by a DIY aesthetic and a strong sense of alternative identity. It was a reaction against uniformity and the herd-following lifestyle, which included the Shoreditch corporate-cool look that could be purchased on the high street or in any department store. Just as the street boutiques were, these events became showcases for talent.

What was unique about these events was the organiser's skill in handpicking innovative characters with distinctive talents to provide the evening's entertainment. An event could include anything from live music to an improvised catwalk show. Performers and punters alike were all into one creative pursuit or another, and this was reflected in their imaginative looks. We started using the word 'curator' to express this new fusion aesthetic. With its new definition, this term would cross into the mainstream, becoming a marketing term used to connote cool. Away from the commercial gaze however, these events were first and foremost a means of alternative expression. While celebrity-obsession was growing in the mainstream, these were 'anti-celebrity' environments. Kudos was earned through the amount of creativity and genuine innovation exhibited and not by the amount of newspaper columns indiscriminately filled. Just as the first generation of Hoxton parties had been 'platforms of social exchange', to quote Gregor Muir in *Lucky Kunst*, the second generation's events had that same potential. This is the fundamental difference between an overground cool party and an underground one. What made the underground events unwittingly hip was the concentration of people attending who would go on to make an impact on the mainstream style and communication industries. For this reason, the underground parties would begin to attract those in the business of being the first to know.

Dressing Up

It goes without saying that the underground clubs were the places to be different. What happens after a decade of dressing down? People started to dress up again. As trends are cyclical, the time was ripe to revive what the previous subcultures had rejected. Style took centre stage in this emerging Hoxton scenario. Yawning at the mention of anything to do with 1990s 'comfort dressing' and its lovechild, the overground 'Hoxton cool' look, it was time to bring on some sartorial eccentricity. Everyone went bonkers: the more absurd the outfit, the better. Music did of course have a role, although it played second fiddle to style. Someone with a huge squash positioned on their forehead (laced up around the head to make it stand) was hardly going to hit the dance floor. Ornamental vegetables, shimmering catsuits, 18th-century French wigs, faces fully painted in fluorescent green, were all looks that didn't lend themselves to sweating, so unnecessary movement and dancing were out. Of course, by the end of the evening, make up would have run and wigs and vegetables would be askew as people succumbed to the beats. Fundamentally though, this club experience was about dressing up.

Mei Hui Liu's Secret Rendez-vous was a seminal event of the new creative wave. Occurring sporadically and in different locations across London (and even in Paris), it was *the* party to be at from around 1998 until 2002. This is where musician Patrick Wolf did his first performances. This is also where Cast Off: the Knitting Club first went beyond the local pub on the day I realised that my granny was hip. Designers Pauric Sweeny, Jas M.B., Junky Styling, Patrick Soderstam and Henrik Vibskov all had their first breaks at Secret Rendez-vous. Characters who would make their mark in years to come, such as Carri Mundane and Philip Normal, were regulars. Here, they would have their first taste of an extravagance that would nurture their vision of the world as seen through a neon-bright lens. Many up-and-coming stylists, journalists, future bloggers and other types of opinion formers also attended. When I first met Mika, the Parisian Hoxtonite, we thought we did not have friends in common until it transpired that he had been at the first Parisian Secret Rendez-vous. The one-degree connection always pops up on the scene.

Just as Secret Rendez-vous was beginning to fizzle out, a new shindig was about to erupt: Kashpoint. The brainchild of Matthew Glamorre (later co-hosted with scenester Jim Warboy), and also held sporadically and in different venues, Kashpoint was the mother of all dress-up bashes. A club for the 'gloriously disaffected', as Glamorre often referred to it, Kashpoint was home to the most extreme dressers. There was no party like a Kashpoint party; second-generation Hoxton is greatly indebted to it, as this was the club night where the nucleus was formed. Performance artist, event promoter, DJ, music producer and wordsmith (though he does not tend to list writing as one of his talents), Glamorre's influences include some of the most flamboyant and forward-thinking personalities, including one of London's greatest club icons, Leigh Bowery. A larger-than-life character, Bowery is best known for his celebrated club night Taboo, held throughout 1985, and for the way he inspired musicians, artists and fashion designers until his untimely death in 1994. Glamorre, together with Richard Torry, was a member of Minty, Bowery's band. Around 2000, Glamorre and Torry got back together to re-form a very unique musical trio called Siren Suite. The third member was Bishi, a second-generation Hoxtonite par excellence as well as a talented musician, who went on to make a few critically acclaimed albums produced by Matthew.

It is perhaps no coincidence that I first met Matthew Glamorre at a club night hosted by Steve Strange in 2001, the same year Kashpoint was launched. A key figure in the new-romantic movement and frontman of the seminal 1980s outfit Visage, Steve was the creator of the legendary Blitz club. Gathering together the kids who were the younger exponents of the punk movement (which included Steve himself), Blitz was one of the first post-punk instalments in London's subcultural history, and it had a global influence. The seeds of extravagant and strange dressing, sown by punks in the late 1970s, came to bloom with the new romantics and futurists who congregated at Blitz in the early 1980s. Blitz was also a prototype for the club business – that of an outside promoter filling an otherwise empty club with his or her own punters and sharing the takings.[4] The Blitz aesthetic would partly inspire the second-generation Hoxtonites, not least because we were all 1980s kids and the first MTV Generation who worshipped synthetic music and the cult of the visual.

Elektroklash

In terms of the second-generation Hoxtonites' musical identity, two regular club nights became emblematic. On Monday nights, there was Trash at The End founded by debutant DJ Erol Alkan. On Wednesdays, there was Nag Nag Nag at the Ghetto, organised by veteran promoter Johnny Slut (charismatic keyboardist of the 1980s goth-glam band Specimen), and Fil OK, with whom Slut often DJed. While it is difficult to sum up the eclectic range of music played at these clubs, the term 'elektroklash' is most commonly used and this is certainly the dominant genre on the second-generation Hoxtonites' playlists. Here, the first and second wave of 1980s dance music (considered too 'poppy' for ravers in the late 1980s) was reworked into a new synthetic sound, combining house, electro and pop with new elements. This genre was not represented in the charts at the time but the antagonism between mainstream chart pop and alternative music that had defined previous subcultures was not as pronounced among second-generation Hoxtonites. For example, playing the odd Britney Spears tune didn't dent a DJ's credibility, which takes me back to the point that music was just one identity signifier of this alternative network.

Elektroklash is one of the post-Ecstasy electronic dance movements that operated on the margins. This genre was devised and adopted by those who desired a more creative space within dance music. New York and Berlin were the two most prominent cities from which this sound emerged, with London's underground clubs later embracing it and providing a fashionable, extravagant touch. New York-based DJ Larry Tee and Berlin-based DJ Hell are considered pioneers of this scene. Fischerspooner (also New York-based), Chicks on Speed (an international trio formed in Munich before moving to Berlin), Peaches (Berlin-based Canadian) and the French artists Felix da Housecat and Miss Kittin (and The Hacker) were among the leading acts associated with this scene. These artists tended to be multidisciplinary. Their stage performances took cues from a wide spectrum of influences and were often very theatrical; perfectly in tune with the second-generation Hoxtonites. Two volumes of compilations called *Futurism*, released by the short-lived label City Rockers, are among the musical documents that best encapsulate the range of artists and the buzz from this period. In fact, label founder Phil Howells was allegedly the first to bring the Scissor Sisters to the UK before they were famous, but they never played their gig because their equipment failed (rumour has it that someone had opened a fridge door, which overwhelmed the small venue's power supply). Scissor Sisters would become one of the most successful commercial exponents of this scene even though their fellow New Yorkers, the more theatrical Fischerspooner, had more impact on the underground scene during its incubation period.

Elektroklash artists continue to have respectable careers and fan-bases around the world but they never became mainstream chart material, with a few exceptions. For example, Fischerspooner did manage to chart and get an appearance on *Top of the Pops* in the UK in 2002 solely on the basis of sales of their single 'Emerge' (on the scene, this song was a true anthem of the period). New Yorker James Murphy and his critically acclaimed outfit LCD Soundsystem got major airplay pretty much from the outset, in 2005. For most part though, elektroklash's influence on the mainstream would prove to be a more diluted version of its original sound. The late noughties' chart successes of Lady Gaga and La Roux represent the commercial extrapolation of what the elektroklash scene originally pioneered. Both flamboyant in looks and sound – considered novel in the youth media sector – it had all been done years before in underground clubs on the global Hoxtonite scene. A less obvious influence is the way elektroklash artists, and more generally, DJs from this scene, began to produce more mainstream artists to give them an edgier sound, be it Chilly Gonzales collaborating with Jane Birkin and Philippe Katerine in France or Erol Alkan with Franz Ferdinand on their third album. These are just two examples; there are many more.

The combination of dress-up clubs and elektroklash in the early noughties provided the foundation for a new movement that would go on to shape the style and communication industries, the development of which we shall follow. Their 1980s-influenced style-and-music combo would eventually become a force in the mainstream. Kashpoint splintered into a series of new club nights, out of which third-generation Hoxtonites would form their universe. This scene was fully commercialised from around 2007. Out of the ashes of the original dress-up clubs, new club nights would rise (and later fall), but none of these clubs and the fashions surrounding them would fundamentally change the principles of the movement – this was evolution rather than revolution. This means that the intricacies of the many microtrends in and around the nucleus that Hoxton is still adept at generating will not be the subject of my story, but before we take a step further in our crossover trajectory, there is another, larger bubble, among the second-generation network that needs to be explored separately. This 'bubble' had also been around since the turn of the millennium but would only be picked up by marketing companies towards the end of the noughties. Because of the seemingly different styles of dress and music from those of the Kashpoint crowds, it could easily have been confused for a different scene or indeed a new scene, but it wasn't: it was all part of the Hoxtonite network.

The Dandy Hoxtonites

Another reaction to the morose 1990s habit of dressing down was represented by the dandy scene. A 21st-century post-punk movement reminiscent of the Bright Young Things of the 1920s, the dandy characters were promoters, musicians, designers, curators and various occupations in between, just like the rest of the Hoxtonites. Theirs was a contemporary interpretation of sartorial and bohemian lifestyle periods from the late 19th century up to the early 1960s. If you went to dandy-orchestrated events (even festivals), you would be treated to an edgy take on the performance traditions of vaudeville, burlesque, peep shows, carnival balls and circuses, as well as interpretations of historical movements ranging from futurism to gothic horror literature. Some strands within the network would be more rockabilly (such as the band The Penetrators) while others would spin 1940s records on gramophones.[5] The dandy-influenced trend became increasingly mainstream at the end of the noughties (in fashion, advertising and entertainment industries), filling the void following the full commercial exploitation of the 1980s revival. For example, Paloma Faith, who began to enjoy mainstream chart success in 2009, was a prime exponent of the Hoxton dandy scene. (She was the lead singer of The Penetrators before going solo.)

The more widespread commercial impact of the first strand (the 1980s-influenced dress-up and elektroklash combo) would create an artificial division between the two, but that's how marketing operates. In real life, everyone from either strand knew each other and came together in various forms of social exchange. The different cliques fed off each other. Other than the different dress sense and music, all the major strands of the second-generation Hoxtonite scene shared the same set of ideals, which is why they formed a movement, like the subcultures before them. In isolation, each could be a fad. Put together, you get a bigger movement that, combined with maverick businesses, led to a paradigm shift, which is where we are headed.

The First Circle in Hip's Continuum
The New Underground Ethos

It is essential to unearth the new set of values that governed the second-generation Hoxtonites in order to understand the sense of unity between the different bubbles that made it a larger movement. That set of values, in turn, was the point of identification for emerging maverick businesses. They would adopt subcultural idioms to challenge the status quo and unleash a new market of early adopters, just as MTV and other cool brands had a decade earlier. At the same time, tracing how the ideological shift occurred will unravel the conditions that led to a sea change in cool marketing. If cool in the 1990s was all about being street, cool in the noughties instead became rather chic.

Forget Irony

Around the time the knitting hype was gaining ground, I got a call from a planner working for one of the most successful cool advertising agencies to emerge from the 1990s creative boom. He wanted Cast Off to take part in an advertising campaign for a famous (inevitably cool) shoe brand. He was looking for unusual (read strange) clubs. The knitting club was among the chosen ones. There was another underlying motive: if you were a cool communication agency, to have some connection to knitting had become essential. It showed your clients that you were at the frontier of trends, the compulsory attribute that set apart a cool agency from a more conventional one. Before seeking our agreement, and assuming that we would accept the offer, the agency had already invested creative time in producing knitting-related storyline templates for their forthcoming campaign. Their pitch to us was that we should feel privileged to have been chosen by this (admittedly) successful advertising agency to feature in an advertising campaign for an (admittedly) iconic brand. This was a hint of a problem, though, as we saw it as a sell-out. If Cast Off was going to do it, 'it' had to be the right message – and Rachael and I did not feel that the agency's viewpoint was right for Cast Off. It is not so much that we were hostile to the idea of Cast Off being in an advert per se, it is just that we didn't like the creative direction of this particular one; it was an ironic take.

Implicitly, the shoe brand was being positioned as hip because, of course, it was not 'us' (the brand + the customer) who were weird, in spite of the odd choice of people featured in the adverts. Rather, the weirdos were the ones in those clubs. We (the brand) were just being ironic. Weren't we cool (and by extension you if you purchased our shoes)? Well actually, no – irony was passé. We refused to take part in this advertising campaign because irony went against the ethos of Cast Off.

Forget irony. That tone no longer reflected the new underground ideology. The corporate cool sector was still using irony as a selling tactic but the hipsters who would drive future style and communication (of which Cast Off was part) were forming a new ethos. If we go back to the time before irony became a marketing tool, you may remember that irony was initially a device used to assert new ideological principles against the dominant rock ideology of authenticity. Emerging in the era of rock hegemony and inheriting beliefs founded upon the truism that anything that was not rock was naff, the new subcultures needed a clever tool to bypass that hurdle. A particular form of irony – based on self-mockery, self-deprecation and parody – proved to do the trick. This fad among the various post-punk subcultures subsequently became a brilliant marketing tool that went on to define the communication tone of the 1990s cool marketing era.

However this ironic tone of communication – born out of the necessity to assert an alternative identity – lost meaning when its commercial potential superseded the drive for diversity.

As the nature of hip is to reinvent itself through a rejection of what it previously patronised, so the rise of über cool brought with it a new understanding of authenticity. If the 1990s was an emotional decade where style triumphed over content, hip in the noughties marked a return to more functional roots. Authenticity was no longer ironically inauthentic. Instead, it was defined through an appreciation of the product and the nature of its production rather than a preoccupation with its packaging. A reaction to the 1990s hi-tech, fast-paced, visually-computerised world where MTV ruled, über cool was all about reverting to an old-fashioned, low-tech, slow-paced cosmos where knitting became the new rock 'n' roll. Technology would fit into this aesthetic but it would not be the driving force. Technology is certainly a medium that facilitates the creation of communities, but it is not in itself a community or a leading-edge trend. While the corporate-cool sector (synonymous with youth culture now) threw themselves at the next wave of technology (digital television and the emerging Web and mobile platforms), assuming that technology would equal cool and youth, the next wave for those in the know emerged elsewhere.

If what was previously cool was about manipulating mass culture and its imagery by removing it from its original context and holding it up for ridicule, the new cool (or über cool) was about looking at artefacts with conventional purposes from an innovative perspective. Rather than producing more, it was about salvaging what was already out there and giving it a modern twist. Examples include: Cast Off's original spin on knitting (previously considered a granny's hobby); the wave of designers who applied recycling as a method such as Junky Styling (who transformed old suits into edgy outfits) or Squint (who turned Victorian furniture into funky home décor); the wave of designers who applied traditional craft methods to unconventional materials (such as the way Tatty Devine used acrylic, which became their signature, but also reclaimed wood, leather and veneers as if they were precious materials to create exquisite jewellery); the new use of period entertainment by the dandies (burlesque, vaudeville and so on); and the 1980s revival spawned by dress-up clubs and elektroklash, which became a dominant trend in the second half of the noughties.

All of this action was seemingly eclectic, which was a nightmare for trend-spotters, but there was order to this chaos. Here, it is useful to go back to the 'existential' questions that hipsters were asking themselves: 'Am I a designer, DJ, promoter or knitting instructor?' One person could be all of these things. It was about fusion. This refusal to be compartmentalised went against the grain of the 1990s lifestyle segmentations and product categories. This shared mindset among scenesters in turn provided the foundation for the creation of the new early-adopters market (or the new youth, if you wish), which a new wave of maverick businesses would unleash. This fusion was not random; not every designer, DJ, promoter and knitting instructor fitted into the scene's ethos. What they all had in common was an aptitude for crafts. The intensity that went into crafting your medium of expression (jewellery, furniture, clothing or indeed, a performance) and the idea (challenging convention, breaking down boundaries, reinterpreting tradition) would be what gave it value.

Celebrate Crafts

The combination of labour-intensiveness and a creative approach determined the value of any given product. In terms of actual pricing, it was racked up to premium. I mentioned earlier that Rachael's guitar bags were priced like designer bags. This was a bold statement for an unknown designer – and the whole scene valued the fruits of their own labours to a similar degree – but still, there appeared to be a market among the Hoxtonites. Street boutiques, which specifically stocked new designs, and the new breed of stores and street markets scattered around them (whether in Hoxton, Paris or Berlin) were all beginning to attract a similar type of customer. The DIY approach of the still-anonymous scene that thrived on pushing boundaries was countering the over-produced mass-consumption trend where 'celebrity' was used to communicate aspiration.

Beneath this penchant for craftiness was a growing eco-consciousness. 'Craft' was not just a word to describe a trade characterised by its means of production; it stood for a way of life. Reclaiming craftsmanship became a way of claiming a right to diversity in an increasingly homogenised society. It was an anti-consumerist stance. It was also about inspiring creativity and responsible consumption. It was about curiosity – enquiring about heritage, questioning modes of production, asking about provenance. Whereas in the 1990s, it was all about being vegetarian on moral grounds, now it was okay to eat meat as long as it was sustainable and ethical. It was also about showing an open-mindedness and inquisitiveness rather than mindlessly consuming. It said that you did not have to buy everything off the shelf. You could make your own things and add a personal touch. Rather than seeking gratification through the purchase of labels, it was time to find a reward in human interaction and to put a value on labour. This type of proposition would prove to be highly motivating for consumers. It is just that someone had to make that first step. A wave of maverick entrepreneurs were the first to take that risk – the first to find a spirited soul in the underground scenes. From there, these beliefs began to attract more partisans, thus forming a mainstream trend, which I shall explore in the next chapter.

To reflect this new wave of crafty hipsters, the word 'artisan' began to appear in the media (rather than the word 'craftsman' – perhaps that had stale and dull connotations). Being an artisan signified an alternative lifestyle to the homogenised, mass-produced and format-driven mainstream. Artisan trade is, by definition, small-scale, handmade and labour-intensive. The finest ingredients; crafted by the finest craftsmen. Attached to production is a sense of pride, as artisans invest love and care in their processes. Customer satisfaction is considered recognition of artistic merit rather than a happy economic exchange. By virtue of being alternative, being an artisan became hip. Consequently, former signifiers of uncool (a farmer in wellies or a person knitting) became cool. To turn the least-fashionable hobby (was there anything less cool than knitting?) into a hip microtrend was so far from the 'bling bling' mainstream. This is where Cast Off came in.

The craft aesthetic became a powerful representation of the new hip wave. The antithesis to modern, fast-paced, convenience-oriented living, craft suggested the cosiness of the home environment. It revived the feeling of comfort associated with nostalgia for the parental homes (and the type of décor that had become unfashionable in the 1990s), a granny's recipe for wellbeing or the smell of home-baked cake. In contrast to the minimalist loft-design aesthetic (the cheaper version of which could be purchased flat-packed at IKEA), what this lot were telling you was that you could use your granny's furniture instead of chucking it away. It needn't be bedsit furniture. With a bit of love and care, it could become a perfectly pleasing piece of interior design. At the same time, it showed you cared about the environment. If IKEA's ironic advertising campaign ('Chuck out your chintz!') had been emblematic of 1990s cool, then now it was time to bring back the doilies and chuck out the irony.

A symbol of this new cool crossing over into the mainstream was the wallpaper revival. In the first half of the noughties, there was no sign of wallpaper in representations of modern affluent living as seen in magazines or estate agents' windows. Cool lifestyles were denoted either by bare brick walls, or bare white walls for the less well off. Meanwhile, underground, wallpaper was becoming fashionable, but it was still not sold in mainstream shops and so you had to do your research to find some. Traditional wallpaper (Osborne & Little, Cole and Son) was, well, too traditional. In search of something edgier, you either scouted car-boot sales or Greenwich Market in south London (the word on the street was that you could find rolls of original 1970s paper), or alternatively, you might be part of the inner circle and therefore know where the odd designer might be producing and selling it in the boutiques of second-generation Hoxtonites. The London-based design house Timorous Beasties were among the first to revive wallpaper. Personally (I have wallpaper, of course!) I got mine over the Internet. It travelled all the way from Texas from a tiny store that sells all things flamingo-related, as I fancied a flamingo motif (nothing else would do).

Pubs and hair salons frequented by scenesters would be among the first public places to pick up on this underground trend. The music industry and cool media sector followed. If you were in a band, for instance, you might have your picture taken with a wallpaper background for your publicity shots. That way, you were cool. Ditto if you worked for a cool communication agency. Consumer home-decoration magazines would also start featuring wallpaper. Trendy chain-bars and high street stores were at the end of the crossover continuum. Estate agents' offices in expensive neighbourhoods (like Shoreditch) incorporated wallpaper as part of their décor while the photographs of the lofts they were selling showed bare-brick walls now combined with one papered 'feature' wall, to be on trend. When wallpaper became a mass trend towards the end of the noughties, new designs were widely available. For hip living, you could purchase limited-edition wallpaper at a premium price designed by the likes of Meg Mathews (former Britpop wife whose 'rock and skull' collection retailed at £85 per roll) or catwalk designers like Julien Macdonald and Basso & Brooke at £60 per roll (limited-edition series designed for Graham & Brown, wallpaper specialists who revived their brand through a number of funky collaborations). Similarly, the traditional wallpaper company Cole and Son commissioned Vivienne Westwood to design a range in 2009. By the end of the decade, every self-respecting sort with a cool-design home had one papered wall (admit it, if you are reading this book, you are most likely one of these sorts). The label for this design element became 'feature 'wallpaper' so widespread that even mainstream DIY stores such as B&Q sold them (and advertised as part of the January 2010 sales).

Irony, the ultimate marketing tool in the corporate-cool empire, had no place in the kingdom of über cool, now heir to the hip throne. Its set of values had been founded on nurturing crafts. To use a self-mocking tone to express your authentic belief not only makes no sense, but could even be construed as offensive. Fundamentally, there was honesty in what you did, as the producer. Your medium of expression was alternative and therefore different from accepted norms, but it was not to be ridiculed. This is not to say that über cool had no sense of humour; it is just that the tone was different. You didn't need to take yourself seriously, but there was no need for self-mockery either. Self-mockery instead gave way to a type of quirky, tongue-in-cheek humour. This was about gently poking fun at aspects of the industry in which you operated. Rather than parodying convention, it was about doing conventional things in an unconventional way. The tone with which you expressed your own non-conformism was subtle, often clever and at times even provocative.

Examples that convey this sense of humour include Cast Off knitting patterns, Tatty Devine jewellery and KIND knitwear. At the more provocative end, the works of Marjan Pejoski (of swan dress fame) and André (graffiti) embodied this aesthetic. The same applies to music if you listen to some of the lyrics of elektroklash performers, especially those that critiqued, through the use of shocking language, the uniform shopping-mall-and-celebrity-culture symbolised by designer clothes and surgically enhanced definitions of beauty. For example, Miss Kittin's song 'Frank Sinatra' ('Do you know Frank Sinatra? He's dead.') is about the 'beautiful world of MTV' (cynical, of course). It depicts hanging out with 'famous friends', making small talk, drinking champagne at VIP parties and having sex in the back of limos. 'To be famous is so niiiice,' she sings. 'Suck my dick. Kiss my arse.'

The Birth of the 'Street-Chic' Ideology

Just as MTV reconciled rock and television by aligning itself with the ethos of the underground to redefine hip, so the second-generation Hoxtonites merged their world of 'street' with the world of 'chic', thus signalling the next shift in subcultural ideology. This would result in these two polarised worlds becoming one, so that hip was no longer opposed to being chic, instead becoming rather chic itself.

Traditionally, the world of chic (ie the luxury sector) and the world of street (ie subcultures with their own ideals and hierarchies) had been at opposite ends of the fashion-and-lifestyle continuum. There was a certain stigma attached to the world of couture, which was seen as alienating. Historically, subcultures (as style cultures) defined themselves *against* high fashion. Ever since the (British, working class) subcultures first appropriated elements of (upper class) bespoke tailoring (teddy boys wearing Edwardian suits in the 1950s), they had been defiant. Defiance as a means of identity expression characterised the 1960s counterculture. In the 1970s, punk's vigorous anti-establishment stance was reflected in its DIY approach to music and fashion. The subcultures that proliferated post punk continued that tradition. New romantics reacted to the early Thatcher era with its conservative politics of individualism and consumerism by making statements through androgynous and epochal sartorial escapades. Street fashion operating on the margins that was embraced by the style press (*The Face* and *i-D*) was clearly defined against the likes of *Vogue*.[6] In the same vein, streetwear – which became the generic term for the comfort-dressing of subcultures that crossed over to define the main style of the 1990s – was perceived as being the antithesis of high-end designer labels. Streetwear was part of an organic culture, which was inspired and created by 'the street' (hip hop, rave and skateboarding). In contrast, high fashion was perceived as elitist, lacking the sense of pride that street cultures attached to their style of dress.[7]

This is not to say that street style was irrelevant to the high end of fashion – on the contrary. It was anything but. Street style served as an inspiration for high-end designers but the end product would still debut on the catwalk and be stocked in luxury stores. At the same time, the street influence was not necessarily obvious, as it was often subsumed in the new design. As Robert Elms wrote in *The Way We Wore*: 'What was actually happening was that the more savvy designers were cleverly tapping into the stylistic energy of Britain's streets, nicking ideas, refining them into international brands and selling them back to us: Gaultier forever popping up in London clubs, studious Japanese types with notepads in Camden Market. British youth culture was becoming a feeder system for haute couture.'[8] This practice was adopted by many couture fashion houses, and would continue throughout the 1990s and noughties, with Hoxton becoming a prime pool for this type of style fishing.

What changed in the noughties is that the Hoxtonites would slowly but surely infiltrate the world of high-end fashion by starting to call the shots, to the point that street-led fashion would become institutionalised. This process occurred somewhat organically. Two developments in the mainstream style industries left a gap for innovation, which created an opportunity for Hoxtonites: the over-exposure of streetwear and the negative impact of Cool Britannia on London's status as a fashion capital. The Hoxtonites, who were operating on the margins of fashion, provided an answer to this crisis of innovation. The subsequent acceptance of the scene by the fashion establishment, including the world of high-end designers, was a natural progression.

The Over-Exposure of Streetwear

Streetwear was very influential in the 1990s – it became the style that defined the decade. It encompassed every demographic and lifestyle, not just youth culture. What had started as functional wear that prioritised comfort over appearance – ie the baggy trousers and T-shirt look of ravers and grungy skateboarders, or sportswear in hip hop – turned into a major trend. Such was the potency of cool marketing. One of the most powerful symbols of this trend, combat trousers were so 'in' that they temporarily rendered the ultimate sartorial expression of casual cool – jeans – out of fashion. The denim mega-brands such as Wrangler, Lee Cooper and even the iconic Levi's, with their 501s, seemed outdated. In fact, the downward spiral was catastrophic for Levi's: between 1997 and 2000, they lost over 50 per cent of their young consumers. It took a brand development agency to apply market segmentation and consumer-driven innovation to revive the brand with new products such as Levi's Engineered Jeans.[9]

Jumping on the casual-wear bandwagon, the luxury-fashion sector introduced sportswear. In 1997, Prada Sport started the trend, followed by most of the high-end brands. Even classic brands such as Chanel started to produce sports ranges and related accessories. Designer sportswear became a comfortable yet viable alternative to the suit. 'Smart casual' became an office staple. As the trend spread beyond high fashion and into the mass market, the high street began to emulate the catwalk at an ever faster pace, delivering many replicas of smart-casual wear. At the same time, the pioneers of streetwear themselves – now big enterprises – started to introduce premium lines such as Phat luxury wear (around 2005). Traditional sportswear manufacturers also started to produce designer ranges (such as Stella McCartney for Adidas in 2002, which extended into a long-term partnership). The premium end of streetwear pretty much became the uniform of the corporate-cool creative industries, including the dotcom sector. Brands such as Stüssy and Maharishi, which reinvented urban camouflage, became signs of being effortlessly hip yet still 'down with the street'. Just like luxury sportswear, the street-cool look spread into the mainstream until over-exposure killed its hip credentials. By the mid-noughties, even among the originators of the streetwear subcultures, a consensus emerged that it had become so mainstream that it was left with nothing interesting to say.[10] As far as new subcultural blood was concerned, bar the occasional thrill such as grime (a microscene that would fully bloom under the patronage of third-generation Hoxtonites), there was little to get excited about among those who had seen it all before and indeed, done it all before.

There would, however, be a crossover between street culture and that of second-generation Hoxtonites – an affinity with elements of a Japanese aesthetic brought into London's alternative circles via the 1990s subcultural route. There has always been a connection between Japanese and hip in Europe, the UK in particular. Wearing avant-garde Japanese designers in the 1980s, such as Comme Des Garçons and Yohji Yamamoto, became the new black – and it was 'always black'.[11] At the turn of the noughties, the inclusion of a Japanese aesthetic element into what constituted hip reflected a mutual fascination between London's underground culture – where there was a contingent of Japanese students in art schools – and Tokyo's equivalent, to which British DJs and other subcultural exponents were making ever more frequent excursions. Wearing obscure Japanese street brands was a signifier of cool. In fact, this was part of the overground Hoxton look at the turn of the millennium and became the corporate-cool uniform. The look was prominent enough to be parodied in *The Shoreditch Twat*. A person's cool credentials could be gauged by the question 'Have you got a Japanese girlfriend?' The joke made a statement about fashion victimhood, but in the fanzine's true cynical style, it also made fun of the notable number of white and black British guys who *did* have Japanese girlfriends. Wearing the right clothes, coupled with a Hoxton Fin and having a trophy Japanese girlfriend, epitomised the Shoreditch wannabe, who truly looked the part (in other words, like a twat).

Second-generation Hoxtonites moved away from street culture and streetwear, but they retained some elements of the Japanese approach to ideas of rarity and uniqueness. In Japan, unlike Europe and the States, there was no division between high fashion and street fashion. Brands such as Bathing Ape would create a sense of exclusivity by producing limited-edition products.

'Ordinary' clothes thus became more desirable and commanded a higher price. Closely related to this definition of what might constitute something special was the idea of collaboration between two brands or individuals. Consequently, the streetwear consumer and the high-fashion consumer in Japan could be one and the same person, whereas in the West, the common link between subcultures that influenced the 1990s was precisely the fact that they defined their style *against* high fashion. In Europe then, Bathing Ape was a cool label, but part of streetwear culture (that would cross over into Hoxtonite culture).

Another aspect of the Japanese ethos that would gain ground in the new scene was the idea of diversification. For example in Japan, music and clothes could constitute a whole, whereas in the West they were separate worlds that only merged via brand extensions, as it were, such as Def Jam Records into Phat Fashions or mega-club music brands producing limited-edition clothing ranges. When that did occur, though, there was still the separation between streetwear and high fashion. Even when streetwear brands became premium, they were still not seen on catwalks. The two were also separated in shops. For example, when labels such as Stüssy, Maharishi or Evisu were sold in luxury department stores, they were compartmentalised into the 'hip' division – in a different section from the luxury fashion labels. (Having a streetwear section is what made London's department store Selfridges hip in the first half of the noughties.) Equally, an association with the high end of fashion could be perceived as a sell-out (here, hip hop and Tommy Hilfiger spring to mind as examples of 1990s cool marketing).

Second-generation Hoxtonites embraced both the idea of diversification and the merging of street and high fashion. This shift was partly influenced by a fascination with Japanese culture, especially among those who actually travelled to Tokyo, which was still relatively rare. It was partly intuitive and unwitting, because the Hoxtonite scene was naturally starting to express its own sense of self-worth as being on a par with high fashion (rather than high street, or indeed street). The production was small-scale. The scene was also innately collaborative. Concepts such as limited editions and collaborations – initially be seen as markers of distinction in the incubation stage of the second-generation Hoxtonite scene – would eventually turn into cool marketing tools by the end of the noughties.

London's 'Catwalk' Fashion Post Cool Britannia

The second development that would lead to the shift in subcultural ideology was linked to the malaise that struck London as a fashion capital. The fashion industry, as one of the creative strands that had contributed to the Cool Britannia phenomenon, began to suffer. The story goes something like this: the peak of the Cool Britannia hype in 1997 coincided with the first catwalk presentations of two radical British designers, John Galliano and Alexander McQueen, for two of the greatest French fashion houses. Galliano, frequently dubbed the *enfant terrible* of fashion, was newly in charge of Christian Dior's couture and ready-to-wear. Before that, he had been chief designer for Givenchy, a position that he had occupied since 1995. The Givenchy vacancy was, in turn, filled by another Brit – McQueen – highly regarded, but considered another *enfant terrible*. Hailed as the most ingenious graduate of his generation, McQueen was only 27 when he took up his new post in Paris. The prestigious appointments of these two wild boys were perceived to be risky by the conservative fashion industry. Much of their radical influence evoked the legacy of underground London and the uninhibited experimental spirit they'd both had experienced first-hand: Galliano was a Blitz kid and McQueen a first-generation Hoxtonite (his studio was in Hoxton Square itself). The influence of iconic scenesters such as Leigh Bowery on McQueen would prove to be enduring, as shown when McQueen's collection (A/W 09–10) was revealed in February 2009, the styling of which paid homage to that continuing source of inspiration.

The reign of two radical Brits at prestige couture houses, combined with the Cool Britannia mood in arts and music, contributed to a renewed enthusiasm in the fashion world for London-bred talent. Their unconventional attitude helped revive the reputation of London as a place of eccentricity, which had first been shaped by the doyenne of punk, Vivienne Westwood, herself now firmly established in the high echelons of fashion aristocracy. The hype resulted in other prestigious fashion positions being offered to prominent alumni of McQueen's generation: Stella McCartney signed a contract with Chloé, Clements Ribeiro took over at Cacharel, and Julien Macdonald later replaced McQueen at Givenchy in 2000, following McQueen's defection to the rival Gucci Group (to whom he sold a 51 per cent stake in his business). The downside to this was that London's hottest talent began to desert its catwalk. In the early noughties Stella McCartney, Hussein Chalayan and Clements Ribeiro all began to show their own collections at Paris Fashion Week (though exceptionally, Macdonald stayed in London). Luella Bartley began to show in New York, followed by Matthew Williamson. London had become a victim of its own hype.

Cool Britannia hype, however, was not the only reason for this mass exodus. Talent defection was also related to London's perennial problem of inadequate financial infrastructure. British designers at home could neither benefit from government support (the first substantial cash injection would be ten years in the future) nor the local fashion industry for back-up. In this sector, the 'industry' was a euphemism for the three main luxury fashion conglomerates: LVMH (Louis Vuitton Möet Hennessy), the Gucci Group (part of Pinault-Printemps-La Redoute, or PPR) and, to some extent, the Prada Group. Between them, these three bought up most of the high-fashion brands. Somewhat understandably, given their Franco-Italian heritage, they favoured the Paris and Milan catwalks over London. (Added to this, the bulk of the fashion business is concentrated in the first two cities.) Unless poached by one of the big groups, a designer's unique talent – previously considered an asset – could turn into a liability. For example, a designer could run into problems that would affect his or her ability to deliver their collections to buyers – cashflow problems that would hinder production, for example. This led to absurd situations, where high-calibre designers literally had to fight for their survival.

For example, Hussein Chalayan had to miss a catwalk season amid rumours of bankruptcy after being named British Designer of the Year for two consecutive years (1999 and 2000). Chalayan later bounced back in 2002, when he started to show his collection again, this time in Paris. From there he went from strength to strength, and in 2006 received an MBE for his services to the fashion industry. A couple of years later he was appointed creative director at Puma and also received backing from the Gucci Group for his label. In 2009, an exhibition celebrating his contribution to fashion was held at London's Design Museum. However, it could so easily have gone wrong – not for lack of talent but through lack of financial support. Similarly, before Chalayan, Galliano had famously left London, disillusioned, to have a stab at showing his collection in Paris in 1993. He struggled to scrape together the money for it and had to rely on his friendships with supermodels including Naomi Campbell, Christy Turlington and rising star Kate Moss, who all dropped their usual large fees to help him out. That show would prove to be a turning point for Galliano because that was how Bernard Arnault, chairman of LVMH, noticed him. Arnault subsequently appointed him at Givenchy. Galliano has remained in Paris ever since, with 'foreign' financial investment backing his signature label.

As if this exodus from London Fashion Week weren't damaging enough, there was also an ironic twist to this tale. The cool Brit pack, by now no longer 'common people' but 'celebrities' in their own right, were actually wearing Prada. In *Lucky Kunst* Greg Muir describes how Miuccia Prada invited Damien Hirst – then on a trip to Florence with an entourage that included Jarvis Cocker – to a supermarket sweep at her headquarters in Milan. Muir's anecdote reminded me of my own time at the MTV Awards in Milan in 1998, at the peak of the Cool Britannia sell-out. Limousines were literally doing round-trips from Hotel Principe Di Savoia to the high-end shopping Mecca that is San Bambilo. Prada (and the Miu Miu diffusion line) was compulsory. Even the unlikeliest Brits were caught up in the frenzy. I spotted Skin, the lead singer of Skunk Anansie, at the Miu Miu store. I remember being a bit surprised. A Britrock chick, whose kudos was owed in part to her anti-feminine look (skinhead, jeans and workmen's boots), even she had caught the Italian glamour bug. Dressing down, which had been the essence of the indie scene's anti-establishment ethos, was truly over, as the scene became a commercial success and 'Britpop' a mere marketing label.

September 2001 was particularly depressing for London Fashion Week. From a business perspective, the 9/11 terrorist attacks on New York put the beleaguered London catwalk under further strain, with even fewer international press and buyers visiting. London's catwalk was effectively left with a handful of big names, such as Paul Smith and Margaret Howell. While perfectly respectable, neither was the type of designer upon which London had built its extravagant reputation. As the fashion industry began to privilege the safer formula of heritage revival over radical innovation (which tends to happen in times of crisis, when fashion reverts to conservative money), attention turned away from London towards a new generation of designers, mainly from Antwerp and Paris. Their approach was innovative but also commercially aware. There was a focus on the product rather than the whole package around it. This reflected London's unique attitude to fashion that echoes the underground club influence. Names such as Véronique Branquinho, Raf Simons and Bernhard Willhelm (of the Antwerp school) and Xavier Delcour, Alexandre Matthieu, Gaspard Yurkievich, Olivier Theyskens and Haider Ackermann (of the Paris school) stole the limelight. This is not to say that there was no fresh talent in London from this period at all. Labels such as

Eley Kishimoto and Sophia Kokosalaki still waved the cool flag. Overall though, London was, as one press report from 2002 said, 'bereft (again), quite the most unfashionable event in the world... You could be forgiven for just washing your hands of the whole shebang, as if Cool Britannia never happened.'[12] London's nonexistent fashion status was even the butt of a joke in the fashion satire *The Devil Wears Prada*. During the fashion season, the main character, the outrageous editor-in-chief of a fictitious American fashion bible 'always skipped London, like everyone did, [and only] went to Milan and Paris'.[13]

The Beginnings of London's Rise from the Ashes

The impoverished London catwalk and the city's nonexistent status as a fashion capital, combined with the streetwear fatigue, provided an opportunity for the new hip scene. When the prospect of London as a fashion capital looked bleak, away from the gaze of west London (where London Fashion Week officially took place), the East End was gradually becoming the focal point for an emerging fashion community bursting with new talent. The incubation period for this developing scene in the first half of the noughties coincided with the global mainstream fashion industry's return to a no-risk approach.

This relative lack of interest in London among the fashion elite allowed for the gradual development of a new scene, founded upon the new 'street-chic' aesthetic. There was time for experimentation, making mistakes and learning from them. Experimentation would crystallise into a new trinity: a platform for edgy fashion (acting as a talent incubator), maverick communication tactics (that would develop into professional PR and communication agencies) and underground clubs (media for creative expression and networking). These provided the groundwork for the trend that would sweep both high fashion and high street – as well as the communication industries – by the end of the decade. Two cliques from the second-generation Hoxtonite network were central to this development. The division between the two is artificial but it will help outsiders understand how powerful the influence of Hoxtonites became. Let us call them 'The Michael Clique' and 'The Mandi Clique'.

The Michael Clique

Among the first to seize the initiative was Michael Oliveira-Salac. Michael had made a name for himself in the build-up to Cool Britannia through his street-culture magazine *Blow*. Set up in 1992, *Blow* was part of the underground movement that provided an alternative to the post-yuppie mainstream. In contrast to the style pointers used in glossy magazines to connote 1980s affluence and opulence, the fanzine-like *Blow* was about 'military trousers' and 'looking poor', as Michael put it. The first issue of *Blow* featured the novice fashion label Antoni & Alison on the cover. This duo went on to become one of the symbols of London's individual style and they remain one of the city's most credible independent labels with a loyal international fan-base of stockists and customers to this day. The choice of the cover and the alternative content set the tone of *Blow* as a countercultural outlet. It became the voice of the cool youth culture that corporate brands were seeking; they hoped to build their 'street' kudos by advertising in the magazine.

Like all the scenesters who had witnessed the build-up of Cool Britannia, Michael lost interest once it peaked: 'You knew that once Cool Britannia was discovered, it was no longer cool.' It was time to move on. *Blow* magazine folded but the many fashion connections that Michael had established would prove to be key for his next career move, a venture that he fell into rather than planned. The many phone calls that Michael was still getting in the aftermath of Cool Britannia from the more radical end of the fashion press and buyers' spectrum acted as a catalyst. As many of the calls were enquiries about London's avant-garde fashion, this led him to set up an off-schedule catwalk guide in 1999. It was called *Blow's Off-Schedule Guide* (to maintain the edgy association with the now-defunct magazine). It was inspired by Alexander McQueen's idea of an 'off-schedule' fashion show, which is how he had fashioned his own first, DIY, catwalk show.

Blow's Off-Schedule Guide began as a listings guide during London Fashion Week, coherently promoting the catwalk shows of the growing number of new designers who were not officially showing on London Fashion Week's runway and who were therefore not listed in the official 'on-schedule' guide. *Blow's Off-Schedule Guide* was the first directory of London's fresh talent operating on the margins. From the point of view of fashion professionals, it became a useful working tool, as it told you who the designers were, where they were showing and at what time, allowing comprehensive and coherent access to what would otherwise have been scattered and obscure raw talent. Logistics notwithstanding, the other important aspect of this guide was its authentic connection to the emerging underground scene. The content of the guide gradually developed from just catwalk schedule-listings into an editorial that separated the good from the

Dad, a unique character, has always had a penchant for the leading edge (be it arts or innovation of the scientific kind); here hanging out with Salvador Dalí at his place in Paris (1970s). Mum was a scenester and photographers' muse (on the slopes in the 1960s).

On tour in 1990, on our way to do a live show from Tuzla; as ever, getting into trouble then trying to make good by charming a policeman: (top from left) the driver, a policeman, Lida, Bafta, Neven, (bottom from left) Zoka, Senad Z., Darko and, separately, a pensive Boro Kontić. A press advert for Omladinski: 'the second programme is always the first'.

The 'big M', the three letters that defined a generation; MTV VJ Pip Dann in my beloved houndstooth jacket reporting on the first Sarajevo Film Festival (1992), which was also the first alternative report about the war that celebrated life under siege; Justin Eade on the right (with Nick Wickham, director of 120 Minutes) at the MTV Christmas party in 1992; German guards on the Berlin Wall, just after its collapse in November 1989, when MTV equalled freedom.

VICTIM FASHION STREET BY QUINTESSENTIAL HOXTONITE MEI HUI LIU

Mei Hui at her boutique in Fashion Street (2003) with 'rag dolls' by Rachael Matthews on display. Martin Ahearne made his debut modelling for Victim before becoming a successful male model, pictured here at Off Schedule London Fashion Week 2004. Alex Box also started her career working with Mei Hui and went on to become one of the most influential make-up artists, illustrated here by Victim catwalks February 2006 (bottom right) and 2007 (above right).

ВОСТОЧНОЕ ПЛЕМЯ

Epitomising London's avant-garde, the duo behind Kokon To Zai, Saško (Sasha) Bežoski (front) and Marjan Pejoski posing in their boutique in Goldborne Road, London, for the Russian 'edgy' magazine Hooligan *(November 2009). This shoot was orchestrated by* Hooligan's *London-based stylist/journalist Masha Mombelli and photographer Mila Nesterova. Below, test running the catwalk and backstage for KTZ SS 2010, On/Off, London Fashion Week.*

KASHPOINT, THE FIRST BATTLE OF THE BOUTIQUES
(OFF SCHEDULE LONDON FASHION WEEK FEBRUARY 2004)

In hindsight, Kashpoint Battles of the Boutiques were seminal moments on the Hoxtonite scene that drew all the key players from the second generation and provided the platform for the third to develop. Bottom left, the host Matthew Glamorre with Lotta, a prominent scenester.

*Gary (a.k.a. Fifi), rescuing the 'big needles' after the security check at the
Eurostar; André's Mickey welcoming Cast Off with a special tag; punters
learning to knit (incidentally including Sarah, my friend since the first
day of nursery school, in the denim jacket) followed by crazy dancing with
wool. This was the night that kicked off the knitting and DIY craft trend in
France, still going strong at the end of the 00s decade.*

La Johnson 2001, (top row left to right): Chloé Poux, Samuel Boutruche, unknown, Perséphone Kessanidis, Michaël Huard (Mika), Johanna Senyk, Aurélie Castex; (bottom row left to right): Lionel Bensemoun (Lio), Armel Morlan, Benjamin Moreau, Fatou N'Diaye, André Saraiva. André's graffiti on Essex Road, Islington (before it was converted into luxury apartments); examples of André's commercial collaborations (a CD compilation from his hip private club Le Baron (co-run with Lio) and Vitamin Water bag, both sold at colette in 2010).

Top Left, Amechi Ihenacho, a Hoxtonite Dandy par excellence and The Pimpette and Ranx (top right) 'squatting' at the Halloween party (2003) at the Great Eastern Hotel (now Andaz) organised by the seminal Whoopee Club, with unknown punters. Bottom left: fly poster for the more 'street' Hoxton Pimps and Pimps DJ Johnny Reckless, 31st December 2004. Though distinct scenes, Hoxtonites in the first half of the noughties were all friends checking out each others' events.

A different kind of humour has replaced the irony that characterised 'cool marketing', illustrated here with Tatty Devine (Rosie Wolfenden and Harriet Vine wearing the 'best of' Tatty Devine) and the 'back-stabber' jumper by KIND deluxe knitwear.

Mandi Lennard wearing a dress by Roksanda Ilinčić, hat by Chanel and boots by Louis Vuitton, in London, December 2008. Michael Oliveira-Salac outside the 'main tent' at London Fashion Week, February 2008.

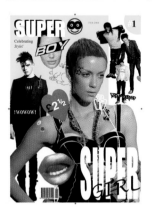

The evolution of Steve Slocombe's creative vision from Blow's Off-Schedule Guide *via* Superblow *into* Super Super *magazine. The ladies once dubbed the 'queens of nu rave': Namalee Bolle, 2007 (top right) and Carri Mundane shot by Tim & Barry, all invited by JCDC for a catwalk and image retrospective, respectively, Athens 2008.*

*The much-hyped club night and the only
place to be for a few fashion seasons.*

Francesca Forcolini's Labour of Love in Islington. The Parisian colette, the mother of concept stores: its notorious water bar and exclusive collaborations (Piper/ Louboutin and Hilfiger/Haring).

Pierre Hermé's Macarons et Chocolats boutique in rue Cambon, Paris, designed by Olivier Lempereur and his heavenly Ispahan. Third Floor in Barcelona (c. 2004) and P.U.R.E. magazine cover (003 volume one, 1999).

bad (not every young designer had the same future star potential). This analysis began to serve as an early directional pointer and from 2004 it would develop into a way of talent-scouting fully endorsed by the fashion establishment. In this capacity, the guide acted in conjunction with Blow PR, born in 2002 as a natural extension of Michael's connection with many young designers. What had started out as a guide (providing a platform for designers to promote their shows during Fashion Week) morphed into a professional relationship (providing them with a platform for representation and promotion during the rest of the year).

Originally situated in a tiny room above a Soho pub next door to *Tank*, one of the visionary magazines that encapsulated the spirit of this new wave of Hoxtonites, Blow PR was a hub of new talent and it operated within the ethos of the scene. Mei Hui Liu, Tatty Devine, Marjan Pejoski and many other key designer names from the early second-generation Hoxtonites would all have been associated with Blow PR at some point. This concentration of exciting names, in turn, brought in other like-minded designers. For example, Amsterdam-based KIND (designers of deluxe knitwear) joined Blow for this reason. The Indian designer Manish Arora and the British-Brazilian duo Basso & Brooke are just two examples of fashion designers who emerged from obscurity to become international success stories thanks to Blow PR. It was in fact Michael, one of the greatest connectors on the second-generation Hoxtonite scene, who introduced me to Ashish. Ashish made his debut off schedule in February 2004, to become an instant hit with the fashion connoisseurs. This demonstrates exactly what the second-generation Hoxtonites' scene had become – the early indicator of future trends.

Blow PR operated in stark contrast to flashy PR companies. At first, Blow was almost a sanctuary for the designers that the mainstream PR agencies would not consider. This was partly because these 'young designers' were too radical in terms of how they created their outfits, and partly because they would have not been able to pay the kind of fees that corporate retail clients paid for the publicists' services. At the same time, Blow PR was also promoting its designers in an unconventional way, reflecting the approach of the scene in general. Unusual fashion shows and collaborative events were the norm. By the late noughties, established agencies would begin to emulate start-ups like Blow. In fact, nowadays, larger PR companies take on young designers for free, just to boost the street profile of the company. The fashion industry now expects London-based PR agencies to have cool designers on their client list. Back then, though, Blow's was a risky business that needed to work its way towards establishing credentials among the fashion establishment.

The greatest strength of *Blow's Off-Schedule Guide* was its grassroots connection. With each new issue (which coincided with each new fashion season) it was becoming an ever more elaborate insight into the second-generation Hoxtonites' underground culture more generally, and not just the fashion. *Blow's Off-Schedule Guide* started to feature reviews from the scene, particularly highlighting the club side. It highlighted select designers (not just those represented by Blow PR but from a rich palette of emerging alternative talent). Features were styled in the context of a developing scene. At the same time, the contributors were themselves new and edgy stylists, make-up artists, editors, journalists, promoters and other hip PRs who shared Blow's unconventional approach. They were all authentic hipsters, creatives or individuals with the nous to spot emerging talent. Not only were their voices authoritative within the scene, but they would also go on to become barometers of talent for the mainstream. For example, contributor Andrew Tucker later became one of the main talent scouts for the British Fashion Council; Robb Young went on to become a fashion writer for the *Financial Times* and the *International Herald Tribune* as well as adviser for the prestigious Swiss Textile Awards and a high-profile Japanese distributor; Hywel Davies a writer for the *Independent* and *Dazed & Confused*. The list goes on.

The off-schedule set-up gradually cemented its position as the barometer of cool. If journalists, stylists, fashion buyers and anyone interested in leading-edge culture wanted to reduce the risk-factor associated with new talent, whether that was separating the eccentric from the plain stupid, or ensuring that the talent had at least some of the potential for longevity that fashion professionals required, *Blow's* was one of the few places they could turn to during this scene's incubation. Identifying this authentic underground kudos is essential in any hip crossover story. We know by now that in order for hip to have an impact outside its own clique, it has to be endorsed by the opinion formers first. This cannot be orchestrated in the boardroom, which is something that Channel 4 attempted to do, and failed.

For a few fashion seasons (somewhere between 2002 and 2003, inclusive), this British television channel tried to compete with *Blow's Off-Schedule Guide* by commissioning a communication agency to print a guide called *Off*, published parallel to *Blow's*. However, the problem that Channel 4 encountered was a lack of credibility among the audience it sought to reach. *Blow's Off-Schedule Guide* was, and is, aimed at an industry that contains a high concentration of professionals (or future professionals) who are the first to know. For them, Channel 4's guide, which profiled young designers via biographies and listings of cool places (their favourite clothes shops, record shops, cafés and so on), did not cut the mustard. Even commissioning Nicola Formichetti (a scenester with street kudos) to do the styling for what proved to be the last issue of *Off* did not help, because the result was a series of beautiful but ultimately vacuous photographs. They were out of context. Channel 4's guide looked more professional than *Blow's* stapled version, but its content lacked immediacy and rawness, unlike that produced by the guys behind the styling and stories of the original.

In contrast, *Blow's* was the authentic voice of the underground. This link to the underground was crucial in a period of free-flowing innovation. Originally, neither Michael nor his contributors were making money out of the guide. Everyone wanted to be part of it though, because it was about commitment to the new wave of creativity. We were witnessing a scene in the making – the nearest thing to a subculture in that day and age – and *Blow's Off-Schedule Guide* was part of this developing movement. It encapsulated that energy. It was not just about alternative fashion but the whole package – from street boutiques and market stalls to key clubs and the music they played. Blow's guide also provided critical commentary on the state of the mainstream as viewed from the margins, which helped to articulate what the alternative was about. At the same time, contributors were not afraid to poke fun at the scene with pieces such as 'Blow's psychometric test', which evaluated your fashionista potential. *Blow's Off-Schedule Guide* had it all. It was the platform where scenesters could express themselves without commercial constraints. In the few years prior to the rise of Web 2.0, this guide was the most immediate way of accessing the second-generation Hoxtonites' scene, and the most up to date. It was produced at a time when a high concentration of opinion formers gathered around London Fashion Week, but it became much more than a listings guide – it was an insight into a buzzing underground scene. It was like a blog and a social networking site combined – before blogging and Facebook took off.

From here we can see how the fusion between street and chic occurred, via its organic connection to the catwalk and London Fashion Week. As Michael told me: 'Up to 1999, I never went to London Fashion Week. I had no interest.' With the shaping of the new underground scene, this mentality would morph into an ideological shift that was driven by the street but came alive within the parameters of the chic world. Most importantly, it did so on its own terms. The off-schedule set-up was, in fact, the actual 'young designer' industry I mentioned earlier. It was not just about radical fashion design, though; the scene also began to influence the mainstream style and communication industries. When it matured, it naturally shifted to 'on schedule' and became accepted by the fashion establishment. The establishment had followed the underground trend, not the other way around.

From Blow to Superblow

A defining moment occurred in September 2004, when *Blow's Off-Schedule Guide* became *Superblow*. From this issue and during the two fashion seasons in 2005 *Superblow* took the format of a compact magazine with cutting-edge content, covering the essence of the second-generation Hoxtonites' network. The overall artistic direction of *Superblow* was taken over by Steve Slocombe. Steve had just left the street magazine *Sleazenation* (relaunched as *Sleaze* following his departure, before folding), where he had worked as editor-in-chief since 2000, until a major editorial disagreement with its owners. Steve's frustration with *Sleazenation* stemmed from his feeling that it was no longer the first to push boundaries, which he had unsuccessfully tried to address with the senior management. A bona fide scenester himself, he had been on the Hoxton circuit since the 1990s, having worked for YBA Wolfgang Tillmans for three years before joining *Sleazenation*. Steve had flair and potential. He believed that what was happening on the second-generation network was 'the future' but that *Sleazenation* was not even adequately responding to, let alone driving the trend. It was still overwhelmingly about street culture.

An epiphany for Steve had been discovering Kashpoint. A friend who worked at the magazine took him to Kashpoint (to show him something 'different'). At the door, 'a guy wearing an aubergine on his head' greeted them. Little Richard – an enormously creative dresser whose sense of individual stylistic expression and exhibitionism is an art-form – obviously had the same effect on Steve as he did on me when I first saw him (though then, he was more about squashes – which must have been out of season on this occasion). That sight alone was worth the door charge, recalls Steve who, as a cool magazine editor, only had to flash his ID to get into any club for free. Kashpoint, though, did not care about magazine IDs or VIPs – you had to look the part. For Steve, Kashpoint was 'definitely the purest form of people coming out of the stone after years of nothing happening. It was fascinating. The music was great but people were not dancing. They weren't even talking to each other. They were eyeing each other. They were trying to compete with looks... this where the first seeds of the [19]80s revival that would go on to shape the next decade were planted.'

What *Sleazenation* had failed to realise, *Superblow* was only too happy to promote: it became the organ that engineered the transition of underground scenes into major trends. By turning *Blow's Off-Schedule Guide* into a magazine for a couple of crucial fashion seasons during the scene's maturation period (2005), Michael gave Steve the longed-for opportunity to push boundaries. By Steve's own admission, *Superblow* was the 'experimental platform' that helped him to develop his own creative direction. Essentially, *Superblow* adopted the street-and-chic aesthetic of second-generation Hoxtonites and the way they expressed their values through various media (collaborations, catwalk shows, DJing, club nights). Complementing the guide was Steve's street boutique Stefan's Superstore. Operating on the principle of underground network connections, this store was a word of mouth affair (no window, you had to buzz to get in, etc). An example of Michael's role as 'connector' was when he *connected* the Superstore with his promising young clients Basso & Brooke. This duo literally turned up at the Superstore with a tea-towel and oven glove in what would become their signature print to ask if they could sell it there. (Who would have thought then that some five years later, the First Lady of the United States, Michelle Obama, would be sporting Basso & Brooke?) Stefan's Superstore also became the hub for future (third-generation) Hoxtonite stars. Equally important were the clubs inspired by Kashpoint, which would in turn spawn their own scenes. *Superblow* highlighted all the key influences from the second-generation Hoxtonites (from designers to clubs) but the variety of visual expressions were streamlined into one coherent look. The visual aesthetic of *Superblow* planted the seeds for what would later become the nu rave phenomenon, hailed by the international media and cool-brand industry as the 'next wave of youth culture'. The turning point for this crossover came with the launch of *Super Super* magazine in 2006, which also symbolically marked the arrival of the third-generation Hoxtonites, as will be detailed later, in the 'Influence on Style and Communication' chapter.

From then on, *Blow's Off-Schedule Guide* reverted to listings, albeit now professionally produced. Today, the guide is an official part of London Fashion Week, fully recognised by the British Fashion Council. Around the same time,

Blow PR turned into a 'proper' business, moving into a large space in central London and now operating as a globally recognised fashion PR for unique yet commercially viable talent. By the end of the decade, innovative designers had become a USP for London within the fashion industry. Agencies such as Blow PR were the first port of call for stylists and other opinion formers in search of radical design. Their authentication of a designer acted as an official blessing of cool. What to the rest of the world was a unique new wave of extravagant young artists in the music industry who emerged at the end of the decade was, more often than not, the result of stylists scouting the few London-based PR agencies with that edgy reputation. Think Katy Perry wearing Manish Arora's designs at the MTV Awards in Japan in 2009 (Arora having been represented by Michael from the start of his career). Think Lady Gaga wearing Bernard Chandran or Florence and the Machine wearing Qasimi at British music festivals and various public appearances in 2009. Both designers were represented by Blow PR at the time. However there are other agencies with equal reputations, notably including Mandi Lennard's.

The Mandi Clique

The other main strand shaping the zeitgeist from the second generation's network was also composed of the trinity of fashion incubation, communication spreading and clubs. It also espoused the street-chic ideology and it would also turn out to be a major factor in hip's commercialisation.

The fashion incubation element is, first and foremost, associated with Fashion East and its host venue, the iconic Old Truman Brewery in Brick Lane. This was part of the off-schedule fashion set-up. Fashion East was launched in 2000 but the story begins earlier, around 1996, when the Truman was taken over by Ofer Zeloof, a man whose name may not be familiar, but whose philanthropy played a significant role in nurturing the creative spirit of the East End as symbolized by the Hoxtonites. To implement his philanthropic vision, Mr Zeloof contacted Lulu Kennedy. Lulu was a scenester from the area, whose experience included organising raves and working at Kensington Market and local art gallery, The Boiler House, two days a week. Lulu's was not a conventional CV by any means, but it was perfect for what Mr Zeloof had in mind. The idea was to start populating the Truman Brewery with creative types. Lulu knew people simply from hanging around. Having said that, there weren't that many places to go locally, but the ones where everyone did congregate – notably The Bricklayers Arms and 333 – proved to be important in sealing friendships between people who would go on to become influential on the trendsetting scene. In the period from the mid-to-late 1990s, The Bricklayers was managed by Pablo Flack. David Waddington was a barman, and Pablo also ran club nights at 333. (Remember those names.)

Cheap rent was one of the Truman's greatest assets in attracting creative types when it first opened its doors. You could get a large studio for something like £30 per week. To the credit of Mr Zeloof, rents there stayed affordable compared to any other local spaces, resisting the staggering rise in property prices following the area's gentrification. The affordability of space has been fundamental in fostering genuine creativity in the face of the merciless commercialisation of this neighbourhood. The Truman remained an oasis untouched by the hungry developers throughout the spectacular property boom of the noughties. In the period immediately post Cool Britannia, the Truman was home to three main innovative types: artists, 'webbies' and young fashion designers. Other than its regular tenants, the space was also let out for parties. For example, the visionary 1990s outfit KLF, notorious for their controversial burning of one million pounds, did some of their events there. Likewise, fashion designers started to frequent the Truman and host catwalk shows for nominal sums of money, or in some cases, for free. Hussein Chalayan was among the first to host a show there in the late 1990s. Another alumnus of the Truman was Giles Deacon, who went on to become one of London's most critically acclaimed designers in the second half of the noughties. Note that in terms of degrees of separation, or connections, we can here see the beginnings of a new bubble within this Hoxtonite clique. Giles was a friend of David Waddington's from The Bricklayers pub. As teenagers, they had attended the same art college, before both going to Central Saint Martins. They were even flatmates for a while, living within walking distance of The Bricklayers in the warehouse-party period of 1990s Shoreditch.

The idea for Fashion East was born out of a desire to provide support for young fashion designers. As with everything else in my story so far, Fashion East started as an alternative initiative that had initially been frowned upon by the establishment, only to become one of the most respected fashion incubators of London Fashion Week. Fashion East acts like a grant for young designers in the early stage of their careers. It provides all the necessary tools to stage a catwalk show, which consists of a free venue as well as the production and post-production support. It is almost like a rehearsal in catwalk staging, an experience that the recipients can benefit from for up to three fashion seasons afterwards. Fashion East was launched as a non-profit project and it remains so, the Truman continuing to support its day-to-day running. The rest of the financial support is generated through sponsorship. Fashion East was originally listed off schedule and attracted the core fresh talent from the area. There was a lot of stuff around, but Fashion East selected the cream of the crop. It became an instant hit on the scene and, from their initially hostile stance, the fashion establishment would grow to like it a lot.

Equally, the early recruits would grow into some of the most recognised fashion labels. For example, fashion darling Tatty Devine was the first accessories brand to be showcased through Fashion East. Clothing labels such as Blaak and PPQ would become hot tickets at London Fashion Week. In fact most of Fashion East's protégés would go on to have successful careers, though occasionally promising talent did not follow through. A now-defunct label called House of Jazz, which generated a lot interest while it lasted (2000–2004), springs to mind. One half of the House of Jazz duo was Pablo Flack, who swapped club-running for designing innovative clubwear, together with design partner Hazel Robinson, a fashion graduate who moved to Shoreditch around 1995. After the demise of House of Jazz, Flack would reinvent himself by going back to his first love (hospitality), but House of Jazz provides a neat link to the next important element in this trendsetting trilogy – PR guru Mandi Lennard.

'PR guru' is a bit of a self-referential joke because Mandi, like all the characters in my story, is a maverick. Mandi's strength lay in the way she bridged the first and second generations of Hoxtonites and nurtured the third generation to create a hip powerhouse. Before becoming one of London's most respected PRs, Mandi was on the scene. With the motto, 'I had nothing, so I had nothing to lose', this northern lass from Leeds set up her own PR company in London in late 1997. With one rented desk above Browns' showroom in central London for £20 per week, and just one client (*Dazed & Confused* magazine, who paid £150 a month for her services), Mandi braved this world. Of course, there was no way of knowing then that the trio who set up this magazine in 1992 – Jefferson Hack, John Rankin Waddell (known simply as Rankin) and Katie Grand – would each become as influential as they did on the global cool scene, through their professional and personal relationships.

Mandi's introduction to *Dazed & Confused* was via Jefferson Hack, whom she knew from *Colors*, Benetton's innovative magazine, the launch of which Mandi had been involved with while working for Marysia Woroniecka, a famous 1990s London PR figure. Incidentally, Mandi began her career as retail manager for Benetton in the late 1980s. She lists the company's founder, Oliviero Toscani, and the founder of *Colors*, the late Tibor Kalman, among her greatest influences. If you are a 1980s teenager, and especially if you are female, you may remember how this brand broke new ground as much in terms of fashion design as in terms of advertising, with its iconic United Colors of Benetton photography, including the controversial AIDS-victim advertisement (from 1992). In those days, Benetton was one of those cool brands with an ethos based on pushing creative boundaries that attracted the like-minded, which is how Mandi and Jefferson 'immediately clicked'.

Through him, Mandi met Rankin and Katie. Katie was wearing a pair of Chanel stud earrings when the two first met, Mandi recalls. Mandi had a similar pair that featured the Dior logo. They, too, immediately clicked. A professional relationship with friendly overtones (or the other way around) led to Mandi continuing to work with *Dazed & Confused* in the decade to come. Inadvertently, Katie Grand would prove to be another crucial connection for the future, as possibly the most influential stylist-cum-editor to cross over from the first-generation Hoxtonite scene. Katie's conquest of the mainstream fashion industry began when she was poached by the magazine publisher Emap in 1999 to be fashion director for *The Face* whilst preparing a then-unnamed publication where she would be editor-in-chief: *Pop* was launched in 2000. Her CV would also boast consulting roles for some of the most prestigious luxury brands and 'celebrity' clients. Eventually Katie left *Pop* to launch a rival magazine called *Love* in 2008, owned by the publisher Condé Nast. Mandi was in charge of PR for both magazines.

Mandi moved to east London around 2000. Her first office was at Shoreditch Town Hall, which operated a bit like the Truman Brewery in that you could get a square foot for something like £2.50. Consequently, the venue attracted a community of creatives. Mandi's neighbours were scenester Pam Hogg and YBA Gavin Turk. (Unlike Truman's, prices went up from £2.50 to £18 per square foot within a few years, which drove the original community out.) Mandi's interest in young designers arose during this period of the scene's incubation. Being right at the place where it was all happening obviously helped foster that interest. Coincidentally, when we were reminiscing about the good old days, Mandi cited Rachael's guitar bags as one of the early 'wow' indicators that some fresh energy was simmering in the neighbourhood. This new creative outburst was not focused in any way at that time, but it was definitely in the air.

Among Mandi's first protégés was Kim Jones. Graduating from Central Saint Martins in 2001, Kim would later hold a few high-profile appointments for high-end and high street brands before taking up the role of creative director of Dunhill in 2008. The two stayed in touch. Mandi was also associated with Fashion East early on, at first via House of Jazz and then through Belgrade-born designer Roksanda Ilinčić, who showed her first collection in 2003. After the demise of House of Jazz, Pablo Flack would partner up once again with David Waddington, his friend and one-time barman from The Bricklayers Arms, to open a leading-edge restaurant-cum-cabaret venue in 2004. Bistrotheque was purposefully located further out in east London, to avoid the Shoreditch area, which was already too commercialised for their liking. Again, Mandi took care of the PR. Thus the prestige venue was added to the prestige magazine, widening the client portfolio beyond fashion but retaining the all-important first-to-know angle. Last but not least, Mandi became the guardian of a new wave of young designers, who became the third-generation Hoxtonites, including Gareth Pugh, Cassette Playa and House of Holland. These designers had their first taste of the fashion limelight via Fashion East but, in their case, there was a twist, which proved a coup for Mandi, while they benefited from her connections and expertise. To fully understand their rise, and by extension the way Hoxtonites crossed over to influence the mainstream style and communications industries in the late noughties, we need the final ingredient, which is the all-important club connection.

Golf Sale and Family

Enter Richard Mortimer. Richard moved to east London around 1998. I met him around 2001 at Tommy Guns, the first hair salon in the area that was not specialising in old-lady hairdos, preferring instead to concentrate on the equally retro Hoxton Mullet before the famed Hoxton Fin came along. For the girls, 'T-parting' was all the rage. This look would cross over to become the footballers' wives' favourite style, with shorter, lighter hair on top and darker, longer bits at the bottom, usually accentuated with hair extensions. Mandi met Richard at the hair salon, just like I did. Back in the day, we all went to the same salon, it being the only hip option in the area. Richard's claim to fame, however, would not come through hair styling but through his ability to put on a damn good club night.

Like most on the scene, Richard used to go to Nag Nag Nag and a club night at Café de Paris called Merkin, hosted by party-organiser Miss Dee with the help of Boy George. As the popularity of Nag Nag Nag was waning on the scene, Richard felt compelled to organise a regular club night to which he could invite friends. It was called Golf Sale, and it happened every Sunday night. It was held at the Lux Bar, (after the cinema that had previously occupied the space), which in turn became the Hoxton Bar and Kitchen under new management. Having learnt a lesson from Nag Nag Nag – that if a club night is over-hyped but does not change, it gets watered down – Richard wanted to avoid that fate. Golf Sale only lasted for one year – but in that time it made a significant impact on the scene. 'Golf Sale is dead', said the title of the piece commemorating its closure in *Blow's Off-Schedule Guide*, with a send-off stating that it was 'the only Sunday night to be seen at in 2004... for one groovy year only'.

Golf Sale may have been dead... but long live Family: club-king Richard's next club night was born. It was the same concept but in a different Shoreditch venue. Like Golf Sale, it was promoted only through word of mouth. The change of name and venue allowed for the core group of punters to regroup and start attending the new night, leaving out the wannabes who had started to frequent the club because the magazines told them it was cool. This is what the scene calls the 'spectator' versus the 'participator' crowd. A good club host knows how to distinguish between who is authentic and who is a wannabe. This selectivity makes the regulars feel like they belong and is also why it is important to have the right person on the door. That person must know how to distinguish 'important' people from those that are less so, because the subcultural hierarchies operate that way, and you need to treat some guests with more care than others. This should also all be done with subtlety.

The main pulling power of Richard's club night came from the über fashionista crowd, who used it every Sunday as a catwalk to parade their individual outfits and also to form connections with the like-minded. Uninhibited behaviour went hand in hand with that creative dressing. The thrill of being daring has always been the core component of London's trendsetting clubs – and that freedom of expression could occasionally turn into debauchery. This was never gratuitous, but it was nevertheless the kind of indulgence that could be tolerated within the confines of the 'family' but perhaps less so by 'spectators'. Hence the club's exclusive door policy, although entrance was free. Often interpreted as a form of elitism – a feature of any scene – the need for screening the punters was an essential means of preserving the intimacy of the club. Restriction of access, in turn, contributed towards its desirability.

The music policy of the club was largely based on Richard inviting friends and people he was a fan of to DJ. This meant that an array of artists and fashion designers took to the decks, as well as musicians, on their days off, as it were. These ad-hoc DJs included YBA Sam Taylor-Wood; designers Roland Mouret, Giles Deacon, Kim

Jones and Katherine Hamnett; musicians Chicks on Speed and DJ duo Queens of Noize. Musically, it would also pay homage to the contemporary but increasingly irregular Kashpoint, and to its predecessors: Blitz, Taboo and Kinky Gerlinky, a 1990s club staged on the cusp of the dressing-down era. Matthew Glamorre DJed at Richard's club nights on a few occasions. In fact, a lot of the Kashpoint crowd moved over. Boy George also occasionally spun records. However, there was not much excitement over DJs, at least not initially. You just turned up at the club and someone played records. In spite of the surprise element, a few resident DJ names began to be associated with the Family night, such as Jerry Bouthier and Princess Julia. These guys – Jerry in particular – would begin to shape the aural identity of the club, which was eclectic but very much grounded in the elektroklash ethos.

Family was not promoted. Even so, the distinct looks of the punters combined with the calibre of famous guests frequenting it started to attract publicity. That is how Richard joined forces with Mandi. When Richard felt he needed to screen the press, who were getting very curious about this new sensation, he turned to Mandi for help. She would send the odd newsflash here, put in a good word there, nothing more, and this proved very effective. By the summer of 2006, when Kokon To Zai joined forces with Family to celebrate the store's anniversary, it was evident that something big was about to happen. As was customary, Kokon invited their own 'family', which consisted of names such as Björk, who flew in especially to DJ, and the regular supporters of the label. Mandi also sent a newsflash to her network.

Word about this party spread like wildfire. A huge crowd of people – far more than anticipated – congregated outside the venue on Curtain Road, making it impossible to get to the entrance. It could have turned sour for me, as I arrived quite late, having travelled back from Paris where I was working on a project, especially for the occasion. The mentality was still about attending a party to support your friends, and not because the party itself was fashionable. I found myself utterly desperate when I realised that there was simply no way of getting through the crowd. It was by pure luck that Sasha spotted me from the inside. He got the security to somehow pull me (and my plus one, the curator Wilhelm Finger) through the crowd into the venue. It proved to be a night to remember.

At the height of its popularity, Family ceased to be. The thirst for more, however, was insatiable. There was no doubt that the scene had reached the 'tipping point'. The incubation phase was over. It was time for the epidemic to spread. Before long, Richard, along with Mandi, would create a monster. Family would give way to the phenomenon of a club night: a hip storm that swept all fashion capitals.

2. New Mavericks: Risk Taking and Diffusion Platforms

'If I'd asked people what they wanted, they would have asked for a better horse.'

Henry Ford, car-manufacturing pioneer on the Ford Model T (1908)

Paris, March 2009

'I bet that these two are going to the same place I am…' I prefer walking down Rue de Rivoli to taking the Métro on this gloriously sunny day. Instead of minding my own business, I become intrigued by the pair walking in front of me: he speaks in American English while she speaks fluent English with a French accent. 'They're probably not a couple… perhaps business acquaintances,' I think. Nothing clearly denotes their 'type', but I can surmise that they are creative professionals of some sort. The further we walk, the more I am convinced that they'll take the same right turn as me, and… bingo! They do. Will they turn right again? Yes! Our shared destination is the concept store, colette, at 213 Rue Saint-Honoré. Guillaume Salmon, Head of PR at colette, is having a smoke outside (a habit he has since quit). He greets the couple, clearly part of the initiated circle. I congratulate myself on having guessed their destination as well as their 'consumer type'. Guillaume then says 'hi' to me – colette may be the most fashionable concept store in the world, but there is still the touch of a local pub about it. Every time I go to colette, there is bound to be someone I know there, even if it is colette's own staff popping down from the office to the store or its restaurant.

I was going to the restaurant myself on that occasion. I sat at the bar for a late lunch/early supper. I was not even halfway through my meal when a familiar figure appeared. Before I saw the face, I clocked a pair of sexy boots coming down the steps, worn by someone in an extravagant cape, the next thing given away as the heels descended. The full silhouette revealed my friend from London, Alexia Somerville. We have known each other since the early noughties. A Hoxtonite who became inspired by *P.U.R.E.* magazine, the influence of which will be evident by the end of this chapter, Alexia's career followed the typical hip trajectory of paying her dues. She had first explored new ground at *P.U.R.E.*, followed by projects with photographer Nick Knight and the late fashionista Isabella Blow, who always had an eye for young talent. Alexia was by now an established stylist, and her portfolio included magazine editorials, an array of commercial clients, styling for music videos (Robbie Williams, Pink, George Michael) and personal styling for actress Rachel Weisz. Alexia was in town for Paris Fashion Week.

In fact, it felt like the whole of Hoxton was in Paris. I moved tables to sit with her, and we had pudding and coffee. Funnily enough, we spoke about this book. Alexia then shot off to a catwalk show. I wanted to have a quick look around the store before I went to my next appointment, and again, I bumped into another familiar face. This time it was a French woman I'd met once in London during a presentation at the Frieze Arts Fair. It's a small world. I must admit to being a little bit surprised to see this lady at colette. She was more 'old money', with an Hermès bag and sporting the timeless Parisian chic of striped shirt, trench coat and moccasins. I would never have associated her with colette but then again, 'when a thing is current it creates currency', and colette was so current that it attracted a diverse crowd.

What didn't happen before colette became so fashionable were large package-tour-style visits to the store. Upon my arrival that day, and to my horror, a coachload of tourists had also arrived, which is why I went to the restaurant first. One by one, they dutifully hopped off the coach, the guide rushing them. Rue Saint-Honoré is a narrow one-way street, where it is impossible to overtake. If any vehicle were stationary there for long, all the traffic behind would come to a halt, upsetting the already-impatient Parisian drivers who honk even when the car ahead of them is waiting at a red light. Once off the coach, the assembly was so large that they blocked the pavement outside colette. The guide spoke to them about this landmark in a language I could not decipher. They took photographs of the window displays before entering.

The central display within was a life-sized Barbie doll. Colette was collaborating with Barbie for its 50th birthday celebration. Designer Jeremy Scott, whom colette had supported since he'd started out a decade earlier, had been commissioned to create a Barbie-themed clothing range (for humans). A series of other limited-edition items, ranging from jewellery to chocolate, had also been made for the occasion. This was accompanied by a collectors' series of dolls, demonstrating Barbie's evolution and clad in outfits specially designed by a series of fashion designers, including Hoxtonites Gareth Pugh and Roksanda Ilinčić. In fact, Hoxtonite Mandi was looking after Barbie's PR account for this occasion. The birthday cake had arrived for Barbie's party that night, which was also the closing party for Paris Fashion Week. Anything hosted by colette is a hot ticket. Just a few days before, the store had been taking part in another Fashion Week-related event: a collaboration with the magazine *Fantastic Man*. As ever, the party pulled anyone who was someone on the scene – there having been a genuine connection between scenesters and the store before it became the epitome of marketing cool. Interestingly, I saw Malcolm McLaren leaving as I arrived. A founding father of punk (the original DIY culture that inspired generations of subcultures) hanging out at colette's party, where the Hoxtonites toasted their own achievements – things had gone full circle.

Colette is now at the top of its game. The company regularly deals with leading corporate brands, but has remained a family business. Colette Rousseaux is still hands-on. That she's the person I most frequently bump into during my sporadic visits to the store is proof. She was there on the day of Barbie's party, wearing her trademark trainers (high-top Converse in a flowery canvas – no doubt some limited edition), pleated skirt, white T-shirt and a sweater casually tied around her waist. She appeared to be discussing the floor layout with one of the staff, taking notes as they moved from section to section. Another time I noticed her was during the May holiday the previous year. Not only was she working (Parisians are notorious for taking long weekends in May), she was actually doing the most basic entry-level task in retail – stocking shelves. Then, her trainers had been neon, combined with a grey pleated skirt and matching grey top. She always says hello to me with a big smile, though I am not convinced she actually knows who I am. I think it is more a matter of greeting a familiar face, as any good hostess would. Another sign of hospitality is the cleanliness of colette (the store, not the lady!). Staff unobtrusively, but constantly, wipe surfaces – be it at the bar or in the lavatories. Occasionally, you will spot someone discreetly spraying air freshener. To me, this meticulous attention to detail is a sign of respect for the customer.

This is not to paint colette simply as a wonderland where Barbie dolls come to life and the air smells of roses. It is a business that employs some 50 staff and currently (in 2009) holds the hip crown, which is as challenging as it is flattering. To stay current, the pressure to reinvent is constant. As we know, when a trend leaves its underground origins and heads for the mainstream, its original maverick spirit becomes somewhat diluted. Success generated from hip effectively selling out also generates a lot of criticism, and colette is no exception. Arnaud Sagnard's book *Vous êtes sur la liste?* (Are you on the guestlist?) is entirely dedicated to putting this (Hoxtonite) Parisian scene (dubbed 'La Hype') under critical scrutiny. It depicts this world as cynical, where consumerism and conformity pass for creativity and open-mindedness. Among the undisputed leaders of La Hype is colette. Sagnard describes colette's tenth birthday party in 2007 in Paris as 'one of the biggest events of the year' where anyone who was someone in the French hip world (*'la quasi-totalité de la branchitude française'*) could be found. Many were turned away from the venue owing to sheer numbers.[14] Described as a party lacking substance, it was attended by punters abiding by La Hype's rule with no one really knowing why they were there, yet knowing that they couldn't afford not to be. The conclusion he draws that La Hype, supposedly comprising the avant-garde, is little more than a bunch of sheep.

Sagnard is not the sole critic of the scene, but what we have to bear in mind is that his book, published in the summer of 2008, primarily documents events that took place in 2007 – the year when the trend reached its peak. This is also the year that the term 'La Hype' appeared in the French *Le Petit Robert* dictionary for the first time. Commercial success was gradually building in the maturation phase until it was fully commercialised in 2007, when a series of landmark events occurred, colette's birthday being a symbolic example. By definition, when hip is commercialised, it is no longer hip underground. We reached the end of the maturity phase for hipsters earlier in the story. However, the commercial impact the Hoxtonites had cannot be fully understood without incorporating the idea of diffusion platforms into the incubation and maturation phases. Colette will serve as a prime example here.

Colette falls into the category of 'concept store' and it is indeed the pioneer and most famous exponent of this type. Just as MTV, in its incubation period, was a diffusion platform that acted as a chasm translator, the role of the new diffusion platforms is the same. MTV was also a lifestyle environment, adopting the vernacular of emerging subcultures that it associated with first-hand, and translating it into a language palatable for the mainstream. Colette took on the same role. In a world that was more fragmented than in the 1990s, there were four types of diffusion platforms across different market categories, which, other than retail (fusion boutiques and concept stores), included food (farmers' markets and couture gastronomy), hospitality (couture hotels) and the publishing sector (a new breed of street-chic magazines). Parallel to this, we need to include the rise of a new breed of maverick businesses that would grow into household (product) brands. I shall start by looking at those, to establish how a new market is unleashed (that being the fundamental difference between creating a trend that would make its mark on mass-market consumption and creating a fad). This chapter is about the mavericks that took a risk and by doing so, challenged the status quo.

THE BIRTH OF THE NEW PREMIUM CONSUMER
The New Mavericks

So far, we have established that hipsters carry the bug that spreads to wide sections of the population, while maverick businesses infected by the hipster bug are fundamental in converting it from incubation stage to pandemic. The 1960s, (Frank's 'homeland of hip'), provides the prototype for this model of social contamination. With the advent of the counterculture in this decade began the marketers' fascination with the youth market, a segment constructed by non-conformist businesses that embraced their 'revolutionary' idioms. Having lain somewhat dormant through the inflation-troubled 1970s and conservative 1980s, the hip virus resurged with a vengeance in the 1990s with MTV becoming the archetype of cool. In the noughties, the principle of hip's trajectory from a small group of taste-makers towards mass-market acceptance remained the same – but the protagonists were new. The emergence of the second-generation Hoxtonites post Cool Britannia coincided with the emergence of maverick businesses sharing their values. From that union the niche market segment that is the holy grail of marketing – in other words the 'new youth' – was born. That elusive segment of early adopters, who represented the next concentric circle in the hip continuum following the alpha trendsetters, contained the precursors of the new hip consumption trend that would later spread into the mass market.

Going against the concept of innovation as seen through the prism of risk-management in the corporate sector, a breed of entrepreneurs (start-ups that would develop into well-known brands) and artisans began to think of innovation in radical terms. Instead of robust consumer and market research, their approach was more intuitive. At the heart of this approach was the belief that a shared passion for what their business stood for would be the way to reach the customer. At the same time, a number of pioneering brands and unbranded businesses, which had already been operating on a niche scale for years (or even decades) became fashionable, and part of this rising trend, because they shared the same set of values. All were independent small-scale operators. In one way or another, all were eco-aware, broadly pertaining to organic and natural products and practices that took into consideration environmental, humane and health concerns. This key ethos created a kinship between these unrelated businesses, which would ultimately lead to the formation of a market category in its own right. Though diverse and geographically dispersed, what these mavericks all had in common was a vision that challenged the established production and distribution models. Their approach necessitated a quantum leap.

Innocent is an example of such a forward-thinking start-up. Launched by three college friends in 1999, it made smoothies from 100 per cent pure fresh fruit, using eco-responsible production methods. The business began modestly by selling smoothies at a music festival in London. Rumour has it that the only consumer research Innocent did was to ask festival punters to put their empty bottles into a 'yes' or 'no' bin and, on the basis of that result, the three partners would decide whether or not to quit their day jobs and embark on a new career producing smoothies. They did, of course. However, unlike the enthusiastic festival punters, experts judged this product to have no chance of success. With no preservatives or additives to lengthen the life of the drinks, the concept was doomed to failure – or so they predicted. Hi-tech packaging gave it the longest possible shelf life but this 'fresh produce' approach still did not match the rest of the products stocked in supermarket fridges (which contained preservatives), and it was thought that Innocent would therefore never reach supermarkets. Ignoring this prediction, the trio stood by their ethical ideals. Having eventually managed to raise some capital, and after many rejections, they started their small venture.[15] Rejections came as no surprise given that this happened during the dotcom boom, when venture capital was pouring large sums into the new media economy. Humble products such as smoothies were deemed not cutting-edge enough.

Most of Innocent's early sales were concentrated in high-end cafés, gyms and sandwich bars. A fresh smoothie was more expensive than its average mass-market equivalent (with preservatives) but, by tapping into an unconventional distribution network, Innocent specifically targeted a niche market that would be the first to adopt this healthy, natural product – and pay a premium for it. Innocent grew at a remarkable pace. In less than a decade, the company's turnover reached nearly £100 million with no business debt and a market share as high as 65 per cent in the UK. Innocent became a mainstream brand available in supermarkets. The next stage of expansion was export. As is the case with many maverick business stories of rags to riches, Innocent eventually sold a share of its company to a multinational (in this case, Coca-Cola) in the spring of 2009. Other diversification strategies included fresh-fruit smoothies specifically targeted at kids and a brand extension into the pre-packed chilled food category (particularly aimed at office workers on the go) in the form of fresh vegetable-based meals.

As for veteran brands that became fashionable at this time, the German-based Dr. Hauschka skincare range is a prime example. The company was developed in the 1960s by medical chemist Dr Rudolf Hauschka, and the cosmetologist and nurse Elisabeth Sigmund. Inspired by the teachings of turn-of-the-century Austrian-born philosopher Rudolf Steiner, this brand pioneered the 'anthroposophical' method to skincare and treatments. At the heart of this philosophy is a holistic approach to the human body. Using homeopathic principles, the brand also works on an understanding of how everyday life processes affect the skin and how plants can act as medical remedies. Dr. Hauschka's brand is also known for being ethically and socially responsible. WALA (Heilmittel GmbH), the company that manufactures the skincare products, owns and works its own gardens and is a certified biodynamic producer of primary ingredients, which means respecting the balance between man and nature. WALA is also owned by a trust that stipulates that it cannot be sold to shareholders.

Its marketing is based on consumer education about the product. Instead of following market trends, this is a market leader that stuck to its principles and became trendy by accident. People are willing to pay a premium when they believe that they are getting the best of science combined with the best of nature, and all of that without having to worry about labour exploitation issues. In spite of this seemingly anti-consumerist approach, Dr. Hauschka is a multi-million-dollar business. The new trend documented here undeniably helped to generate wider awareness about this brand. With Dr. Hauschka being first endorsed by hipsters and subsequently stocked in hip stores (ie diffusion platforms), then receiving celebrity endorsement (Madonna, Julia Roberts, Kylie Minogue), the brand gained a greater market share in the noughties. Dr. Hauschka may not have actively sought 'celebrities' but it does recognise that this kind of publicity helped its expansion.

Being part of the new wave that challenged the status quo, it was only natural for these brands to adopt the tone of the new hip in their brand and advertising communications, where irony no longer had a place. Just think of the naive imagery used on Innocent products. The childlike graphics reflected the honesty of the product, the quality of which, in turn, justified its premium value. In fact, Innocent tapped into the Cast Off hype by encouraging customers to make hand-knitted caps for smoothies as part of a charity project. Knitting as a medium of expression was earthy and cosy in contrast to the sophisticated packaging of disposable trendy products sold at high-end and high street chainstores, which connoted a certain cachet but were, for the most part, devoid of values beyond conspicuous consumption. It fitted Innocent's brand image perfectly. By the same token, there was no need to cushion Dr. Hauschka's bold statement about the brand's '40 years of unparalleled quality' with an ironic undertone: its natural products genuinely are among the best that can be found on the market. You pay a premium for their quality, not their label. The brand is unapologetic about this. Dr. Hauschka does not rely on strapline differentiators because it has a truly unique proposition. The message is transparent, with no small print. That is what you pay for. Whether that's 'Because You're Worth It' (L'Oréal) or you need to 'Take Care' (Garnier) or 'Love the Skin You're In' (Olay), perhaps it is for you to decide and not for the brand to tell you.

Initially, word of mouth was an essential promotional tool in both cases and, as ever, the best. What helped the crossover process on the one hand were diffusion platforms as an essential first port of call when selling these types of products. On the other hand, it was their affinity with the hipster's new understanding of authenticity premised on the nurturing of crafts. Mavericks and hipsters in this way started to complement each other. Growing media exposure about underground movements such as second-generation Hoxtonites and select new businesses triggered the necessary publicity that created consumer interest for the new trend(s). By extension, this surplus of publicity helped the businesses to grow. In some cases, this interest culminated in the acquisition of a small independent business by a larger corporation, which would then start commercialising the products on a mass-market scale. In other cases, independent brands would be strong enough for continued success without needing, or indeed wanting, to be acquired. However, what really generated profits (and corporate interest in these types of companies), was the fact that there was actually a market for their type of 'eco' product, large enough to reach a critical mass. This was no fad.

The New Individualism
The key point, here, is that the mavericks who took a risk unleashed a new market. There had not existed a market for natural produce, no matter how ethical or organic. The same goes for what diffusion platforms had to offer. Once again, we need to look at the opening up of this new market in terms of a response to new individualism. In the 1990s, satellite television became the technology that facilitated the first wave of identity fragmentation, in a response to the rising

individualism. The marketing lifestyle segments were the first to express this need but radical consumerism also mirrored the need for a new kind of identity politics. That is what made cool marketing so, well, *cool*. This consuming vision, which shook up the establishment, came to constitute the mainstream market.

Just as MTV had to construct an audience for music television back in the day (which it did by applying segmentation – extracting a well-defined segment from the mass market), it was now the turn of the new entrepreneurs to effectively challenge that model. They needed to extract a new niche market segment from the various lifestyle fragments constructed in the 1990s in order to start carving their own space in the commercial brand landscape. The kinds of categories devised in the 1990s did not encompass the essence of the emerging consumption patterns. These mirrored the new underground movements, whose eclecticism sprawled across established lifestyle segments and product categories. This is where the fusion mindset previously discussed is central to expressing the need for a new individuality. However, the refusal to be compartmentalised as dictated by the mainstream could only truly be an expression of individualism as long as the 'non-categorised' products also reflected a set of ideals.

From the early adopters' perspective, the attraction was what was dubbed the 'nurturing of crafts'. This proposition was genuinely meaningful to them. Here, the affiliation with underground scenes was useful for the maverick businesses and artisans when reaching for this early adopter. By sharing or adopting underground idioms, the businesses were able to articulate those values as a benefit to the consumer. There was a functional benefit (the naturalness of the product and the health aspects) underlined by an emotional benefit (consciousness, ie responsible consumption). Another emotional layer was that in this scenario, time itself was redefined as having value – as a luxury, if you wish. It was not just about purchasing a product but also about how and why you purchased it. The experience (of shopping, staying at the boutique hotel, or whatever) became itself part of what you were buying into as a customer. This was not just about buying 'organic' at the supermarket. It was about the market experience (it was an outing, a place to hang with similar types, as well as a place to buy something different), and statistics would later emerge confirming this. The crafty aesthetic – as opposed to the minimalist aesthetic that came to signify cool – became shorthand for expressing all those values. Celebrating crafts or artisanship was a step ahead of the mainstream. No one was operating at the margins in order to be hip, but became labelled as such by others.

At the same time, by adopting the street-chic ideology of the underground scenes, the mavericks were able to differentiate their products and experiences from the homogenising consumer trends in the luxury market (which, in turn, the high street followed). Pitted against the label-mania and 'celebrity' endorsement of affluence, there was the labour of love. Catering for individualism by offering a meaningful story behind the product justified putting a premium price on such alternative products (be they smoothies or skincare) and experiences (shopping at the market or concept store, staying at the boutique hotel). The producers offered a genuine product of their passion and the customer purchased it in good faith.

Certainly with the Hoxtonites and the way they priced their guitar bags or recycled outfits or plastic jewellery – almost as if they were designer gear – it was a matter of putting estimated values on their own labour and innovative design. There appeared to be an enthusiastic market out there for what they had to offer, which was encouraging. Was it arrogant; elitist? Perhaps. I am conscious that this may be the perception of some critics. However, what I do know for a fact is that the intention of any hipster (as a conferred label) was to exercise a genuine right to diversity. Remember, for every cheap garment on the high street, someone, somewhere, is paying the price. While the scene is not necessarily about making grand statements about the world, for the bulk of the protagonists in this story, the 'eco' orientation is a lifestyle; it is personal. For example, I still go out of my way to the little shop in order to refill my Ecover washing-up and soap bottles so that I do not waste the packaging (in spite of having access to a recycling scheme). Going to the little shop is a hassle, especially when my nearest supermarket is Planet Organic, the über trendy eco-outlet which, surprisingly, doesn't provide a refill service. It takes time, and time is money, but that is my choice. I pay a premium for certain products (skincare, chocolate, washing-up liquid, clothes, art, that sort of thing) but I do not own a car. Would I like to have a car, sometimes? Yes, but I cannot have it all. And I am not the only one who prioritises this way.

For maverick businesses, emerging product brands and diffusion platforms alike, it was often a matter of taking a well-educated risk. It was indeed conceivable enough that people in gyms – especially if they were dedicated enough to pay a membership and exercise regularly – were likely to want a fresh fruit smoothie to reward their efforts. This was not so much because *they* were worth it (to paraphrase L'Oréal) but because the professed 100 per cent fresh fruit content was worth it. This was simply common sense. It is just that there weren't any fresh smoothies in gyms until Innocent bothered to do the rounds. The market was developing. Punters were willing to pay a premium price, not because they had money in abundance, but because it enabled them to shop meaningfully while getting a real health benefit, and also to express a sense of individualism. This type of consumption was not just about alternative choice; it was also about positive choice. Inevitably, this trend would be co-opted and turned into a fashion devoid of values but, for some people, it is still a genuine and considered lifestyle decision.

The New Early Adopters

In the period post Cool Britannia and the first half of the noughties, 'cool' was still the domain of corporate-cool brands who were investing considerable sums of money in cool hunting to keep track of the supposed latest trends. Cool hunting – a product of the 1990s that truly worked for cool brands in that it helped them take a leader position – was still very fashionable. Cool hunters employed various methods, notably revolving around observation techniques (or 'ethnography'), to unearth the next big thing. Cool hunting was the way to walk the line between risk avoidance and staying a step ahead. Naturally, cool hunting gravitated towards youth culture, not least because of the powerful myth that young people and style leaders are one and the same. In this context, as explored when I first set the hip scene in Part One, Shoreditch became a cool-hunting Mecca. In a desperate attempt to keep ahead, though, cool hunting was falling prey to whimsical fashions. By the time findings from the street were reported back to corporate headquarters and had been through the system, the 'in thing' was no longer in. The fundamental problem was not really fashion's whims, but the fact that wannabe culture was often mistaken for cool. The wannabe types, which were the products of marketing segmentations, were essentially the Postcode Plonkers and the Shop DJs. Shoreditch was scouted for its club and bar culture where wannabes congregated and thus became a byword for fashion-victimhood.

Meanwhile, the hipster (read alpha trendsetter) was elsewhere. Those interested in what the alphas had to offer were worlds apart in their mindset from the Postcode Plonker, in spite of sharing the same geography. My friend Rachael from Cast Off perceptively coined the term 'Islington Mother' as a humorous stereotype for the kind of consumer we were after for the short period when Cast

Off flirted with the fashion retail world. Later, this stereotype would morph into the 'Yummy Mummy'. Why Islington Mother rather than, say, Hoxton Mother? In the late 1990s and early noughties, Islington (more precisely the Angel area) was the wealthier neighbourhood adjacent to Hoxton, dubbed hip by the press – until the baton was passed to Shoreditch following Angel's gentrification. Islington had been a *bit* rock 'n' roll: it boasted a lot of left-wing media types (it was a Labour borough); the first organic pub in 1998, The Duke of Cambridge (or simply 'The Organic Pub'); and it hosted London's first farmers' market (on Sundays from 1999). Some of the first upmarket boutiques to offer an alternative to the world of mainstream high fashion and design also set up shop in Islington. I live there, so a lot of this knowledge was accumulated first-hand. The Organic Pub is literally my nearest.

The other main customers we sought were of the 'geek chic' persuasion. We used this description (later popularised with the publication of the book *Geek Chic*, 2005) to describe the meritocracy who made money off the back of the dotcom boom. The 'webbies' were real innovators and Shoreditch boasted a high population of them. However, the speed of their trajectory from underground to mainstream was quite spectacular. The dotcom bubble's growth, fuelled by venture-capital investment in the late 1990s, was every bit as dramatic as its burst in the early noughties. This meant that for the crucial period of this new market's incubation, these innovators suddenly came into money, and had a surplus of spare cash. From 'geek' to 'chic' they went, but their mentality did not change overnight. They happily spent their income on nurturing crafts.

Then there were the first-generation Hoxtonites, whose commercial successes had taken them from being struggling artists to wealthy ones, plus the second-generation Hoxtonites, who also fitted into this pattern of consumption behaviour. This all added up to a by-no-means negligible market. If you multiplied it by the pockets of like-minded people in other urban centres, the numbers were even more impressive.

What I am talking about here, though, is not the size of this market, but its potential to become an arbiter of taste. This developing market of early adopters – whom I dubbed the New Premium Consumers (NPC) in precursor articles for this book published in the marketing trade press – was a market that was worth a premium for brands. This was because its constituents were thought to be indicators of early trends and also because this segment was willing to pay a premium price for the products and experiences that fitted their lifestyle. Traditionally, in the eyes of marketers, this had been the domain of youth culture, even though we have established that this was something of a myth. In both the 1960s (when cool was born) and the 1990s (when cool marketing reached its peak), the original trigger of a new trend was non-conformist rather than youth. Neither were the maverick marketers of the 1960s or the 1990s interested in the silent majority, at least not initially. Only after you have identified a new trend on which to establish your business do you go for a larger market share. In the case of hip, this trajectory happens in concentric circles spreading from the nucleus of alpha trendsetters, to the inner circles of opinion formers and early adopters outwards, towards the early and late majority. Here, the early adopter is the NPC. Its segments, such as the Islington Mother and the Chic Geek, are very different from the Postcode Plonker and the Shop DJ, the cool wannabe types.

Neither the NPC, who acted in the capacity of spreading the trend outwards, nor the new brands that emerged from this period were in any way concerned about being cool, or indeed, related to the corporate cool sector. And yet, the consumption trend first adopted by the NPC would spread towards the mainstream. When we look at diffusion platforms more closely, we shall trace that crossover and put some statistics on the trends emanating from each diffusion platform. In contrast, the corporate cool sector, though still profitable and cool among the young demographic, was no longer leading trends. While MTV in the early 1990s emulated the language of underground subcultures and was the first to know, in the early noughties it increasingly distanced itself from 'the street' and its flagship programmes became all about 'reality' TV and alleged celebrity. Its language was similar to that of the tabloid press rather than a fanzine. MTV (and the like) was now the status quo.

The new underground was an alternative to the corporate cool. As this new trend started to cross over, a number of maverick brands from this period would start earning the accolade of 'cool' from the Brands Council, including Innocent and Dr. Hauschka, which also goes some way to showing how they set a trend. Around the same time, MTV lost its cool-brand status. It appeared that corporate cool hunters missed the new bug. They, first and foremost, still concentrated their hunt on the street (primarily focusing on a demographic and on peer leaders – neither of which was now automatically synonymous with style leaders). They never thought to look at places such as the margins of high-end fashion or food markets, because neither was traditionally cool. And yet, off-schedule fashion or

Black Block in Palais de Tokyo or farmers' markets were the hubs for the new scenes moulding the street-chic ideology. The NPC occupied a niche between the corporate cool (as in street culture) and the traditional luxury sector. This was unusual. But then, hip moves in mysterious ways. Mainstream youth culture would later catch on, especially by discovering the third-generation Hoxtonites. By then the trend was no longer leading-edge; in other words it had been sifted through new chasm translators (whereas before cool brands like MTV had acted as chasm translators).

As the NPC trend started to expand into the early majority, new segmentation studies began to emerge, pinpointing this type. One such study dubbed this segment 'the Mass Affluents' and suggested that it was one of the fastest growing groups in the affluent sections of society.[16] A generation of self-made rich people, they were defined as high-income, high-achieving individuals. They were determined to pursue a more conscious and ethically-minded lifestyle, less conspicuous than the 'bling-or-bust' affluent equivalent driven by celebrity culture and the branded 'It' bag. Hard workers, ardent travellers and responsible consumers, the Mass Affluents were understated about their display of wealth. 'Discerning', 'provenance', 'considered' and 'timeless' were just some of the words you might have associated with them.

This segment was part of the luxury sector rather than the youth sector, which corroborates the line of argument in which hip consumption (as in being a step ahead) is a mindset, not a demographic. Market studies would emerge to further support this segment's role as a trendsetting one, using attributes that defined the NPC as the next commercial opportunity.[17] They urged brands to look beyond the 18–30 segment (still the marketers' favourite demographic), to other sectors (notably luxury) and older segments, who not only had more money, but whose behaviour was a greater 'predictor of general consumer trends'. The Mass Affluent (or the NPC, call it what you will) is effectively Generation X or the first MTV Generation grown up, with good jobs, but still non-conformist. This generation earned their money. Their mindset was different to those that had benefited from the rise of 'quick' or 'easy' money derived from the various speculative economies, which fed the luxury industry (more of which in the final chapter when I address identity politics).

In contrast, the youth demographic was now shrinking in size.[18] Unlike during the 'youthquake' of the 1960s, the population was getting older (with some governments even considering raising the pension age). In the UK, for example, the population is projected to become older gradually, with the average (median) age rising from 39.3 years in 2008 to 40.0 years in 2018 and 42.2 years by 2033. As the population ages, the number that will increase the fastest is at the oldest age. Whereas in 2008 there were 1.3 million people aged 85 and over, this number is projected to increase to 1.8 million by 2018 and to 3.3 million by 2033 (effectively more than double in 25 years).[19] Couple this with changing lifestyle trends, notably high divorce rates (meaning that singlehood and dating are no longer just the realm of 'young' people seeking 'the one' to settle down with). Socialising and related industries now extend beyond the youth market but the economics of pleasure (clubbing and bar economics, music festivals, music charts, TV ratings) are still overwhelmingly focused on 'youth'. By the same token, empty nesters are not all automatically qualifying for a Saga holiday (there is variety in the 'silver' market just like there is among youth tribes, the favourite material for market segmentations).

The purchasing power of young people was also significantly deteriorating – fact. In Western societies today, 'there are more better-off oldies and fewer indebted youngsters', as Dick Stroud put it in his compelling argument about the power of the over-fifties.[20] The recession that hit at the end of the noughties only intensified this downward spiral. Also, there was a plethora of studies suggesting that ideologically, young people were more conservative and lacked the ethical framework of the previous generation.[21] This led some youth expert journalists to dub Generation Y the 'vanilla generation', a debate I shall pick up on later.

Finally, even the belief about young people being early adopters of new technology (a particular favourite among the corporate cool at the turn of the millennium), was challenged. For example, statistics quoted in Penn's *Microtrends* state that the average gamer is 33 years old (as of 2006), with gaming thus becoming 'the biggest pastime of adults, not children'. You could play the devil's advocate and argue that this is precisely because when you hook them young, you keep them loyal (as the marketing mantra went), but how do you then account for the statistics which indicate that one of the fastest growing gamer groups is mothers over 45, who play when their children are at school? The same could be said about social networking or usage of mobile phones. Gone are the days when kids showed parents how to use the video recorder or nudged them to get satellite television so that they could watch MTV. For every techno whizz-kid in one household, there is an avid techno-dad in another, whose Blackberry is his 'second life'. Old dogmas are changing. One must be open-minded when it comes to identifying microtrends, particularly those with leading-edge potential. Unless the net is cast wider in the first-to-know search, those who need to know (fixated with chasing youth) will run the risk of becoming the last to know.

AN ALTERNATIVE TO THE MAINSTREAM CONSUMER RETAIL SECTOR
The Mainstream Retail Market Trends

In 2001, Prada opened its flagship store on Broadway, New York City. A retail plot of some 23,000 square feet in a prime location, it was designed by superstar architect Rem Koolhaas of OMA (Office for Metropolitan Architecture), and reportedly cost some $40 million. This grandiose design concept was later replicated in Los Angeles, Tokyo and Shanghai. The opening ceremony of Prada's cathedral to luxury brand-worship in New York symbolically inaugurated the age of bling. Fashion retail in the first half of the noughties was marked by the rise of lush mono-label stores. Clothing brands (high-end, as well as high street by emulation) were also diversifying into accessories, footwear and perfume, all of which could be purchased in their flagship stores. And yet, for all the provision of variety, whether in Paris, London or New York, it seemed the high-end stores and high street chains had the same window displays. Luxury was what equalled status, across the board. No longer was the focus on craftsmanship – not least because a lot of production was being outsourced from small artisan ateliers to overseas factories where labour was cheaper. Desire for luxury goods was further heightened through the medium of celebrity-red-carpet magazines.

While fashion retail brands were thinking grand, the mass grocery retail sector started to think small. At the turn of the millennium, supermarket giant Sainsbury's announced a major push into the convenience-store market with the launch of its new brand, Sainsbury's Local. This was a mini-market or a 'tennis court-sized [...] around 3,000 square feet' version of the store (to quote a spokesperson). A move that was, above all, a response to loss of market share to competitor Tesco, it also meant that Sainsbury's Local entered into a price battle that undercut the traditional cornershop and smaller grocery chains such as Spar. The local formula would prove to be a successful one and was emulated by Tesco itself as well as other supermarket brands, from Marks & Spencer in the UK to Monoprix in France. At the heart of Sainsbury's strategic decision to open the local stores were consumer needs that had not previously been catered for (remember, this is the age of insight-led marketing). The local stores were for 'people with no time', thus putting convenience at the centre of innovation strategy. Though the move was towards smaller shops, the overarching retail strategy for both local and large stores was 'category management', ie products sold in small, discrete groups, as discussed earlier in 'From Street to Boardroom'.

The hospitality industry was going through a similar process of market consolidation and homogenisation in spite of the diversity of services on offer. Whether five- or two-star accommodations in whatever part of the world, the trend for hotel brands was to deliver the same level and quality of experience, commensurate with the number of stars. Marketing strategies were for the most part centralised, adhering to one brand proposition and aiming to deliver that promise across diverse markets. This was coupled with the arrival of new money, especially from ex-communist countries. The needs of these small but extravagantly wealthy segments would put their stamp on the luxury end of the industry, keen to dip into their deep pockets. Finally, the rise of extreme luxury resorts in the guise of six- and seven-star hotels in places such as Dubai would also set new standards of luxury service expectation.

It was difficult to argue that there was no choice in the mainstream. Whichever sector you looked at, there was plenty of stuff to consume. The corporate market was constantly investing resources in innovation to stay a step ahead of the competition. You might have thought that there was no room for more. And yet, another new trend would emerge premised on the need for diversity in a world where we appeared to have reached the 'paradox of choice'. How come? The issue was not so much the paradox of choice (ie too many varieties of jam). The paradox was that corporations had to operate within their own limitations, which meant that as a corporation, you needed to be innovative – but not totally. Corporate innovation was channelled through pre-determined categories, for fear of stepping out of line (perceived as a risk). What you got was constrained innovation.

Every now and then, there is a genuine 'Eureka!' moment but, more often, 'innovation' is used to describe upgrades from double- to triple-velvet toilet paper or added aloe vera for extra comfort on your bum. This is OK as long as brands compete with each other within their category (whether it be loo roll or washing powder) because all corporations are constrained by the same imperative of trying to be innovative while still managing risk. The challenge comes when someone from the outside, with a greater investment in risk-taking, comes along. Imagine recycled toilet paper? Or no toilet paper at all! Imagine something like soap and water instead… Bonkers? Think again. If you open your eyes to cultures with as-deserving derrières but where toilet paper is not the norm, you will find that toilets with water jets are commonplace in public places. In Japan, they have washlets. Washlets are the hi-tech cousins of the bidet, specifically created for public places. They are so sophisticated that they even have a dryer for the end of 'the cycle' as it were. In Muslim countries, it has always been part of the culture to wash rather than use paper. It is common to find toilet cubicles with a shower-type option, or a jug in less sophisticated premises. The point is that if you step outside what's familiar, you never know what you might find. This openness to diversity (or curiosity) is what new diffusion platforms would need to adopt. (Incidentally, the colette store also adopted the washlet – let's see if the trend takes off.)

The Alternative Consumption Trends

It was against the homogenising tendency (within which the corporate sector has to operate) that new opportunities arose. This is how the diffusion platforms, which are above all retail environments, managed to find their niche. This is also why the kinship between maverick businesses and hipsters was essential. Mutually dependent, together they would create an alternative network of consumption. The diffusion platforms are the missing jigsaw piece in our alternative-world puzzle. Though diverse, geographically dispersed and often unrelated (just like the new maverick brands), diffusion platforms shared a common vision that challenged the established distribution networks. Their approach, too, necessitated a quantum leap.

Instead of thinking within market categories and well-defined consumer segments, the new wave of diffusion platforms was more eclectic. It was all about fusion. It is helpful to go back one more time to the questions that the hipsters had grappled with: 'am I a designer, an artist, a DJ, a promoter, a retailer or a knitting instructor?' One person could be all. This fusion mindset – or a refusal to be categorised – is also relevant here, in the consideration of diffusion platforms. In the emerging market you could sell candles, skincare products, bars of chocolate, books and clothing items under one roof, with a pile of flyers by the till listing the evening's entertainment. However, the mentality was quite different from that of the supermarket, where products were categorised (all the chocolates together with the rest of the confectionery) or the mono-label store (a diversity of articles but all from one brand) or indeed the department store (a diversity of articles and brands but all departmentalised, hence the name). Also, in most cases, the new brands associated with the new diffusion platforms would not be available in mainstream outlets – yet.

The new diffusion platforms created a sense of complicity with their customers by highlighting the labour of love aspect; they had something special to share with you and they hoped you would like it. And, once again, just as with the maverick brands, it was often a matter of taking a well-educated risk. It was indeed conceivable that people who were curious enough to step into that intriguing place that looked like a store but had no window display would be willing to pay extra for a limited-edition item from that store. Or that people who made an effort to ask around about a nice place for a short break (thus avoiding tourist brochures) would indeed pay the extra money to stay in that boutique hotel recommended by a friend of a friend. Or that someone who made an effort to go the farmers' market on a specific day, between specific times and in the odd postcode where there was one, would indeed purchase something, even if only a slice of home-baked cake with a cup of Fairtrade coffee or a box of strawberries. However, it would be wrong to assume that everything in concept stores or markets was expensive. Some stuff was dead cheap, either because it celebrated the 'everything for a pound' shopping sector (Hoxtonites love a bit of tat and anything trashy) or because it was second-hand (before it turned into 'vintage'). The main point was that it was different. You just had to have the confidence to buy it. The main customer in these new diffusion platforms was the NPC.

However, this was not about stocking a shop with any old bar of chocolate, candle, skincare product or piece of kitsch – or indeed a random flyer. On the contrary, it was very selective. The choice was sifted through a specialist knowhow process, or 'curated', a term increasingly used to describe this skill. The curator was guided by street-chic ideology, where the alternative environment was roughly composed of both a new definition of street that celebrated craftiness (artisan and 'granny nostalgia' elements), with the established definition of street (select streetwear and an affinity with exclusive Japanese brands), with curios and trinkets, with exclusive luxury items and, last but not least, with kitsch (select mass-market products). Another important aspect of diversity was the retail experience itself. The value of time in this context was less about maximising convenience and more about the quality of the time spent, be it in the discovery of a curio that made you smile for a second, or a magnificent stay at some chic lodging.

The approach was mainly intuitive rather than researched, but it nevertheless unleashed the early adopter market. Embracing the street-chic ideology, the new diffusion platforms were environments where the mentality of the street market was effortlessly blended with elements of luxury service and experience. It was about reclaiming craftsmanship and personalised service.

Diffusion platforms emerged in each of the retail sectors covered by the mainstream (fashion design, grocery, hospitality, publishing) to provide an alternative retail experience, and they even challenged those categories themselves. A *pâtissier* might act like a designer, doing seasonal, twice-yearly cake collections. A fashion shop might also double as an art gallery or a massage parlour. A magazine brand could also be an events promoter, and so on. That mentality would start breaking down the boundaries that were the legacy of the 1990s cool brands that became mainstream, an approach that would also leak into the mainstream market over time.

Fusion Boutiques and Concept Stores

Fusion Boutiques

With their curated array of products, fusion boutiques began to provide a new kind of shopping experience. Their basic premise was a desire to introduce the customer to something different. It was all about the labour of love. Fusion boutiques were small, independent stores, where the owner was often a designer. They were closely connected to an independent network of designers, artists and artisans and they thrived on supporting the new. They were similar to the original Hoxtonite street boutiques like Victim, Kokon To Zai and Black Block, but with a nuance; they had emerged in the maturation phase of the scene and operated within the fashion retail industry tempo of seasonal buying, though with more investment in risk-taking in terms of brands stocked compared to their mainstream equivalents. They would often be the first to showcase new talent and provided a much-needed platform for emerging designers. Though fashion tended to be the main focus, they sold anything from interior design items to books, if it felt right. Often, they also acted as galleries. Labour of Love and Beyond the Valley in London are prime examples of fusion boutiques.

Initially, these boutiques were scattered around London, Paris, Berlin and other cities. The only way to find out about these stores without stumbling across one was through word of mouth. When Rachael and I went to Paris to look for outlets to stock Cast Off in the early noughties, we asked friends for recommendations. That is how we found out about Surface to Air via a scenester called Diane Pernet. Surface To Air would metamorphose into a seriously cool venture, while Diane would become one of the most respected voices in fashion, as will become evident in the next chapter. We didn't know that then, of course. We combined our friends' tips with literally walking around Paris to spot shops that felt right. There was no other way. Rachael and I were not the only ones with that predicament, which is why the 'Very' style guides began. Very produced their first guide between September 2000 and February 2001 and acted as a curator, selecting all the places of interest for those who considered knitting cool. In 2002, *Shopping Addict* listed the new boutiques in Paris.[22] By the mid-noughties, this type of fusion boutique had become a category in its own right, with professional guides such as *Paris Chic and Trendy* listing 'cool boutiques'.[23] By this time, though, the trend was increasingly mainstream. In 2007, the magazine brand *Wallpaper** began to produce their own city guides, emulating the fusion ideology of the new scene. Even the Cool Brand Council would pick up on this, awarding Beyond the Valley its 'cool' label.

Concept Stores

Concept stores were a must in the new cool listings (when these listings were a novelty). Concept stores were similar to fusion boutiques, but larger. They were like novelty department stores, even though they were primarily aimed at focused market segments (initially the NPC) rather than the mass market. They were not so much about labels as anti-labels, offering something different from luxury flagship stores or the high street. There are only a handful of true concept stores, but their reputation in fashion and beyond is massive. Similar stores mushroomed but the originators remain the reference points. Concept stores are all individual, with their own idiosyncrasies.

Corso Como 10 in Milan has been around since 1991, inspired by the iconic British 1970s brand Biba. It was redesigned as a concept store in 1999, with a café-restaurant added to its eclectic layout, which offered an edgy but chic alternative in Milan's über stylish but somewhat conservative fashion landscape. IdeB in Brussels was opened in 2005 as a 'lifestore' where the idea of a Parisian *hôtel particulier* (a grand, private urban house) was applied to a retail environment. Here, you walked from one salon to another, each offering its own top-of-the-range selection of luxurious and unique ready-to-wear, accessories, lingerie, jewellery, beauty products and interior-design items. One salon was a massage parlour. Another was a bar area. Quirks included acting as a mini-booking agent for the Ritz hotel. There was also a philanthropic aspect to the store; the profits from certain items went towards charitable foundations.

And now for something even more radical: Dover Street Market, London's concept store, opened in 2004. The name still confuses many people as they think it is a food market. The brainchild of Rei Kawakubo from the Japanese ultra-modern label Comme des Garçons, Dover Street Market echoed her non-conformist stance. It celebrated the spirit of London's street markets, especially inspired by Kawakubo's memories of Kensington Market. In Dover Street different 'flavas' and fragrances mixed to connote an almost folkloric vibe. This was juxtaposed with forward-thinking design elements. Its industrial architecture was so bare that it was almost brutal. Yet the selection of items in the store (ranging from clothes to food) and the way they were displayed were exquisite and stimulating. The result was an atmosphere of graceful and subtle elegance.

Last but not least, the aforementioned colette of Paris, the mother of all concept stores and the undisputed style leader, or *prescripteur de tendance*, in the local vernacular. When colette was launched in 1997, at the same address it occupies today, it was off the main shopping track. Its concept was so radical that fashion insiders gave it no more than six months. Colette was breaking so many industry rules that it was almost bound to fail, but instead it set the tone and the industry followed.

Colette looked different. It was larger than an ordinary boutique but much smaller than a department store. In any case, it operated neither like a 'normal' boutique nor like a department store. For starters, colette did not dress its window as one would ordinarily do – in a showy fashion – which is the whole point of a shop window, really. Colette was understated and at times so minimalist that its windows did not look like those of an open and functioning shop. The unsuspecting pedestrian could easily pass by without realising that it was a shop at all. Inside the store, its displays broke with convention, too. If you expected to find clothes in one section and shoes in another, or all the garments by the same brand grouped together for your convenience, you were in for a surprise. It did not work like that chez colette. The display and layout was very stylish, but it did not follow any rules and changed on a regular basis.

In retail terms, colette committed heresy. Items were bought in small quantities. For example, the store would order a dress in a few sizes but only one or two per size. When it sold out, that was it. This went against the grain of established fashion-buying principles, where you ordered in large quantities and then, if an item sold, you would re-order it. Consequently, there was only a small number of fashion designers or brands that colette could work with, because for most, it made no commercial sense. Of course, that was intentional: colette did not want to work with any old brand, either. It preferred the idea of difference and exclusivity. The small quantities allowed for frequent change. Exceptions to this rule were items such as books, which did get re-ordered. Over time, colette also developed a rapport with certain brands and partners and worked regularly with them.

This initial 'small quantities' tactic developed into twin ideas that would not only become colette's trademark, but would also be among the main cool marketing tools for the noughties – collaborations and limited editions. As colette's fame as a hip store grew, brands started working with the store in the colette way in order to raise their status and tap into the opinion-forming market that colette was effortlessly reaching. The benefit was mutual: the brand got access to the colette customer while the store got an exclusive limited edition. As ever, the manner of choosing whom to collaborate with was done through intuition. At the beginning, collaborations were with obscure brands (some of them developed by colette). Over time, 'everyone' would want to work with colette. Examples included Hermès (with a limited number of watches) and even a collaboration with Gap or indeed Barbie for 'her 50th'.

Colette was endorsed by second-generation Hoxtonites at first – be they Londoners, Parisians or the like-minded from any other part of the world – because they recognised a kindred spirit in colette. That is how, over time, hipness was guaranteed. Originally it was about having the same ideals and aesthetic sensibilities. At the heart of colette's policy was the idea of fusion. This refusal to be categorised echoed the scene's creed. Colette's savoir faire, or 'curating', was second to none. Colette and the Hoxtonites loved the same things. This was because they shared the same street-chic ideology, with colette epitomising street chic at a time when it made little sense to anyone outside the scene. Colette really understood the ideological shift that had occurred and managed to capture it – not because it did loads of focus groups to find out about its customers, but because colette was its own customer. Colette Rousseaux and her daughter Sarah Lerfel (the main buyer for the store) have a simple buying policy based on liking and not liking stuff. Choices for the store reflected their own respective styles, which happened to be a mix of streetwear and fashion (hence my earlier descriptions of what Colette Rousseaux was wearing on the occasions our paths crossed).

As I've already established, streetwear was cool, but it was nearing overkill: it needed an injection of something new. For a short period at the turn of the millennium, a trend called 'couture streetwear' emerged. London labels in this vein included Vexed Generation and Silas and Maria. Colette immediately picked up on this, even though it was partly 'couture' (literally 'high culture' – that is, high fashion – the antithesis of streetwear). For streetwear purists, couture versions would not be their thing (although the more open-minded would see the potential). This trend of couture streetwear was itself a fad, but the collapsing of the divide between street culture and high-end fashion was not. This was not just about style; this was about a new set of ideals, as established in the 'New Underground Ideology' chapter. While streetwear and street culture would retain their own sets of ideals (skateboarding, graphics, music) but eventually become the symbol of corporate cool, the new hip was in part a reaction to that.

Colette embraced some elements of streetwear and street culture, but it would also broaden its horizons to encompass luxury wear, items from Cast Off the knitting club, music not associated with street culture, a new breed of magazines, food and so on. Its brand positioning was not street culture. Guillaume Salmon, colette's PR man, expressed this when he spoke to me: 'We love street culture – 'le street' – but not *just* street culture. We love video games but we also love the knitting club. We are, above all, about curiosity. We dig things that are different and we like to showcase them.' Colette was in fact *the* shop for Generation X – who grew up in the sense that they now had jobs with responsibilities, perhaps mortgages and even children – but hadn't changed their outlook; the original MTV Generation that led the way in the 1990s was still non-conformist and hedonist. They still liked to keep up with the latest trends and were willing to pay a premium for items and experiences that fitted their lifestyle. The difference was that they had more money than their counterparts a decade earlier, when 'premium' corresponded to the '3Cs' (CDs, cafés and clothes). And even if they weren't making a lot of money, they would prioritise spending in such as way that they might consider treating themselves to something curated by colette, rather than a designer label.

A lot of things sold at colette were in the premium price bracket, but it was not about splashing money around; again, it was about the labour of love. Colette was a Mecca for the hipsters, opinion formers and early adopters long before it was listed as a must-see destination in tourist guides. What colette sold was not to everyone's taste, but it hit the spot for the aficionados. You paid a visit to colette to look around as much as you did to shop. Some stuff was really dear. Other pricing was relatively reasonable. If you could not afford a luxury item, there was always a book, CD or Cast Off's embroidery kit. To some, a DIY embroidery miniature record-sleeve replica might have seemed a silly waste of time and money. For colette, it was charming. In fact, it was so charming that some of colette's team actually bought them for themselves. Might not the customer want to do so, too? And if that was too expensive, there were always the *Fraises Tagada* (cult Haribo sweets). What better way to forge a connection with your customer then by sharing sweets? If you were born in France between 1967 and 1977, then your daily trip to the *boulangerie* to get your after-school treat (*Fraises Tagada* were sold from a big jar) surely brings back sweet memories. Maybe you'd forgotten all about it until one day, the little delicacies resurfaced cheekily at the colette counter. Colette tacitly encourages you to be naughty – buy as many as you want! Go on, while your mum's not looking…

The sweets are an example of the way colette managed to hit the right note with a generation and become its chosen lifestyle environment (just as MTV had once been 'lifestyle television'). Colette's notorious basement water bar is another good example of this. Rumours circulated at the time about a bar that sold still water at super-inflated prices, causing outrage but generating huge amounts of free publicity into the bargain. Colette's people are the first to admit that a water bar is a daft idea in isolation, but it was not in isolation; it was in colette's restaurant, which was specifically designed for those who do not have nine to five jobs. Whereas the bulk of Parisians would have their lunch breaks between noon and 2pm, at colette, you could have lunch any time and even bring your laptop if you wished. Once again, this reflected the way the leading faction of the grown-up MTV Generation now worked. For those types, it was always a matter of mixing work and play; rigid office hours did not apply. The menu also featured dishes that reflected the rising trend of couture gastronomy as well as awareness about food provenance. By the mid-noughties, this would become a major issue for consumers and in this context bottled water would prove to be one of the fastest-growing market sectors. Colette was not crazy – it was simply a step ahead of the market.

Farmers' Markets and Couture Gastronomy

Farmers' Markets

The first farmers' market in the UK opened in 1997 in Bath, emulating the feel of a small-town or rural market. Apparently, 3,000 people turned up to sample produce made by the people who sold it. In June 1999, London Farmers' Markets pioneered its own scheme in Islington. The idea behind it was simple: to provide Londoners with fresh, local food and to provide farmers with an outlet to sell their produce to city people. Farmers' markets in London operate a strict policy: all producers must raise, grow or bake everything they sell (no middlemen allowed) and they must come from within 100 miles of the London perimeter (considered as the M25). This radius is reduced for markets outside of London. All farmers' markets are certified by the National Farmers' Retail & Markets Association (FARMA), which controls quality and standards so that consumers can be confident that they are buying from the farmer and not a wholesaler. Though not certified as a farmers' market, Old Spitalfields Market, the original hub for Hoxtonites, was also partly a food market where many farmers were selling their produce direct (this ceased when the market was redeveloped). London's equally trendy Borough Market was faced with a similar predicament as redevelopment plans were announced, but managed to survive and flourish as one of the capital's top gastronomic destinations. The farmers' market scheme proved to be so popular that by the end of 2007, there were 15 certified farmers' markets in London, with an estimate that this market trend funnelled £3 million back to the rural economy each year. In the UK in that same year, there were 550 farmers' markets across the country with an estimated income of more than £220 million a year.[24]

Considered at 'the vanguard of the British food revolution', the rise of farmers' markets and other foodie markets (basically those non-certified by FARMA), coupled with independent stores selling food products from small producers (many of them online), sparked off a trend indeed. By the mid-noughties, organic food had become the key growth market sector in Europe. Valued at £0.8 billion in 2000, it rose to £1.6 billion by 2005 in the UK alone. Research revealed that the growing consumer awareness about the harmful effects of processed food, coupled with the perception that organic food was tastier, both contributed to the rise of consumer demand.[25] Supermarkets were all jumping on the organic bandwagon, with giants such as Sainsbury's reporting 18.4 per cent growth in organic sales year on year.[26] Interestingly, figures showed an overall decline in the percentage of organic sales made by supermarkets for three consecutive years (from 81 per cent to 75 per cent) at the height of this trend due to consumer concerns over issues such as food miles and a limited range of organic products being available in the supermarkets. At the same time, farmers' markets registered significant sales increases of 33 per cent, plus an equally healthy increase in 'box schemes' (farms delivering seasonal produce directly to customers) and an even greater rise for small independent retailers, who saw their sales rise by 43 per cent.[27] This pointed to a microtrend – a niche target-market for whom consciousness and quality were more important than convenience, and who preferred alternative outlets to supermarkets, even if they did stock organic food ranges. That positive organic growth picture was even healthier in Germany, Europe's most developed organic food market, now valued at £3.5 billion, with Berlin being Europe's biggest 'organic' capital (home to the largest organic store, opened by the LPG chain in 2007).[28]

A series of high-profile corporate takeovers further underlined this trend. These included the acquisition of Fresh and Wild, London's leading-edge organic supermarket, by the American natural-food supermarket chain Whole Foods (2004). Other high-profile corporate acquisitions across product categories included that of Rachel's Organic dairy, a small family business, by Horizon Organic Dairy of America in 1999 (itself acquired by Dean Foods in 2004), L'Oréal's purchase of Kiehl's (2000), Cadbury Schweppes' purchase of Green & Black's chocolate (2005) and Colgate Palmolive's purchase of Tom's of Maine (2006). However, the healthy profits of brands that refused corporate money, such as Dr. Hauschka, Weleda and Nature et Découvertes are indicative of consumer interest in sustainable consumption. By the end of the noughties, much mainstream advertising focused on 'eco' messages heralding 'naturalness' (no 'baddies' in food), provenance, ethical orientation, awareness about the environment and tradition. Think Stella Artois' '1366 challenge' campaign with the 'Four Precious Ingredients' strapline, Coca-Cola's pledge that they'll never add preservatives or artificial flavours, PG Tips tea's 'ethical alliance', Anchor butter's 'free-roam cows' (for 'free range') butter, Heinz's 'free-range eggs' mayonnaise, The Naturals' sweets with 'only natural colours and flavours', and so on.

It is in this context that we must locate colette's water bar. In the early noughties, when studies began to look into the emerging bottled-water trend, the figures indeed confirmed the growing consumer awareness and concerns over amounts of artificial additives, caffeine, alcohol, calories, salt and fat content in food and beverages. This began to drive the demand for bottled water in particular, making it one of the fastest-growing market sectors. Between 2000 and 2004, in the UK alone, sales of still and sparkling bottled water increased by as much as 46 per cent. Research showed that consumers were taking heed of the health advice to drink eight glasses of water a day. This was coupled with the belief that bottled water was a healthier option than tap water.[29] The launches of Fiji and Dasani water in the UK in 2004 are interesting here. Both were bottled still-water brands and among the top sellers in their category in the USA, with international expansion ambitions. The former was driving the health-consciousness trend. The latter was responding to growing market interest, triggered by the leading-edge sector.

Dasani, owned by Coca-Cola, was a spectacular flop, well documented in the British trade press at the time. Assuming that a successful brand in the USA, combined with the healthy market prognostics for the category would automatically translate into success, Dasani appeared to have taken market opportunity as a given. Its first faux pas was its failure to realise that in the British psyche, the image of purified tap water – effectively Dasani's proposition – was inevitably conditioned by memories of 'Peckham Spring', the title of a 1992 episode of the enormously popular sitcom *Only Fools and Horses*. The main character, lovable rogue Derek 'Del Boy' Trotter, had chanced upon a new 'business venture' (euphemism for a dodgy deal) that consisted of bottling tap water from his council flat and reselling it as 'Peckham Spring'. Del Boy was literally tapping into the trend of middle-class people discovering French bottled water when it first arrived in Britain. Named after his working-class neighbourhood, it implicitly made fun of this la-di-dah fashion. Indeed, to paraphrase Del Boy, what could be more 'natural' and 'ancient' than the River Thames, its source? Beyond the unfortunate association with Peckham Spring, Dasani's proposition also appeared weak simply because there were many other brands from clear, natural springs already competing for this space on the shelf. A new market entrant had to do better, which Fiji understood.

Originally owned by Canadian entrepreneur David Gilmour, Fiji water began manufacture in 1996 and was distributed in the USA and Canada thereafter as 'natural artesian water'. Fiji was bottled at the source (Fiji) according to stringent quality standards in order to preserve the goodness of its special minerals. The water company paid a royalty and a lease fee to the landowners and set up a trust fund to provide health, hygiene, sanitation and education facilities in the area's villages. Although a business, it clearly had a philanthropic aspect. (A few years later, when Fiji became successful, a contentious issue became the environmental impact, but according to a company source, in an attempt to reduce carbon emissions the water travels from Fiji to its UK destination in special ocean vessels.)[30]

Fiji was built as a premium brand. It was among the first to realise the potential of bottled water as a response to the growing consumer consciousness about wellbeing. Fiji offered a combination of health benefits (purity), transparency (a company standing by its values) and passion (the story of one man's love for the island and giving back to the community that gives us Fijian water). Its target market were early adopters who would be willing to pay the premium price in good faith. Consequently, the launch of Fiji water was a matter of finding the right channels to reach the right consumer segment. To this end, the brand image in the UK was built through select third-party endorsements and relationships with the press, such as product placement at Fashion Week or on offbeat television series such as *The Sopranos*. Fiji was sold in select stores such as Fresh and Wild (now Whole Foods), bars and restaurants. The ultra-fashionable Japanese restaurant chain Nobu claimed to boil its rice in Fiji water.

In 2004, Fiji was acquired by Roll International, a private company owned by a husband and wife team. Incidentally, this was the same team behind the success of POM Wonderful, the pomegranate juice. By turning a small, inherited field into the United States' largest cultivator of pomegranates, they had created a market for the juice of a fruit that only 4 per cent of the US market had heard of in 2002. This, in turn, opened up a new industry for foods with high antioxidant properties. Sold in high-end cafés and delis first, supermarkets picked up on it and began to sell pomegranate juice in their chiller cabinets. At the same time, conveniently peeled and packaged fresh pomegranate began to be sold, with plastic cutlery included. Raised consumer awareness of fresh antioxidant juices in turn put pressure on ambient carton juices. For example, the American company Ocean Spray was a market leader in the early 1990s when it first brought cranberry juice into the UK. However, with the growing demand for fresh juice such as POM, carton juice became the poor relation. To jazz up Ocean Spray, the company picked up on the 'antioxidant' fashion. Their advertising campaign (from British television, circa spring 2009) featured a humorous take on the health-spa trend. We saw one woman going through all kinds of elaborate mud baths to cleanse her body 'from the outside', implying that to do so would be purely cosmetic, while another simply drank a glass of Ocean Spray, full of antioxidants (as claimed by the advert). This implied that the cleansing effect happens 'from inside', without you having to suffer in the name of beauty. To accompany the advert, information about brand heritage, health benefits and ethical awareness (cranberries are sourced from a cooperative of farmers) appeared on the company's website.

As with any trend that becomes fashionable, the original good intentions were open to abuse, whether by phonies passing as farmers at farmers' markets or the supermarkets' attempts to cash in, but the integrity of specific individuals or corporations is beyond the scope of my story. In the UK in 2009, a government report suggested that there were no nutritional advantages to organic food, dubbing it a 'lifestyle choice'. Many people were unconvinced by the findings of the report, but it did spark public debate. However, the merits (or otherwise) of organic food are also beyond the scope of this book. Our topic is the crossover of this trend from the underground into the mainstream, how the Islington Mother acted as an early adopter, and how her consumption behaviour inspired the mainstream consumer's psyche.

Couture Gastronomy

Parallel to the street-market-led organic trend, there was 'couture' gastronomy, a new niche market that owed a lot to particular pioneer artisans who began to apply a multidisciplinary approach to the art of food creation. Pierre Hermé was the father of this 'haute pâtisserie'. Dubbed the 'Picasso of pâtisserie', 'pâtissier provocateur', 'genius chief pâtissier' and even 'Dior of pâtisserie', Hermé was (and is) indisputably one of the greatest contemporary food innovators. Descending from a family of three generations of *boulangers* (and *pâtissiers*), he served his apprenticeship at the reputable Maison Lenôtre, where he admitted to developing his passion for the trade. He mastered the tradition only to break with it and single-handedly provide what is probably the greatest contemporary challenge the pâtisserie world has seen. He makes cakes like designers make clothes.

Pierre Hermé boutiques look like concept stores. With their smart combinations of dark colours, select materials and lighting displays, they are almost reminiscent of hip nightclubs. The windows are dark and understated, bereft of the traditional display of cakes. The interiors are an unlikely combination of pharmacy-cum-jewellery-store with meticulous attention paid to the display of products, service and packaging. You walk out of Hermé's as if you'd just walked out of Tiffany's, carrying a bag emblazoned with his ultra-modern logo, rather than the traditional cardboard cake box. Interestingly, the first Pierre Hermé boutique was opened in Tokyo in 1998, followed by a *salon de thé* in 2000. More innovative concepts followed in the mid-noughties, including a 'chocolat bar' strategically positioned in the Omotesandō area where the big fashion houses are. The first Paris boutique opened in 2001 and the second in 2004 followed by a *'chocolat et macaron'* boutique. (The plan is to open an Hermé boutique in London in 2010, having had concessions in places such as the Food Hall in Selfridges prior to that.) There was no difference between products stocked in France and Japan because Hermé's approach was creation-centric rather than consumer-centric. In other words, he did not begin with 'what the customer might want' – instead, the starting point was the marriage of flavours.

Chez Pierre Hermé, indulgence (*'gourmandise'*) is a holistic experience; Hermé has perfected the art of tantalising the senses. The pleasure of eating is to be savoured in stages. There is something almost burlesque about the unveiling of the different layers. First, there is the anticipation, looking around, absorbing the environment, smelling. You are teased into the boutique and spoilt for choice. Once you have made your purchase, the experience is followed by the pleasure of unwrapping and discovering what is inside, and then admiring the creation to arouse your senses. Each cake looks exquisite. When you finally take your first bite, the anticipation is not over – only then does it truly begin, because what you see is often not representative of the taste. The surprise might continue with an unexpected flavour like *'chocolat azur'*, traditionally made of chocolate and lime but modernised by the addition of exotic *'yuzon'*, an Eastern citrus fruit. Alternatively, the surprise may come from unusual textures. A cake that looks like a macaroon from outside – which you might therefore expect to be crunchy – turns out to be melt-in-the-mouth tender. Or you might find a cake wrapped up like a sweet.

Hermé did not just bake cakes. He designed them. In fashion, research is one of the most important parts of the creation process, whereby forward-thinking designers look for inspiration (and that can come from anywhere). By way of analogy, inspiration for Pierre came from different sources, most often his worldwide travels and curiosity about anything, rather than an exclusive concentration on bakery. Innovation resulted, above all, from this exploratory stage. Once the ideas for new cakes had been sketched and prototyped, the tasting began – rather like a fitting in fashion. However, this was not done with professional tasters, but with a 'nose'. This term is fragrance-industry jargon used to describe a professional who creates perfumes. Pierre believed that the distinction between fragrance and flavour was artificial. If anything, he judged the sense of smell to be a more developed and a truer way of assessing flavour, rather than relying on taste. Moreover, a 'nose' would have a richer vocabulary to convey taste sensations than a chef. When the new *prêt-a-manger* creations were all ready, they were inaugurated twice a year in Hermé's own version of a catwalk show.

Hermé is credited with introducing new flavours into the field of pâtisserie, as well as colours, textures, layouts and ways of presentation. Even temperature was considered. In addition to new creations, there were staples, including the signature Ispahan (a rose macaroon with fresh raspberry and lychee). In fact, innovative macaroon flavours were what made Hermé famous. Until he came on the scene, the range of flavours was pretty much stuck in the early 1900s, as demonstrated by renowned Parisian house Ladurée, which invented the macaroon as we know it today (biscuit-crust sandwich filled with ganache). Among Pierre's most experimental flavours was the ketchup macaroon, served chez colette for the store's fifth anniversary. A recently published book featuring Hermé's macaroons, simply entitled *Macaron*, is also sold at colette. Since Hermé set the tone in the Parisian pâtisserie landscape, Ladurée also introduced 'seasonal' macaroon flavours and other types of pâtisserie outside their traditional canon, including items such as a rose and violet *religieuse*, a cake like a round, two-tier *éclair* which traditionally only ever came in chocolate or coffee flavours. Other household names such as Fauchon and Hévin subsequently refreshed their staples as well as modernised their looks. Places such as Le Délicabar started to offer 'couture' snacking. Paris had never been short of superb food but Hermé upped the game by setting an innovation challenge to the *gastronomie* clique.

Another notable ongoing trend in couture gastronomy is culinary alchemy. Here, the culinary genius looks to chemistry and physics for inspiration, literally engineering provocative dishes consisting of radical flavours, textures and colour combinations. Pioneers include British chef Heston Blumenthal, who came on the scene around the same time as Daft Punk. Just as they had dispelled the myth about French rock, Blumenthal did the same for English cooking. His Fat Duck restaurant was awarded three Michelin stars in 2004.

Anyone for snail porridge? Or ejaculating cake, perhaps? Blumenthal seems obsessed with the weird and wonderful possibilities of blending the most unlikely ingredients, like some mad scientist character. I watched him on television as he attempted to recreate the 'Drink Me' potion from *Alice in Wonderland*. A subversive and imaginary recipe from an enchanted tale, it contained five or six flavours ranging from butterscotch to turkey meat, but this did not appear to deter him. And he did succeed in creating layers of liquid, each with its distinct flavour. He also devised a special test tube-inspired glass (a beaker with a glass straw) with which to sample this delicacy, one flavour at a time. It was impressive. Similarly, Spain's Ferran Adrià (of the internationally acclaimed elBulli restaurant) developed his famous bite-size creations in his 'laboratory' (as opposed to his kitchen).

More generally, there was a movement among the design, arts and culinary communities, which involved designing not only the food but also the experiential art of eating, and curating events around this theme. There were also individual collaborative examples of 'couture food', though this was not quite the fusion trend that boffins like Blumenthal or craftsmen like Hermé had initiated. Nevertheless, Jean Paul Gaultier's designer 'baguettes' are worthy of mention. They were intended for a Cartier Foundation installation in 2004 and involved iconic Gaultier garments, such as Madonna's corset, being shaped from dough and then baked. Beyond artistic merit, what was interesting about this was that Gaultier's contribution – the idea for which had been driven by his own passion for the craft of baking – coincided with a more general revival of the traditional baguette, following a steep decline in quality. Bakers began to reject industrial methods of production in favour of the old ways, bringing the declining number of traditional baguettes being sold in France in the mid-noughties back up from the downward spiral to a fifth of the 30 million now consumed daily.[31]

Finally, in the context of holistic sensual experiences, it is also worth noting the trend of '*haute parfumerie*'. This involves the creation of personalised fragrances using natural, premium-quality ingredients. Leading names include the London-based Roja Dove and the Parisian Frédéric Malle, who calls himself an '*éditeur de parfum*'. This type of perfume creation was about subverting the conventions set by the fragrance industry. All the major perfume brands were owned by a handful of corporate companies and reduced to trusting a few industry noses, with the result that they all hit the same top-and-base notes for fear of commercial failure, which in turn resulted in over-familiar scents: 'if in doubt, put in vanilla' (one of the four most popular scents according to market research). Radical parfumiers at this time also began to diversify by producing nutritional products. Miller Harris produced fragrant teas. In a collaboration with Comme des Garçons, Amsterdam's sweet-shop, Papabubble, invented the 'taste of Comme des Garçons', a powdered candy that matched the fragrance of a particular edition of Comme des Garçons perfume. Customers also got one sweet when they purchased the perfume.[32] In its water bar, colette sells Shigeta floral water, which combines water bottled at source with aromatic oils. Sold in one-litre bottles to take away, you can either drink it diluted with water or use it as a facial lotion. This particular trend is perhaps best illustrated by a 2009 advertisement for Dr. Alkaitis's Therapeutic Skin Food, which stated 'if you can't eat it, don't put it on your skin'. The same principle later extended into mass-market cosmetics, such as Urban Decay's Marshmallow Body Powder.

Couture Hôtellerie

The bottom line here is that time is a luxury. 'Couture hôtellerie' was all about blurring the distinction between being at home and being in a hotel. It was about dropping the formalities of the latter and adopting the cosiness of the former to deliver an experience that mirrored home comforts while giving you that little bit of extra indulgence that you wouldn't associate with being at home. Returning to the diffusion-platform model, we have the street version of establishments, which I shall call 'chic lodgings', and the concept store equivalent – boutique hotels.

Service and *savoir faire* rather than superficial or ostentatious décor was at the heart of what drove this trend; an intuitive reaction to what was happening in the luxury chain sector, whereby 'service' had increasingly been confused with marketing politesse rehearsed to perfection, but often devoid of any meaning. You would have immaculate hostesses to escort you from A to B, catering for your 'every need', but the moment you actually needed something simple that necessitated common sense (rather than something that fitted into a marketing box), you would get a blank face. Here is an example.

During a business trip in the mid-noughties I stayed in a luxury hotel in Moscow owned by a prestige five-star chain – not because I had a generous client but because all the other business hotels were booked up. As the hotel had a spectacular view of Red Square, it would have been a sin not to find those extra 30 minutes for breakfast instead of having it as usual, on the go. Tea with toast was very dear but it seemed worth it to savour that moment. (How often does one get to drink tea overlooking Red Square on a gloriously sunny day?) Anyway, to cut a long story short, it was a disaster: the waitress did not know the difference between one type of brew and another. First she brought me one I did not order. She didn't bring any milk. By the time she did, the tea was cold. She made me feel uncomfortable for being demanding, even though she had wasted both my time and money, and expected a tip regardless. As I walked out of the restaurant into the long corridors, I was looking forward to inspecting the old masters on the walls that I'd been too busy to observe earlier. To my horror, they were recently painted replicas.

Those shortcomings in décor and service were exactly what a new wave of lodgings and hotels sought to provide an alternative to. More than just the difference between fake and original art and furniture, though, it was all about creating an environment for the customer to feel at ease in.

Chic Lodgings

'Chic lodgings' are family-run places (usually the owner's home), which manage to combine the simple, heartwarming welcome you might associate with your own home with the sophistication of a luxury hotel. Once again, there is a product-centric approach rather than a consumer-led one. The host has a home to offer; this may not be everyone's cup of tea, but for the right customer, the 'labour of love' factor is evident. The customer's experience relies entirely on the hospitality of the host. '*La relation humaine d'abord, l'argent après,*' (human rapport before money) as one owner of a *maison d'hôte* (a type of chic lodging) in Paris put it. It is all about the attention to detail, from the choice of linen or soap, to the design of the place and the selection of (original) artwork – not forgetting those personal recommendations for that little café or bakery round the corner.

My friend Paul Reynolds decided to convert his 300 square-metre (or so) apartment in Barcelona into a guesthouse when he moved there from London in around 2002. He called it The Third Floor. An interior designer-cum-artist, Paul epitomised the second-generation Hoxtonites' approach to fusion. Translating his art into space, he decorated the flat following his wildest fancies. Aware of the preciousness of time to his potential guests, he decided that The Third Floor would have no check-in or check-out policies, that room service would run 24 hours a day (he would be on call), that breakfast would be served at any time, that a 'pampering room' was essential with treatments available 24/7, and that the food would be freshly homemade. On top of all this, he would only accept one customer at a time – but they could bring friends (the place slept 12 comfortably, though any kind of adjustment could be made to suit the customer). Paul would also give his recommendations for off-the-trail places to go in Barcelona.

Paul's apartment is just one example of the many chic lodgings scattered all over the world. Word-of-mouth, press reviews and select online portals are the only way to find these places. 'Chic lodgings' are a microtrend, so statistics are difficult to come by. In Paris there were some 300 *maisons d'hôte* in 2005.[33] By 2007 this number had tripled. By 2009, a conference was even organised for this micro-industry, boasting 45,000 beds in France alone. In neighbouring Switzerland, they called it 'bed and breakfast' in reference to its English origin but with the added tag '*haute gamme*' to stress its upmarket status. Official figures in 2007 showed that there were 800 chic lodgings in Switzerland (270,000 nights in terms of occupancy by number of guests, which was a 50 per cent increase compared to 2005) and a plan to list 1,000 establishments in the 2010 official Swiss tourist guide.[34]

Boutique Hotels

Boutique hotels have famously been described as 'homes away from home'. They provide individually tailored service based on exquisite style and anticipating customer needs. Their design is often undertaken by eminent designers and architects, rather than by impersonal developers. The first boutique hotel, Morgans in New York City, was opened in 1984 by the Morgans Hotel Group. Its proposition was based on combining work and play, a lifestyle previously the preserve of the hipsters, but by then becoming more mainstream. It should come as no surprise that this early boutique hotel was the brainchild of one of the greatest hipsters, Ian Schrager, one of the duo behind New York's legendary Studio 54. Often dubbed 'ultra hip', Schrager's vision for a unique place to stay (over a decade ahead of its time) later became the blueprint for über cool hotels.

Though the Morgans Group would launch a few more properties before the late 1990s, the year 1998 signalled a turning point and the beginning of a new trend. Symbolically, this was marked by the launch of the first W Hotel in New York City by the Starwood Hotel Group. W became synonymous with urban boutique hotels, through a branding exercise that turned service into a commodity. By renaming the hotel's reception desk (or 'front desk' in American

English) the 'welcome desk' and replacing the word 'service' with 'whatever/ whenever', they focused on personalised service and extended the concept to some 30 properties within a decade. In 1999, Morgans inaugurated the high-profile St Martins Lane Hotel in London, followed by The Sanderson and a number of other international launches.

The boutique hotel went on to influence the hospitality industry across the board, including the beach-hotel sector and package holidays. From a scattering of unique, high-profile properties, the boutique hotel grew into a new category in its own right. This included targeting the business market segment by offering lower rates. A number of players began to vie for position in the second half of the noughties. Tapping into the needs of business travellers whose way of life revolved around 'seamlessly merging personal and professional activities', in 2007, the Global Hyatt Corporation launched Hyatt Place as its mid-market range and Andaz as the five-star version. Interestingly, the Great Eastern Hotel in Shoreditch (later rebranded as Andaz), once host to many chic second-generation Hoxtonite events, was the first in its series. Starwood launched their W-influenced Aloft Hotels, with attention to design combined with hi-tech office/entertainment centres, at more affordable prices (and a virtual version on Second Life to test new products). And in 2007 Marriott recruited none other than Schrager (who left Morgans in 2005) to consult on the launch of lifestyle boutique hotels to be opened under the Marriott umbrella.

Street-Chic Magazines

During its short life (spring 1999–spring 2001), *P.U.R.E.* magazine dictated the zeitgeist. As a true innovator and trend-incubator, it proved to be an instant hit among opinion formers from its first issue. Once again, in the case of this diffusion platform, there was a product-centric approach. The magazine's vision reflected the lifestyle of its editorial team; readers were invited to be part of the cool fraternity. In contrast to the corporate publishing industry, where creativity and freedom of speech were constrained by advertising pressures and rigid celebrity contracts, *P.U.R.E.* was an acronym for 'provocative uncompromising radical entertainment'.

The aim of *P.U.R.E.* was to provoke its contributors to look beyond the obvious and to think outside the conventions set by corporate-owned publishers in order to challenge them. It was uncompromising because it did not have to pander to mass consumer trends or corporate policy. It was radical because it liked to surprise. It was entertaining because it did not take itself seriously, in spite of its penchant for analysis (rather than simply reporting what was in). Here, the tongue-in-cheek, provocative humour that characterised the Hoxtonite scene flourished, manifesting itself in the magazine's art direction.

A lot of *P.U.R.E.*'s non-conformity reflected the editorial team's own life on the edge, somewhere between the underground and the underworld. Creative risk-taking was often inspired by the magazine's own entourage, who were a colourful bunch of people. It ranged from flirting with high society in west London to entering the risqué world of the grotty striptease joints in east London. Juxtaposing influences from such contrasting worlds, the results were often stunning. *P.U.R.E.*'s production bordered on art: the inventiveness of the magazine's layout, the creativity behind the editorial, the quality of photography and even the choice of paper it was printed on – all were exquisite. The team also hosted novel events, which were not focused on the DJ, or getting sponsorship from video game companies, or beer to attract cool kids. *P.U.R.E.* was the antithesis of that world.

The magazine both embodied and shaped the emerging 'street-chic' underground ideology to become the voice of second-generation Hoxtonites, and the core team was very much part of the east London scene. Its founder, Mike Lake-McMillan, was a debonair man equally at ease in the underground club scene as at sophisticated gatherings. There was something gentlemanly about Mike even though he looked like a typical rock star, in his leather pants. He had an air of polite ambiguity about him, leaving you wondering whether he'd spent last night at an S&M club, in a five-star hotel room smashing TV sets, or under a duvet with a hot water bottle. James Mannox, the art director, was a fine arts graduate with a skill for translating conceptual stories into visual forms. Jo Perfect, the editor, had been an original member of the *Dazed & Confused* staff when it was a seminal street publication in the early 1990s. No longer excited by *Dazed*, she was ready for new challenges. Last but not least, Carla Peretz was in charge of ad sales. A unique character, Carla combined military discipline (she had been a tank instructor in her native Israel) with the charm of a Playboy bunny, her GI Jane skinhead combined with sexy bright-red lipstick perfectly illustrating this contradiction. The rest of the team consisted of leading photographers, stylists and art directors for whom *P.U.R.E.* represented a forum of uncompromised artistic expression. Equally important was the army of new stylists, editors, journalists and artists who were in search of platforms where they could exercise creative freedom. With a superb sense for striking the right balance between sophisticated and dirty, *P.U.R.E.* had a stylish exterior but was a fanzine at heart.

P.U.R.E.'s editorial policy was to encourage all its contributors to take the time to consider what they intended to achieve and what route they might take to get there. The focus was on curiosity about anything new and different. *P.U.R.E.* thrived on discovering new talent from across the board. This meant that it defied categorisation and favoured the fusion approach, challenging the 1990s-style fragments and categories. *P.U.R.E.* also categorically rejected trend-spotting. Instead, it acted as a curator. Its intention was to document moments in popular culture not just because they were timely, but because the team wanted them to become timeless references. Art director James used to describe their approach with a fashion analogy: 'We are not trying to spot the latest trends, which is what publications do. We tend to feature what we consider interesting. So, for example, in fashion, we might not search for the latest trendy white garment but we may feature some interesting items that happen to be white.' By avoiding cool hunting, *P.U.R.E.* became effortlessly cool. Being the first to know meant that *P.U.R.E.* was directional. What was featured would often appear later in mainstream magazines, because opinion forming types (avid readers of the magazine) would transmit the knowledge.

With its non-conformist stance, *P.U.R.E.* began to challenge established publishing industry practices. There was no category in the official Audit Bureau of Circulation (ABC) for a magazine like *P.U.R.E.* To begin with, it offered a new model to advertisers. It did not fit the demographic criteria used to define target readership. With its editorial mix, the magazine was equally targeting females and males and 'all those in between', which was a huge contrast to the trend of lads' mags such as *FHM* and *Maxim* or established female press such as *Elle* or *Marie-Claire*. Furthermore, the 'age' category stretched beyond the youth market (either defined as 15–24 or 18–34) towards Generation X (its makers were in their thirties or older) and even the baby boomers, encompassing all those who shared an interest in the same lifestyle. *P.U.R.E.*'s readership was an international group of early adopters who bought into the magazine's attitude.

The next challenge was distribution, on a number of levels. First, *P.U.R.E.* didn't fit easily on the magazine shelves (which category: Fashion? Women? Men? Youth Culture? Music? Art?). Second, its price was in the premium bracket at £6.95 (compared, at the time, to £2.70 for *Marie-Claire*; £3.20 for *Vogue* and £4.20 for *Wallpaper**). Third, it was aimed at an international readership (sold in over 20 countries) but with a standard international issue, as opposed to the trend for localised versions of successful magazine brands (*Vogue, Marie-Claire*, etc). Finally, *P.U.R.E.* began to be sold in unconventional outlets, such as art galleries, bookshops, museums, street boutiques, concept stores and the like, which added to its complexity. In spite of all this, the sales of *P.U.R.E.* indicated that there was clearly a market for this kind of magazine. London's renowned store for fashion publications, R. D. Franks, used to order 80 copies at a time and sell them all, indicating that there was a specialist community of avid readers. A pilot scheme at mainstream newsagent WHSmith's busy Victoria station branch saw them taking on ten copies which sold immediately, resulting in their re-ordering another 30.[35] This was promising for the distributor Comag, who took on *P.U.R.E.* via its specialist division.

P.U.R.E. was short-lived (due to a set of unfortunate circumstances) but its legacy lived on. In the distribution chain, the magazine niche carved out by pioneers such as *P.U.R.E.* grew into a magazine category in its own right. Already in 2001, *Spruce* (backed by *Wallpaper**) and *AnOther Magazine* (backed by Jefferson Hack, the founder of *Dazed & Confused*) were launched, emulating the format. Other publications from this varied and edgy, but chic, sector included *Tank, Numéro, Jalouse, Wonderland, Above Magazine* and even the design publication *Nest* and the art publication *Modern Painters*. The French publication *Citizen K* was among *P.U.R.E.*'s greatest fans. I met Frédéric Chaubin, its editor-in-chief, at a dinner party in Paris following the inauguration of Palais de Tokyo in 2002. He was full of praise and admiration for *P.U.R.E.* and admitted that he was both inspired by it and encouraged to find a clear editorial direction for his own publication. Today, *Citizen K* is a major international player in the chic magazine market.

Interestingly, while *AnOther Magazine* became *P.U.R.E.*'s most obvious competitor when it came out, *P.U.R.E.* did not consider *Dazed & Confused* a competitor at all. It was perceived as 'too youth oriented' and 'the magazine equivalent of MTV'. A few years later, *Dazed & Confused* would reformulate its editorial strategy. It aligned itself with the Hoxtonite network as it was becoming among the hottest on the global opinion-forming circuit, meaning that if there was something to know, *Dazed* knew it first. The magazine also launched a digital version, employing an early high-profile blogger as its editor. This combination of the right connections and the ability to provide immediate coverage of anything worth knowing about put it right back at the heart of the zeitgeist. *Dazed & Confused* once again became a platform for cool communication involving collaboration opportunities, rather than just pages and pages of advertising. One such partnership would involve the Cool Brands Council, whose *CoolBrands 2008/09* book was distributed with the magazine.

Unlike *Dazed & Confused*, which gave itself a new lease of life, two of its contemporaries folded in 2004. The first, *Sleazenation*, was re-launched as *Sleaze* with the arrival of its new editor Neil Boorman, as mentioned previously. However, Neil's sense of humour proved too cynical. The first cover featured a burning photograph of the ultimate manufactured pop product and footballer's wife par excellence, Victoria Beckham. This was coupled with opinionated and ideas-driven content, rather than simply lists of information. However, questioning mindless celebrity and consumption was out of step with mainstream youth culture – the advertising target market for *Sleaze*. Similarly, the one-time style icon *The Face* was no longer relevant, partly because its half-hearted references to street style would soon be made redundant by street style blogs and partly because it lost its edge by choosing to follow the mega-celebrity path, featuring the likes of David Beckham and Beyoncé as cover stars. What was this magazine about? It was sending mixed messages. Religiously read by hipsters since the early 1980s, they'd defected a long time ago. The fact that it sold out to a mainstream publisher did not help. Even so, the downfall of these magazines was not so much indicative of them being uncool as it was of a youth culture at the crossroads.

The turn of the millennium was a period when the meaning of cool was being reassessed, and the magazine industry – as a main medium for identity expression – would feel this effect. Cool hunting was all the rage. In this scenario, cool and youth culture were synonymous. However, the mainstream youth sector was becoming celebrity-obsessed, what with MTV going down the reality-TV route and *Big Brother* occupying the centre ground of mainstream youth culture, with magazines like *Heat*, heavily patronised by young readers, dedicating their coverage to its 'stars'. 'Cool' became a misnomer. The alternative to this was street culture, which allowed corporate brands to differentiate their own corporate-cool world. Street culture was cooler than 'celebrity' culture, yet it was effectively the sell-out of a scene that had been discovered by the commercial world when MTV and cool brands brought it into the spotlight, in the build-up to Cool Britannia.

As such, street culture was not about responding to the next ideological shift because the nature of hip, and by extension, what makes capitalism reinvent itself, is hip's reaction to what it had previously patronised. And so street chic became the next hip ideology. Who you defined yourself against was as intuitive as it was a conscious rejection of other ideologies, notably those of 'celebrity' and 'street'.

Here, a conversation with Guillaume Le Goff proved enlightening for my understanding of how this ideological shift manifested itself in the magazine market. I met Guillaume in London at the Kokon To Zai store around 2008. He was in London for a street-art opening nearby, so he'd popped into Kokon To Zai because he was a fan of the brand. If I remember correctly, the art show was being hosted by the Lazarides, a leading street-art gallery. Its founder was credited with discovering British street artist/megastar Banksy, or rather for bringing him to prominence, because in Hoxton in the early noughties, you could walk around and see his graffiti all over or go to Cargo (a bar) and see half the walls covered by his stencils. By the end of the noughties, the starting price on his salvaged works at art auctions would be in six figures, with 'Cargo nightclub' listed as its place of origin.

Guillaume was the founder of the French street culture magazine *Clark*, launched in 2001. Guillaume's influence was the Beautiful Losers and this magazine was his labour of love. It was dedicated to promoting street culture (emanating from skateboarding), graphic art and (urban) music. It was passionate and independent. However, unlike *P.U.R.E.* during its brief life, *Clark* was never really embraced by the Parisian network of La Hype or indeed the London-based Hoxtonites. The truth is that I had never heard of *Clark* until I met Guillaume. I sensed a feeling of rejection when he spoke of La Hype. *Clark* had never been solicited for any kind of collaboration or mutual project. Guillaume's predicament made me think. The real reason for the lack of interest was not a conspiracy. *Clark* was 'street' – but it was not 'street chic'.

In business, this distinction is a matter of positioning. Guillaume Salmon of colette had talked about colette's brand positioning as not being 'street culture' and he spoke for the scene when he said this. Similarly Kitsuné, a key Parisian label from La Hype that I shall look at later, had the same feeling about 'streetwear'. *'Surtout pas,'* (absolutely not) was their reaction, expressed by Jacques Shu from the Kitsuné team. Among the subculture, the distinction was ideological. *P.U.R.E.* magazine intuitively adopted this ideology because it had been inspired by the scene. Though the rejection of street culture is perhaps less drastic now that the Hoxtonite scene is commercialised (in that some of its exponents have reinstated elements of streetwear), it was strong in the beginning when the scene was incubating. Streetwear (that which defined itself against high fashion) was noticeable by its absence. In the 'dress up' underground clubs, no one was into streetwear, and by extension, street culture. It would have been like asking a punk to hang out with a hippy; ideologically, it did not work. The Hoxtonite scene was eclectic but there was the commonality of a shared set of ideals. That is why the dandy scene blended with the Kashpoint scene, even though they sported completely different styles (sartorially and musically). This was still the same group of street-chic friends. Street culture was not their world just like it was 'not the same family' for colette, as Guillaume Salmon would say.

This new ideology would come to redefine cool communication in the noughties, as well as influence the style industries. Hoxtonites were the hidden influencers, and many of them capitalised on this trend. They would turn their play into business and become major purveyors of cool for the corporate sector, as we are about to discover.

3. Influence on Style and Communication Industries

'Once something goes mainstream, for me it is over'

Ian Schrager

HOXTON, JULY 2008

'Fuck fuck fuck. I forgot... SO sorry. Shall we say 3pm? Do you want to pick me up at my office?'

Richard expresses his sincere apology for forgetting our mid-morning appointment, and after a bit of diary juggling we decide to meet later on that same day to enjoy the pleasant weather and the long, light early July evening. We have a drink outside the Hoxton Bar and Kitchen in Hoxton Square, east London, which is local for both of us. Richard is in charge of entertainment at this venue on Sunday evenings where the popularity of his club nights has led him to branch out into organising the after-parties for book or album launches and fashion shows, thus bringing a trendy crowd to the Hoxton Bar on other nights, too.

'Rich – on your bike. Get that sexy arse into Da Kitchen!' I courteously remind him, shortly before 6pm to be on the safe side. 'I am there already,' he replies.

Not only did I immediately forgive Rich for not remembering our rendez-vous (after all, he had been known not to turn up for a *Vogue* interview), I was actually grateful for his time. Despite being busy, he'd kindly agreed for us to have a proper sit-down when it suited me, as I wanted to pick his brains for this book.

Richard Mortimer is in demand: a man of the moment, a master of the zeitgeist. When I met him, he was fresh from the launch party for Jean Paul Gaultier's new perfume, Ma Dame, for which model Agyness Deyn was the face. Richard was the 'cool purveyor' for this high profile event. We have reached the stage in our crossover story where Hoxton had become the favourite pool for cool fishing. Richard's network was possibly the hottest. Bringing on the hipsters – a handpicked posse of around 40 à la mode London people to give Gaultier's event an edge – fell under his remit.

Just a few days before, Richard had kickstarted his new club night, Ponystep, at the Hoxton Bar, which would regularly take place on the last Sunday of the month until the end of that year. Ponystep then moved to Paris for the first half of 2009 and came back to its UK home in time for London Fashion Week in September. Ponystep also acted as the flagship party for Richard's latest venture, an online magazine of the same name featuring fashion, art and beauty. In this context, Ponystep became a mobile club night, lending its flair to various occasions. Monsieur Gaultier's perfume launch was among the first to buy into the Ponystep experience. Many similar opportunities would later present themselves.

The first Ponystep party at the Hoxton Bar was co-hosted with Kitsuné, the über hip Parisian music-cum-fashion label with a graphics studio arm in London. This being the domain of 'the first to know', there had even been a launch party for the launch party. Ponystep's official launch had taken place a month before the Hoxton premiere at the more upmarket Sketch in central London. Sketch is owned by Momo (Mourad Mazouz), a hip restaurateur connected to the underground scene. The Ponystep official launch was a lush affair. Being the ace event, the crowd was a touch more high-profile than the punters on a regular night, as Richard's designer friends Bella Freud, Roland Mouret, Giles Deacon, Gareth Pugh and Henry Holland all showed up. The all-important behind-the-sceners were also present, including Katie Grand and a mix of models, fashion editors, stylists, photographers and all-round poseurs, without whom there would have been no party. Reports from select parties formed a section of their own in Ponystep's online magazine. The morning after, photographs were displayed on the website for viewing, as a testimony to the previous night's shenanigans. This tactic would soon become a widespread cool marketing tool.

The next 'big' Ponystep was in August the same year, to celebrate Gareth Pugh's achievement. He had come a long way in the short period since his graduation from Central Saint Martins in 2003. He did his first DIY catwalk show at Kashpoint in February 2004, a zany affair that was listed as part of Off-Schedule Fashion Week. Kokon To Zai was the first boutique to stock his collection, accompanied by a small exhibition. Kashpoint appeared off-schedule once more in September 2004 in another bonkers bash called Battle of the Boutiques, where the most respected underground multi-label street boutiques 'competed' for the title of Best Design. Gareth Pugh paraded here on behalf of (the now-defunct) Stefan's Superstore. From there, he went on to show his collections as part of Fashion East, an already-established talent incubator by the time he hit the catwalk. Exposure through Fashion East, in turn, netted him the fashion award New Gen for two consecutive years (2006 and 2007). By then, Gareth had teamed up with maven Mandi Lennard, who looked after his PR. To top it all, the following year he received the prestigious ANDAM award, which came with the substantial cash injection of €150,000 and the right to stage his collection in Paris, the most prestigious runway of them all.[36] Reminscent of Galliano and McQueen's trajectories from London to Paris, already I am finding press reports where Pugh is dubbed an *enfant terrible*. I begin to wonder whether a new definition for that phrase should be entered in the dictionary: 'Radical London designer connected to the underground scene who makes the transition to Paris amid speculation among the fashion establishment that the choice of said designer is a risk.'

Gareth would be making his Parisian debut in September 2008, followed by an aftershow party organised by Richard. Or would he? Shock horror, the Eurostar was only running a limited service. As London's fashpack was preparing to cross the Channel for their bi-annual pilgrimage, they had to frantically look for alternative transport. Gareth had the extra pressure of his show being scheduled on the first day of Paris Fashion Week. In crisis situations of this type, it pays to have a good PR. Unfazed, Mandi had already organised aeroplane tickets to be on the safe side. Luckily, some of us managed to get on to the limited Eurostar service, which meant a very early start; it was also running at reduced speed and unable to confirm arrival times. In the Eurostar waiting lounge, I found a weary Richard sitting next to Dean, who looked sleepy, and Roísín, who looked lovely, even at this ungodly hour. Dean Mayo Davies was a journalist, who was also fashion features editor for *Ponystep*. Roísín was Roísín Murphy, former lead singer of Moloko and later a solo artist, famed as much for her cutting-edge style as for her voice. Roísín had been sporting Gareth's designs since his early collections. I couldn't help but notice she was the only person with more luggage than me, though I knew she wasn't staying in Paris for as long as I was. (I was to be there for the duration of Fashion Week.)

Though being in Paris for Fashion Week could be a lot of fun and an opportunity to catch up with globe-trotting friends, one had not to forget that it was first and foremost about business. It was just that in some cases, the line between the friends and professional networks got somewhat blurred. With that blurred line in mind, my loyalties would be with colette and Kitsuné, who were co-hosting the closing party for Fashion Week at Le Régine. This was a new venue and one of the hippest nightclubs in Paris, owned by Lio and André, who had come a long way in building a hip empire since we first met them in the incubation stage of the scene. In fact, the same club was Ponystep's Parisian residence. Hence, I *had* to stay until the end of Fashion Week. The reason I was booked on an unfashionably early train is that the catwalk show of my friend's label, Ivana Helsinki, was scheduled on the first day, even earlier than Gareth's.

Ivana Helsinki was a second-generation Hoxtonite enterprise away from Hoxton (the clue's in the name!). Very much adhering to the ethos of fusion and nurturing of crafts that governs this scene, Ivana Helsinki was not just a fashion label, but a universe – of which clothes were just one aspect. The label was also about film, music, art, graphic design and experiential communication, including collaborations with select partners and brands. This universe first came into existence in 1998, coinciding with the incubation period of the Hoxtonite scene in London, partly as a reaction against the mainstream fashion trends in Finland, which favoured clothes of international provenance (Milan, Paris, London) over local clothing. Paola Suhonen, Ivana Helsinki's designer, began to produce clothes at home, inspired by the immediate environment and proudly honouring her Finnish roots. She was a keen snowboarder, who'd connected to the new rock 'n' roll world by watching MTV when it was a pioneering channel in Europe. She began her career making clothes for female snowboarders, thus producing garments in the tradition of seminal snowboarding and skateboarding clothing brands – ie functional wear that couldn't be found in other shops.

Ivana Helsinki was also a reaction against the 1990s trend of 'categorising'. The label responded to the new individualism, intuitively adopting the fusion mindset and shifting its set of values from 'street' towards incorporating 'chic'. In so doing, Ivana Helsinki became a quintessential street-chic label. And it is through this shared set of values that I met Paola's sister, Pirjo, who looks after strategy and marketing for the label – a true family business. Pirjo had come across an article I wrote about the NPC and diffusion platforms for *Brand Strategy*'s December 2005/January 2006 issue (*Brand Strategy* was a trade publication dedicated to brand innovation that became a high-profile recession casualty in 2009). Pirjo felt compelled to get in touch because my article was the first to identify the essence of brands such as Ivana Helsinki as well as their customers and distribution networks. From virtual beginnings, our friendship became real at the first opportunity, which was in Paris. Ivana Helsinki was the first Finnish fashion label ever to show at Paris Fashion Week. September 2008 was their third season. I knew I could just about make it to the show if the Eurostar got into Gare du Nord on (anticipated) time, though I was running against the clock. That I'd miss the cocktail reception beforehand seemed pretty certain.

'Are you coming tonight?' Richard asked me with a hint of secrecy, but I knew exactly where he was going with that question. He meant, was I going to the 'Gareth aftershow', with the intention of tipping me off as to where this was. There was no point competing in the first-to-know race with Richard: if something were worth knowing in our world, he was always among the first to know. (During the fashion season, there is a lot of hush-hush surrounding parties. In that already exclusive world, there's always something more exclusive. Sometimes these exclusive parties are impromptu, so word of mouth is the only way to discover them. This is not unique to fashion. Big awards ceremonies, film festivals and art fairs all practise similar exclusivist policies.)

However, on that occasion, I was a step ahead, for I'd spoken to Maxime in Paris, the PR for Kitsuné's music division. I already knew that Gareth's aftershow party was to be at Chez Moune, though I must say that I had been a little bit surprised as to the choice of venue. Chez Moune was a 'closed-door policy' lesbian cabaret club in Pigalle that I vaguely remembered as being situated in the 'exclusion zone' (for us children growing up in that area in the 1970s). Back then, Montmartre was split into three: the sex-trade district in Pigalle at the foot of the hill; the artists on La Butte de Montmartre, which is the top of the hill; and, in between, the popular Rue des Abbesses (now a fashionable address among trendy types) and Rue Lepic (ditto, because the famous café from the film *Amélie* is situated there). The 'exclusion zone' began at the bottom of Rue Houdon, the street where our primary school was situated, which is effectively Place Pigalle. The zone encompassed Boulevard de Clichy as well as the area on the other side of Place Pigalle, which is where Chez Moune was. Why would Chez Moune let Richard have a fashion party there, I wondered?

The answer I discovered a few days later when I picked up a copy of *Pariscope*, the weekly guide to what's on in Paris. In the section entitled 'La Hype', dedicated to the hottest news, I read that 'the kings of the night life [and team behind] Le Baron and Le Paris Paris, Lionel and Alain, are the new proprietors of Chez Moune.' Surely they meant André, not Alain? But when it came to La Hype, timing was everything. This listings magazine was rushing to tell the public that they were the first to know about this new hip venue, even if it meant getting the proprietor's name wrong. For me, *Pariscope*'s news was already 'so last season'. Gareth's aftershow party had been held there before the news about the venue's new management had even gone to press. I should have guessed that a connection was lurking somewhere between Chez Moune and the network, because in the world of my promoter friends, party venues were rarely random choices. They were always made based on personal recommendations – adhering to the principle of degrees of separation.

The Hoxtonite network, which was scattered around little urban enclaves at the beginning of the noughties, had become a fully connected global community by the decade's end. The scene was bound by mindsets rather than physical proximity. The geographical distinction became especially irrelevant between London and Paris. No longer a tale of two cities, when it came to networks dubbed hip or La Hype (depending which language you preferred – though within the scene many spoke franglais), Paris and London had become one. Indeed, as JCDC (Jean Charles de Castelbajac) put it: 'London and Paris don't exist anymore. There is one city called Londonparis, [and] the new Métro is called Eurostar.'[37]

Reaching the 'Tipping Point'
The Scene's Consolidation
Rewind for a moment. In our chronicle, 2006 was the year before the storm. Richard's club night Family had ceased to be while at its peak, leaving everyone waiting for the next thing. (This would be a club called BoomBox, the precursor to Ponystep.) At the same time, *Blow's Off-Schedule Fashion Guide* (*Superblow* for a few fashion seasons) became a new magazine called *Super Super*. Part of the same network of Hoxtonites, both the BoomBox tribe and the *Super Super* tribe would cause a big stir. Each tribe had its roots in the off-schedule fashion tradition and in seminal clubs such as Nag Nag Nag and (particularly) Kashpoint, which marked the incubation phase of the second-generation Hoxtonites. Each tribe took shape during the maturation period of the scene, between 2004 and 2006. The trend reached its peak in 2007, (just as Cool Britannia had ten years before).

In 2007, both the BoomBox and the *Super Super* kids hit the headlines big time. Although use of the word 'kids' suggested that there was a new youth culture out there (and that's certainly how the media spoke about this new phenomenon from east London), the tribes associated with BoomBox and *Super Super* (specifically the nu rave fad) were clearly a product of the second generation's subculture. Each set-up brought with it new individuals who went on to do their own clubs patronised by youngsters, which is how the scene spread from the nucleus and gained energy. However, the leaders of the tribes who formed the nucleus were still Generation X (in terms of mindset and age) or borderline Generation Y (in age, but adhering to the X mindset).

Let me put this in the historical context of subcultural evolution to make this point clear (as it is fundamental to the overall hypothesis of this book). If we look at punk in the late 1970s and the new romantics at the turn of the 1980s, the latter had been around during punk but were too young to 'officially' go to clubs and gigs. In that sense, new romantics didn't come out of nowhere but they evolved from punk, and were clearly inspired by it. However, they went on to form a distinctive subculture of their own with a new set of values (use of synths and self-conscious hype) and aesthetic sensibilities (music and look), which then crossed over to form a global trend. As such, they were a reaction to punk just as punk had been a reaction to the overblown and corporate rock culture of the early-to-mid 1970s. When ravers came along, they were reacting to the new romantics, who had by then sold out (playing the star system and wallowing in 1980s excess by wearing designer suits, producing lush music videos, drinking champagne and dating supermodels – a new concept – who famously didn't get out of bed for less than £10,000). Ravers dressed down, became anonymous and bypassed elitist club door policies by moving to fields – until they too sold out, and along came the second-generation Hoxtonites seeking an alternative to the mega club and superstar DJ.

With the third-generation Hoxtonites, this reactive model doesn't apply. The third generation is part of the second generation's evolution and its formation coincided with the commercialisation phase of the second-generation scene. Exponents of the third generation were labelled as hip, for sure, but by the time they came onto the scene – as prominent individuals or collectively, under the umbrella of BoomBox or nu rave – the scene had lost its cutting edge. This does not make the individual perpetrators less hip. It is just that the third generation came about as the second-generation Hoxtonites' scene reached maturity. Like it or not, the scene had, by then, been discovered by the commercial world – albeit the more adventurous brands and agencies, who were ready for a new story. Things could not be kept underground for long.

More importantly, if the trajectory of hip happenings relied on the practitioners being the first to know, then the third generation did not bring about a new set of values. The third generation did not rebel against the second (why would they – they were the same scene). This means that third-generation Hoxtonites took for granted the 'street and chic' ideology of the second generation and they adopted its means of communication (events, collaborations, the hip circuit), and even operated in the same postcode. What happened, though, is that the third generation evolved into a new, cool package – a commercialised version of the second generation (and fully endorsed by it). The rise of the third-generation Hoxtonites was therefore the culmination of a trend rather than a whole new raw subculture with a new ethos that challenged all that the scene had previously patronised. It was the Hoxtonites' 'tipping point'.

The third generation's rise coincided with a market need for new ways of communicating the cool factor to the mainstream. The luxury brand sector needed an image refreshment to counter the detrimental reputation it had acquired thanks to the 'nouveau riche'. The cool youth sector was desperate for a new 'street' thing. Dance culture, rap, graffiti and skateboarding had all reached the point of commercial overkill. Even manufactured pop starlet Avril Lavigne was singing about a 'skater boi' in the pop charts. Things could not get any more mainstream. Both sectors (luxury and youth) would resort to Hoxton as the one significant source of cool.

Younger and more commercially savvy than the second generation, the third generation was ready to oblige. Parallel to this, key characters from the second generation were turning to more commercial enterprises. In fact, the second generation would have a major influence by harbouring the third and managing its commercial success. There was no discontinuity between the two generations, let alone rupture. It was the same scene: the BoomBox strand ran direct from the 'Mandi clique' while the 'Michael clique' led to nu rave.

The rise of the third generation also coincided with a new technological development: the advent of Web 2.0. From then on, pressure on anything creative would be high, as the discovery of the latest thing happened faster. This, in turn, meant that if there were something new, there would be less time for it to develop. This is also a challenge that faces any future subculture. The second-generation Hoxtonites were perhaps the last true London subculture, as their incubation stage occurred before the advent of Web 2.0, and therefore away from the trend-spotter's gaze. By the time the third generation took shape, self-promotion became the norm. Scenes became platforms for showcasing individuals, rather than subcultural collectives. This is not to undermine the impact of the third generation, but it does raise some ideological issues, which I shall examine in the next chapter.

BoomBox

Described as 'the best weekly party in the world' by veteran London club reviewer Dave Swindells, BoomBox became a real sensation. Swindells' word is not to be taken lightly. When it comes to London's club history, this man has seen it all: from the extreme dress-up of Taboo that shaped trends in the second half of the 1980s to the extreme dress-down of Shoom, the seminal house club, which kickstarted the rave scene in the 1990s. BoomBox, in its own place and time, had a comparable influence on the next generation of clubs. BoomBox only lasted for about 18 months but its impact on the Hoxtonite scene was deep. From this nucleus, it caused a storm among the global opinion-forming network, as news of it gradually spread outwards through hip's concentric circles. The aftershock of such a powerful and fashionable earthquake is often felt for longer than the actual club's life. Ephemera is the essence of a club like BoomBox – by the time everyone's heard about it, it's gone. The impact of BoomBox should therefore also be measured in terms of the opportunities it opened up for its instigators once it had been laid to rest. Even Ponystep would gain its kudos by virtue of being 'the new thing by the guys behind BoomBox'. Off the back of the sensation BoomBox caused within the edgy fashion community, even prestige brands such as Jean Paul Gaultier would want to be associated with the latest hype so as to be on trend among opinion formers.

So what was BoomBox? Ostensibly, it was simply the club night that followed Family. The difference was that by the time it became BoomBox, Richard knew much more about running a club and was developing a network based around his vision. Another important difference is timing. Unlike Family and its earlier incarnation, Golf Sale, BoomBox, when it arrived, came to epitomise the carefree creativity of London's fashion scene at a time when there was renewed interest in the city's extravagant style. As Richard said: 'Everyone wanted to be the first to come.' For all the aura of sophistication surrounding BoomBox, its main attraction was its simplicity: it was a social club in a bar on a Sunday night that drew the arty and fashionable local crowd, as opposed to those who scoured Shoreditch in search of indiscriminate entertainment (at least until word spread). 'Come and be fabulous' was its motto. By this time, a whole dressing-up Hoxtonite scene had sprung up – from the seeds sewn by Kashpoint. (Whereas the Kashpoint crowd had been about DIY sartorial experimentation at its purest, almost bordering on performance art in some cases, the BoomBox dressers were a touch more sophisticated.)

By this point, there was another new wave of young designers directly inspired by the clubs and the off-schedule designers of the early noughties, who had paved the way. By the time the new guys hit the scene, fashion incubators and awards were already in place, the resources of which they benefited from early on in their careers (unlike their predecessors). There was a style known as the 'local designer look', Gareth Pugh being a prime example. The other dominant look was created out of the charity shop dump-bins. Occasionally, there was some nudity, such as bare breasts. This look had been around since Family. A local 'band' called No Bra, in existence ever since the early days of Kashpoint, springs to mind. No Bra was the brainchild of Suzanne, a singer and performance artist, who occasionally sported... no bra. I have also seen her happily wearing a moustache. Even though wearing no bra never caught on in mainstream clubs, it was that kind of free spirit that made the underground experience unique. Other than extravagant clothes, there was a lot of make-up at BoomBox. Many punters made such an effort to paint their faces that they truly became works of art. However, there was not one single dress or make-up style that could be called the 'BoomBox look'. Rather, freaky dressing in general became its identity, coupled with uninhibited behaviour. Impromptu performances would often take place. All of this contributed to the thrill of being there.

The door policy at BoomBox was stringent. It was free to get in but the crew reserved the right to turn people away. If the queue outside got too long, the promoters prioritised friends within it, the regular clubbers who made an effort to dress up and people who could spread the word (obviously, you had to know who these were). It was vital to have the right 'door bitch'. 'Exclusivity keeps them wanting more' became the rule governing BoomBox. Of course, this is also where the dreaded 'Are you on the guest list?' would be asked. The question became synonymous with the absurd rules and regulations imposed by club security, which often got in the way of having a good time. Unfortunately, though, that is the nature of the game once the hype kicks in. On high-profile nights, the process of getting into a BoomBox-branded club could be frustrating. Outside special occasions, BoomBox started to draw 'people who read about it in magazines'. It was not a wannabe club to begin with, but became so owing to the fact that it became the place to be seen. This is why it was killed off at precisely the moment commercial success seemed inevitable.

A Club for the Fashpack

What was different about BoomBox was that it was fashion-led rather than music-led. Contemporary overground clubs were working on the principle that their DJ(s) had pulling power, a mentality inherited from rave's sell-out. These clubs, many based in east London, were the corporate-cool alternative to West End 'celebrity' hangouts. The most credible were the 'muso' parties, such as private events organised by promoters like Ranx. People were coming to these for the DJ's credentials and out of a shared passion for the music (rather than because the DJ was famous), but these parties didn't draw the fashion crowd – people went there to dance. At BoomBox, in the tradition of predecessors such as Kashpoint and Nag Nag Nag where the dress-up crowds first congregated, you could be forgiven for not being able to get down to it because your elaborate outfit might have condemned you to standing with your back against the wall.

Promoting the fashion network was Mandi Lennard's contribution, even though she tended to underplay her role. She talks about her own part in spreading the BoomBox bug with humility, preferring to give credit to Richard. Either way, what is certain is that the two gelled, and shared a vision of clubbing that set a precedent. Already, Mandi had pushed Family. It was only natural that she would do the same for BoomBox, which also happened to come at the right time commercially. BoomBox would become the star of Mandi's portfolio which, you may remember, also included magazines (*Dazed & Confused*, and later *Love*), venues (Bistrotheque), 'it' designers (Gareth Pugh, Cassette Playa, House of Holland) and the hottest behind-the-sceners (Katie Grand and her ilk). This network was the very essence of hip from Hoxton.

It was unusual to have a fashion PR as a club promoter, but why not break the rules? 'BoomBox', however, had no regular mail-out, no website, no MySpace page; it remained as 'Family'. So if you wanted to find BoomBox, you had to type 'family London' into search engines. Unless you were a true Hoxtonite, it was unlikely that you would know that. Frequenting independent record shops, the conventional way of finding flyers for offbeat clubs, did not help either. Instead, Mandi intuitively applied the street and chic aesthetic, which meant that in terms of distribution, totally new avenues were explored. For example, flyers were placed in select fashion boutiques. Ditto with press requests. For press coverage, chic publications were favoured over streetwear and culture magazines – far from the traditional homeland of club cultures. Moreover, there was a 'no camera' policy. BoomBox did not trade on 'celebrity' in spite of the impressive number of famous people regularly attending the club. Any kind of exposure in any type of tabloid press was actively discouraged.

In its heyday, the BoomBox punters were a mix of gay and straight, young and old; men, women and those in between. What the club also managed to do marvellously was to bring the three generations of Hoxtonites together. Wolfgang Tillmans, Sam Taylor-Wood, Roland Mouret, Sophia Kokosalaki, Luella Bartley, Katie Grand, Giles Deacon and Roksanda Ilinčić are just some of the Hoxtonites who were regulars. The thrill of the club also attracted eminent names from the fashion world, including Hamish Bowles, Pat McGrath, Katherine Hamnett, Hedi Slimane, Judy Blame and the late Isabella Blow. 'Celebrities' would also pop by including Naomi Campbell, Natalie Portman, Kelly Osbourne, Siobhán Donaghy... but if there were 'celebrities', BoomBox made them hip (briefly) and not they it. The true stars of BoomBox were the BoomBox 'regulars', the men and women, the androgynous and the transvestites, who all lived to dress up for their weekly dose of carefree flamboyance. Out of that lot, a few names would emerge and go on to have international success in the fashion arena. This eminent third generation of Hoxtonites came to life with a little help from their friends: the BoomBox kids who gave them their underground aura and the second-generation Hoxtonites who had created the platforms on which they could develop. They include designers Gareth Pugh, House of Holland and Cassette Playa, model Agyness Deyn, the resident DJs and the less visible (but equally powerful) behind-the-sceners. The power of the Hoxtonite network is truly visible in the way BoomBox catapulted its clique to international hip iconography.

Gareth Pugh fully benefited from this connection, in that his trajectory to the mainstream ticked all the relevant boxes. In terms of underground connections, Gareth was originally part of an art collective called the !WOWOW!, who lived together in a squat in south London. Matthew Stone was the artist most associated with this concept. The squat lot also included Hanna Hanra and KT Shillingford, both DJs and stylists-cum-magazine editors. Hanna also ran *The Pix* fanzine with DJ and former Blitz kid Princess Julia, who famously appeared in the iconic video for the new romantic classic 'Fade to Grey' by Visage in 1980. KT (now using Katie!) became Fashion Editor at *Dazed and Confused*. Gareth gained his hip kudos via all the relevant hubs, including Kashpoint, Kokon To

Zai and Stefan's Superstore, then became a focal point for the *Super Super* nu rave tribe (including Carri Mundane, more of which in a moment). Gareth flourished through his association with the BoomBox network, which ultimately lifted him to the heights of high-end fashion (from Kashpoint via Fashion East to ANDAM).

Henry Holland burst onto the scene in 2006 with humorous slogan T-shirts making fun of the local fashionista community ('UHU GARETH PUGH') as well as fashion's establishment ('DO ME DAILY CHRISTOPHER BAILEY'). Bailey was the creative director of Burberry. Isn't it great when someone whose endorsement can make a difference finds an in-joke funny? Indeed it was, as Henry's case would prove. Katie Grand introduced Holland to Mandi, and his trajectory was similar to Gareth's: Fashion East in September 2007, followed by a first solo show on-schedule in February 2008, and the New Gen award from the British Fashion Council a year later. This was also accompanied by collaborations with brands and guest appearances on youth TV. In the same year that Henry was printing his T-shirts, his childhood friend and former flatmate Agyness Deyn was signed by a model agency. Agyness too, had support from the Hoxtonite network, including a series of covers for *Dazed & Confused* as well as the cover of *Pop* magazine, which was very high-profile for a new model. Her prestigious Burberry and Gaultier advertising contracts would soon follow.

Music at BoomBox

Dressing up was paramount at BoomBox, but there was of course, also music. The mix was eclectic because the music policy was based on Richard getting friends to DJ but even so, there were resident BoomBox DJs. These were a mix of non-muso types who took to the decks, and 'proper' DJ/studio-producer types. They included the artist Matthew Stone from the !WOWOW! collective, DJ Rokk, Nathan Gregory Wilkins, Colin Toogood and Andrea Gorgerino who initially did the warm-up set and would go on to DJ with Jerry Bouthier under the name JBAG. Jerry was the DJ who had defined the BoomBox sound. Reflecting his own tastes and experiences, pop and disco tunes to make people go wild on the dancefloor were heavily laced with elektroklash. He achieved a distinctive sound through his use of software such as Ableton, and this was replicated live in JBAG's DJ sets or in the studio. The duo became increasingly sought-after by established musicians seeking cool new DJs to remix their material. A JBAG album is also planned at some point.

Born in Marseille, Jerry moved to Paris as a child. A typical member of Generation X, ruled by rock's ideology of authenticity, he grew up listening to English and American records in the era when French rock was still like English cooking. His affinity for London was first developed through his passion for punk and later nurtured by *i-D* magazine, a publication that could only be found in small, independent stores in France. One such independent store was New Rose in Paris (associated with one of the rare French indie labels in the 1980s). Jerry used to wait outside New Rose for record deliveries from London on a Tuesday night, having learnt to avoid Saturdays, when punks would lurk and steal newly bought records from unsuspecting kids. (Incidentally, the other important French indie label at the time was Bondage Records, run by Marsu, the character I introduced when talking about my alternative music playlist on Radio Sarajevo. In this small world, Jerry and I discovered that Marsu was a mutual friend.) Jerry moved to London in the 1990s, inspired by rave. He worked as a DJ and music journalist until he became disillusioned with the scene's sell-out in the late 1990s. He would return to music through discovering Fischerspooner and elektroklash. His introduction to the Hoxtonite scene was via Kokon To Zai, which he frequented for records, subsequently becoming Kokon To Zai's music advisor and DJ. Jerry had met Richard through Sasha (of Kokon To Zai) at a party for YBA Sam Taylor-Wood (Sasha occasionally DJed for her). Jerry became the resident DJ at both Family and BoomBox and would later headline Ponystep with Andrea under the JBAG moniker, as well as work with him in the studio.

JBAG were part of the new wave of DJs who reacted against the cult of the superstar. Their hip status as perceived outside the scene was primarily due to them being part of the underground rather than because they were promoting a new music genre, as had been the case with house DJs. The way the tracks were mashed was more indicative of a personal musical identity than a particular genre, albeit with elektroklash overtones. Opportunities in the music industry beckoned due to their technical skills. However, even the less technically accomplished DJs from the network got DJing opportunities, simply because the BoomBox label could be attached to their names to connote cool.

It was through Jerry that the connection was made with Parisian label Kitsuné. The brainchild of Gildas Loaëc and Masaya Kuroki, Kitsuné (meaning 'fox' in Japanese) is best described as a creative factory. Its main line of business was a record and clothing label, with a graphic studio called Abäke based in London. Masaya primarily looked after the fashion side. An architect by training, he applied fusion thinking when it came to clothing design. Kitsuné was a premium clothing label, focusing on the quality of materials and an artisan's approach to production. Its clothes offered contemporary interpretations of classic designs. It collaborated with the likes of Pierre Hardy, whose work experience included Dior, Hermès and, more recently, Balenciaga, and whose career is inextricably linked to a Parisian network of artisans who service the major couture houses. Kitsuné clothes are sold in their eponymous boutique in Paris – a small, understated shop with no window display. They are also sold at select stores, such as colette and a series of pop-up boutiques abroad. In the true spirit of the second-generation Hoxtonites, Kitsuné embraced the street-and-chic aesthetic and would define its identity as 'not being streetwear'. This point is especially pertinent given that Gildas was among the fathers of French dance music and the French version of street culture associated with it. (He was the artistic director for Daft Punk.)

The Kitsuné music label was a clever response to the music industry's crisis of profitability. Instead of investing time and money in developing bands, Kitsuné became known primarily for producing music compilations with a distinct sound. Essentially, it made the elektroklash sound more palatable to the mainstream by bringing a series of new artists to the fore, combining their sounds with elektroklash classics. A lot of the new music would be dug out of the few remaining independent record stores or by scouting on MySpace. The first Kitsuné compilation was released in 2003. Acts on the Kitsuné label included Digitalism (their first signing) and Hot Chip, whose debut album they produced. Digitalism were later co-signed by the major EMI for global distribution. With the signing of The Cazals, a Shoreditch outfit, Kitsuné would also spend some resources on developing acts. They also released the first maxi for The Klaxons. This was a timely signing, as The Klaxons were associated with the nu rave phenomenon, the next big thing in youth culture as far as the media were concerned. The Klaxons thus became the soundtrack of a scene widely associated with the *Super Super* tribe, although (as we shall discover shortly), there was in fact no connection there beyond marketing hype.

The rise of Kitsuné corresponded with a need for innovation in the youth sector. Music festivals needed new blood. Radio and music television stations also began to take notice. Just as Fashion East was a talent incubator for fashion, Kitsuné became the music equivalent. Gildas and Masaya's image as trendsetters was further enhanced by DJ slots, which brought them on to the club scene and into the field of live events, generating complementary revenues for music sales. Given that London's club scene was more vibrant than Paris' and that the majority of Kitsuné acts were anglophone, it made sense to connect with London's club culture to bring the music to life. The Hoxtonite connection was the perfect opportunity. Gildas and Masaya first started to DJ at Family, and continued to collaborate with BoomBox.

In 2007, the year the Hoxton underground trend reached its peak, Kitsuné hosted BoomBox parties during Paris Fashion Week. BoomBox in Paris was the hottest party of the season among the fashion community. It came right at the moment when the Parisian fashion scene was ready for an injection of new energy. The equally exhilarating second BoomBox party, during Paris Fashion Week in October that same year, was also the launch of the Kitsuné BoomBox compilation CD, mixed by Jerry. This is the musical document that captured *l'air du temps*. Kitsuné would continue to collaborate with Ponystep, starting with the Ponystep launch party in London, mentioned at the start of this chapter.

BoomBox made a huge impact in 2007, not just on Paris Fashion Week, but also on the London Fashion circuit and even Europe's most conservative fashion capital, Milan. The prestigious trade show Pitti Immagine invited a posse of around 50 BoomBoxers to make an appearance there and bring the London flavour, all under the careful supervision of Mandi. For both Mandi and Richard, BoomBox brought further opportunities to stage similar events for luxury brands, and later a series of high street brands and 1990s cool brands. For Jerry, BoomBox was a turning point in his career. To paraphrase him, he was not cool until BoomBox came about. After that, though, opportunities opened up for him as a solo act as well as for JBAG to DJ at fashion shows and aftershow parties at fashion capitals across the globe. No longer was he just DJing for Hoxtonite designer friends; Jerry's list now included Vivienne Westwood, Jean Paul Gaultier, Dunhill, Möet et Chandon and the lifestyle management club Quintessentially. In the music world, a JBAG remix became highly sought after. Kylie Minogue, S'Express and Siobhán Donaghy were among the artists queuing up. Beyond commercial gigs, Jerry and Andrea also travelled the world DJing at underground clubs, meeting people who shared similar affinities, something close to their hearts.

The last BoomBox party was held on 31 December 2007. BoomBox will be remembered as the organic club that charmed its way into the fashionista universe through its friendship-cum-work way of operating. The greatest thing about BoomBox was not the way it attracted 'celebrities', but the way it managed to make its mark on the opinion-forming scene by imposing its own rules and selecting its own people. BoomBox defied the age of 'celebrity', if only for a short while, in that it managed to make rule-breaking and innovation worthy of attention, countering the ubiquitous famous-for-being-famous trend. BoomBox became so hot and refreshing that 'celebrities' were suddenly willing to take a trip to east London to be seen there, a place which had a completely different energy to the glitzy West End hangouts. Inevitably, BoomBox created its own celebrities, for that is how we communicate in this day and age, but its legacy – that it attracted opinion formers by being carefree – will remain.

The Super Super *Tribe*

Super Super magazine broke many rules when it hit the shelves. With a cover featuring a mash-up of images rather than a single dominant one, eclectic layout and colourful content that was a cross between a fanzine, *The Face* and a glossy magazine with a hint of tabloid trash, it was just as well that it was not widely distributed. Strikingly different, it could have alienated the mainstream magazine consumer. Instead, *Super Super* found its spiritual home in independent bookshops, select boutiques and concept stores where sales of the magazine would by far outnumber those made by conventional newsagents (50 to 100 copies sold in a boutique compared to between one and three copies in an ordinary newsagent).

At the beginning, it was also difficult to convince advertisers of its worth. The industry tried to locate *Super Super* in the same bracket as *i-D* and *Dazed & Confused* but remained puzzled and therefore reluctant to take a bite, because *Super Super* clearly looked different. For the first few issues, it was a novelty on the scene, but quickly its core readership crystallised into 12- to 25-year-olds. Advertisers saw its potential in reaching this young demographic. For this group, the magazine became the alternative to the corporate-cool vision of youth culture dominated by 'celebrity'. *Super Super* became profitable within a year. From an initial print-run of around 5,000 copies, *Super Super* expanded into 62,000 copies distributed in 40 countries around the world within two to three years. It is a bi-monthly publication and, at the time of writing, remains independent.

A direct descendant of *Superblow*, the off-schedule fashion guide, *Super Super* was the 'voice of the future', as founder Steve Slocombe said. It was the magazine that *Sleazenation* could have been but never became for fear of taking the risk. When Steve had tried to change it, he got fired. The transitional phase at *Superblow* allowed Steve to experiment and create a vision for his future magazine. At *Superblow*, a publication aimed at the fashion community, Steve had used a mix of contributors including iconic names from the recent past (Judy Blame and Isabella Blow) as well as up-and-coming scenesters. What transpired was that the vibrant new breed had so much to say that there was scope for *another* brand new magazine to focus just on that. *Super Super* was born out of the idea of promoting this scene and its DIY, fun approach to fashion and, more generally, lifestyle.

Super Super was an organic product of the scene typified by off-schedule fashion, Kashpoint and all the usual suspects. Many microtribes proliferated from this network. A new generation of kids would live the scene's ethos; *Super Super* would document it. Like any tribe, the *Super Super* tribe had its leaders. Though he looked the part and lived and breathed the culture, Steve took a step back from the limelight, preferring to leave the prominent role to his associate, former *Sleazenation* pal and flatmate, Namalee Bolle, who acted as editor-in-chief. *Super Super*, just like BoomBox, thrived on the camaraderie of the second-generation Hoxtonites.

The Tribe Leaders

The offspring of a love affair between two penpals – a Dutch man and a Sri Lankan woman in a situation that could have easily been a movie – it was perhaps no surprise that Namalee would grow up to be a leading lady and a natural in the spotlight. After falling in love through their letters and first meeting in Sri Lanka, Namalee's parents eventually settled in Guildford, in London's commuter belt. Unfortunately for the imaginative Namalee, Guildford was no Hollywood. As a teen, she dreamt up Technicolor scenarios to escape the dullness of suburban life, which uneventfully unravelled in black and white. Her favourite Christmas presents were back issues of *The Face*, which she would savour for weeks. She avidly read Julie Burchill, a British journalist with a punk attitude and great fondness for feminist politics, whose career began at the iconic *New Musical Express*. Namalee was also fascinated by club flyers from the early 1990s, inspired to try to envision what this alien, yet enticing, world might be like. A defining moment for her came in the form of a gift from a boyfriend. It was a copy of *i-D* magazine (hard to come by in Guildford) featuring a mixed-race girl on its cover (the first she'd seen). The vivid image of that 'hardcore, sexy girl in trainers and the word "ragga" beneath' stuck in Namalee's mind. This was inspiring for a mixed-race kid growing up in an overwhelmingly white community.

Being both different and the rebellious kind, Namalee spent her teen years refusing to conform. Naturally curious, she questioned everything. At school, this did not always go down well and at times resulted in her being called into the headmaster's office, a serious offence for one brought up to respect institutions. Aware of her daughter's penchant for trouble, Namalee's poor mother decided to enrol her on a course at the Surrey Institute of Art and Design, hoping that she'd channel her anger into creativity. Namalee studied fashion promotion and illustration. She continued to rebel though, questioning assignments, an attitude that was not necessarily conducive to getting good grades. She eagerly embraced subcultural literature, which sealed her anthropological interest in fashion. She combined this with an equally keen interest in other aesthetic forms, especially cartoons and jewellery. These elements laid the foundation for her future interest in expressing her identity through fashion, which she would also apply in her professional role as a stylist. (In stark contrast to 1990s minimalism, *Super Super*'s creed was 'maxi maximalism'.)

Namalee first encountered the Hoxton set-up around 1998, the hangover period of Cool Britannia. When she moved to London, she immediately went in search of *Sleazenation*, the street magazine that she had (surprisingly) discovered in Guildford. It was 'rude, direct and amazing and taking the piss out of cool culture'. She loved it. She joined the team and worked in fashion editorial. Simply by being in east London, she connected with the Hoxtonite community and later met most of the future *Super Super* crew at Kashpoint. Like Steve, by now the editor of *Sleazenation*, she related to the underground scene, increasingly believing that the new direction for the magazine should come from there. Trying to replicate that energy in editorial, however, did not go down well. 'I suffered for my beliefs,' Namalee recalled when I quizzed her. 'Carri [Mundane] also walked around and people laughed, but now, the whole world is looking like Carri.' Indeed, the editorial style that would give rise to maxi maximalism and eventually nu rave (which Namalee and Carri would be crowned the queens of) was too cutting-edge for advertisers to see its potential.

Carri Munden, nicknamed 'Mundane' at university by her friend and fellow student Philip Normal, is the designer behind the Cassette Playa label. Carri and Philip met at Westminster College in London. They noticed each other as they both stood out. Philip thought that Carri 'looked like a pixie'. Carri thought that Philip 'looked like a weirdo'. Carri modelled for Philip's first show at college. Their friendship, based on a mutual love of neon colours, cyberculture and music, developed from there. Outside of college, they typically hung out on the second-generation circuit (by now, you know the tune). They both graduated in 2003 and, for a short period after graduation, became the duo 'Normal and Mundane'. The name was the ultimate irony as their style couldn't have been further removed from normality or mundanity. However, this was not the 1990s cool marketing use of irony. In the words of Philip: 'It wasn't a joke. We weren't trying to be funny.'

Unusually for aspiring fashion designers, Philip and Carri happily worked as stylists. Their first assignment was styling the then-unknown Pete Doherty (just starting out with The Libertines) for *Superblow*. They never actually designed together but presented their early work as that of a duo. After graduation, they showed their clothes for two seasons at Kashpoint's Off-Schedule in 2004. When *Super Super* was launched, Mundane and Normal were part of the core team. Carri was given the title of 'fashion editor-at-large' while Philip became the 'fun fashion editor'. Philip went on to develop a fashion line that he still sells at Camden Stables market, preferring to stay on the sidelines of the mainstream fashion industry. An oasis of unique pieces amid a sea of mass-produced fashion, Philip's little shop stands out and is doing quite well. He sells his own designs as well as stuff by friends.

Unlike Philip, Carri did play the fashion game, albeit with her rebellious streak. While still at university, Carri had an unconventional vision as to how she'd express herself as an aspiring fashion designer. The early noughties, when she was a student, were still dogged by 1990s-style categorisation. You were either a designer, a stylist (which was still not widespread as a vocation at that time), a fashion buyer or a model (no degree needed for that one). If you also aspired to use the medium of film or to DJ, then it got really confusing. The idea of a multidisciplinary career was embryonic. Fortunately, Carri had a supportive tutor in Zoe Broach. Zoe was one half of the design duo behind Boudicca, one of the funkiest off-schedule labels at the time. Coming from an emerging east London set-up, Zoe realised Carri's potential as the scene headed towards fusion and encouraged her to 'build her own world'.

Cassette Playa, Carri's label, was a product of that fusion. When it was launched (in February 2005 at Stefan's Superstore) it had a unique aesthetic inspired by influences from the Hoxtonite scene, but its identity was also shaped through collaborations with various individuals from the creative industries, especially musicians and select brands. In the world of the fashion industry, Cassette Playa is now positioned as one of the Hoxtonite 'street-chic' labels. This means that Cassette Playa commands a premium price and is stocked in concept stores such as colette in Paris or Dover Street Market in London but also in select street boutiques, including Kokon To Zai. In Fact, Marjan Pejoski's catwalk show was the first that Carri ever attended and it set the tone for what she aspired to. The two sporadically collaborate through Marjan's diffusion line KTZ. The acceptance of Cassette Playa by the fashion establishment has had a lot to do with its endorsement by the most credible incubators. Cassette Playa made its official debut in September 2005 with Fashion East, as part of the brand-new initiative called MAN, aimed at showcasing new menswear designers on London Fashion Week. Cassette Playa did showcase there for four seasons while being part of Mandi Lennard's portfolio of clients. Endorsement by the right network of people combined with underground connections at the right time meant that Cassette Playa made it big: this happened in 2007, the year the establishment all wanted their own piece of edgy Hoxton.

Alongside Cassette Playa the label is the role that Carri herself has played in driving the new look, which, as Namalee said, led to many Carri clones. There was indeed a time when Carri looked strange when she stepped outside the Hoxton clique (where everyone looked weird). She wore baggy T-shirts, leggings (before American Apparel made them retro-chic), denim hotpants, trainers, chunky jewellery (a combination of plastic and fake gold) – and all of this in fluorescent colours and eclectic prints. Coupled with her trademark fringe, long Barbie-doll hair and 'spazzy specs' (as dubbed by *Super Super*), her look could not have been further away from what was sold as cool on the high street. Her 'spazzy specs' are clear-glass spectacles in a large plastic frame. They are not quite the Cazals that Run DMC used to sport; neither are they the nerdy black-framed glasses associated with geek chic. They are more like Clark Kent's (though Carri would not count Superman as an influence, it's the best I can do to convey the image, unless you are British, in which case think Su Pollard). From being considered 'weird', within a few years, spazzy specs would become a must-have accessory.

In isolation, Carri's look might have remained her own. However, with the launch of *Super Super*, it became instrumental in shaping their signature style. By the second half of the noughties, there was a whole underground scene of dressing up, which was not yet reflected in the mainstream. Other than BoomBox, which left its own legacy, what made the scene truly vibrant was the series of clubs that flourished after Kashpoint. They brought the scene to life and expanded the network outside the original inner circle to include a new generation of followers.

All You Can Eat, Antisocial, Nuke Them All, Calling All Tribes and Gauche Chic are just some of the ephemeral club nights from this period, each with their own charismatic tribal leaders. This universe would be the inspiration for photoshoots in *Super Super*. Being one of the main stylists for the magazine, Carri started picking up on items from the pool of Hoxtonite designers and dress-up clubs that fitted with her Technicolor cartoonish vision. Then she'd accessorise the looks with her specs. Namalee did the same with her own aesthetic, giving it her own colourful edge, and so did the other contributing editors.

The Nu Rave Fad

Though these looks were wildly eclectic, there was method in the madness. Although there was, by no means, a single look that could be described as the *Super Super* look (just as there was not one definitive BoomBox style), a dominant trend did get picked up by the mainstream: baggy trousers and T-shirts, colourful trainers, cartoons, glitter and sequins, coloured-in faces, plastic toys, baseball caps, heavy 'neckbreaker' necklaces, a lot of neon and the 'spazzy specs'... This was combined with *Super Super*'s own street lingo. For example, the word 'new' was spelt 'nu'; 'trends' as 'trendz'; 'specs' as 'spex'; and so on. Last but not least, there was the *Super Super* logo: a yellow smiley face with dark circles around the eyes. The idea behind it was to connote the mixture of influences on *Super Super*, or the 'mashing up' of influences (not to be confused with how the term 'mash-up' is used on mainstream radio stations such as Radio 1, which the underground scene not only dissociates itself from but defines itself against – 'Radio 1, what is that?', Philip Normal raised his eyebrow). *Super Super*'s logo was not neon glow-in-the-dark yellow, but it was a smiley, just like the rave symbol of the late 1980s.

Next thing, the media started to talk about 'nu rave'. This became the hottest youth trend, even though there never really was a true nu rave subculture. Ironically, the scene from which nu rave unwittingly sprang was a dress-up scene specifically reacting against the 1990s dressing down spawned by the likes of rave. Nu rave was not about house music. It was not an Ecstasy culture. The only apparent connections were the smiley logo and the term 'nu'. However, this trend emerged at a time when the mainstream youth sector desperately needed a new story. Nu rave coincided with the commercialisation of the second-generation Hoxtonite scene. It co-opted the third, more youthful generation of Hoxtonites of which *Super Super* was the nerve centre. Nu rave essentially became the reductionist marketing label that picked up on the hype and use it to sell a cool new (life)style to the wannabes (early majority) in the marketing circles. In the nu rave scenario, *Super Super*'s smiley logo became nothing more than an empty signifier of cool used to sell a look devoid of meaning. It did not signify what the scene was about at all (unlike the smiley that had signified rave in the late 1980s and all the moral panic surrounding it).

Every style needs a soundtrack, and somehow – mostly through the music press and mainstream music radio – The Klaxons and Simian Mobile Disco became the kings of nu rave. There was no organic connection between those bands and the underground scene but who cared? It was selling records. We know that Kitsuné (The Klaxons' and Simian's label) established its link to the Hoxtonites via Jerry Bouthier, Family and BoomBox to form a longer-term partnership, rather than basing the relationship on the fad of nu rave. But nu rave was the necessary trigger that helped sell this elektroklash-based genre to the mainstream chart buyer. By the end of the decade, new acts had emerged within this genre, such as Lady Gaga and La Roux, but they had no authentic connection to the scene, other than perhaps borrowing clothes from the PRs, notably Michael (of Blow), via their stylists (some of them Hoxtonites, depending on the act).

Parallel to the nu rave hype in Britain, there was the phenomenon of 'fluo kids' in France or more precisely, Paris. Just as in Britain, this was to be a short-lived fad. It was based around five or six blogs that came about (with Web 2.0 – the process of crossing over was now speeding up). The most obvious was the blog Fluokids. What was spectacular about these crazes was their swift rise and the way the commercial brands threw themselves at them. There had been a desperate need to inject something new into the youth sector. Suddenly, anything branded 'fluo' commanded a high fee. Casper C, one of the bloggers, would later become a DJ and get gigs off the back of that trend.

The other tribal leader was Pedro Winter. Former manager of Daft Punk, and the man behind the label Ed Banger, Pedro was commercially experienced and truly grounded within a subculture, rather than the superficial hype of nu rave. Essentially, the Daft Punk clique created what may be called French rave culture, with influences that broadly include British rave, Chicago house, early 1990s warehouse parties, grunge and skateboarding. Pedro's career fits into the hip model of crossing over from the underground into the mainstream by paying your dues. He therefore knows a thing or two about entrepreneurship premised on mixing work and play, for he is a product of subcultures that defined the 1990s cool marketing. Daft Punk truly brought some innovation into the music landscape in the 1990s, not just in France, but globally. Pedro – he DJs under the name Busy P – would benefit from the fluo craze.

However, just like his friend and former partner at Daft Punk, Gildas from Kitsuné, Pedro realised only too well the importance of a real underground club connection. He saw that this real connection was in London, not Paris. Parisians are simply not as bonkers as Londoners; the free spirit of London's clubs is second to none. Pedro connected with BoomBox via DJ Mehdi, a high-profile signing on the Ed Banger label, whom Richard once invited to DJ at The Hoxton Bar and Kitchen. Realising that BoomBox was the hip place to be, Pedro subsequently contacted Richard. Justice (signed to the Ed Banger label) later DJed at BoomBox – for free – before releasing their single 'D.A.N.C.E.'. This became one of the greatest hits of the summer of 2007, winning them two MTV Europe Video Awards that year. This was followed in 2008 by Grammy and MTV Award nominations in the US, a market notoriously resistant to music imports in general, and dance music in particular. Pedro regularly popped by to DJ at Ponystep and became a regular during the same club's Paris residency. Together with Kitsuné, Ed Banger created the second wave of La French Touch in this period.

Like everyone else concerned, *Super Super* went along with nu rave. The media hype helped shape the magazine's credibility in the mainstream. With headlines such as: 'Responsible for shaping virtually the entire nu-rave fashion scene' (*Independent on Sunday*), it would have been foolish not to go with the flow. In 2007, the year of the 'tipping point', just as BoomBox had come to signify hip in the world of high fashion, *Super Super* became the cool voice of the next generation. From 'driving the next wave of youth culture in the UK' (*International Herald Tribune*) to being 'simply the most exciting and influential new youth brand in Europe' (brand manager of K-Swiss), *Super Super* was hot. Luckily for them though, they did not believe their own hype based on nu rave, because if they had, their lifespan would have been considerably shortened. By the end of 2008, nu rave was already over.

Luckily, there was something beyond nu rave, albeit less bombastic. The style and music promoted by *Super Super* simply reflected the network of connections and personal tastes of the magazine's contributors. In terms of overall style, *Super Super* was above all, a product of off-schedule designers whose work would later become the highlight of London Fashion Week and even Parisian catwalks. The street-chic ideology was by now simply taken for granted. There was no questioning whether or not it was part of high fashion – it was. The original designers from the scene whose pieces had been instrumental in creating *Super Super*'s colourful and upbeat feel included Basso & Brooke, KTZ, Noki, Tatty Devine, Ashish, Manish Arora, Gareth Pugh and Christopher Kane, to name just a few. The off-schedule look was intertwined with street style (in clubs or day to day), for the two were originally all part of the same network. This was literally a matter of: one day you wear your mate's clothes and next thing you know, Madonna wants it or Beyoncé buys the whole capsule collection at Top Shop (which is what happened to Ashish, the designer friend that people on the scene most associate me with). The *Super Super* style also incorporated an element of sportswear in a more explicit way. Up until then, the scene had sneered at sports brands but now it was OK to bring them back – with a twist.

At the same time, another important influence from the world of high fashion was Jean-Charles de Castelbajac. A visionary designer who mixed pop art, cartoon art and street art with high fashion, he produced some of the most iconic fashion designs of the 1970s and 1980s. His aesthetic provided an inspiration for many key figures from the scene. Namalee discovered his work in the early noughties and did a feature about him for a British magazine at a time when he appeared to be forgotten. A few years later, it was Carri's turn to befriend him; a rapport that first developed through MySpace. They later met on a photoshoot in preparation for Castelbajac's 2007 retrospective exhibition 'Gallierock' at Paris's Fashion Museum. This photoshoot was done by über hip photographers Tim & Barry. By then Castelbajac had adopted his street name, JCDC. This was the way London's grime scene, another crew genuinely fascinated by his clothes (without necessarily realising that he was a 'proper' designer on Paris Fashion Week), referred to him. London's edgy scene loved JCDC and he loved them back. The exhibition described at the opening of this book goes some way to explaining why JCDC commands respect on the scene. In spite of his success in mainstream fashion (he even had a major retrospective at the Victoria and Albert Museum) JCDC remains genuine, connected to his street roots, uncompromising in his designs and constantly in search of new challenges. This mutual respect and admiration worked out to everyone's advantage. JDCD brought cachet to up-and-coming talent. It return, he gained a new generation of youthful followers. Everyone parties together!

Grime

The connection between Grime and the *Super Super* crew is a good case study for my main hypothesis, namely that you need a hip authenticator in order to be accepted by the mainstream industry. Grime was a movement from east London first spotted around 2002. It had a hip hop attitude but it was British – its musical origins lay in 1990s jungle and drum 'n' bass and the UK garage scene from the turn of the millennium. The main exponent of grime became the Mercury Prize-winning Dizzee Rascal. Despite the award, Dizzee didn't achieve huge mainstream success at the time, in 2003. Grime had potential – and it was indeed often cited by the disillusioned fathers of street culture as being the one interesting new youth culture that they felt excited about – but somehow it never really crossed over. Instead, it became ridiculed as the music of petty adolescent criminals, disparagingly referred to as 'hoodies' or 'chavs'. This was accompanied by headlines about crime and violence, which was enough to scare the brands off. Ironically, grime was not a violent culture at all. It was, in fact, a reaction to ostentatious UK garage culture (which had indeed been associated with a series of shootings). The UK garage outfit So Solid Crew was particularly scrutinised, but they came from a different scene to Dizzee. Back then, he'd been a 19-year-old kid rapping on pirate radio and at rave parties about his day-to-day council-estate life. He did not have access to the elitist UK garage clubs.

The arrival of *Super Super* contributed towards changing the perception of grime. The connection between the crews, to use the jargon, was organic. Steve and Namalee had already had dealings with Dizzee at *Sleazenation*, which was the only magazine that put him on the cover when he won the Mercury. Another link to the grime scene came through Carri. She first met Chronik and Tempa from the Slew Dem Crew (from east London) through the photographers Tim & Barry. Like Carri, they had modelled for JCDC. Another link was through JME, founder of the grime record label Boy Better Know (BBK), whose co-founder was Skepta. JME modelled at Carri's first catwalk show. BBK, in turn, were mainly associated with Roll Deep. One of the founding members of that crew was grime artist Wiley. Wiley liked to sport Cassette Playa. Carri also styled a video for the grime crew Ruff Squad, of which Tinchy Stryder is a member.

When *Super Super* burst on to the scene at the same time as BoomBox they further boosted London's hip reputation by getting exposure at Paris Fashion Week; it hosted a launch party for online fashion network IQONS. *Super Super* would also subsequently do two seasons at London Fashion Week, sponsored by MySpace. For that occasion, they supplied goody bags that included a CD, which was heavily skewed towards grime. This mutual endorsement meant that the mainstream media was now prepared to accept the grime package as cool. Youth culture needed a new style-and-music combo. Nu rave's fad had been short-lived; grime, by contrast, had a proper grounding. It subsequently became big in the mainstream UK charts, with Dizzee, Wiley and Tinchy Stryder having a string of chart-toppers in 2008 and 2009.

However, *Super Super* was not a grime magazine. Aside from grime, the musicians initially featured in the magazine were Hoxtonites including Patrick Wolf, Bishi, Paloma Faith, The Noisettes and Mathangi (Maya) Arulpragasam (better known as M.I.A.). It was a mixture of looks and music styles, but they all had a personal connection with someone from the scene or were themselves part of it, with looks heavily influenced by Hoxtonite designers. Rather than being 'grime', 'nu rave' or any other label, *Super Super* is a magazine about being the first to know. It adopted the ethos of the second-generation Hoxtonites and translated it for mainstream youth culture. The *Super Super* universe was no longer either/or, black or white, high fashion or street fashion, but a mash-up of different elements, subjectively filtered in order to distinguish what was hot from what was not.

INFLUENCE ON THE STYLE INDUSTRY
In Search of the New Black

The style industry's cyclical search for 'the new black' began afresh when innovation ran dry. When fashion was in need of a new story, all eyes turned to London, the eccentric fashion capital neglected by fashion's big hitters during the first half of the noughties. By that time, London's underground scene had matured into a hub where radical ideas thrived. Here, prominent characters and more specific talent-incubators would emerge. With the ever-growing interest in the Hoxton scene, coupled with its constant growth, these platforms would transform radical underground styles and practices, once perceived as anti-establishment, into something more palatable for the mainstream fashion industry.

The underground influence is visible in the way both high-end and high street fashion adopted underground idioms. In this context, there were two main strands of influence: on the one hand, the British Fashion Council focused resources on turning London's unique position as the most diverse and creative fashion city into a brand. On the other, the street influence was 'directional'. This meant that it shaped the overall trends found in mainstream fashion stores.

The BFC and London's 'Edgy' USP

The British Fashion Council (BFC) was established in 1983 as a non-profit organisation in charge of representing, promoting and otherwise supporting British fashion. This included the orchestration of the bi-annual London Fashion Week. Traditionally, London Fashion Week was predominantly a west London affair, associated with the world of high-end fashion. The East End had no 'high' fashion until the rise of the second-generation Hoxtonites (except, perhaps, for Alexander McQueen, an Eastender initially working in Hoxton Square). In the first half of the noughties, the style division between west and east London still operated, but the fashion establishment was growing curious about the eastern commotion.

The BFC has always been partial to new talent. As early as 1993, it set up a sponsorship scheme called New Gen (as mentioned earlier) intended to act as a launch pad for new designers. New Gen was awarded in the form of a cash sum to be used to fund a catwalk show at London Fashion Week, together with free usage of a central venue and a free stand at the London Fashion Week Exhibition, the main BFC-endorsed trade show. The fashion year always runs a season ahead: when the winter collections are about to appear in stores, next summer's outfits are appearing on the catwalk, and vice versa. A New Gen designer either got sponsorship for the catwalk show, the static exhibition or both. The New Gen sponsorship scheme was usually awarded for a few fashion seasons; an average of three but never exceeding four. New Gen winners from the 1990s who went on to enjoy international success included Antonio Berardi, Clements Ribeiro, Julien Macdonald, Matthew Williamson and, last but not least, Alexander McQueen, who received the New Gen award in 1993, its first year. Interestingly, McQueen only received support for the static exhibition rather than the catwalk show, which might have been part of the reason he chose to stage his own DIY off-schedule catwalk.

In 2000, it was the turn of Marjan Pejoski to receive New Gen. He pretty much stole the show straight from graduation with what 'eyewitnesses' remember to this day as the most weird and wonderful display of extravagance. Marjan's catwalk show was more of a conceptual performance than a traditional fashion runway show. Björk's notorious egg-laying swan dress emerged from this early period of Marjan's work. Other prominent New Gen recipients from 2000 include Boudicca, Sophia Kokosalaki and Maria Chen's self-titled but now-defunct label. Maria was among the first designers from the radical new wave to be offered a creative director's role at a chainstore (All Saints), thus signalling the early beginnings of the mainstream's interest in this rising generation from the East End.

Maria's case is symptomatic of the predicament designers found themselves in. The problem of having to balance enormous creative drive with equally enormous business pressures did not go away, with or without New Gen. Creative accolades and publicity are one thing – running a business is another. In the vast majority of cases, designers are not salesmen, but new designers can rarely afford to take someone on to fulfil that specific role. A situation then occurs (endemic in London) whereby select British fashion schools – which many consider to be the best in the world – coupled with the cyclical emergence of energetic, experimental club scenes, tend to produce talent with the ability to break rules and set new agendas. This, in turn, means that a London-bred designer can be catapulted into the media spotlight and generate the same interest from fashion buyers as the established high-end brands, but without any comparable infrastructure to back them up (whether to produce and distribute collections or to pay for advertising in magazines). This was why many of London's star alumni either suffered serious setbacks (like Hussein Chalayan and John Galliano before him) or simply disappeared, unable to withstand the multi-layered pressures of having to deliver a collection every six months. Alternatively, they had to reluctantly give up their own collections and settle for full-time employment, as in Maria's case.

However, in the noughties, this situation started to change for the better. In this context, the BFC took a proactive role via a new strategy specifically designed to ensure these situations would no longer occur. This change was prompted by the rise of the second-generation Hoxtonites or, in other words, the 'young designer' phenomenon. As mentioned previously, the term 'young designer' (like YBA before it) was coined to refer to the new wave of designers who embraced the Hoxtonite spirit. It was more than just a label, though. It was obvious that this new generation, for all its striking eclecticism, shared an ethos and an overall aesthetic.

Off-Schedule became the hub for this new entrepreneurial breed of fashion designers, who were very much embedded in punk's DIY tradition.

They formed a collaborative and mutually supportive international network on the margins of mainstream fashion where they could all thrive. For example, if you took Marjan Pejoski in isolation, you could say it was just another label, albeit radical, like McQueen or Galliano. However, what you also had was Kokon To Zai. This was a multifaceted concept that included a boutique, where other similar designers were sold. There was also a synergy with underground clubs, a link to music movements (elektroklash, as well as emerging artists from the scene) and a relationship with arts and DIY crafts (new talent within the same aesthetic, such as avant-garde artist Franko B, as well as YBAs). Other designers/street boutiques functioned in a similar way.

Alongside the inventive individuals on the scene, there was a new breed of maverick businesses such as Blow PR, Mandi Lennard, Lulu Kennedy and an array of other individuals and small companies, shaping the rules of the scene or adhering to them early on. Initially, for little or no money from clients' fees (thus having to think how else they might get funded), they provided the important aspect of development that young designers needed but could never afford through a mainstream PR. Equally importantly, there were spaces like the Truman offering cheap rents. There were magazines like *P.U.R.E.*, *Tank* and *Flux* (based in Manchester but fully embedded in London's Hoxtonite scene) that were very much part of the network, who would start promoting this new wave. Last but not least, there was the support of scenesters who had made it following the first-generation Hoxtonite hype (in that they were now employed by luxury houses). For example, Katie Hillier moved to designing accessories for Marc Jacobs but she remained a friend and collaborator of both Luella Bartley and Henry Holland. Behind the scenes lies an intricate web (and that's where the opinion-shaping power is).

By the time the third-generation Hoxtonites emerged, the Hoxtonite model was already in place. This lot were neither interested in Zara nor Prada for their own careers as designers. They wanted to break the rules. They all went to Kashpoint and the nights that emerged in the wake of it. They all worked or congregated at Kokon To Zai, Victim and the like. They were all inspired by conceptual catwalk shows such as Marjan Pejoski's. They all had a tip or two from the likes of Michael, Mandi or Lulu. By 2004 (the beginning of the maturation of the Hoxton scene) it was becoming increasingly evident that a new energy was bubbling up and that it was worth taking notice of it.

With this in mind, the BFC put into operation a new scout initiative specifically aimed at unearthing talent from this new wave. A team of three, later reduced to two, began to operate as talent-spotters. Andrew Tucker, a fashion writer and lecturer and key contributor to *Blow's Off-Schedule Guide* was paired up with Sarah Mower, a British fashion journalist specialising in cutting-edge fashion, who wrote for two of the most prestigious fashion publications, American *Vogue* and style.com. Originally, there was also Yeda Yun, the buyer for London's renowned fashion boutique Browns Focus, but she relocated to Italy when offered a buyer's job at Prada. All this goes some way to showing how the hidden influential types grew out of the original nucleus of the second-generation Hoxtonites' scene.

In the first year of this new scout initiative, designers Giles Deacon and my good friend Ashish Gupta were discovered as 'hotshot' new names from the buzzing Hoxtonite fashion scene. They were both awarded the New Gen and subsequently became key designers on London Fashion Week's circuit. As we know, Giles had been part of the of the Hoxton clique since the early 1990s, though he later lived abroad while working for high-end French and Italian labels, before returning to London around 2002. Ashish, back then, was in Blow PR's portfolio. Both he and Giles are Central Saint Martins graduates. The recognition of Giles and Ashish came to symbolise what was hailed as the exciting beginning of London's comeback as the most innovative capital of fashion.

Other talent initiatives were subsequently created, all dedicated to discovering and fostering new talent in some way. Each contributed to what became London's brand of the most innovative fashion capital. This organic network of talent hubs comprised Fashion On/Off (in 2003), Fashion Fringe (2004) and Vauxhall Fashion Scout (2008). On/Off and Vauxhall Fashion Scout offered low-cost venue solutions for new designers. Fashion Fringe was a talent competition set up by fashion historian and writer Colin McDowell in conjunction with the sports and entertainment conglomerate IMG, which launched the career of Erdem. In September 2009, Blow PR added its own preview of coming attractions on London Fashion Week, called 'Blow Presents'. There would not just be 'pure' fashion designers but also related talent, such as Charlie Le Mindu's hairdressing catwalk. In November 2009, the BFC announced the launch of the *Vogue* Designer Fashion Fund to provide support for designers in the UK. All of these were welcome developments that took place in stages from the mid-noughties to cement London's position as a unique breeding-ground for talent.

In spite of some crossovers between the various initiatives, they tended to be mutually cooperative rather than collaborative. According to Sarah Mower, who was appointed by the BFC in 2009 as Ambassador for Emerging Talent, a stacked system will most likely be put in place over the coming years. Alongside talent-fostering initiatives, The Centre for Fashion Enterprise was established as a mentoring scheme, providing workspace and professional consultants for fashion designers on the London Fashion Week circuit. This centre was set up in recognition of the need for London-bred designers to turn their style agendas into viable business strategies. Basso & Brooke, Erdem, Marios Schwab, Richard Nicoll and Manish Arora are just some of London's internationally recognised designers who have benefited from this scheme.

In the developmental stage of the Hoxtonite scene, by far the most influential incubator became Fashion East, the talent hub located in the Old Truman Brewery. In 2003, Fashion East received sponsorship from Top Shop and was transferred 'on schedule'. This coincided with the maturation of the scene. Between 2004 and 2006, this platform was the place of discovery for a new wave of designers emanating from the Hoxtonite scene, who rose meteorically to international fashion fame. Around 80 per cent of New Gen winners came out of Fashion East, including Jonathan Saunders, Marios Schwab and Gareth Pugh, all now star international designers. With its credibility growing exponentially with every fashion season, Fashion East became a key destination for fashion professionals during Fashion Week. Not only would they get three designers showcased for the price of one, as it were, thus saving valuable time in hectic schedules, but they also knew they were not wasting their time. In September 2005, MAN, an initiative to raise the profile of menswear designers, was launched in partnership with Fashion East and the high street chain Top Man. Fashion East was reassuring in the sense that the designers showcased there were likely to at least stick around in the industry, if not actually become future stars.

It was increasingly evident that London had more to offer than passing eccentricity. In 2005, the BFC itself went through a restructuring process. Aside from a revision of its own book-keeping, it developed a strategy in tune with London's USP, which was essentially 'young designers'. London Fashion Week became a self-supporting event. At the same time, the BFC began to concentrate resources on becoming a sales and marketing strategy nerve-centre – a resource that upcoming designers had lacked. From then on, efforts were concentrated on building London's young designers into a brand. London by name, cosmopolitan by nature: cutting-edge innovation, always part of London's identity, directly related to its street fashion and subcultural heritage, was to be formally acknowledged. The world's fashion elite would start to take notice of London.

An immediate result of the BFC's restructuring was the launch of the Fashion Forward initiative in 2006, the year before the underground trend explosion. This scheme took the form of a substantial cash prize and access to business mentoring. The aim of Fashion Forward was to provide much-needed funding and professional advice for designers who had already built up a reputation in the field to take them to the next stage of expansion. At this crucial phase of career development, where there is a buzz about a designer, hype often is higher than the funds to deliver on the promise; it is difficult to reach a position whereby the business of an independent fashion designer is sustainable. For this reason, a cash injection is needed. The first two recipients of the Fashion Forward award were previous New Gen winners Giles Deacon and Jonathan Saunders, followed by Jens Laugesen, Jonathan Saunders, Richard Nicoll, Roksanda Ilinčić and Sinha-Stanić. The next wave of recipients were Christopher Kane, Erdem and Marios Schwab, who received the sponsorship for three consecutive seasons.

The year 2007 in some ways echoed the Cool Britannia of 1997. London was seen to be at the epicentre of creativity once again. New names that emerged from the maturation period of the scene went on to gain international recognition, including Jonathan Saunders, Christopher Kane, Marios Schwab and Gareth Pugh. Their pulling power for London in this buzz year was coupled with the presence of a good number of high-profile designers who had built up their careers during the incubation and maturation stages of the scene's development, as well as the household names from previous generations, all showing in London. To add extra élan, 2007 also saw the return from New York of Luella Bartley, who has subsequently remained in London, and Matthew Williamson, who decided to celebrate his tenth anniversary also at home. This celebration came with a bonus: music was provided courtesy of none other than Prince, who emerged from his hiding place in the front row to surprise the audience with a live performance. A year later, Vivienne Westwood, who had long-since absconded for the runways of Paris, began showcasing her Red Label collection in London. Though somewhat more modest than Prince, her choice of DJ for the catwalk show nevertheless represented a nod to Hoxton: none other than Jerry Bouthier, who went on to play at all her shows and aftershow parties internationally. Their connection was organic: Murray Blewett, Westwood's personal assistant of over 20 years, was a regular at BoomBox, where Jerry was the resident DJ.

On-Schedule in London in 2007, the 'tipping point' year, was a far cry from the impoverished incarnation of the early noughties when home talent sought asylum on international runways. London even experienced a trend reversal, in that it was not just the Brits returning home – the Yanks were coming with them. Marc Jacobs decided to launch his younger collection, Marc, in London. This was accompanied with a store opening and party. Essentially, Jacobs' choice of London over New York for his younger line meant that London was not just cooler than any other fashion capital, but it was simply the coolest place on Earth. Jacobs pulled in eminent names who would not ordinarily have been seen in London. Perhaps it was just hot gossip, but rumour also had it that the godmother of fashion, American *Vogue* editor Anna Wintour, flew in just to see Gareth Pugh's spring/summer 2008 show in September 2007. No longer did the devil wear Prada, it seemed London events were now back in the fashion elite's diary, rather than being non-events that 'everyone skipped'.

To cap it all, in December 2007, the British Fashion Council received a substantial cash injection from the London Development Agency (LDA). This was long overdue under the Labour government, especially as they'd come to power on the basis of their Cool Britannia credentials a decade earlier. While the YBAs had benefited from the Cool Britannia hype in terms of governmental grant schemes (see *Lucky Kunst*), fashion (especially street fashion) remained a footnote, despite its contribution towards London's status as a global fashion attraction. Its contribution to the overall perception of the UK as a creative place was finally recognised through the LDA's three-year funding package. Reminiscent of the days when Britpop bands went to Downing Street, it was now the turn of the fashpack to toast their achievement with the country's leaders. This was to celebrate British fashion (a term referring to any designer based in London, regardless of their national origin) and the BFC's 25th anniversary in 2009. The festive mood continued after the party. The summer of the jubilee was marked by a series of announcements about high-profile designers 'returning to London' from international runways for September's Fashion Week, notably Jonathan Saunders, Burberry, Matthew Williamson, Pringle and Clements Ribeiro. (It should be noted that the governmental organisation UK Trade and Investment has also participated in supporting the BFC, which notably contributed toward setting up the initiative London Showrooms.)

Essentially, London Showrooms is a pop-up trade showroom in Paris, used during Paris Fashion Week and first tested as a concept in 2008, then replicated the following year. The Showrooms are under the supervision of Anna Orsini, the BFC's Head of International Relations and a long-serving executive. A vastly experienced fashion sales strategist, Anna's background in bridging gaps between cutting-edge designers and relevant fashion buyers goes back to the 1980s, most notably through her work with Belgian designer Ann Demeulemeester. Demeulemeester is part of what is known as the Antwerp Six, a group of avant-garde designers who pushed the boundaries of fashion in the 1980s. Anna and Ann remain friends and business partners to this day, a synergy that the initiated eye can spot in Anna's understated but effortlessly chic personal style. In simplistic terms, the idea of a showroom for young designers from London in Paris was intended to generate sales that they would not otherwise achieve.

In the context of this story, the BFC-endorsed showroom acted as a chasm translator. The main client of any trade show is the fashion buyer, probably the most risk-averse link in the fashion chain. To get the buyers' attention, a designer needs proof that s/he is a viable investment. Publicity itself is not enough. From a buyer's point of view, being under the patronage of the BFC indicates that the designer on show is unlikely to fail to deliver his or her order (by going bust or missing deadlines, for example), which had happened in the past and contributed towards London's unfavourable reputation. From the designer's point of view, access to trade shows in Paris is expensive and selective. Simply having money does not guarantee access to a stand. For example, the prestigious Tranoï operates exclusionist policies. The alternative is to be part of an independent showroom, but more often than not, such showrooms do not attract the elite of the fashion business.

The showroom excursion from London to Paris during Paris Fashion Week is like a compromise between building London as a fashion capital and respecting the established ways of fashion business, where Paris has the upper hand. In terms of business (ie collection sales), a fashion professional could be forgiven for bypassing London but one cannot bypass Paris. This goes beyond anecdotal evidence into the hard reality of the fashion business, where buying patterns have been established for years and are unlikely to change in the near future. Couture fashion is by definition Parisian; it is where the heritage is. The fact that the largest luxury fashion groups – LVMH and the Gucci Group – are French (or Franco-Italian) also plays a part in the Parisian fashion monopoly. The big buck remains in Paris and the big-brand big-budget contracts are brokered in Paris. Any other fashion spending comes after these big contracts have been fulfilled. The other large business centres are Milan, where many prestige Italian houses tend to operate, and to some extent New York. The buying is done over the short period of a few days during Fashion Week at the many trade shows. Competition for buyers' attention is huge. With the BFC's endorsement and the power behind that institution (for the BFC is after all, the official ambassador of British fashion) the London Showroom was able to attract some of the most prestigious buyers and press, as well as help generate sales for all the designers featured. Most of the designers there increased their amount of orders and opened new buying accounts.

Rendez-Vous Showroom in Paris

Notwithstanding all the positive and welcome efforts of the BFC in the Parisian fashion market that would otherwise not have been available to young London designers, there is another showroom whose role deserves to be acknowledged in this context. In fact, following my line of argument about being the first to know, that particular place is where it was originally at. The real risk-taker when it came to chasm-translation between the underground and the mainstream fashion business was the seminal showroom called Rendez-Vous. In the early stages of development of the Hoxtonite scene, you can see how access to Paris would have been like vaulting a mountain. Rendez-Vous was the first to attempt getting over that obstacle. Set up in 2004, after a few tentative attempts under another name a few seasons earlier, Rendez-Vous was a trade show specifically for 'young designers' of the second-generation Hoxtonite kind, not just from London, but from anywhere. However, London was the key source of this new breed of talent. A partnership between two scenesters, Nic Jones and Jérémie Rozan, Rendez-Vous was one of the early chapters in the developing tale of the two cities, London and Paris.

Waving the British flag was Nic Jones, a Shoreditch regular before his relocation to Paris. His fashion background manly involved working with the hip label Vexed Generation at the turn of the millennium. Vexed Generation were associated with very distinctive couture-like sportswear and combat gear combined with highly original cuts as well as stories behind the clothes. They were among the original second-generation Hoxtonite cutting-edge labels, making clothes that were political. For example, their 'shark coat' was a response to the government's proposed bill to tackle public disorder by installing more surveillance cameras on the streets. This jacket had a hood that zipped up all the way up to the eyes, rather than stopping at the neckline, thus masking the wearer. Vexed Generation were also one of the early labels to adopt the fusion approach to fashion, where clothing was just one element. When it came to hosting some good, fun events, I remember them collaborating with *P.U.R.E.* and creating some truly exciting noise about the new underground.

Jérémie Rozan, the French half of Rendez-Vous, used to run a street boutique in Paris called Surface to Air, as recommended to Rachael and me when we went boutique hunting for Cast Off in Paris. Surface to Air in its original form had been a soulmate of the London street boutiques, incorporating arts, fashion, events and an open-minded collaborative approach to projects. What I called fusion is what Surface to Air referred to as 'multidiscipline'. Their attitude was an alternative to the mainstream Parisian fashion retail landscape, but akin to places such as colette. Unsurprisingly, Jérémie loved the idea of the knitting club and he took on Rachael's ragdolls. We loved the shop in return.

Surface to Air grew into a 'multidisciplinary' creative hub. Nowadays, it can be mapped on to the same collaborative-cum-competitive landscape as Kitsuné. Surface to Air diversified into clothing design (with mono-label boutiques in a number of cities across the world, including a Parisian base), communication consulting and film and video production. Their greatest claim to fame, at least in terms of the buzz it generated, was the music video for Justice Vs Simian's 'We Are Your Friends', directed by Jérémie. This clip is as famous for its artistic merit as for the controversy surrounding Jérémie's acceptance speech at the MTV Europe Music Awards in 2006, when Kanye West stormed onstage to complain that he should have received it instead. In 2008 Kanye remixed Daft Punk's 'Stronger' into a global chart hit, without realising that there was a connection with Justice through the Ed Banger label. (Remember, Pedro Winter used to be Daft Punk's manager before he set up Ed Banger records and signed Justice.)

The trade show Rendez-Vous was born out of a need to provide a sales platform for new designers in the fashion business capital. Set up in Paris during Fashion Week and offering relatively affordable prices for stalls in comparison to other trade shows, it quickly became a hit among young designers. What was unique about Rendez-Vous was that it respected the rules of the scene, not least because Nic and Jérémie were scenesters themselves. This meant that it was a 'curated' trade show rather than one that applied rigorous professional rules. This open-minded – or multidisciplinary – approach allowed for a range of talented designers to expose their work. Having a party to launch and close the event was *de rigueur* – the unwritten rule of the Hoxtonite scene is to always have an event to celebrate something new. Rendez-Vous thus functioned as a networking opportunity as well as a place for friends to hang out.

By its organic nature, Rendez-Vous attracted the hidden influencers of tomorrow, be they future star bloggers or indeed those who would one day decide to tell the tale in a book about being the first to know. The second-generation Hoxtonites and their equivalents from other cities across the world came out in force, from the Amsterdam-based deluxe knitwear brand KIND to the Sydney-based art collective The Kingpins, both personal favourites whom I count among my friends. The Kingpins I met at Rendez-Vous, while Mr and Mrs KIND were another connection through Blow PR; my friendships, nurtured via constant globe-trotting, are typical of how this network operates. Rendez-Vous also attracted the hipsters from previous generations, who thrived on the independent spirit it embodied, such as regulars Antoni & Alison or even Jean Charles de Castelbajac, whose marvellous cartoon-vision extravaganza stand I spotted there next to Antoni & Alison in February 2008. Instead of hectic selling and buying, Rendez-Vous became a showcase experience that other showrooms would later emulate.

Initially perceived as a risk, Rendez-Vous grew into what the industry often now refers to as the leading 'directional' trade show. For the professionals who visited, it represented reduced risk due to its selection policy, which had grown stricter. From the buyer's point of view, a designer at Rendez-Vous, though radical, had potential longevity and would deliver their order on time and in agreed quantities. It also saved them time, as a one-stop-shop for the new and edgy; they no longer needed to search for showrooms scattered around Paris. Rendez-Vous grew bigger over time and, inevitably, became more professional. Some designers defected to other showrooms but Rendez-Vous is still going strong. In 2009, it set up a showroom at New York Fashion Week, thus expanding its network across the Atlantic, as well as globally via an online trade show that same year. Of course, there are other showrooms during Paris Fashion Week for 'edgy talent', now including London's pop-up showroom, but Rendez-Vous is still among the more high-profile ones (read 'safer') as far the mainstream industry is concerned.

Of interest here is another trade show that operates within the cool bracket, called Bread & Butter. This was another case of party people deciding to do a trade show. Its original location in Berlin (after a short stint in Cologne) was perceived as funky in the early noughties. At first it attracted some of the Hoxton scene, not least because they invited 'cool' people like Mei Hui Liu to showcase there and paid for her trip. However, as Bread & Butter developed, its orientation moved towards streetwear, which was not the Hoxtonite aesthetic. In 2005, Bread & Butter moved to Barcelona. On the scene, this show was perceived as a 'jeans and trainers' one. In contrast, Rendez-Vous was 'street and chic' just like the scene, and located in Paris, which is where the high-fashion industry operates. As we know, the Hoxtonite scene was more akin to high fashion, a world within which they were forging their own space of identity, rather than streetwear, which became a byword for corporate cool. There was not a deliberate boycott of Bread & Butter. It is just that it was not very relevant. As it happens, it was not as cool either, because when it comes to being a step ahead, the world of Rendez-Vous (representing Hoxtonites and La Hype) was where a number of jeans and trainers brands started to fish for cool once they needed a new story (I shall look at some examples in the last section of this chapter). Bread & Butter would buy into the Hoxton cool, too. For example, in 2009 they collaborated with *Super Super* on a Berlin-based event. They got the cool image association, and *Super Super* got a physical presence in Berlin, where the brand had not done any events before. However, when it comes to sales, the prominent third-generation Hoxtonites, notably Cassette Playa, go to Rendez-Vous, leaving Bread & Butter as a potential avenue for any future diffusion lines.

Sustainable Fashion

Finally, in terms of leading-edge initiatives that emanated from London Fashion Week, there was eco fashion. In 2006, the BFC launched its eco/sustainable initiative, called Esthetica. Esthetica was a division within the main exhibition hall entirely dedicated to eco fashion. It was curated by Orsola de Castro of the eco label From Somewhere, which she co-founded with business-partner Filippo Ricci. Orsola had been part of the Hoxton scene in the build-up to Cool Britannia. But by the time she started her label, she'd moved away from east London to cater for the upmarket media types of Notting Hill and the Primrose Hill set, who were less edgy than the Eastenders. Orsola's passion and true commitment to sustainability played a huge part in setting up Esthetica, but From Somewhere was not directly part of Hoxton's hip circuit, post Cool Britannia. When it came to boosting the eco trend Hoxton-style, the scene's ambassador was the pioneering label Junky Styling.

Back in the day, Junky Styling were very radical, just like the rest of the Hoxtonites. They were known as 'the bunch who turned jackets into trousers'. Needless to say, from the outside they were perceived as yet another weird lot from Hoxton rather than the precursors of a trend that would influence the fashion establishment. Unlike an ordinary fashion label, Junky Styling was more of a holistic concept. They adopted the second-generation Hoxtonites' fusion approach. Clothes were the main aspect of Junky Styling but music had always been a big part of their aesthetic and so was the attention to visuals, such as the design of promotional materials. The main designers were Annika (Anni) Sanders and Kerry Seager, coupled with a loyal and long-serving team including David and Eric (operating more backstage) and Coco and Krt (on the frontline). Pop around to the Junky Styling shop at 12 Dray Walk, Truman's Brewery, just off Brick Lane and you are bound to meet at least one of the crew on the shopfloor.

What made Junky Styling unique in the incubation period of the second-generation Hoxton scene was the way they were breaking rules, not just in fashion production (through recycling) but also with their overall attitude. In true punk DIY style, nothing was impossible. Armed with a small bank loan and the idea of producing unique outfits for people who did not want to bump into someone in the toilet queue wearing the same thing, their journey began. With no formal qualifications in tailoring, Junky Styling invented their own style by re-cutting clothes rather than devising patterns. The result stood out. It had the feel of streetwear but it was made out of 'proper' suit fabrics, not least because they recycled classically tailored suits. With no boutiques to stock them initially, they started to sell in a cubicle-sized stall at Kensington Market before moving to their permanent home in Dray Walk in July 1998, making them among the earliest denizens of the Old Truman Brewery.

Their early catwalk shows were collaborations at Rendez-Vous and later at Kashpoint's Off-Schedule Battles of the Boutiques during Fashion Week. These shows were a riot. Friends turned up to have good time, whistling and cheering in the crowd, while the models paraded. Then everyone stayed for a party. Junky Styling has since become an established label on London's fashion circuit but a contingent of friends still attends the shows, though possibly now outnumbered by fashion professionals. This also means that the friends now behave relatively respectably, only cheering if male models take off their shirts. Also interesting about Junky was that their models included non-professionals. They cast women and men from a broad age spectrum as well as those of unconventional sizes, way beyond the dreaded size zero. The growing publicity that Junky Styling was getting as an underground outfit also contributed to their becoming ambassadors for sustainable fashion. They celebrated a decade in business in 2009, with the publication of their book *Wardrobe Surgery* in which they share their experiences and give tips for making new garments by recycling old ones.

In February 2009, the Sustainable Clothing Action Plan was introduced within the BFC, aimed at raising awareness and commitment regarding the negative impact of 'throwaway' fashion. Some 300 large companies, ranging from high street retailers to manufacturers, came on board seeking to make positive changes in the environment as well as the workforce in worldwide fashion. As Orsola rightly pointed out, these 'board level' decisions were necessary in order to have a wider impact on production and conditions of labour, as opposed to the small independent labels' decisions to recycle. This action plan was supported by the Department for Environment, Food and Rural Affairs (Defra). The recognition of the eco agenda is perhaps one of the proudest legacies of the second-generation Hoxtonites' movement, for it was at least partly influenced by the nurturing of the 'craft' set of values governing this scene and the commitment of individual labels such as Junky Styling.

Directional Trends

The second strand of the scene's influence on mainstream style is the way it became 'directional', providing a source of inspiration at the first stage of product creation. Basically, the designer needs to be inspired. Something needs to trigger his or her imagination and they then take this in a more focused direction to create a season's collection. The creative process in fashion design can also be looked at through the lens of risk. The more innovative a design, the more risky it is perceived to be and vice versa. More conventional may be less risky, but is in danger of being boring. Most mass-produced fashion operates somewhere in between. It aims to be fresh (so that the consumer wants to buy something new) while finding methods to reduce risk (if it is too different from what the consumer is used to, it may not sell). With this in mind, broadly speaking there are two approaches to fashion design: the creativity-led approach and the trend-led approach.

The wave of new designers emanating from the Hoxtonite scene would all fall into the first category, the creativity-led approach. This did not mean they operated in a vacuum, but that they tended to follow their instincts. They produced what they liked and hoped that their customers (buyers and ultimately people wearing their designs) would like it too, rather than producing to be on trend. The small boutiques and concept stores all shared this relatively risky approach, and so a kinship between them developed.

The trend-led approach is about minimizing risk. The industry of retail fashion design – as with any corporate brand industry competing in a busy market – relies on different types of consumer-focused research to best manage risk and deliver an image both desirable to the target audience and, ultimately, profitable to shareholders. For example, when Levi's designed the engineered jeans to reverse their falling sales, they followed consumer research cues to get a sense of creative direction. To satisfy the need for this consumer-focused research, an industry of fashion trend-forecasting developed, catering for the design teams within clothing retail companies. Fashion forecasting was not a novelty but over the last decade, it has almost grown into a science.

As fashion became 'disposable', with new designs being churned out at an increasing rate, inspiration still had to come from somewhere. This is where companies such as WGSN come in. They hunt for trends around the world, so that you, the designer, don't have to. It is all there at the click of a mouse. Their business model principally relies on online subscription to their service, which gives access to a large pool of data. Not only did such trend forecasters become relevant at the first stage of garment production – providing inspiration, but they also forecast into future seasons. These directional guidelines for various stages of garment design into the future are put in a broader context of lifestyle and consumption trends. Finally, their online search filters are intricate and targeted at various positions within the retail industry (a creative director will not be looking for the same trend cues as a junior designer) as well as different sectors of the industry (knitwear designers will favour different online services than shoe designers).

So far, so good. Problems start, though, when all brands subscribe to the same forecasting services and plainly follow the same directional guidelines. If everything is served on a plate, complacency – the enemy of creativity – sets in. From the second half of the noughties onwards, a crisis of innovation occurred. It was increasingly difficult to differentiate between the various brands on the high street, as looks were becoming uniform. This created an opportunity for the hipsters to fill a gap, but before looking into this, I want to highlight the case of Top Shop, a high street brand that took a well-educated risk by associating itself with Hoxtonite fashion. Ultimately, this creative risk afforded this brand a market-leader position in its category, as well as gaining them a 'cool brand' accolade from the Cool Brand Council. Competitors in this category are brands such as the Spanish Zara and the Swedish H&M.[38] Both are cases of local brands, which expanded globally by rolling out a model of fast-paced production of trendy clothing.

The Case of London's Top Shop

To better understand what made Top Shop's approach original, let us look at what Top Shop was not. The majority of high street brands in the first half of the noughties, including Zara and H&M, embraced the popular trend of delivering designer looks – as worn by celebrities on the red carpet – at affordable prices. As the number of celebrities grew to include all the reality-TV contestants and the number of awards ceremonies grew to celebrate just about anything, there were plenty of opportunities to be 'papped' (photographed by paparazzi). Female consumer magazines and related websites satisfied their readers by providing ready-made looks from high street stores that emulated high-end fashion. Weekly gossip magazines did the same. New online retail businesses such as ASOS.com (an acronym of 'as seen on screen') built their brand entirely on selling replicas of designer wear at a fraction of the designer price.

Around the mid-noughties, one-off collections (known as capsule collections) by high-fashion designers for high street brands became all the rage, as the proposition of delivering designer items at affordable prices proved very attractive to consumers. H&M were among the first to use this as part of their sales strategy. The first collection was Karl Lagerfeld's in 2004, a model then replicated using other designers. Capsule collections by high-end designers for high street chains became the norm. As a rule, capsule collections would sell out instantly amid rumours that these exclusive pieces could fetch higher prices than designer 'bargains' on eBay, thus feeding a micro-industry of fashion touts. Extending this principle beyond fashion, 'affordable luxury' became a common way of generating significant sales in the mass market. Examples include Manolo Blahnik's shoehorn for Habitat or Evian's festive water bottles (which they sell over Christmas and New Year in select markets) designed by the likes of Jean Paul Gaultier, Christian Lacroix and Paul Smith. Though technically not a novelty (in 1987 the French pasta company Panzani commissioned Philippe Starck to design pasta shapes) the resurgence of this type of alliance between the high street and high-end designers responded to the more general consumer trend of 'trading up'.[39] Over time, celebrities began to lend their names to capsule collections, such as Lily Allen for New Look or Beth Ditto for Evans.

Top Shop, however, started to think differently and became a trendsetter on the high street. Instead of red carpets, Top Shop scouted the dirty streets of Hoxton. At the same time, it started to forge a partnership with the British Fashion Council. As early in the development of the Hoxtonite scene as 2002, Top Shop became the sponsor of the New Gen award. In 2003 (for the 2004 season), Top Shop extended its sponsorship to Fashion East. In 2005, it added its support the new fashion initiative called MAN, the collaboration between Top Man and Fashion East. Parallel to this, Top Shop introduced the 'boutique' concept to its flagship Oxford Circus store in central London – a space where young designers' collections were sold, cheaper than their catwalk collections. Anything that was hip, Top Shop would do: whether that was introducing a vintage section or talking to the knitting club (a project we decided not to do but Top Shop was nevertheless looking to capitalise on this trend early on). As Hoxtonites upgraded from 'young designer' to the very happening and respected, Top Shop created a category called 'designer' where esteemed Hoxtonites (for most part past New Gen winners) create capsule collections. (At the imminent start of London Fashion Week February 2010, the last fashion season before this book goes to print, the designer collections in store are those by Ashish, KTZ, Jonathan Saunders and Ann Sophie Back.) Top Shop also employed cutting-edge designers as creative consultants. All of this contributed to the store building a hip image.

This is not to say that Top Shop had underground kudos – it didn't. It is a corporate brand and so, by definition, cannot have street kudos. In fact, many young designers felt aggrieved that Top Shop scouts were appropriating their designs without payment. They felt vulnerable, especially at the incubation stage of the scene's development, when it was still only partially in the spotlight. For every commission to produce a capsule collection for Top Shop, there was a lot of free picture-taking, as it were. Another practice that created resentment among young designers was that of buying one outfit, only for the buyer to deconstruct the pattern and then mass-produce it. This 'borrowing' particularly affected designers who made one-offs or limited ranges and sold those unique garments in upmarket or street boutiques for premium prices. Once these garments were available on the high street for a fraction of the price, that started to negatively affect both the young designer and the small boutique, who would struggle to compete. Because of this, a number of hip designers refuse to collaborate with Top Shop, although they are increasingly in the minority as market forces are simply too strong to fight against. If Top Shop seeks to collaborate, the answer from the vast majority of designers is 'yes please'.

From a brand-positioning perspective, Top Shop deserves credit. In comparison with its peers (or competitors), Top Shop was edgy and alternative. Top Shop took a creative risk by associating itself with the Hoxtonite scene, which subsequently put it in a brand-leader position. It was undeniably delivering a trendy product, which earned the brand a good reputation among opinion formers, who shopped at Top Shop and put it on a par with a designer labels. Through word of mouth, even foreign creatives on a trip to London would go to Top Shop for edgy outfits at decent prices. This edgy association is what made Top Shop's reputation. Much of this was attributed to brand director Jane Shepherdson, who had joined the company in the late 1990s to reinvent its image – and did a great job.

Street Style Blogging

The street-led trend that would later spread into the mainstream once it needed a novelty injection was the phenomenon of style-scout blogging. It began around 2006, with the rise of social networking sites and blogs, became very popular in 2007 and was all the rage by 2008. It simply involved the posting of photos taken on the street of interesting-looking people. 'Street style' is not a new trend. It can be traced as far back as the school of photography pioneered by the Seeberger brothers in the early 1900s when they started to take photographs of elegant women on fashionable promenades in and around Paris. This type of sartorial reporting is cyclical. The British style press of the 1980s (*The Face* and *i-D*) forged their 'alternative' identities using this principle. While *Vogue* was all about the catwalk and high fashion, the street style shots were showing what people were wearing on the streets or in clubs. In the 1980s, when the world of high fashion had no connection with street fashion, 'street style' in the hip press was truly a revelation. Youth magazines of the 1990s, such as *Sleazenation*, also worked the theme. The first half of the noughties was obsessed with 'celebrity' fashion. And when 'celebrity-look-fatigue' struck, it was time for street style to return. A new breed of bloggers emerged with a good eye for spotting alternative dressers whose looks had the potential to cross over into the mainstream. These shots, posted daily on the blogs, acted as indicators of future trends.

Nowadays, if you take a stroll down to hip neighbourhoods such as Shoreditch, you can see dozens of scouts walking around with cameras, snapping fashionable dressers. Hordes of young people happily oblige, dressing up in the hope that they'll be spotted. On the scene itself – for, unsurprisingly, the old-settler Hoxtonites do stand out with their styles – there is a reaction against this trend. Should a scout ask you for permission to take a photo (which many do not), the tacit understanding is that you'll say no. The reason for this is that they may wish to take your photo for the purpose of ripping off an idea or for a third-rate blog that no one wants to be on.

Only a few years before, you might happily have posed because the odd style scout's interest in your look was a celebration of individuality as well as a free advert for the designer you were wearing. (Alternatively, they may have been working for Top Shop!) Around this early period, a few bloggers started to generate a sizable number of daily hits. Communities formed around their blogs, with visitors regularly posting comments and creating stories. Among these bloggers, a handful stood out. The most high-profile were The Sartorialist and Facehunter, both part of the first-to-know nucleus. The Sartorialist, Scott Schuman, is based in New York but is respected by Hoxtonites worldwide.[40]

Facehunter – aka Yvan Rodic – is a Hoxtonite.[41] He was the guy always present at the right parties. His trademarks were 'spazzy spex' and his camera. He took photos of punters and in exchange gave them his tiny card that stated only his blog's address (he'd started blogging in 2006 – and it goes without saying that he stopped wearing the specs when the trend took off). Though a lone hunter, he burst on to the scene when the Parisian contingent of the third generation was forming. His was one of the blogs that got noticed as part of the new wave of Parisian-based agitators, together with the multidisciplinary collective Andrea Crews, the party-documenters Laperolog and bloggers such as Uglysmile or indeed Fluokids. This Parisian third generation of 'Hoxtonites' very quickly connected with the second generation to form the wider network that would become La Hype. Due to the focus of his blog, Facehunter moved to London, the home of street style. By now, remember, London and Paris were different postcodes of the same super-city that used Eurostar as its Métro. Initially, taking pictures for his blog was a passion on the side, which he subsidised with a job in advertising, but he soon dropped the day job in favour of full-time face-hunting. Within the space of a couple of years, this type of blogging had taken off, and

Facehunter was a household name in this micro-industry.

With the rise of Facehunter, The Sartorialist and the like (there are literally hundreds of such websites but only a handful of them are high-profile), ordinary people wearing extraordinary clothes became an inspiration for those who did not wish to follow models on a catwalk. Hip was no longer about 'celebrities' but about style blogs. Consequently, designers within corporate brands began to turn to these blogs for style cues. Once again, it was about chasm translation. Bloggers with the most hype and therefore the most credibility eliminated risk (providing directional guidelines) and saved time (scouting the streets for you). Today, street-style shots are the norm, whether on *Vogue* online or at a professional trend agency. Out of this street-scouting trend, the 'cool' look that combined high street fashion with a piece of designer wear and something vintage became hip (referred to at times in the press as 'the trilogy'). By now, you were catering for the high street consumer. The high street items signified great design, affordable price and disposability – so you could change them often. The designer element equalled cachet. If you couldn't afford the real deal (or a good fake), there were also now fashion designers' high-street capsule collections worth queuing for. Then there was the cool that came from vintage. It was no longer about rummaging through charity-shop stock in the hope of finding the item you wanted, though, because it had all been selected for you (and presented undamaged, ready-to-wear).

What were once simply called 'second-hand clothes' (and the ultimate cheap clothing) were instead labelled 'vintage' and could command a higher price. Vintage was no longer about rare old clothes or the imperfect rejects found in charity shops that you might turn into your own with a bit of tender loving care. It was also no longer the choice of the select few, as vintage stores were now located in hip urban areas on the tourist trail. You even found it in high street shops as other chains followed Top Shop's lead. Namalee from *Super Super* springs to mind, shaking her head in despair as she spotted what looked like a 'vintage' section in the mass-market chainstore Primark. 'Vintage' was used to label their own disposable fashion items from a couple of months before (or something like that, in their fast world) which they'd charge a fraction more for. Through overexposure, the word 'vintage' became drained of meaning. First formed by a tight-knit community of lovers of bygone eras, vintage trade fairs went big. In 2008, Paris introduced Le Salon du Vintage, the only type of trade show it had previously lacked. In 2009, one of the two main vintage trade shows in London went mass-market with a stand at Clothes Show Live, the UK's biggest fashion fair.[40] Milan never really caught this bug, always preferring brand-new designer wear, but a 'vintage workshop' was launched there in 2005, mainly aimed at the design industry for research purposes rather than the general public.

Parallel to style scouting ran opinion blogging, essentially written by those who were the first to know. They acted as authenticators of what was hip and worthy of attention. Among them, the much-respected blogger Diane Pernet deserves a mention. Once a designer herself, Diane lived and worked in New York City in the 1980s. Leaving the city and her fashion-design career behind, she decided to move to Paris. She thought New York in the late 1990s was a 'sad place', with high levels of homelessness and crack addiction. She turned to fashion journalism and filmmaking instead, as well as becoming an early blogger. A passionate spotter of emerging talent, and possessing a keen drive to democratise fashion, Diane's daily blog about hip events and people from all around the world also served as a window into fashion for people outside the metropolis. At least, that is what Diane hoped for. In a similar spirit of exchange, IQONS is an online social networking community dedicated to talent-promotion across the board, ranging from fashion designers to photographers, with a global reach. Diane was among its founding team.

Whether opinionated or with a good eye for spotting stylish people on the street, bloggers themselves became a source of cool. As ever, hip was premised on knowing stuff before anyone else, which came from being with the right people in the right places. As knowledge grew, the bloggers offered scope for hip image-building. As they started to form communities and receive more and more hits, the most high-profile ones also began to attract advertising revenue. At the same time, bloggers in person started to provide the cool-factor for brands, who would seek events-based collaborations with them. This neatly leads us into the effects on the communication industry.

INFLUENCE ON THE COMMUNICATION INDUSTRY
The 'Curated' Event and the 'Hip Circuit'

The interest of the mainstream communication industry in the underground scenes coincided with a crisis of innovation when it came to communicating the cool-factor. In a climate where brands had to pay increasingly more for increasingly less consumer attention, brand communication began to focus resources on getting free media coverage. This meant redirecting some investment from costly advertising and focusing instead on tactics that would get you press attention. With this in mind, brands (brand managers or their agencies) began to turn to underground events and to seek scenesters who'd provide the hip element to act as a press hook. Scenesters were getting a lot of press without even having to pay for a PR.

The scenesters' conquest of mainstream brands came about through their being solicited by established communication agencies to work as the cool arm on specific client briefs. Or else, they set up their own small communication agencies (usually somewhere between event management and PR), thus bypassing the middlemen and taking corporate budgets away from established communication agencies. Finally, some people from the scene were directly employed in brand marketing clientside (meaning they worked for the brand) on cool credentials alone. We have already seen how the Hoxtonites became purveyors of cool for image-building and how their influence was visible in the style industries. What remains to be seen is how the communication industry more generally adopted subcultural idioms, just as the guerrilla-style marketing once employed by scenesters became the cool marketing of the 1990s, and subsequently spread beyond the cool-brand sector.

The origins of the new cool communication were in the 'curated' underground event of the early noughties, which was a reaction to the branded mega club and superstar DJ (and their colossal fees). The underground scene began to adopt another kind of entertainment away from the mainstream's attention, whether it was dress-up clubs such as Kashpoint in London, or private parties such as those organised by La Johnson in Paris, or indeed Cast Off's knitting parties and other themed events. Common to all these events was the way they acted as promotional platforms for new talent as well as networking webs for the similar-minded. These occasions attracted the non-conformists who rejected compartmentalisation within the established worlds of arts, crafts, fashion and the in-between industries. At the same time, the concentration of alpha trendsetters at those parties would in turn attract opinion formers. This is where the commercial value of such gatherings began to germinate.

Initially, the scenesters themselves solicited the interest of brands. This scene was not hostile to branding, but rather than indiscriminately seeking money at any cost, it was more a matter of trying to do things on your own terms. Essentially, you needed a brave and bold brand manager to become your partisan within the corporation. So, if you were Cast Off looking for a commercial partner, you wanted to work with someone who understood the spirit of Cast Off rather than someone who wanted to play it safe by doing an ironic advertisement about the knitting club because knitting was hyped as cool. It was in search of funding for events that the word 'curator' began to creep into the second-generation Hoxtonites' vocabulary to convey the fusion principle to outsiders. In the underground definition, a curator is someone who fuses seemingly eclectic elements (products, artefacts, networks of people) into a coherent theme for a one-off occasion. This is how a word traditionally associated with museums – and thus (perhaps unjustified) dullness – assumed hipness. The curator began to act as a 'chasm translator'. The curator's kudos became an asset in reducing the risk-factor to which the industry is so adverse. The curator became the person who could guarantee the right hip crowd both by separating the mediocre from the hot (choice of showcased talent, including DJ) and by having the right network of contacts (access to the right scenesters).

Emulating the underground, the mainstream industry started to use the word 'curator' to signify hip. For example, the music festival Bestival no longer simply listed the acts on the bill. Instead, the festival was 'curated', as the magazine advert pointed out. Put like that, the word 'curator' became a signifier of distinction. It told you that Bestival, the intimate festival with carefully selected acts, was cooler than Glastonbury, where thousands of people congregate in the fields to see megastar headliners. This new definition of curator would also be used in the arts world. For example, in London's Victoria and Albert Museum, exhibitions are curated as they always have been, but the person who is invited to choose the selection for a Friday Late event open to the public is now also called a 'curator', a label that confers leading-edge kudos. It suggests a person able to organise a press-worthy cool event that opens up the museum space to a wider public.

Other than the right network of people, there was also the right network of regular events around the globe that hipsters naturally started to frequent owing to the nature of operating in cross-categorised worlds. By bridging the gap between underground arts and fashion and the more established industry, the contemporary arts and high-fashion cliques began to open up to wider audiences. Typically, in the early days of the scene, you would hang around Fashion Week in London because of Off-Schedule, where the catwalk would be just one aspect of the all-round festivities. Already, this was unusual, because traditionally subcultures kept away from the world of high fashion. Then you would also start crossing over to Paris during its Fashion Week, at first congregating around the showrooms for young designers, most notably Rendez-Vous. The scenesters' presence at art events was also noted. Whereas before, contemporary arts fairs (Art Basel, Frieze, La Fiac), just like Fashion Weeks (London, Paris, New York and to some extent Milan), were a matter of specialist knowledge, they had now become lifestyle environments. As my friend Mika, the Parisian scenester, put it: 'In places like Miami Art Basel, there are the specialists in arts and there are people who come to party.' Equally you were interested in emerging smaller music festivals hosted by mates that promoted new talent, which you could find scattered around from Corsica to Iceland. And so select music festivals, too, became part of the pilgrimage. All these regular gatherings morphed into what became known as the hip circuit. Once the commercial world became interested, these events would become regularly-occurring platforms for promotion, in that brands would specifically time their product launches to coincide with them and their high concentration of alpha trendsetters and opinion formers. What had started as DIY logistics grew into a series of more exclusive events with strict guest lists, not least because a lot of scenesters grew into 'names'.

This is how hipsters came to be solicited by brands to orchestrate events for them. Beyond using 'curator' as a label for cool, the advantage of this approach was that a brand could get talked about without sacrificing a huge advertising budget. Essentially, brands shifted from sponsoring events towards hosting them. It was no longer about sticking up a logo as a sponsor to build an image. Instead, it was about providing an experience for a smaller, niche-targeted crowd of opinion formers who would start spreading the word.

Edouard (Ed) Rostand's explanation of this industry mentality shift is quite pertinent. Ed was another prominent character from La Hype, his hip status fully asserted via his proficiency in beginner's knitting. (Ed and I met through co-hosting a knitting party in Paris.) One of Ed's learning curves at the school for cool came during the period when he was commercially pitching a new music festival in Corsica called Calvi on the Rocks, co-organised by the Lio and André clan. They started that venture in 2002 to provide a feelgood place for friends away from the metropolis, rather than for money. (In the beginning the aim was to not lose too much rather than to make any.) In attempts to find commercial partners, Ed's pitch stated that 100 of the right people in a small, select venue could have more impact than 5,000 in a mega club. That logic applied specifically to Calvi given that the friends were all somewhere between alpha trendsetters and opinion formers, combined with credible musicians who were intimate supporters, notably those from the elektroklash scene and the Kitsuné and Ed

Banger labels. The connections were all first-degree. However, this mentality of seeing value in small but well-selected numbers came to extend beyond music festivals into the brand communication industry more generally.

Ed's case is also a good example of a scenester without previous corporate experience who got a corporate job on cool credentials alone. He was recruited by MySpace for its 'in house' marketing team when the company was setting up an office in France at the end of 2006, but he retained his underground connections. Ed's fascination with alternative club culture had begun with 'a big musical slap' in 1998 when he was introduced to the Respect night at Parisian club Le Queen. Up until then, he only ever went to places that played chart music. Having experienced what he described as an 'incredible energy and adrenalin rush' at Respect, he made a point of never attending a mainstream club again. For the next three years or so, Ed made it his mission to discover anything that there was to discover about alternative nightlife in Paris.

A stroke of luck had also landed him the part-time job of working on party listings for the (now-defunct) website parissi.com at the time when the web industry was still in its infancy. That is how Ed developed his network of underground contacts, which crossed over to become that new hip elite dubbed La Hype. His 2006 appointment at MySpace illustrates the corporate shift in mentality because it coincided with the period when hip – as shaped by the second-generation Hoxtonites (or La Hype in Paris) became a desirable currency. I remember this vividly because Ed and I had lunch just after his interview with MySpace in London. Ed was unsure whether he was going to get the job because he had no corporate experience, but it was precisely his underground network of connections combined with the web angle that won him the post. Perhaps even a year before, his appointment would have been too risky – but now the time was right.

Collaborations and Limited Editions

What became most fashionable from the idea of bridging different worlds was the concept of 'collaborations': the principle of joining a mass-market brand with a more prestigious one from the arts, fashion or hip circuit in general, in order to create a limited-edition product or experience that would build the bigger brand's image and produce a press-worthy story. Consequently, the launch party – inevitably an event involving hipsters in some way – became the norm; the necessary hook. Though not a novelty in itself, the 'collaboration' assumed a central role in noughties cool marketing. There were a couple of main collaboration trends where the second-generation Hoxtonite scene was the cool-purveyor. One was focused within the luxury sector; the other was the new marketing of the cool (ie being a cycle ahead of the consuming crowd – or at least appearing to be by association with bona fide hipsters). Both were image-building exercises.

By creating a link between hip artists and the brand's own values, luxury brands could increase their cachet. This was especially relevant to brands in image-crisis due to the impact on them of the nouveau riche and 'massification', both of which I shall look at in the next chapter. Calling upon hipsters to orchestrate such collaborations was a way of being on trend (though the association between arts and luxury sectors was by no means new, Hoxtonite hipsters provided a fresh image). That type of collaboration would principally be aimed at opinion formers rather than the general public, such as the project between Veuve Clicquot and artist Ann Veronica Janssen, themed around the colour yellow in 2007, or Swarovski's 'Unbridled' project and book (in which they commissioned a series of designers and artists to make wedding-related items using Swarovski crystals, launched at Paris Fashion Week in 2008).

The principle of fusing of the worlds of art and branded goods to create an inclusive experience began to occur in the consumer market by emulation. What I mean here is that the target market became the early majority rather than the opinion former. Brands started to communicate their brand values to the public by hosting events rather than simply sponsoring them. However, there were still launch events, often exclusively for the inner circle and the press.

Let me use an example from the motoring industry to illustrate this, as that sector latched on to the trend early. In this new scenario, the car industry started speaking the art language by moving out of the car showroom context and into a gallery space where, traditionally, a brand-new commercial product such as a car would have no place. As a brand you could have sponsored an event but the event itself would never have been 'polluted' by commerce. That was all changing. Creatively, it worked this way: before, car manufacturers would borrow arts cues and incorporate them into their design and advertising communications (such as the Citroën Xsara Picasso). With the new trend the car brand began to provide an experience aligned to the brand values, as in the case of the Volkswagen Scirocco Studios, in 2008. This was a curated project in which a series of artists were invited to use the car as a springboard for design inspiration. A travelling exhibition of the artefacts produced toured a number of UK cities holding private views as well as a series of parties in collaboration with *Intersection* magazine (a sister publication of *Dazed & Confused*). A dedicated website was set up, including the unavoidable section featuring photos from the parties intended to communicate the youthfulness and hipness of the occasions. Similarly, Nissan collaborated with *Dazed & Confused* in 2008 and commissioned street-art projects to promote the Qashqai vehicle and communicate its 'urban' brand values. Nissan also sponsored an exhibition of street art at Tate Modern in London that same year as part of the promotional strategy. At the same time, there was a mainstream ('above line') advertising campaign, including television adverts. The brand continued to rely on this type of experiential communication with its Cube Store project, a combination of cutting-edge events from fashion to art to launch the new Cube car model, which took place in Paris, London and Berlin in 2009.

Communicating Hipness

Not all collaborations are hip. For example, collaborations in the luxury sector such as that between the Bugatti Veyron Fbg and Hermès, or Louis Vuitton's tribute to Stephen Sprouse bags, or the L'Or de Jean Martell edition of cognac in 120 bottles designed by Dragon Rouge, and so on, were a matter of status. The item (car, bag or drink) did not suggest 'I seek a sense of individual style and therefore I am cool' but rather 'I am extremely wealthy'. This is a different kind of distinction from the self-conscious elitism nurtured by hip, which is about being the first to know. As soon as hip begins its trajectory towards the mainstream, it becomes diluted, because you are already a circle away from the immediate hip clique. In the vast majority of cases, brands that seek to communicate hipness via collaborative events really need to do a separate event for the initiated circle, because unless you reach the opinion former, you won't get the relevant publicity.

There are two main marketing tools that convey the sense of privilege that comes from being the first to know: rarity and frustration.

Rarity is communicated via a limited-edition product, resulting from a collaboration between two parties (the hip one and one seeking hip by association). Usually, a limited-edition product commands a premium price, even though, more often than not, there is nothing exclusive about the way it was produced other than its being limited. The hip element comes from your choice of collaborator and how you promote and distribute your product. An example of a guaranteed signifier of hip, combining the right name, promotion and distribution channels would be a collaboration with the concept-store colette. Once discredited on the grounds that the limited-edition approach to store buying would never take off, the colette method in fact led the way. Though the market for collaborations is now becoming saturated, colette still manages to represent the cool (its position remains unchallenged at the time of writing).

More generally, the (global) Hoxtonite network continues to provide a universe of ready-made signifiers of hipness that brands can co-opt. We have seen many examples of this already, such as Jean Paul Gaultier's perfume launch. The cool-brand sector also adopted this trend but lagged a step behind. What I mean by this is that the first brands to seek out hipsters for their services were from the luxury sector before the cool (youth) brand sector started to recruit Hoxtonites for hipness. Once again, the reason is that cool, for them, meant 'street' before it became 'street chic' by which time they were no longer market leaders. The trend of cool brands collaborating with Hoxtonites really took off around 2007 and fully flourished in 2008/2009. The Hoxtonites were afforded the most high-profile brand-communication projects. For example, Carri Mundane (Cassette Playa) designed a limited-edition pair of trainers for Nike (2008). Reebok collaborated with *Super Super* and used Namalee as the face of its Freestyle campaign in the UK (2009). Henry Holland (House of Holland) was sought after by brands ranging from Levi's jeans (he created a premium range for Levi's 501s) through to Wrigley's Extra chewing gum (he designed its limited-edition packaging) and Nintendo Wii (he designed limited-edition customised accessories for the Sims, a project that involved other Hoxtonites, too). The list of both second- and third-generation Hoxtonites collaborating with brands is long.

Extending this principle of communication, the wider (non-cool and non-luxury) market brands started to follow. The business model here partly relied on sales and partly on generating 'free' publicity, measured in inches of newspaper columns. Such was the theory. In practice however, brands were left with the question: was it worth it? The issue of ROI (return on investment) became crucial. Not every collaboration was viewed as a successful move by the marketing practitioners. For example, the collaboration between Peroni Nastro Azzuro beer and designer Antonio Berardi had a lukewarm reception. Berardi designed a limited-edition range of accessories called Peroni by Antonio Berardi to be sold in upmarket stores. Many brand-industry insiders perceived this as a gimmick, myself included when I was asked to comment. Peroni's response was that this was an image-building exercise and that the strategy had increased their sales by

25 per cent.[43] I am still not entirely convinced about the appeal of an upmarket accessories range sponsored by a brand of beer, even if created by a bona fide designer. Where is the cachet in that?

The fact that a trend is in vogue in the communication industry does not mean that it is right for every brand. Let us examine another case, where a mainstream brand *did* adopt a cool trend in a relevant fashion to boost its own image. When unveiling their redesigned brand identity, Kuoni Travel Ltd resorted to collaborative events and related communications in 2008/2009 in order to reach the opinion formers first, even though their redesign first and foremost affected the consumer. By evolving from merely a 'holiday' brand into a 'lifestyle' brand, Kuoni retuned various aspects of their service to the customer (from introducing a concierge service to individualised holiday activities). With this change in emphasis they wanted to tap into the NPC market; they decided to communicate the lifestyle values via word of mouth rather than directly targeting the consumer (with, say, an advertisement in a Sunday paper). As part of this exercise, they acted as sponsor to designer Osman Yousefzada at London Fashion Week and collaborated with the Serpentine Gallery. Kuoni was clear in its strategy. This type of communication was not about sales but about a long-term investment in building the brand's profile. You could not buy a bag called Osman for Kuoni in department stores, but you did get a Kuoni-branded canvas goody bag if you were in the select circle of those who attended Osman's catwalk show.

Frustration marketing is a way of nurturing the cult of being the first to know by keeping the information tightly guarded in order to convey a sense of mystery. Treat 'em mean, keep 'em keen. Hip is dictated by the right hype, usually ephemeral. Currently, the currency of La Hype or the Hoxtonites is valued high. As a result of this, brands are keen to tap into these networks. This is where the dreaded guest list rears its head – during the inevitable launch party for the limited-edition product. The principle is that if you are in, you are on it, and if not, you have to find out through blogs. The moment you log on to find out, you're already in the next circle on from the core hipsters who have already been there and done that. You are, however, still far cooler than the early majority, who don't even know the blog exists. The principle of frustration marketing is as relevant among the opinion-forming circles (as notably critiqued in Sagnard's book *Vous êtes sur la liste?*) as it is on the mainstream entertainment-industry circuit through the promotion of VIP parties. Once by definition exclusive (in that you couldn't pay to get in), now you can purchase a ticket for an 'aftershow party'. Music festivals in particular use this practice and wannabes fall for it – and post their photos on Facebook to prove it.

Pop Ups

From limited-edition products, the trend extended into limited-edition environments in the guise of temporary spaces: pop-up stores, restaurants, galleries, showrooms – even pop-up hair salons. Many brands would start doing pop ups.

The pop-up store was, if not pioneered, then certainly turned into a trend by Rei Kawakubo's label Comme des Garçons (CDG, as of lately).[44] They referred to these temporary stores as 'guerrilla stores'. Guerrilla stores made a statement against the gentrification of the luxury fashion retail business. Against the high-end mainstream trend of building shopping cathedrals, the guerrilla store's dogma was: to be outside city centres, in a space where rent was cheap; to employ people with no retail experience; to sell both new and old stock; and last but not least, to open for up to a year then disappear. The aesthetic of the store was 'nothing' – essentially leaving the bare industrial space as found. The advertising for these guerrilla stores was the antithesis of the lush campaigns that characterised the luxury industry. The brand used fly-posting, citing only the country code and postcode. You either got it – or you did not. The first guerrilla store opened in 2004 in East Berlin. A series followed across the world, always using the country-and-postcode principle. In 2009, CDG started to open up 'pocket stores'. As the name implies, these were tiny boutiques selling only a handful of staples and of-the-moment products, including wallets, fragrances, T-shirts and collaborative items that changed seasonally (such as 'collaboration' Speedo/CDG swimwear).

Pop-up restaurants followed a similar principle. You opened a temporary eatery in a space that would not normally be a restaurant. The purpose was as much about brand image-building as about operating a hospitality business as such. The Hoxtonites behind the (permanent) Bistrotheque restaurant and venue first started to use this technique when they opened a temporary restaurant over the 2006 Christmas period in east London called The Reindeer, which was a Santa's grotto for grown-ups where they hosted a series of performances (concert, theatre). The duo's uniqueness – first-generation Hoxtonites Pablo Flack and David Waddington, remember their names? – lay in their flair for identifying future talent. For example, this is where I met the singer Mika before he became famous. This idea was replicated in November 2008 when a temporary restaurant called Flash was opened at the Royal Academy of Arts, with a series of high-profile collaborations between artists, fashion designers and brands to produce anything from plates to chandeliers. Also in 2008 in London, The Double Club opened for a duration of around six to nine months as a collaborative art project between Swedish-based German artist Carsten Höller and Fondazione Prada. The Double Club was a public space that offered a mix of entertainment (especially live music) and hospitality (restaurant, bar and launch-party venue). Here again, the hip was provided by the Hoxtonite network, with Momo (of Momo and Sketch fame) being in charge of hosting the restaurant and Richard (BoomBox) in charge of 'Western' music and related festivities. The venue was open-house but the promotion was very carefully orchestrated to rely on word of mouth as much as possible. Another notable trend at this time was people turning their homes into pop-up restaurants. (Of course, some were more exclusive than others.)

Pop-up galleries involved staging temporary exhibitions in non-gallery spaces. Exhibits in these cutting-edge environments often served as indicators of hip art that the mainstream art world would later follow. Pop-up showrooms used unconventional spaces such as art galleries to act as showrooms for buyers during Fashion Week. Up-and-coming hair stylist Charlie Le Mindu and jewellery design-duo Tatty Devine also utilised the pop-up idea by turning a section of the Tatty Devine store into a hair salon once a week. This exchange also inspired a quirky collection of dressing-table accessories for the hair and jewellery courtesy of Tatty Devine, but using Charlie's logo. Theirs was an example of the creatively-inspired collaborations that had characterised the early development of the scene, rather than being a marketing stunt. It may well spark a continuing trend. This would not surprise me in the slightest, as so many ideas have been appropriated from this scene.

When underground practices primarily serve marketing purposes, the amount of risk-taking is reduced. Once platforms of social exchange, events had turned into cool marketing tools by the end of the noughties. Here, hip was no longer used as an expression of diversity but as a means of homogenising the market to sell a product. In other words, it was sell-out time.

4. Diversity versus Homogenisation

'Revolucija? Nama je dobro, mi nenamo pojma,
dok oni se časte, mi jedemo govna.'
('Revolution? We're all right 'coz we're clueless and dumb.
While they're living the Life of Riley, we live like scum.')

From the play *Nakaze* (Bosnian adaptation of *Creeps*)

ISLINGTON, OCTOBER 2008

Sunday morning, and I was absentmindedly channel hopping. Eventually I settled on T4, Channel 4's youth-branded slot, because I spotted designer Henry Holland on screen, our foremost third-generation Hoxtonite. Henry was co-hosting a show called Frock Me with Alexa Chung, a top youth TV presenter.[45] To my mind, there was nothing interesting, let alone inspiring, about this show. It was like watching QVC or The Shopping Channel. I was told about the latest collaboration between H&M and a designer label. This time it was Comme des Garçons. I also found out that Dr. Martens boots were back in fashion (you needn't be a fashion insider to know that this was old news). The fashion-conscious kid who wanted to be the first to know would have scouted street style blogs, which had been featuring shots of people wearing boots (Dr. Martens and other varieties) for a while and had already moved on. Nevertheless, I was told that Dr. Martens were 'really cool' and 'authentic' but the show delved no further into why that might be, other than listing which celebrities were wearing them. Or, could it be that this very list of 'celebrity' patrons was what was making them cool? (Silly me!)

A few months later, in January 2009, *Tatler* UK magazine featured three young women posing nude on its cover: Kimberly, Leah and Peaches. Who? I was not a *Tatler* reader but usually I recognised the cover star(s) be they Liz Hurley, Madonna or someone of that calibre. I was intrigued by the 'rock babes' headline, so I parted with my £3.80. I discovered that these ladies were the daughters of 'rock royalty' whose 'sense of style is idolised'. I was encouraged to give a 'big hand for the smash-hit kids'. As I read on, I became increasingly convinced that the only thing worth applauding about this article was its audacity. I was told that the cover girls 'need no introduction' because 'it would be hard to find anyone in the country who doesn't have a vague knowledge of who they are and what they get up to'. I was obviously in that minority. The article then elaborated on each girl, starting with 19-year-old Peaches, whose younger sister, Pixie, had already been a *Tatler* cover girl, as the article boasted. As soon as I spotted the family name, I realised they were Bob Geldof's daughters. I knew who the father was, for sure. Live Aid marked my generation and I do not like Mondays either – but I was not then acquainted with the repertoire of Geldof's daughters. But then... it all came back to me. I *had* (vaguely) heard of Peaches, as a matter of fact, but it was not because of what she did for a living. It was because she had allegedly walked out of Hoxtonite Mei Hui Liu's Soho boutique without paying for a dress. This incident caused unsuspecting Mei some grief at the time, which the tabloid press picked up on.[46] Prior to the dress episode, our group of bona fide Hoxtonite friends had never heard of Peaches, let alone been aware of her status as, if we were to trust *Tatler*, 'the queen of the East End indie scene'.

Tatler's interpretation of Hoxton cool whereby 'celebrity + street = cool' has come to embody the way that the mainstream, in its search for cool-for-profit, has appropriated the second coming of the East End scene (the first wave of co-optation being Cool Britannia, which was parodied in *The Shoreditch Twat* and then on *Nathan Barley*). In *Tatler*'s scenario, the offspring of rock aristocracy was unquestionably, doubly cool: with the 'celebrity' element that came from having a famous parent and the 'street' angle that came from supposed association with the underground East End scene. With that scene now a byword for cool – as redefined by the second-generation Hoxtonites – *Tatler*'s cover girl was nothing less than its 'queen'. The youth TV programme *Frock Me* went by that same ideology, with the screen unification of Holland (street) and Chung (celebrity). In that case, Holland provided the hip element and his kudos was authenticated outside the scene via mainstream exposure, making him a safe bet for cool marketing (in the form of collaborations, as examined in the previous chapter). By the same token, a mainstream youth-TV presenter who had no street credentials could build her cool by supposedly hanging out with the street-cool kids.

The co-optation of Hoxton cool coincided with the scene's shift from the maturation period (circa 2004–2006) to its full commercialisation (around 2007 onwards). The inevitable consequence of commercialisation was the sell-out of the underground scene. The original Hoxtonites – with varying degrees of consent, compromise or resistance depending on the individual – began to operate commercially. The previous chapter explored this in terms of crossover. In its co-opted version, hipness that relied upon Hoxton to supply its symbols and codes began to be communicated via a series of signifiers. 'Being cool' involved things such as: DJing, hosting club nights, being a VIP (or 'on the guest list') or just being and looking the part (if you turned up at enough places deemed cool and got photographed, that in itself also constituted being cool). As a result of this process, DJing shifted from depending on musical knowledge to being an image-building tool; the appearance on the decks of someone even vaguely famous would act as an anchor for a party. As such, it became just about playing records without the possibility of challenging DJ heritage or potentially contributing a new style. The event itself, once a platform of social exchange, became a mere VIP exercise. It has become a self-serving career medium for a new generation of pseudo-cool people, primarily attracting the wannabes, or the new generation of Shoreditch Twats, rather than hipsters. Here, there are two types of 'cool' purveyors.

On the one hand, we witnessed the rise of a new young breed of Hoxton party-promoters, who realised that you could make a career out of being cool through an aggressive pursuit of fame based on nurturing the cult of the individual. Shoreditch was already a byword for hip. All you had to do was to infiltrate yourself into the scene, but instead of promoting the scene and its talent, you put yourself centre-stage. Your goal was to become current to create currency. You were aiming to play the celebrity stock exchange, or Celebdaq.[47] As a result of this process, cool turned from breaking new ground into shameless attention-seeking and relentless self-promotion in order to gain indiscriminate media exposure and accumulate Celebdaq currency. To this end, attending hip events to be seen, and preferably photographed, for the day-after-party sections of social networking sites, blogs and magazines became the norm. The desire for a bit of the spotlight across various media grew exponentially as follows: on social networks and blogs, in any magazine or paper (reputed or otherwise), niche television programme on cable, mainstream television programme and finally, your own television programme (in most cases some kind of 'reality TV'). The summit of the nouveau hip's aspiration is a job on MTV or on a 'youth' programme on terrestrial television (or, frankly, any programme).

On the other hand, the rise of 'hereditary cool' redefined cool as something conferred simply by being a descendant of rock aristocracy. This fast track to coolness comes with social privileges. If we are to buy into the *Tatler* article, it is merit all around rather than lack of: 'wha-hey – [the cover girls are] all actually doing something interesting with their lives'. The first featured cover girl, Peaches Geldof, has an impressive CV including things such as writing newspaper columns for prestigious publications (the *Guardian*, *Observer* and *Daily Telegraph*), TV shows, modelling, commanding a 'large fee' as a DJ and designing a capsule collection for label PPQ.[48] What ordinary teenager would have those kinds of professional openings without a family name and publicity machine behind them? There is a whole clique of celebrity offspring with automatic access to the media, be they the progeny of high-profile rock parents (like Peaches Geldof or the young Osbournes) or those whose parents were once in bands that no one can now remember. Their careers, other than being photographed coming out of a car/party/gym, predictably involve modelling or some kind of reality TV.

For this rock aristocracy offspring, fame is an entitlement. To me this is like communism all over again. Remember *štela* in the former Yugoslavia, where one of the main things that inhibited progress was the privileges awarded to the children of the communist elite simply *because* they were the children of officials? The less-equal comrades among the equal had to 'give a big hand' and express joy that some comrade's offspring had jumped the queue. Inspired by rock 'n' roll, we rebelled against this system. Twenty years on, hereditary cool operates in a similar fashion. The rock aristocracy, once members of the counterculture and now part of the elite establishment, enjoy social privileges that are simply passed on. With previous generations, at least you needed to prove yourself in some way. Often, the 'children of' were in the shadow of their illustrious parent and had to work harder to get recognition, especially if in the same field as the parent (music, film etc). For example, though fashion designer Stella McCartney, when she graduated in the 1990s, may have become part of Cool Britannia because of who her father was, she had nevertheless studied at one of the best schools and actually had a job as a designer (before starting her own label), rather than feeding her career on gossip headlines. The journey to success no longer appears to matter.

When hip reaches its commercialisation stage, the discussion inevitably slips into a battle of value judgements. To critique hip at this stage for being subject to its inevitable fate is kind of futile. Moreover, when it comes to second-generation Hoxtonites, it has already been done. The bitter sentiments about La Hype in Paris expressed in *Vous êtes sur la liste?* could easily be applied its non-Parisian counterparts.

How can the discussion be elevated beyond lamenting the sell-out? I aim to do so by revisiting the discussion of identity politics from the first chapter (the history of hip and attendant identity) and my 1990s hip-and-identity debate examined by using MTV as a case study. Once again, I am interested in the dynamic between diversity and homogenisation. I have already explored hip's alternative set of values during its incubation and maturation (ie crossover) phases in the noughties. In this chapter, I shall look more closely at what hip was an alternative *to*, a trend I call Red Carpet Culture, and explore it in relation to the economic model it is reproducing. Red Carpet Culture is a phenomenon that typified the mainstream of the noughties. It is premised on 'celebrity' whereby being famous – regardless of how or why – is revered above all else. In terms of drivers, there are two interconnected strands that epitomise this trend, which I shall call the Double Bs: *Big Brother* and bling bling. The Double Bs are symbols of the aspirational values of the audiences buying into this 'celebrity' trend. Then I shall raise the question of how the ideology of that culture impacts on the potential for hip to reinvent itself.

THE DOUBLE BS
Big Brother
Traditionally, fame was the result of paying one's dues and was judged according to a set of meritorious criteria. With the proliferation of reality TV, we have seen the emergence of another type of fame, whereby almost anyone could become a star overnight. In the noughties, the famous-for-being-famous model of stardom dominated. The byword for this trend – and one of the original and most successful exponents of reality TV – is *Big Brother*. An idea created by Joop Van den Ende and Johannes (John) de Mol, the Dutch founders of Endemol (the production company behind *Big Brother*), it was first broadcast in the Netherlands in 1999. This format, essentially a response to the problem of how to generate revenue from the new interactive television technology, became an international success story. This included the conquest of the previously impenetrable US television market with regards to 'foreign' formats. Reality-TV contests – and *Big Brother*, as part of that trend – were among the most successful European exports to the US, though interestingly this time around there were not debates to match the American cultural imperialism furore surrounding the implementation of satellite television in Europe in the early 1990s. The Europeans were perfectly happy to export their 'reality' format without any concern for the erosion of American culture.

Local variants of *Big Brother* included *Loft Story* in France, *Gran Hermano* in Spain, *Grande Fratello* in Italy, *Veliki Brat* in Serbia and *Big Brother USA* in the States. The number of seasons it ran for in each country varied. In the Netherlands, it ran for six, ending in 2006. In France, *Loft Story* ended after two series, but similar formats have since replaced it. By contrast, the UK, where *Big Brother* was launched in 2000, became one of the territories where this show ran and ran (until the final series in 2010). There were also spin-off shows, including *Celebrity Big Brother*. Here contestants tended to be minor celebrities, celebrities by association (sister of, mother of, and so on) or has-beens in need of a career-boost rather than current or genuinely famous celebrities.

Each local version had its idiosyncrasies but all shared the same premise: each was a televised contest in which a number of strangers selected by audition consented to live together for an indefinite period of time, during which they were completely cut off from the outside world. Each week or so, a candidate was eliminated by public vote until one – the winner – remained. The motivation for participating, and by the same token *watching*, this programme was also the reason it generated a lot of critical reaction. It actively encouraged – legitimised even – the possibility of becoming 'successful without having to make an effort, notorious without having to work'.[49]

Big Brother celebrated ignorance. It was a world in which intellectual curiosity or critical thinking were noticeable only by their absence, not least because access to any means of communication was banned and bringing books into the house was forbidden. Instead, mundane tasks were set by the production team to incite contestants to outwit (or fight with) each other. This helped combat what would otherwise have been unprecedented boredom because, for all the supposed 'reality', there was no such idle way of life in the real world. Even when the activities were based on 'teamwork', the truth was that each contestant was in it for themselves. There could only be one winner, after all. Consequently, as Vincent Cespedes, the French philosopher and secondary-school teacher who wrote one of the first virulent critiques of *Loft Story* pointed out: 'The contest becomes a perfect model for social hypocrisy where you have to destroy the other while keeping a smile on your face, pretend to like them only to back-stab them, or conspire with another housemate to eliminate the undesirables.'[50]

The intrigues in the house as well as the unravelling personalities of the contestants became, in turn, conversational currency. To paraphrase another French writer, Alain Schifres, we watched *Big Brother* (or *Loft Story*), and therefore watched nothing, and we talked about *Big Brother*, and therefore talked of nothing.[51] This debate occasionally heated up and stretched into burning issues such as '*Cékikapété?*' (from '*c'est qui qu'a pété?*' meaning 'who's farted?') – the notorious line that led the critical public to denounce *Loft Story* in France, based on a genuine episode in the house. Note that in this instance, I am not interested in the use of truncated language, prompted by the advent of technological phenomena such as text messages (or 'txts'), and its alleged contribution to dumbing down, which is how many critics addressed this issue. (As it happens, I personally find aspects of short-cut language both functional and creative.) My point here is about the vacuity of the conversation, the legitimisation of which is symptomatic of the prevalent 'proud to be ignorant' attitude. A good example of what I mean is provided by the British outfit N-Dubz, top-sellers in the UK mainstream music chart. In autumn 2009, they recorded a charity single, a cover of a song by Las Vegas indie band The Killers. Typical of the narrow-mindedness I am talking about, N-Dubz admitted to never having heard of The Killers, their chart contemporaries. Tula 'Tulisa' Contostavlos, the female singer of N-Dubz, was quite proud of not knowing, and of having had no intention of looking up the original single. This lack of curiosity comes as standard.

The complicity between the programme and the viewer that was based on a shared language (albeit impoverished and basic, à la '*cékikapété*') and value system (based on the extent of knowledge about intrigues in the house and, by extension, lack of curiosity about other things) culminated in televised evictions based on a public vote. The last remaining housemate became the winner by default, which is how he or she 'earned' their fame, as it were. What was completely disregarded in this world of perverted reality is that the candidate had no talent to offer to begin with, other than a willingness to consent to humiliation and an ability to exhibit all sorts of 'eccentricities' for the chance of winning money (but more importantly, notoriety): that celebrity was a goal in itself is supported by evidence from UK audition tapes.[52] For wannabe contestants, *Big Brother* began to embody the famous-for-being-famous trend, turning residency in the house into a shortcut to achieving this goal. Would-be contestants began running around in the nude and going to all sorts of extremes to show producers their willingness to do anything to become famous. In turn, the producers encouraged such sensationalist displays in order to counter ratings slumps that were already registering after a few series. At the same time, also to maintain audience interest, they ratcheted up the unpleasantness of the tasks that the housemates had to perform.

The shared culture between the contestant/programme and the viewer was built upon the desire to be famous, as well as the anticipation, for those entering the house, of the life-changing experience of going from anonymity to the red carpet. And yet, at first, it was thought that the show would never work precisely because of the way it had been concocted – as a social experiment on the edge of decency, rewarding behaviour that might previously have been considered shameful. When *Big Brother* was originally pitched to Channel 4 in the UK, the idea seemed too shocking. It was initially rejected on the grounds that the market for 'rats-in-the-cage-who'll-do-anything-for-money' was too narrow and the format was therefore not viable for a commercial network.[53] Contrary to expectation, *Big Brother* not only achieved high ratings – its first series in the UK beat all records and its novelty-factor impact was replicated around the world – but it also reached the holy grail of marketing: the youth segment, which proved to contain its most avid viewers. Consequently, *Big Brother* became a flagship programme (despite the declining ratings once the novelty factor wore off).

In terms of being an idea that no one believed in, which turned out to be a major success, there is a similarity between *Big Brother* and MTV – but the similarity ends there. You can't do a like-for-like comparison between *Big Brother* (and Endemol as a production company) and maverick businesses such as MTV (in its infancy) because *Big Brother* does not fit into hip's historical framework. As with maverick businesses in the 1960s, MTV in the 1990s adopted the subcultural ways of its own generation. It was also a narrowcaster and therefore challenged the status quo and provided an alternative to the mainstream. Consequently, on MTV the early adopter and the youth market were one and the same. Opinion formers were watching MTV because it was at the cutting edge of music, graphics and more generally lifestyle – just like its fans, who became cool by association. That is why advertising on MTV was worth a premium.

Put in the context of the hip framework, *Big Brother* fails to qualify as hip on every count. When it comes to business risk-taking for the television network that took on *Big Brother*, the risk had already been minimised by outsourcing its production to an independent (though the subsequent success did raise the acquisition price). The format had been tested before it was acquired, except in the Netherlands (but the risk was Endemol's, not the network's, and being the first market where *Big Brother* was shown, I can only assume that the television network had the upper hand in negotiating fees). Though it became an annual series, there was no original long-term commitment. Furthermore, unlike MTV, who entered a virgin market (satellite TV) and expanded organically, *Big Brother* came to us through the old technology of terrestrial television. Big Brother was not niche-targeted at the early adopters' market. It was primetime. The advertising model was therefore conventional. In terms of advertising worth, the show might be delivering a young demographic but this was no longer synonymous with the early adopter, the precursor of future trends. The greatest commercial novelty that resulted from the interactive television potential – which was the buzz of the moment in the media industry – was an extra revenue stream from telephone votes.

In terms of ideology, *Big Brother* was not hip either. First, it did not follow the rock 'n' roll model of crossing over and selling out: it was a sell-out from the outset. There was no paying of dues en route to success from an organic culture; it was rather openly about a shortcut to fame, and short-lived glory (with very few exceptions). Instead of paying their dues, the famous-for-being-famous were catapulted on to the red carpet – from obscurity to notoriety – literally overnight. Second, *Big Brother* did not share a rock 'n' roll set of ideals, based on peer culture (or, in the case of the second-generation Hoxtonites, a sense of solidarity among individuals with a penchant for cutting-edge innovation, rather than a group identity as such). Instead, it was all about shameless and relentless self-promotion. It was about 'me', and not 'us'. The cult of the individual famous for being famous *was* the set of ideals in *Big Brother* culture.

How do you communicate 'achievement' when success is unwarranted? You do so through status symbols. Crass materialism became a proof of worth. The ultimate symbol of success was now an appearance on the red carpet, or being a 'VIP'. The aesthetic of the newly famous – and by extension newly rich – was summarised by the expression 'bling bling'. So, just like in the 1960s, when the counterculture reacted to the conformity of the 1950s as summed up by the expression 'keeping up with the Joneses', the hip culture of the noughties became a reaction to keeping up with the Beckhams.

Bling Bling

Bling bling – or simply bling – was the sell-out of street culture, notably hip hop. Bling was about conspicuous consumption. It was about acquiring expensive possessions for the purpose of attaining social status. Its emergence in the late 1990s and early noughties coincided with two microtrends in the luxury sector: the rise of an über wealthy population segment, and the 'massification' of luxury. Parallel to this, bling came to symbolise the mainstream youth culture of the noughties, as redefined by the likes of MTV and *Big Brother* and their 'celebrity' culture.

The main exponents of bling are the nouveau riche. Bling bling males are, above all, rappers (mainstream chart-toppers), footballers and Russian oligarchs. The female equivalents are the 'biatches' (controversial hip hop slang for women who go out with men for their money), the WAGS (footballers' Wives And Girlfriends, whose claim to fame for the most part is being just that) and the '*bogataya bezdelniza*' (a rich female doing nothing but subsidising her lifestyle by hopping between rich men's beds) or the '*tusovshiza*' (the 'It' girl). The 'biatch' phenomenon spawned a reaction, particularly among the Afro-American community, by women professing to earn their own cash and needing neither a man to buy their bling nor wanting to entertain a 'scrub' (male equivalent of 'biatch', who 'sits on his broke ass').[54] This type of powerful, liberated and inspiring black female also eventually sold out to become a strand of commercial R&B subsumed by bling. The bling role models par excellence included rapper P. Diddy (originally known as Puff Daddy, now as Sean Combs), 'independent' ladies such as Jennifer Lopez (or 'J-Lo' – and P. Diddy's former girlfriend) and Beyoncé, footballer David Beckham and his former-Spice Girl wife Victoria, and oligarchs who now have a public profile outside Russia. Most visible in the media spotlight were those who held stakes in Western football clubs, such as Roman Abramovich and his socialite girlfriend Daria (Dasha) Zhukova, herself an oligarch's daughter, whom Abramovich started to date after his well-publicised and hugely expensive divorce.

With the rise of bling bling and the nouveau riche, the concept of luxury was redefined. Essentially, it was distorted. Attributes upon which the luxury fashion houses had traditionally built their cachet, such as discretion, elegance, timelessness and, last but not least, craftsmanship and innovation, were replaced by a different set of values. Luxury became a badge of honour. Discretion was substituted for an ostentatious display of wealth. Elegance was confused with excess often bordering on vulgarity. Timelessness was redefined as transient fashion. This was symbolised by the designer 'It' bag, which became a disposable accessory, going from a 'must-have' to 'so last season' in the blink of an eye. The customer was not buying for style (be it quality, design or even heritage) but to show off. Retailers were perfectly aware of this. As the CEO of a boutique chain catering for the über wealthy said: 'If a person is buying a Roberto Cavalli bag, they're looking at the price tag… The exact same bag would be 10 and 15 per cent higher every season.'[55] Incidentally (or perhaps not so) one of the main ambassadors for this brand was Victoria Beckham, an association nurtured through her appearances at Cavalli flagship store openings or as a guest model on the catwalk.

In Russia, the need to show off newly acquired wealth was even more pressing. Though routinely referred to as an 'emerging' market, this was something of a misnomer. The minority population of extremely wealthy Russians that drove the luxury industry in the decade 1997–2007 were technically expatriates and already avid shoppers in Western European capitals, notably London. Russian-speaking sales assistants were employed by Knightsbridge luxury stores to cater specifically for this market. In the post-communist 1990s, it had been all about head-to-toe Versace, a combo of brassy designer logo-flashing and 'tits-and-arse' parading. This brazen attitude towards splashing money around was well illustrated by the story of Roman Abramovich's former wife Irina property-hunting in London. She briefed her husband's secretary to find her something 'near Harrods', which was as far as her knowledge about her future home city appeared to extend.[56] By the mid-noughties, flashiness had given way to discretion, but not necessarily to a more discerning taste. In the words of Russian *Vogue*'s editor: 'It still has to look expensive and, more importantly, be expensive.'[57]

While the über wealthy were spending like there was no tomorrow, the 'massification' of luxury made it possible for people on lower incomes to acquire luxury items at more affordable prices. In order to cater for the mass luxury market, designer brands started to offer a range of relatively affordable items. The accessible end of the luxury goods market, comprising perfumes, watches and cosmetics, constituted around 55 per cent of luxury sales.[58] According to a Mintel consumer report, the celebrity culture showcasing the latest items – in other words, Red Carpet Culture – boosted the luxury market and raised awareness outside its traditional core of customers. Among the main sales drivers became what the report refers to as the 'celebrity obsessed youth market'. 'Bling things' on the desirable list were baseball caps (Burberry), gift sets (Calvin Klein), keyrings (Louis Vuitton, Prada), jewellery (Tiffany, Swarovski) and underwear (Calvin Klein, Versace).[59] People were spending beyond their means – not to buy a piece of craftsmanship (which used to be what gave luxury houses their cachet) but because they wanted a piece of status. The 'celebrity' aesthetic preached that you would be a better person if you acquired that little designer item. When the original was out of reach a good fake did the job, because it was about the label, not the quality.

This all-out fascination with luxury goods boosted their sales in the mid-noughties but the market buoyancy came at a price for luxury brands. If a brand is built on cachet and its products become widespread, it is by definition no longer exclusive. As the so-called 'undesirables' at the lower end of the market began to appropriate luxury brands, this started to have a negative impact on the brands' reputations. In the UK for example, the rise of the 'new British elite' popularly known as 'chavs' (the term entered the national lingo around 2004), began to give luxury a bad name. What is a chav? By self-admission, chavs are identifiable by their clothes and attitude. They want 'money and a lot of it but don't want to have to work for it'.[60] Their role models are reality-TV stars (particularly *Big Brother* contestants or glamour model Jordan, AKA Katie Price, who appeared on *I'm a Celebrity, Get Me Out of Here* and was subsequently given her own reality TV show on a cable channel), rappers such as Eminem, and footballers and WAGS such as the Beckhams or the Rooneys. The chav look favours tracksuits, baggy shirts (especially football tops), trainers, jewellery and the ubiquitous (Burberry) cap. Rightly or wrongly, chavs came to be perceived as a symbol of the new underclass, and were linked by some to all society's ills, from teenage pregnancy to petty crime at best and gun crime at worst.

The chav phenomenon particularly began to affect the credibility of the traditional British luxury brand Burberry – the average chav's brand of choice. Burberry also 'enjoyed' an unsolicited association with a series of public figures who came to be stereotyped as high-profile chavs, such as soap actress Daniella Westbrook, who was photographed with her baby, with both parties wearing head-to-toe Burberry, and the spoof band Goldie Lookin Chain, against whom Burberry brought a court order, demanding that they destroy the Vauxhall Cavalier they'd decked out in Burberry plaid. Burberry's image was in trouble, though understandably the brand played this down. The appointment of a new CEO in the summer of 2006 led to an almost immediate image overhaul. The new advertising campaign for Burberry, which followed in 2007, featured Hoxtonites such as the model Agyness Deyn and the musician Patrick Wolf, to create a hip image and win back the customer (including a younger demographic) with a fresher look. (This problem was not unique to Burberry – similar trouble affected upmarket brands across Europe, such as the case of Lacoste and *les banlieues* – the

French equivalent of 'chav' – in France. Lacoste also subsequently underwent an image-overhaul.)

Bling fatigue coincided with the full commercialisation of the Hoxtonite scene, in 2007. As luxury brands changed direction by reverting to the values they'd abandoned in pursuit of the new El Dorado, they inevitably sought to project a new youthful image. Here, a brand-new generation of Hoxtonites was fully groomed and ready to oblige. Burberry was just one among the many brands that began to fish for cool in the Hoxton pool, as established in the previous chapter. Given that its origins were in the street-chic ideology, the leap into the world of established luxury brands came naturally. The point of my story was indeed to show how an underground clique that challenged the status quo ultimately went on to influence the style and communication industries. The sell-out of Hoxtonites was inevitable, however unfortunate (or not, depending on where you stand on the sell-out debate) and I don't wish to lament this. The sell-out debate is, in fact, symptomatic of a deeper issue.

That issue is how nearly a decade of Red Carpet Culture premised on *Big Brother* and bling bling has potentially affected hip's ideology and, by extension, its ability to reinvent itself. What we have here is a fundamental conflict of cultural values between the hipster – coming from the rock 'n' roll tradition – versus the wannabe – coming from the famous-for-being-famous school. The disparity between the culture of curiosity fostered by hip and the culture of voyeurism fostered by the Red Carpet value system can be used as a metaphor for the conflict between 'diversity' and 'homogenisation' at the heart of identity politics.

CURIOSITY VERSUS VOYEURISM: THE CASE OF COOL BRITANNIA
Casino-TV Format

In contrast to the culture of curiosity, which is ruled by open-mindedness, interest in the 'other' and celebrating diversity, Red Carpet Culture is a culture of voyeurism. This ideology creates a new 'imagined community' where fame regardless of merit and all the bling bling symbols of success are unquestionable. It governs the bulk of mainstream media as well as youth-oriented media and communication – but I shall continue with my *Big Brother* metaphor to explore this trend. Voyeurism, unlike curiosity, is not about openness towards the other – even though paradoxically, in the case of *Big Brother*, the other was laid bare for our (guilty) viewing pleasure. Instead of celebrating diversity, stereotypes were juxtaposed based on the anticipation that their different social and cultural backgrounds would lead to a clash. There was no sense of fraternity (or sorority) because ultimately, it was all about 'me'. To learn about each other was not what *Big Brother* was about, even though its producers have used this argument to justify the show. I find it very hard to buy into the spiel that the gay Muslim transvestite or any other such character from a niche community was recruited to put human rights issues on the agenda. The line between freak and unique is very thin here. Contestants entered the *Big Brother* house for their five minutes of fame. To believe that the show was a medium for altruism is nothing short of absurd.

Let us look at the evidence. In the UK, this show only really got noticed when the manipulations of 'Nasty Nick' were uncovered in series one. His 'deceitful' ways began to feature in the press, especially in the newly-launched gossip magazine *Heat*, which became *Big Brother*'s unofficial print partner (and more generally a partner to the famous-for-being-famous crowd). This set a precedent. From then on, anything went, from physical fights to prospective love stories with the inevitable 'Have they done it?' factor, to perhaps the most notorious of all – the infamous 'racism' incident in *Celebrity Big Brother*. Here, I refer to the well-publicised episode where Bollywoood actress Shilpa Shetty was bullied by a group of housemates and ringleader Jade Goody in particular, which caused a diplomatic incident. Goody was the notorious *Big Brother* contestant who managed to carve out a lucrative career as a 'celebrity' post *Big Brother* until her premature death from cancer in 2009, the progress of which was put under public scrutiny through carefully orchestrated media 'exclusives'. All this goes to show that without intrigue and scandal, there would have been nothing to talk about. All means to that greater end – 'celebrity' – could be justified. Scandal does sell newspapers, and the rise of the famous-for-being-famous crowd was steadily turning from a ratings dictatorship into a new form of propaganda.

Let me use a metaphor here for the culture of voyeurism epitomised by *Big Brother*, which some readers may find provocative. With *Big Brother* on our screens, we literally watched 'the lives of others' unravel. The boundaries between the private and the public were eroded and we consented to being part of this – by being either a housemate or a viewer. It was supposedly for entertainment but the set-up nevertheless closely echoed the scenario of the Oscar-winning film *The Lives of Others* (directed by Florian Henckel von Donnersmarck, 2006). This film depicts life in East Berlin under the communists where freedom was brutally taken away by the regime. The film focuses on a couple being watched constantly without them realising that cameras were secretly installed in their flat. The differences were that in *Big Brother*, instead of the infamous *Stasi* police, it was us who watched; and instead of unsuspecting citizens subjected to 24/7 surveillance against their will, these housemates had given their consent.

More specifically, the idea of *Big Brother* was borrowed from George Orwell's novel *Nineteen Eighty-Four*. Beyond pastiche, a link can be made between our current glorification of celebrity and the voyeuristic attitude this encourages, and the totalitarian system portrayed in the book. *Nineteen Eighty-Four* is the story of life under non-stop surveillance in a dystopian Britain where its rulers proclaim that 'freedom is slavery'. The supreme ruler is Big Brother, an invisible yet powerful force whose omnipresence is a symbol of communist despotism. Cowed by the constant paranoia created by being watched and fear of being punished, citizens abide by draconian codes. Suppression of thought is the main weapon of coercion. Hence all books have been banned (just like in the *Big Brother* house) while the language, once called English, has been reduced to 'newspeak', a vernacular consisting of only basic vocabulary (something like '*cékikapété*') to make 'any other modes of thought impossible'.

In the 1980s, Orwell's novel enjoyed renewed popularity. Though no one thought that communism would collapse, the seeds of change were in the air, particularly in 1985 with the coming to power of reformist Mikhail Gorbachev in the Soviet Union. Orwell's novel helped strengthen the voices of hope. Referencing the book (along with Orwell's *Animal Farm*, which similarly focuses on the subjects of freedom and oppression) was rock 'n' roll. It meant that you did not agree with a repressive system. It was a stance for diversity. 'Sexcrime (1984)' by The Eurythmics from the soundtrack to the award-winning big-screen adaptation of the novel (directed by Michael Radford, 1984) captured the public mood. ('Sexcrime' was newspeak for 'all sexual misdeeds whatever' in this land of forbidden romance.)

Recently, a number of critics of *Big Brother* (the programme) linked the effects of it to reduced critical capacities. Echoing the Frankfurt School – who provided the first critique of mass culture (and the rise of consumerism) on the grounds of it corrupting the intellect – acting like a 'hypodermic needle' to spread propaganda and ultimately reproduce capitalism – this more recent school of thought sees *Big Brother* as a genuine symbol of a new totalitarianism. It is premised on the argument that the collapse of knowledge is a dangerous trend that breeds consent without resistance. The implication is that the end of thinking – or in other words, the suppression of the culture of curiosity – could have catastrophic consequences for freedom and democracy.[61]

Speaking as a cultural studies graduate, I should reject this kind of thinking. After all, at Goldmsiths College I was taught by eminent scholars from the Birmingham School. This intellectual movement provided the first comprehensible critique of the Frankfurt School. Their response, in turn, became the foundation for cultural studies and media courses around the world. And yet, I find myself intrigued by this recent revival of the Frankfurt School. No doubt, different people watch *Big Brother* for different reasons. It probably doesn't act on everyone who does watch it like a 'hypodermic needle'. I am also perfectly aware that many viewers actually enjoy it. Still, I cannot help but find a correlation between the ideology of programmes such as *Big Brother* and the economic model of mindless consumerism.

Unlike hip cultures, which have always been about challenging the system before the sell-out occurs (they are necessarily co-opted to fuel the system) – *Big Brother* does exactly the opposite. Here, I concur with Colin Sparks, a media professor from the Marxist tradition. (Who would have thought that my long-abandoned Marxist education would be seeing a retro revival?) Professor Sparks wrote an article about *Big Brother* following the outrage caused by the 'racism' incident.[62] Having examined both the economic motivations and the viewing appeal of the programme, he concludes that, although *Big Brother* provides a form of escapism from alienated labour under capitalism (entertainment for the viewer and a gateway to success for the contestant), fundamentally it offers no challenge to the system. On the contrary, *Big Brother* reproduces 'some of the most pernicious effects of capitalism [where] human energy and initiative are ruthlessly exploited in order to make money... Where there is no obvious alternative that can provide a focus for mass discontent, all sorts of more or less magical solutions to the anger and frustration that mar millions of lives are seized almost in despair.' Being prepared to gamble your destiny – be it through playing the lottery or into the hands of *Big Brother* or some other 'talent' contest – are indicators of frustration rather than empowerment. I cannot help but use my communist analogy here, once again. For some, *Big Brother* represents salvation from their mundane lives (and reality-TV talent-contest judges, such as the notorious Simon Cowell, are the new Messiahs). Just like the Supreme Comrade in the days of communism, *Big Brother* will come to the rescue. He does all the thinking so you don't have to.

Casino Economy

Meanwhile, in real-life Britain, this gambling-TV format went hand-in-hand with the unravelling 'gambling' economy. While the media was obsessed with speculating about who was going to leave the *Big Brother* house next, another kind of speculation was going on. In the decade between 1997 (when New Labour came to power) and 2007 (the peak of the trend that was followed by the devastating global economic meltdown), the majority stakes for economic development were overwhelmingly played on financial markets and related professional services. 'For those who make money out of money [tax lawyers, accountants and bankers],' observed Mark Hollingsworth and Stewart Lansley, co-authors of the book *Londongrad: From Russia with Cash*, 'it was a golden decade.'[63] This was coupled with a vertiginous rise in property prices. The accounting, legal and real-estate sectors accounted for roughly half of Britain's growth in the mid-noughties, bringing in around 30 per cent of the national income, more than in any European country and even more than in the USA, the most liberal free-market economy. Cool Britannia – the marketing label that originated from the sell-out of street cultures and should have been synonymous with a youthful and dynamic Britain – became a paradise for the über wealthy. Meanwhile, for the majority of ordinary London folk and foreign visitors alike, London was getting so expensive that Cool Britannia was increasingly dubbed 'Rip-off Britannia' in the headlines.

Elected on the promise of Cool Britannia and to the thumping house tune 'Things Can Only Get Better' (by d:ream), New Labour's landslide victory was supposed to signify a new era. For many Labour supporters, Cool Britannia implied a fairer and less divisive society and a less aggressive free-market economy after nearly two decades of Conservative politics. Even though there has been a lot of criticism of the Britpop and Britart crowd for drinking 'champagne supernova' at Downing Street and selling out, the scenesters at the time were there because they genuinely believed that the party was about change. Whether it was British music or art, it emerged out of the ashes of the Thatcher era, which staggered to an end after a market crash in the late 1980s, followed by recession in the early 1990s. Unfortunately, under New Labour, instead of a 'youthful New Britain', we ended up with the worst recession in living memory and with economic divisions between the haves and have-nots unseen since the gloomy days of the Victorian age.[64]

It may have been a global recession but the UK, and London in particular, had been at the crest of the bling bling wave, and had further to crash. By 2007, at the peak of the upward trend, London had even displaced New York as the financial capital of the world. When everything collapsed in 2008, and plunged into deeper recession in 2009, 'banker' became a byword for morally corrupt capitalism. The Royal Bank of Scotland, who registered the greatest loss in UK corporate history, was just one of the banks bailed out by the British taxpayer. In spite of that, its chief executive walked out with a six-figure pension package for life at the age of 50, amid a huge public outcry.[65] A banker who was being rewarded for losing public money was seen as holding the country in contempt. Politicians and financial regulatory bodies appeared unequipped to deal with this extraordinary scenario. The case of people versus the banks remains open as the City's bonus culture still continues.

That was not what Cool Britannia was supposed to have been. Something somewhere had been lost in translation...

On the one hand, 'Cool Britannia' – supposedly conducive to healthy entrepreneurship – was instead appropriated as a vehicle for driving the City of London. Premised on a gluttonous bonus culture, this economic model was fed by greed. Individuals were taking increasingly big risks before it all collapsed. This 'casino economy' was coupled with the phenomenon of 'parachute bonuses'. Widespread across corporations, these stipulated that executive contracts would be honoured, regardless of individual track records. In that decade, an average chief executive earned 100 times the average salary of a worker.[66] According to a *Sunday Times* report, the richest 1,000 people in the UK have seen their wealth quadruple under New Labour, the collective sum of which was £412 billion in 2007 compared to 'only' £99 billion in 1997 when New Labour came to power.[67] Paradoxically, the top earners, including over 650 directors of British companies, were not domiciled in the UK. This segment benefited from loopholes in the law that enabled them to avoid tax if their place of residence was abroad, in most cases Monaco.[68]

On the other hand, 'Cool Britannia' was reinterpreted as 'tax haven' by comrades from the former Soviet Union. The unrivalled tax-evasion opportunities in Cool Britannia provided the foundation for 'Londongrad'. This was a new enclave that formed in the posh areas of west London as the extravagantly rich Russian oligarchs invaded this patch of land (and the noble British countryside). It included wealthy areas such as Mayfair and Kensington or, in terms of landmarks, anywhere 'near Harrods', as mentioned earlier. The intrigues surrounding the mass exodus of oligarchs from Russia to west London under dubious circumstances are discussed in *Londongrad: From Russia with Cash*, a fascinating but chilling account of how an unprecedented amount of new wealth was acquired by a small group of profiteers following the collapse of the Soviet Union. These fabulously wealthy few came to be known as oligarchs. Despite the questionable origins of this wealth, a costly fast-track visa ensured UK entry. London became the oligarchs' destination of choice. It was not long before they also bought their way into British high society, and formed friendships with politicians across the mainstream parties. Landmark property, football clubs, newspaper empires, art – there seemed nothing the oligarchs' money could not buy.

And yet, the overwhelming conclusion of *Londongrad* is not that this cash had any overall benefit for Britain, bar the industries servicing oligarchs and their lifestyles, which is corroborated by a plethora of literature.[69] On the contrary, the book shows how this influx of what is effectively dirty money had a series of detrimental effects. A handful made a hefty profit from dealing with oligarchs but for the majority, this uncontrolled bazaar of luxury exchange caused more harm than good. The amount of money that these guys brought in provoked all sorts of disruptions among the local communities (known as 'old money') as well as spawning a speculative economy. Anything from values at art auctions to property prices rocketed. It even led to the formation of a 'grey' economy within the luxury sector where deals were sealed on handshakes (no legal documentation) and payments made with 'suitcases full of money'. Some people, though it was offered, declined to operate in such a way. For others, the lure of such extravagant riches was too hard to resist.

The mainstream noughties were a decade so entangled in the culture of voyeurism that it became all about celebrating wealth without any critical distance. The culture of voyeurism had nothing to do with questioning the system, and everything to do with fuelling its economic drive at any cost.

The UK was taking money without investigating its provenance. The 'untaxed rouble' that catered for the lavish lifestyle of a small minority was not just dubious in its origin but for the sheer amount that was taken out of Russia (without being re-invested into that country's infrastructure), leaving utter devastation. This has been a hugely contentious issue between Russia's 'KGB style'[70] government –

Vladimir Putin (and his protégé, President Medvedev) – and the oligarchs ever since both sides came to power, as ever, at the expense of ordinary folk. Against the backdrop of the bling bling dream of a minority that they were supposed to admire, lay a nightmare for over 80 per cent of the country's population (with 30 per cent living below the poverty line) with staggering figures revealing the pitiful state of the health and education systems, the grim reality of life for the elderly and a rising AIDS crisis.[71] As recession kicked in at the end of the noughties and unemployment soared, life for ordinary Russians became even more precarious.

Back in the UK, we were spending money. We did not worry about reimbursement, preferring to embrace the 'buy now, pay later' philosophy without thinking of saving for a raining day. It was jangly ker-ching bells, bling bling all the way. Britain went through a phase of prosperity – or so we wanted to believe. And yet, there were always warning signs. Already in 2006, Datamonitor revealed that the average Briton had more than twice as much unsecured borrowing – overdrafts, personal loans and credit card debts – than their average European counterpart. In 2007, the German publication *Spiegel*, dazzled by the profligate spending of the British consumer, stated figures of 166 per cent of household debt as a percentage of gross disposable income in the UK compared to 127 per cent in the USA. When the market crash happened a year later, it did not just rain on the UK's economy.[72] It was more like a tsunami.

The recession also opened up a can of worms in the public sector in 2009. From local council tax 'surplus' (whatever happened to rebates?) being placed in Icelandic banks (something most of us first heard of when those banks went bust), through to the 'culture of excess' among high-ranking civil servants; it was all coming out. It transpired that executives in the public sector were paid disproportionately large salaries and bonuses. The government vowed to curb this practice (should it ever have been allowed?). And to top it all, the much-publicised MPs' expenses scandal tarnished politicians across all mainstream parties. Uncovered by the 'old-school' investigative journalism of the *Daily Telegraph*, it transpired that MPs, drafting their own entitlements, happily accepted the option to claim back public money to subsidise their private costs for things as outrageous as moats and as pathetic as chocolate biscuits.

Not such a dazzling economy when you started digging, but the culture of voyeurism did not involve being curious and, as such, it had been the perfect distraction from rapacious capitalism. Mike von Joel, the editor of an arts publication, certainly had a point when he spoke about new money, referring to the way the 'bling art for oligarchs' colonised, and some would say polluted, the arts world. Famously, Damian Hirst's diamond-encrusted skull sold for around £50 million to an 'anonymous group of investors' (this secretive way of placing money being common practice among oligarchs). What became most important was how much the piece sold for, rather than what it was. Von Joel's lament over the state of art can be applied more generally to the state of mainstream culture: 'We were supposed to be impressed with the ever-increasing amounts paid for individual works as they unfolded, eulogised in newspapers, television reports... What is clear is that any individual prepared to pay large amounts of money for art in this new highly public arena, would have society, the art trade and the media lining up to lick their boots. And this is the *irresistible* factor for those enjoying wealth without merit in our post rock 'n' roll era.'[73]

This is exactly what I am wondering. The greed of the few came at a huge cost to the many. So consumed by consumerism as to lose all sense of (moral) value and sold out as citizens as to feel powerless and demoralised, has it all gone a step too far in the bling bling decade? Have we indeed entered a post rock 'n' roll era?

THE POST ROCK 'N' ROLL ERA?
Fame Without Merit

So far, I've argued that hip's sell-out was inevitable – but has it even become desirable (a goal rather than a fate)? In its crossover journey, which began in the 1960s, has the definition of hip as understood in the mainstream gone from virulently oppositional (the rock counterculture of baby boomers), via ironically inevitable (post-punk DIY alternative cultures of Generation X) through to becoming its own antithesis (the celebrity culture of Generation Y)? I'm not even considering the new kids on the block – Generation Z and even Generation i. Have we reached a generational precedent in hip's crossover story where the sell-out no longer means anything? Could it be that the emotional rift between the underground and the mainstream, once based on convictions that community ideals had been sacrificed for commerce, has been replaced by a functional, almost Machiavellian attitude where the goal justifies all means?

This is not so much a reflection on a generation as it is on the way the market chooses to construct consumption ideologies. What we mustn't forget is that, as far as the market is concerned, hip is primarily interesting insofar as it opens the door for the wannabe. In our framework, the ability of hip to reinvent itself is also dependent on the readiness of the wannabe to accept it. The interest of marketers in hip always coincides with a need for innovation. Historically, the co-opted hip emulated the minority rebel because that kind of attitude and imagery, when translated into a more palatable language for the silent majority, was a gateway to their pockets. The tone of hip communication has changed over the decades but the principle of hip rebelling against the system – or at least selling that illusion – remained a constant and a powerful marketing tool. It did marvels for Madison Avenue executives in the 1960s (in countercultural terms) just as it did for the cool brands of the 1990s (with irony). En route to the inevitable, hip's trajectory from the underground to the mainstream has always been that of building kudos by paying your dues, crossing over and selling out. That happened to rock 'n' roll just like it did to hip hop and any other subculture you care to mention that became mainstream.

In the decade of bling, a powerful phenomenon began to compete with hip's ideology of authenticity. The famous-for-being-famous opened the door to achieving fame without talent and started to redefine, even erode, the notion of merit. Wanting to be famous and aspiring to materialism is the antithesis of hip, but it has gradually been legitimised, particularly by youth media brands that almost indiscriminately speak the 'celebrity' language when addressing their consumers. It became cool to be famous (for being famous). 'Celebrity' became the perfect risk alleviator for the corporate paranoia. Like it or not, the wannabe – or the mainstream youth market of today that is the future of tomorrow – has been indoctrinated by this Red Carpet ideology. Gone are the days when hip hop or rave called for moral panic in the tabloid press. In the noughties, *Heat* magazine (more akin to a bestselling tabloid paper than a fanzine) sold in bucketloads to the young. 'Celebrity' was no longer just an advertising medium with huge amounts of money being pumped into it (the fees that stars get for being 'the face of…'). It also became a legitimised career path across many industries, without practitioners necessarily having the right skills, or indeed, any skills other than being famous.

Take the example of the Beckhams. They are the golden couple of bling, but what are we actually getting back from worshipping their cult?

David Beckham has long ceased to be the lad on the pitch ('one of us') and become a one-man global brand and advertising medium. Any excuse to nurture his celebrity status serves as a media hook, which is how Beckham grabbed the headlines when he played his 108th cap for England. Essentially a non-event, it provided an opportunity to glorify his status of not-quite-sure-what. He was compared to the legendary Bobby Moore, who also played 108 times. The difference is that Moore led England to its only World Cup victory in 1966. Beckham's team, consisting of some of the most expensive players in the world, not only lost that much-hyped game (a friendly against the European champions, Spain, in 2008) but failed to qualify for the tournament. (The English fans are among the most loyal to their team but England's pathetic exit compelled the BBC – who paid for the rights to the game with the license fee – to make promos in the national team's absence with the slogan 'What team will you support?' in an attempt to soften both the financial and emotional blows.) England's abysmal game at the 2010 World Cup was a wake-up call, with the public increasingly objecting to the players' 'underperformance and overpay'. The football transfer fees provide in themselves enough material for a thesis on ethics. When the media eulogises the obscene £135 million potential transfer of a footballer (Kaka) from Milan to Manchester City (which did not materialise) on the same day that thousands lose their jobs in the midst of the recession in Britain in January 2009, it is simply immoral. The provenance of a considerable amount of the money paying for colossal football wages is equally dubious – but who cares?

David Beckham's missus, Victoria the former Spice Girl, has recently reinvented herself as a fashion designer. (Taking five obvious market segmentation types – something that cool brands mastered, as we've seen on the example of MTV – with no particular talent for either singing or dancing, the Spice Girls were the ultimate product of 1990s cool marketing hype and became one of the most successful commercial acts of all time. In 1997, the year of Cool Britannia, the Spice Girls were glorified at the annual Brit Awards, as their appropriately titled debut single 'Wannabe' sold in truckloads – thus extending 1990s cool from the early majority or the wannabe to the realm of the mass market. Success for the Spice Girls came at the right time – when cool sold out and was ready for commercial exploitation.) But back to Mrs Beckham. The moment she produced her first collection, it went straight on to New York Fashion Week's catwalks with a huge amount of publicity. Earlier chapters explained how difficult it is to become a fashion designer and how the road to success is very precarious. Yet here was someone who was famous but with no training whatsoever in fashion other than wearing clothes, immediately getting the Red Carpet treatment.

Let me use an example closer to Hoxton to follow the argument through. In 2007 Top Shop, the brand that had taken a risk under the guidance of visionary brand director Jane Shepherdson and associated itself with London's 'street' heritage to become a market leader, did a U-turn: it commissioned model Kate Moss to lend her name to a collection. What this move did was to single-handedly erode the merit-based culture of the hipster upon which Top Shop had established its trendsetting image. Rumours of unhappy staff began to circulate in the underground fashion community, combined with talk that Moss's contract had caused a rift between Shepherdson and Top Shop, as it coincided with Shepherdson's departure.[74] The latter is hearsay but the sense of betrayal among 'young designers' was real.

Top Shop was the brand that had built a cutting-edge image thanks, in part, to the Hoxtonites. It also continues to sponsor the New Gen Award on London Fashion Week. At reportedly £3 million, the fee afforded to a person (Moss) not qualified in clothes-making exceeds any fee that an actual designer ever received to design a capsule collection for Top Shop. For comparison's sake, the award from the London Development Agency that the British Fashion Council finally got in recognition of London's fashion legacy in 2007 was £4.2 million. This money was to be spread over three years among all the existing and new talent on London's fashion circuit. And yet, this community contributes to London's cool-city image and, as such, it gives something back. To make another comparison, a worker in Mauritius making clothes for the Arcadia group that owns Top Shop would need to toil for almost 4,000 years to earn the £3 million that model Kate Moss earned in a single transaction for her clothing range.[75] Whether that calculation is accurate is immaterial. It is about the principle. Digging even further, we see that Philip Green, the owner of Arcadia, was among the beneficiaries of the tax loopholes for the super-rich. From that perspective, I guess, £3 million is pocket money. (I am not putting blame on the individual – if the law can be circumvented, then the failure is political, as observed previously.)

As disheartening as these stories may be for a creative seeking to achieve success by challenging the status quo, the cases of Kate Moss and Top Shop and Victoria Beckham and her clothing range reflect a market reality. 'Celebrity' sells – or such is the current belief within the retail sector (in terms of ROI, the distinction between selling the non-designer 'celebrity' collections and measuring their publicity worth remains non-robust and non-transparent). What is certain is that 'celebrity' is a risk alleviator. For as long as that is the case, resorting to a 'name' to generate awareness and sales will be widespread in fashion retail. It is impossible to be oblivious to it. It also begs the question: what is the point of going to college and being driven by the idea that one day it could be your collection up there on the runway if someone else – who has not gone through the process of learning their craft – could so easily be there instead? A similar predicament applies across other industries and it poses a real threat to the future of creativity. If you are an aspiring musician (not simply a descendant of rock aristocracy), which route do you follow? Would you rather push boundaries and suffer for your art, without guarantee of success? Or would you gamble it all and follow the TV talent-contest route, for a greater chance of fame? In that case, forget about perfecting your guitar skills – better train in vocal gymnastics, to achieve the voice favoured by judges on *The X Factor*. In this way your career path is already planned. You are no longer an individual. You are someone who has to fit a format disproportionately glorified by the media.

The Red Carpet dream proved to be particularly compelling for the younger demographic that traditionally rebelled against status gained through 'labels'. Through the use of 'celebrity', the youth sector was made compliant to the economic model of excess (marvelling over the wealth of footballers or 'celebrity' fees). The TV formats of *Big Brother* and *The X Factor* also fitted the excess model. On the surface, reality TV could generate higher-than-average ratings amid an overall ratings decline. In reality, terrestrial television is an old-fashioned technology relying on a dated advertising model. The ratings principle based on prime time has been declining for broadcasters ever since the likes of MTV started to eat into the advertising pie in the early 1990s. With the Internet revolution and the advent of YouTube, music downloads and social networking, MTV's purpose was challenged along with that of the youth programmes on terrestrial TV whose schedules were even more constrained. Naturally, these businesses will fight for their place in the cultural landscape. As long as 'celebrity' appears to be selling (ratings, perfume, whatever) the industry will cling on to it but rather than a real solution to the challenges imposed by the digital revolution, it is a risk allievator soon to run out of steam. The dramatic collapse of time and space spawned by the recent technological advancements means that the marketing and communication industry is fundamentally rethinking its essence. In a fragmented landscape of social networks where content creation and its dissemination happens in real time, there is little room for 'prime time' (and the distribution of both content production and advertising revenue resources will need to be adapted accordingly).

The high fees that 'celebrity' commands – this might be a chat show host (Jonathan Ross was reportedly paid £18 million by the BBC over three years from the licence fee) or *Big Brother* or *The X Factor* producers – not only sustain an old-fashioned business model (on terrestrial television, a medium that ruled in the old economy) but they are also ultimately detrimental for the networks. That *The X Factor* or *Big Brother* or a high-profile chat show host could generate (relatively!) high ratings (particularly among the young) made their producers wealthy people; less so on the terrestrial networks though, as they were forced to make hundreds of staff redundancies. The prime youth radio outlets, notably BBC Radio 1, supposedly 'public services', also disbursed ludicrous sums to cling on to 'celebrity' DJs (or 'talent') on freelance contracts while making redundant around 30 per cent of the rest of its workforce (this wave of cuts began in the mid-noughties). Their management appeared to have forgotten that the unique heritage of the BBC brand is too great an asset for the BBC to be bullied into meeting unreasonable 'celebrity' demands subsidised by the public purse. The justification is often given that the celebrities would otherwise be poached by commercial networks. So what?

The culture of voyeurism has conveniently set all notions of curiosity aside. Adore bling. Desire fame. Don't ask why. That 'celebrity' was a powerful driver among the young was corroborated by many studies suggesting that 'fame' is a top aspiration for Generation Y. Even though the dream of becoming a footballer or a pop star could not become everyone's reality, there was a shortcut to achieving the bling lifestyle. Young borrowers in the UK jumped on the 'buy now, pay later' bandwagon in their thousands, making this the first generation who preferred to spend on credit rather than save. In 2009, with recession in full swing, the Citizens Advice Bureau (CAB) revealed the alarming extent of the debt crisis. Linking 'WAG-like spending mania' to bankruptcy among young people, figures from the Insolvency Service showed that in 2008, over 62,000 young people declared themselves bankrupt. Over 50,000 under-25s visited a CAB in England or Wales in 2008/2009 to get help with debt. Similarly, research by the Reform and Chartered Insurance Institute (2008) revealed that 50 per cent of the 18–34-year olds surveyed had debts (excluding mortgages) up to £10,000 and 20 per cent had debts (excluding mortgages) greater than £10,000.[76]

The second-generation Hoxtonites were a movement that provided an alternative to this trend. The Hoxtonites who achieved commercial success did so because they were innovative (fame through merit), but with its co-optation, the alternative ideals of the scene were subsumed by the Red Carpet. The rise of the nouveau hip and hereditary hip, coupled with the commercialisation of the authentic Hoxtonites, has diluted its original set of values. As with any trend that reaches overkill, a 'celebrity' backlash is inevitable (and it is in fact already happening underground). However, the prospect of instantaneous, gratuitous fame and a bling bling lifestyle has not been without its impact on the idea of hip as a status-challenger. In whatever form hip reappears, it will do so by building on previous ideological precedents. To round off the identity politics, let me use the legacy of Hoxtonites as an ideological shift barometer, even if in a speculative manner.

Attitude to Commerce Revisited

Among the second-generation Hoxtonites, the sell-out, though inevitable, is still frowned upon. The belief in the set of ideals that governed the scene is still omnipresent, even among the hipsters who have reached the 'tipping point' in the trajectory. A hipster (artist, designer, promoter, DJ) has to make money from their talent like anyone else. In that sense, you have to abide by commercial rules. However, there are degrees of concession; retaining control in this way is a form of resistance that helps retain some integrity in the face of all-out consumerism. Often, you will hear: 'We work only with people we like.' You want to make money but not at any cost. For example, an authentic hip promoter would turn away brand sponsorship for a club night if the brand's profile or the sponsor's contractual demands did not fit their vision. What also tends to happen among the scenesters who are in demand by brands is that they balance out their commercial work with work for friends. For example, if you are a DJ, PR or graphic designer, you will charge a different rate for a brand than you would for a friend (who might be a fashion designer, artist or similar). The principle of solidarity among the like-minded still exists. It is not all about money.

With the rise of the third-generation Hoxtonites, there has been a change in the attitude towards commercialism, but this is not so much because of an ideological shift within the scene as it is about context. Hip had reached its maturation phase en route to its full commercialisation. At that point, it was sink or swim. Whether you were an authentic hipster or nouveau hip or hereditary hip no longer mattered. It became necessary to adapt to circumstances where the distinction between the mainstream and the underground was getting blurred. This was a different set-up from the end of the 1990s and early noughties, the period of the second-generation Hoxtonite scene's incubation, when the division between the underground and the mainstream was still clear-cut. The anti-consumerist sentiment was still going strong, which is why the arguments put by books such as *No Logo* or *Culture Jam* resonated with Generation X. In 2001, YBA Michael Landy made a spectacular anti-consumerist statement when he destroyed all his worldly possessions in a project entitled 'Break Down'. Back then, that type of bravery was still a cool statement – but only just. Within a few years, it would resonate with Generation Y as much as hanging Che's picture did with Generation X.

To imagine that there is a life outside consumerism in 21st century Western societies has simply become impossible – even as an eccentric exercise. Neil Boorman's real-life 2006 experiment of living without brands (having burnt only his branded possessions rather than all of them, as documented in his book, *Bonfire of the Brands*) goes some way to supporting this. A lot of Neil's relations (and unrelated people alike) frowned upon his experiment. In fact, the demise of the street-culture magazine *Sleaze*, where Neil was editor, also points to an ideological shift when it comes to consumerism. Whatever the internal reasons for the magazine's closure, its über cynical attitude towards 'celebrity' and consumption did not make sense to celebrity-obsessed youth culture, the demographic it was selling to advertisers.

The mainstream's interpretation of cool (which was the reverse ideology of hip) nevertheless affected the underground. Steve Slocombe – following his departure as editor of *Sleazenation* (the vacancy filled by Boorman) and in pursuit of a different editorial direction at *Super Super* – sums up the feeling of the Hoxtonites when he says that 'it is no longer about being for or against brands'. If you want to succeed in living off your creative work while remaining independent, whether that work is running a magazine (as in the case of *Super Super*) or a fashion label, brand patronage has become an important means of support. The choice is no longer whether one should or should not work with a brand, but which one to choose. This is where one's integrity may be tested: by issues such as sustainability or child labour. The scene's ideals live through these individual choices.

Talking about the sell-out has become too simplistic. Brands are omnipresent. They can play a positive role just as they may have questionable practices. Being 'alternative' is no longer about abolishing consumerism. Rather, it is about offering pockets of challenge within the commercial world as well as finding ways to operate with commercial partners while striving to keep one's integrity. Let us look at a concrete example: the collaboration between Nike and Cassette Playa, which involved both a high-profile cool brand and a high-profile Hoxtonite.

Carri Mundane (AKA Cassette Playa) had established a connection with Nike when working as a stylist. Her personal style involved an element of sportswear, which was reflected in the way she styled photoshoots: she borrowed Nike footwear for them. The collaboration developed from there. Carri produced a line of trainers for Nike in 2008. From her perspective, Nike was a leading brand at the forefront of technology and performance. When it comes to fashion, the brand's heritage was in street culture (or streetwear), something she personally related to. Another consideration was ethical. Surely Nike could not be seen to operate sweatshops, following the bad publicity generated by literature such as *No Logo* – so Carri believed, in good faith. When working with Nike, Carri had creative freedom, which was also an important consideration. The product itself, the Cassette Playa X Nike Blazer, was a way of reaching wider customer-base, who could not afford the premium Cassette Playa line. This is the constant dilemma among the hip as defined by the Hoxtonites, where the ideology of street chic entails a constant need for price justification in response to accusations of elitism. And yet, most often, the production costs are genuinely high and do not translate to high profits in spite of the premium price, which is at least partly why designers resort to external collaborations.

As for Nike, it had a cool reputation to sustain. This was one of the leading brands of the 1990s cool marketing trend. Its image had to be constantly nurtured. To this end, Nike employed staff to act as 'connectors' between the street and the boardroom in places they consider key strategic centres (New York, London and Tokyo). In London, that position was held until the end of 2009 by a character called Acyde, a DJ from the old school whereby 'DJs were preservers of music and history as well as entertainers', whose scenester background afforded him the Nike role. The challenge for Nike was to find something fresh. Nike appeared to be somewhat struggling, as they were uninspired by contemporary youth culture, normally a rich source of ideas. Nike's urban director Fraser Cooke, a Londoner based in Tokyo, talked about how street culture had plateaued.[77] It was not reinventing itself. For people like him, who discovered punk and skateboarding in 1977 when it was all happening in London for the first time, and who hung out with the likes of the Beautiful Losers, rehashing those same ideas yet again is not impressive.

Paradoxically, Nike was complaining about 'passive consumerism' because, as a brand leader, you want the kid who rebels to keep you challenged and not the one who buys into an image (in this case street culture) without asking why. When you don't ask why, you can't push boundaries. If you accept, you do not rebel. While a brand is selling to the wannabe (who consumes without asking questions), it takes the alpha trendsetter to help trigger a new consuming cycle. This was not quite happening in street culture. Nike's feeling also goes some way to support my hypothesis that if you have a limited horizon – in this case the marketing mythology that street equals cool equals youth – then you are limiting your own possibilities for discovering the unexpected.

The movement that released Nike from this predicament was that of the second-generation Hoxtonites. Nike adopted this movement – but not in its incubation phase. The explanation for this is the haphazardness of hip. Hip reinvented itself by adopting the new ideology of 'street chic', which had originally been a reaction to streetwear. Cool hunting happened predominantly in that sphere, until the lack of innovation in 'street' culture made the hunters look elsewhere. That is when Nike started to court the Hoxtonites – by now in their third (more commercialised) generation. Nike captured the nu rave craze as it was waning, but still before the rest of the consuming cycle followed.

An association with Carri, 'the queen of nu rave', was a way to be current. Cassette Playa stood out as 'the most inventive' among the 'cut and paste' that characterised contemporary youth culture, explained Acyde, who drove this collaboration. It was 'an easy way to tap into a market you would otherwise not have access to'. The Cassette Playa X Nike Blazer was launched in London, then New York. Abiding by the rules of new cool marketing, there was a launch event in each city attended by 'cool people', the photos of which could then be found on blogs. Essentially, it all fitted into the model of cool marketing examined in the previous chapter. The next collaboration of this kind was with Dizzee Rascal (Nike X Dizzee 'Tongue and Cheek', 2009) signalling a formal acceptance of grime – now filtered through, this movement was 'safe'. At the same time, in support of the argument that the second-generation Hoxtonites were responsible for Hoxton's 'tipping point' in terms of brands moving into the area, Nike also set up shop in Shoreditch in 2009 (having experimented with the space through a 'pop up' the previous year).

It could be argued that the second-generation Hoxtonites had the luxury of being able to operate underground. This was probably the last subculture that was formed out of the gaze of Web 2.0. Already, with the third-generation Hoxtonites, the online medium was incorporated, notably with the rise of street style blogging (and it was the endorsement of the Hoxtonites that made them hip, not the fact that they were bloggers). The challenge post Web 2.0 is how to survive for long in a world that constantly seeks the next thing. In a desperate race to be the first to know, new ideas get discovered with little time for experimentation or making mistakes and learning from them. That speed puts huge pressure on creativity because it leaves little time for incubation. The next truly hip thing will learn to operate within those constraints.

The pressure of commercial demand on hip was coupled with another reality: the ideological shift that occurred among the silent majority, the mainstream receiver of the diluted underground message. Not only were they consumers by orientation (apparently, this was the first generation that tattoos brands on their body) but in the decade of 'celebrity', they could get their 15 minutes of fame via reality TV.[78] Even that model was challenged by YouTube, as anyone could upload content for the whole world to see. In the mid-noughties, youth market studies revealed that the new generation lacked the ethical framework of their parents. This was used as part of the evidence to corroborate this book's hypothesis that parents are now cooler than kids. The second-generation Hoxtonites' set of ideals (including putting ethical concerns on the agenda) did influence consumption at large, but the silent majority only adopted it as marketing hype because it was cool, whether knitting or nu rave. Looking at fresh studies into youth trends (published late 2009), this situation, in terms of lacking a sense of ethics, has not improved. For example, MTV's latest generational study reveals that ethics are not high on young people's agenda.[79] They would not justify an act of goodness if it compromised their lifestyle. In order words, they may sympathise with issues of child labour in fashion (and perhaps even wear a wristband to support a cause) but that is where their engagement stops. The moment they are on the high street, they will shop at Primark because it is cheaper than anywhere else and they can buy more.

This state of affairs is not a great one. Of course, we could now lament over MTV. If research tells them that their target market is not interested in ethics, then logically they won't bother them with that and then we would criticise MTV for 'homogenising' youth into advertiser segments. A non-argument, as far as I see it, given that MTV or any brand will not naturally sway towards the business of ethics unless ethics themselves – 'eco cool' – become a gateway to profits. This is called capitalism. However, there *are* ways of curbing corporate behaviour, which is a political issue. The corporate sector alone is not responsible for all society's evils. The other option is to lament over the 'vanilla generation' (or '*la boff génération*'), which is how a lot of criticism of today's young, obsessed with *Big Brother* and the like, is voiced. There is no denying that there is something uncomfortable about the 'me' generation, but if the young are that way inclined, could it be that there is something wrong with role models and more generally, society?

Rebellion Revisited

Two decades ago, Generation X was facing criticism for being less engaged in civic duties than its predecessor, the illustrious and groovy counterculture. Alas, it transpired that the counterculture had it wrong. It hadn't changed the world (though at least it had tried). Generation X was going to learn from its mistakes. Less anti-capitalist than the flower power crowd of summer 1967 or those who demonstrated in Paris in May 1968, Generation X nevertheless proved to be as cynical and as rebellious. They just expressed their alternative sense of identity in a way more attuned to their own era of hip hop beats and rave. Politics for Generation X was a reflection of a new sense of individualism. No longer was it about the politics of resistance through style but rather the stylisation of politics. Mainstream political parties did not understand this shift, denouncing young people as apathetic. When MTV rocked the vote, young people turned up in millions to the polls. Amid fashion fads, Generation X fought against racism, learnt about using condoms to protect itself from a deadly virus that could be sexually transmitted and even opposed the war in Bosnia. Acts of citizenship in the 1990s ranged from grand political gestures (abolition of apartheid, collapse of communism, European unification) to smaller-scale activism through causes (Live Aid set a global precedent for the formation of affective alliances through new media technologies).

Inevitably, when MTV became profitable and the market for music television grew increasingly competitive, it left its citizenship battles behind and focused on the most commercial facets of youth culture. (The question lingered, though – should politics have been left to MTV?) At the same time, politicians now understood that cool was motivating. Applying cool marketing tactics, New Labour achieved a landslide election victory on the promise of Cool Britannia. In the decade that followed, 'celebrity' took over the mainstream youth culture.

Citizenship happened in the guise of 'celebrities' promoting causes, or not at all. It became standard for 'celebrities' to do charity and for us to do our bit during highly publicised television fundraising marathons. In order to do good we needed to have fun – a perverted sense of humanitarian duty that became the norm.[80] We actually pay taxes for most of the initiatives that 'celebrities' endorse but it is now conventional for them to be seen to be saving the world and for the political establishment to happily go along with that. Is it any wonder that ethics don't matter to Generation Y?

Generation X was pejoratively dubbed 'Reagan's progeny', 'Thatcher's children' or *omladina* ('corrupted by capitalist propaganda'), for being entrepreneurial and finding a space to operate within the system, which in turn challenged the status quo. Generation Y is New Labour's offspring, the product of the bling bling era of rapacious capitalism. It worships young Internet millionaires or footballers who become rich when barely out of their teens. Unless you make your millions – overnight if at all possible – you are nothing. That is a huge pressure on a young person (or I would imagine so – this book was not a first-hand study of youth culture). There is no alternative in politics – or not much. Voting just so that the BNP does not get in is not democracy. Is it any wonder young people choose to drop out? How can we be citizens if citizenship is not nurtured beyond using consumerist language? The worldwide enthusiasm surrounding President Obama's campaign and victory in 2008 goes some way to showing that citizens are still motivated by an authentic path to success and a willingness to change things. The 'no clear majority' general election result in May 2010, which led to the formation of a coalition government, only confirms that the British voter is aware of the importance of having the right to vote (rather than apathetic) but equally unimpressed by any mainstream party (by voting, we are still reproducing a political system that needs change). Paradoxically, the next gap in the market – the next cool thing – could be in politics. By this I mean a radical political overhaul and a movement from outside the current political system with a genuine set of values, not cool hype.

Generation Y will no doubt come right back at me, the illustrious and ironic representative of Generation X, with their own tale of being misunderstood. My motivation for claiming that parents are cooler than kids was never meant to be a generational rant. In fact, I agree with the Hoxtonites who contributed to this book, who said, 'There must be some cool youth culture, we just don't know.' I sincerely hope that is the case. What we do know is that the notion of rebellion has changed. We have established that attitudes to both commerce and politics have significantly shifted and not necessarily in the right direction, and that this ideological shift will impact on the potential for hip to reinvent itself.

The most recent manifestation of hip that challenged the status quo over the past decade (with considerable mainstream market influence) has come from Generation X once again, rather than being a new attitude brought by Generation Y. Generation X were the originators of trends still considered cool, and whose status remains unchallenged. Nike's Fraser Cooke spoke for streetwear culture: 'That's why so many influential people exist who are part of the original generation that created many of these movements.'[81] Nike's feeling about this lack of innovation in youth culture that truly pushes the boundaries (like punk, hip hop, skateboarding and rave) is widespread. The story of the second-generation Hoxtonites supports this insofar as they were leading edge, but the youth market was not the first adopter in the cycle of the new trend's crossover. (That there are other cool movements outside Hoxtonites is a given – it's just that the Hoxtonite network throughout the noughties has been a fertile ground for cool hunting and a good case-study to assess hip's cyclical reinvention). This also supports my hypothesis that being a style leader is not necessarily the preserve of youth.

This has resulted in a situation where there is less distinction between Generation X and the next in terms of what is considered to be cool. The second-generation Hoxtonites' perpetual need to be a step ahead can also be substantiated with anecdotal evidence from the hipster clique itself, where it is the parents rather than the kids who are actually pushing boundaries. What became notable on the Hoxtonite party circuit from the mid-noughties onwards is that children of hipsters (the faction whose kids are in their late teens or early twenties) take cues from their parents about what is cool and what is not (rather than the other way around). Whereas with Generation X it was inconceivable that you'd hang out with your parents, now it is perfectly acceptable. The parent–child combo of my friend Garfield and his daughter Miquita is a prime example.

On the underground circuit, they do not come hipper than Garfield Hackett. A descendant of Britain's embryonic rave culture and an all-round scenester with experience in the music and television industries, more recently his hip kudos was strengthened through staging street-art exhibitions. 'No sponsorship, no bullshit, just amazing spaces and mind-blowing art,' said a blogger, summing up the feeling about the series of impressive events that Garfield and his partners hosted in London throughout 2008 and 2009. As ever in this story, what you saw there later appeared in mainstream art venues.

In mainstream youth culture, they do not come cooler than Garfield's daughter, TV and radio presenter Miquita Oliver. Miquita is a household name in British youth media. She got her first break when she auditioned at MTV and her career expanded from there on. In the hierarchy of 'cool' within the 'celebrity' system of values, Miquita is at the top of the scale, ahead of nouveau hip and hereditary hip. And yet, for all the VIP parties to which Miquita has access and for all the young stars that she regularly interviews, it seems to me that this girl's heart belongs to daddy. Not only is Miquita a regular punter at Garfield's events but she also brings along her 'celebrity' pals. Once, I remember her high-profile 'celebrity' friends serving drinks behind the bar at Garfield's event – just to be there. Miquita and her crew even patronise the same pub as her poor parents, who moved further east precisely to avoid the 'cool' Shoreditch crowd (in vain, as it turned out). Of course, Miquita's parents (her mother is the broadcaster Andrea Oliver) speak lovingly even when they try to 'escape' the kids, but there is nevertheless a sense of generational difference in attitude. They (the kids) are not like us (Generation X – and of course we implicitly self-congratulate on our hip heritage being 'better').

The case of Miquita and her parents is by no means unique and is suggestive of a couple more points pertaining to hip. One is that it could be that it's no longer cool to rebel against your parents, especially if the parents have authentic street kudos. In some cases, the kids are more responsible than the parents, who remain wild at heart (the 18-year-old son of a famous British actor known for his subversive comic characters went out clubbing with dad and taking party photos, as you now do, and was getting impatient as he was ready to go home but daddy simply wouldn't leave). If you can't beat 'em, join 'em. Rebellion has been replaced by a sense of camaderie. This sense of tolerance and mutual admiration rather than generational rift leads to situations where parents and kids co-host events and organise cross-generational club nights. Only recently, I got a text from Garfield inviting me to a street art exhibition to which Miquita had contributed a mural, inspired by daddy's world to create something original. Together, they have a guest list to die for.

Similarly, Rose Turner, once 'front of house' at the legendary Blitz club, started to co-host events with her son Callum. From a little duckling that we occasionally took to gigs (especially 1980s revivals where 'Uncle Steve' – AKA

Strange – and the gang performed), he grew into a beautiful swan and became a model. His career is on the up. In our fast-paced world of fads, he has already replaced Namalee as the face of Reebok Freestyle (albeit in the male part of the campaign). Hosting events is a natural extension of his professional world. Callum started clubbing with us in his late teens (he will turn 20 in 2010) and has always been in the entourage of people who have pretty much defined London's subcultural street tradition. It is very difficult to reinvent a style (clothing, music, clubbing) if your mother *still* has the original. (Rose worked at PX, the clothing store associated with the new romantics.) A sense of admiration has replaced the instinct to rebel. This is not to say that Callum does not have friends of his age – of course he does – but mum's authentic heritage is as much of an asset as Callum's debutant status on the scene. Once again, with Rose and Callum, you have a great combination for a mixed crowd of veterans with new kids, all at the leading edge.

The other implication arises from the conflict between the culture of curiosity, upon which Generation X was fed, and the culture of voyeurism, which is the staple diet of Generation Y. Whereas traditionally, the market sold images of 'rebellion' as cool, in the noughties cool became dominated by 'celebrity', which is the antithesis of hip, but nevertheless conditions the hip. It was almost as if *Big Brother* became the postmodern phenomenon that MTV was hailed as two decades earlier, but never was. MTV was firmly grounded in rock 'n' roll tradition (and rebelled against the previous heritage) whereas *Big Brother* lives in perpetual short-memory spans, inventing its own cool culture while denying ideals that had existed for a couple of generations. As previously stated, it is no longer about 'us' – it is all about 'me'.

The following thoughts reflect a more personal feeling among the Hoxtonites (whom I have specifically bothered over the past couple of years to help me crystallise my thinking – see acknowledgements) about the state of contemporary youth culture. In spite of the camaraderie between parents and kids (who are more conditioned by the mainstream), hip as understood by Generation X does not sit comfortably with 'celebrity'. As far as the Hoxtonites are concerned, the famous-for-being-famous trend is summed up in one word: bullshit. It doesn't mean you don't have to put up with it and work within those parameters but the culture of voyeurism is not something to be celebrated. It represents everything that hipsters stand against.

Today's heroes do not follow the path of crossing over from the underground, and that is why Generation X still dominates. The original superstar DJs are still the top DJs (in spite of abandoning their street roots for money a long time ago), because they paid their dues. They came from an organic culture. A nouveau-hip DJ or hereditary-hip DJ, who may be paid equally impressive fees, commands no underground respect because they never had any kudos other than 'celebrity'. As far as the hipster is concerned, they are 'parasites'. This is why the 'celebrity' clique – glorified as hip by the media (as in *Tatler*, as mentioned earlier) tags along to underground parties in order to be cool. The difference between them and the hipsters who inevitably crossed over is they do not, organically speaking, belong there. They are not the originators though they are labelled as such. Remember, Peaches Geldof is 'the queen of the East End indie scene'.

Garfield spoke for the Hoxtonites when he said: 'Now it's all about "I want to be famous." Before, being famous wasn't cool. Being a face – now that was cool.' And Garfield is spot on. Whether you were at Blitz in London in the early 1980s or *kafić* Davor in Sarajevo, the punters revered 'the face' (or *faca*). In the former Yugoslavia, *faca* was also the word used to refer to the effortlessly stylish, who did not have to be famous outside the scene, but within that microcosm, were respected, because they did their own thing (*fura svoj fazon*). Generation X was built on the tradition of the individual who breaks boundaries by rebelling against the previous scene. Still, they knew what it meant to be a face and they redefined that notion (with their own dress-code, music and clubs as well as their own commercial and political agendas). In contemporary youth culture, there are no faces. 'Faces' have been replaced by 'celebrities'. That is a different system of values, a rupture within the tradition established in the 1960s.

The greatest challenge for hip, as I see it, is that maybe the new generation do not care about being a face, or worse, don't even get it. Being caught up between the cult of celebrity and the 'cult of the amateur' (to paraphrase the title of Andrew Keen's sobering book about the dangerous impact of Web 2.0 on education, merit and ultimately democracy), the wannabe listens to 'the voice from the telescreen' and unquestionably abides by Big Brother's rules. Fame without merit (but with bling) breeds conformity and no good can come of it. Innovation and greed do not sit well together. One is about breaking down boundaries, the other about accepting the status quo. One could argue that, just like the counterculture, Generation X rebelled but they didn't change the world either. But the point is that we tried. That possibility of challenging the status quo is a key resource in a democratic society. Yes, hip feeds the economic machine by helping capitalism to reinvent itself, but it is also the guardian of diversity. The alternative is to have no alternative, an Orwellian scenario that I want to explore by looking at the case of Bosnia and Herzegovina, before drawing conclusions.

My story began in Sarajevo in 1987, when Omladinski Program became the product of a new scene that developed after the 1984 Olympic Games. This alternative symbol rebelled against the regime where a single ruler, 'Big Brother', was watching us. A generation later, 'it was all right, everything was all right, the struggle was finished'.[82] The communist system of Big Brother is abolished and Big Brother is no longer watching you. Instead, young people are watching *Big Brother*. They love Big Brother (and *Big Brother*). There is no resistance. The Orwellian scenario has become as vivid in day-to-day life as it is sobering in the fiction *Nakaze*, a theatre adaptation of Lutz Hübner's *Creeps* by Sarajevan director Dino Mustafić. This play is a virulent critique of the *Big Brother* phenomenon and the culture of mindless consumerism that it breeds. The rap soundtrack from the play (written by Hamdija Salihbegović and Nedžad Merdžanović, from the band Konvoj) sums it all up: '*Revolucija? Nama je dobro, mi nenamo pojma, dok oni se časte, mi jedemo govna.*' ('Revolution? We're all right 'coz we're clueless and dumb. While they're living the Life of Riley, we live like scum.')

We'll relocate from my adoptive country of Cool Britannia to my country of birth (well, Yugoslavia may no longer exist, but Bosnia is still where I come from). I have already been quite a harsh critic of the Double B phenomenon in the UK and it will get harsher with Bosnia, the case of which I'd like to serve as a warning to all of us about the potential cost for democracy if Big Brother (the Red Carpet ideology) ruled and there were no alternatives. The object is to learn a lesson, and reclaim the resources for hip.

SEX, DRUGS, NO ROCK 'N' ROLL: THE CASE OF BOSNIA AND HERZEGOVINA

'Ignorance Is Power'

Welcome a topsy-turvy world, where *sponzoruše* (pejorative term meaning 'sponsored woman', a local version of the WAG) are the archetypes of being 'well classy' while corrupt semi-literate macho-men rule, with a blatant disregard for any influence that doesn't conform to their insular outlook.[83] This is no longer a case of having no access to cultures beyond your immediate reference, because of 'communist time' or 'the war' – there's just no interest. Here, we have a situation where the notion of hip is almost completely extinct (it is a distant memory that lives on in the minds of those who once upon a time listened to rock 'n' roll and now write blogs about Omladinski Program). With the rock 'n' roll spirit suppressed, the alternative has almost entirely disappeared to give way to the post-war parochial nouveau-riche culture.

The Double Bs dominate. Jelena Karleuša is a role model. A silicone-enhanced pop starlet (from Serbia but popular across all the former Yugoslavia, now referred to as *Regija*), she has the whole package: the aforementioned breast implants, hair and nail extensions, the fake tan that goes with a bleached shade of blonde, Botoxed features, a footballer husband, and she once appeared in a porn video that 'unintentionally' slipped out on YouTube. The trials and tribulations of her life are picked over in the gossip media. Jelena is the definition of a career woman, commanding tens of thousands of euros for live PAs (for there is no music industry to generate profits from selling CDs). Her fee is more important for the public to know about than her music. Her favourite things are 'shopping and designer clothes'. Her advice for success? 'For me, my sexual organ is my brain.'[84] Her musical style? A new wave of turbo-folk, building on the tradition of Yugoslavian neofolk – which symbolised all things 'primitive' – and the turbo-folk that symbolised all the horrors related to war. However, the new turbo genre conveniently ignores its origins.

It is no wonder the past is taboo. The post-war society's elite emerged as a wealthy segment amid a majority who are struggling to make ends meet and cope with the psychological traumas of their recent history. Where once there was the amicable existence of different nations united under one flag before the conflict, now there is a total blank. The nouveau-riche culture is literally brand new and it celebrates Jelena. Those whose memories extend as far back as Part One will see a striking resemblance between this and the neofolk culture. Rich in material possessions, this class have always been cultural paupers. Before, they were ridiculed for their small-minded view of the world. Now they rule the world.

Famously on YouTube, there is an interview with a politician from Serbia (but his kind can be found across *Regija*) in which he made the mother of all blunders. He was boasting about being wealthy enough to invite any pop or folk star of his liking to sing at his feet. In fact, the only musicians who didn't play for him were Beethoven and Chopin. When quizzed by the incredulous interviewer, who thought it might have been a slip of the tongue, our man explained that had he been of the age and stature he was now when they were successful, he would certainly have brought them to play at his feet. It is just that he'd been 'a little boy when Beethoven was famous'.

Of course, not every politician is so ignorant, but those that are cultured are fighting a difficult battle. So far, the tide has not turned in their favour. The situation is similar across *Regija* but I shall primarily concentrate on Bosnia and Herzegovina. The post-war years have been dominated by *lopovluk* ('thieving') among a ruling minority standing in the way of progress. Corruption, which crept in during the conflict and used 'nationalism' as its cover-up, is endemic and widespread. For those who live honestly, it is a daily struggle and the state-imposed taxes and bureaucracy act as a deterrent to healthy enterprise. This is an extremely complex situation and I have no qualification to discuss it. Like anyone else, I get my information from the local media where politics dominates the agenda. There is a strand that specialises in uncovering corruption. They often name and blame individuals and companies by providing irrefutable evidence of wrongdoing, but to no avail. The question on everyone's lips is 'Why is nothing being done?'

Years of accusations without sanctions have created disillusion. People call it *crnjak*, meaning 'dark reality'. A particularly alarming problem is (teen) delinquency. *Crnjak* also refers to a style of TV that has emerged over the past few years. It is a sickening display of morbid voyeurism where charity is sought by highlighting extremely depressing cases of social deprivation and asking for donations from the public. This has in turn created an underclass of 'professional' charity-seekers. The general public needs escapism from bleakness but there is no more communist-style Big Brother to save them. The new Big Brother is capitalist. Reality TV (including *Big Brother*) and turbo-folk are the main alternatives to *crnjak*. It is difficult to find anything else in the mainstream and what there is tends to be imported.

Predictably, war was the start of this cultural limbo (it is impossible to disassociate the politico-economic climate from culture). The noughties became the decade where 'ignorance was power', to paraphrase a banner from Orwell's fictitious land. The clash between the culture of curiosity and the culture of voyeurism is extreme here. The alternative to the trend of voyeurism has so far been almost powerless. After the hangover period from the war in the late 1990s, which was symbolically inaugurated by U2's gig and the opening of the Pavarotti Centre in 1997, during the next hip cycle (1997–2007) rock was unable to survive under the onslaught of *Big Brother* and bling. The odd rock concert (with Western bands) that was held in Sarajevo was only possible because of the enormous passion of the old rockers who organised them. It was never about the money as there is no market for English rock. Such gigs, increasingly rare, are attended by a handful of the urban population: the rock generation and their children, to whom they are keen to transmit urban values. Even bona fide local rock bands from Yugoslavia are 'forgotten'. A handful of mediocre semi-rock bands who could barely make the Top 30 before are now the top bands (and they like it that way, not least because every time an old bona fide rock band re-unites for a tour, audiences are euphoric – there is no doubt that the music is superior). The sound of contemporary bands is folk with perhaps a touch of electric guitar. In fact, it does not even qualify as rock. The most cultured music is now urban folk. Its purveyors, former neofolk singers, are the new A-listers. Once ridiculed by the urban population for their arriviste values, they are now the elite whose 'urban' folk is distinguished from the 'less cultivated' turbo-folk. Before, it was cool to be a rocker, even in villages. Now, cool is not in. It is all about bling and folk has become 'urban' (a contradiction in terms, but nevertheless the cultural reality).

A new generation came of age, raised in this new climate. They went to school in the basement during the war. The mood in the post-war years had little positive energy. It was either *crnjak* (the reality of the majority) or the life of bling (unobtainable for the vast majority). Consequently, years of cultural deprivation during the war and some ten subsequent years of local versions of reality TV-style culture have created a fatalistic climate. The remaining 'old rockers' became tired and disillusioned while the new kids, with more access to information than their parents ever had, don't seem to be equipped with the knowledge to use it. Robbed of their traditions by the war and of their future by brazen politicians, they live in a postmodern state of amnesia and ignorance. They watch *Big Brother* and listen to turbo-folk. What's truly absurd is that the notorious turbo-folk star Ceca is popular in Bosnia and Herzegovina even among those whose lives were shattered by her late husband's mercenaries. By the same token, Pink TV is among the most watched networks. Having somehow succeeded in turning the war years of destruction and deprivation into a prosperous enterprise, its owner emerged as Serbia's greatest media tycoon. He now 'regrets' his former association with Slobodan Milošević and his wife.[85] Pink TV abandoned its nationalistic orientation from the 1990s in favour of a programming strategy aimed at *Regija*. It is wall-to-wall reality TV, talent contests and *Big Brother*.

The author of the play *Nakaze*, Dino Mustafić, sees the climate in *Regija* and the new generation growing up in it as the perfect ground for the development of Marcuse's 'one-dimensional culture'. There is avid consumption of Western consumerist values without any critical distance. This, in turn, says Mustafić, 'annihilates all senses and inhibits any rebellious reflex'. Meanwhile, local culture remains institutionalised and compliant, thus reinforcing the system in which politics and economics are one and the same, where huge privileges are blatantly and ashamedly enjoyed by the ruling minority at the expense of the rest. Well-educated and sharp, Mustafić speaks eloquently, but he is of Generation X. He had the benefit of growing up in a cosmopolitan environment. Back then, we had a fertile 'organic culture' (*organska kultura*), he said. That culture has now been replaced with 'spectacle' (*manifestacija*). It is all about the Red Carpet.

Mustafić is part of the minuscule local avant-garde. Outside theatre (there are about three venues) there is a jazz festival, a bit of classical tradition, the odd art event here and there, occasional books and… (I am saving the best for last) there is an exquisite filmmaking scene in Sarajevo. This should not be confused with a film production industry, for there is none. In Sarajevo, there is not even a decent camera for hire, let alone anything else.[86] How the filmmakers raise funds is anyone's guess. Ironically, we have an expression in Bosnia: 'Doing the impossible using film tricks.' Certainly, the film guys do magic. The country's pride and joy is *No Man's Land*, Danis Tanović's Oscar-winning 2001 film. The lead actor, Branko Đurić (now based in Slovenia), is from Sarajevo's New Primitivs movement, a principal character from both *Top Lista Nadrealista* and *Audicija* – a generation of actors still unsurpassed. His band, Bombaj Štampa, was also central to Sarajevo's New Primitivs' musical identity.

There is a whole gang of directors from Sarajevo who are regularly achieving success at international film and theatre festivals, so much so that it has almost become an expectation, locally, for them to win prizes. The feverish local media attention that this inspires has almost become a problem. The focus is on what they wore on the red carpet, with little interest in the process of filmmaking (a huge struggle) and the creative journey (a way of seeing ordinary things through an extraordinary lens – a unique talent that requires nurturing). Aida Begić, award-winning director of the 2008 film *Snijeg* (snow), talks of this phenomenon in terms of a negative 'energy' that is 'inhibiting progress'. Being curious and 'having the right to diversity' is not in the interest of 'some individuals' for whom the status quo is perfect, Aida says. This is why there is no new generation of talent. Young people give up too quickly, but they cannot be blamed because the local climate is what it is. Unlike Aida herself, a member of Generation X who at least has 'memories of living in a society with a system of moral codes', people in their twenties now have no such values to cling to.[87] This is a problem that the Red Carpet Culture (that of voyeurism) is not going to solve.

Sarajevo's filmmaking scene should not be confused with Sarajevo Film Festival (SFF), where these local films are indeed shown, often premiering there. Unlike the organic culture of filmmakers, SFF is an example of spectacle (a display of Red Carpet Culture). The festival began under siege as a sign of defiance against the aggression wrought upon Sarajevo, but has since been appropriated by the current director, who runs the festival as his private enterprise. Though by no means a political festival, it has nevertheless enjoyed a privileged position among the local dignitaries, which means that it receives a disproportionate amount of the annual budgets dedicated to culture. This is a contentious issue. While most people recognise the tourist value of the festival and the buzz it creates during the week or so it takes place, intellectuals are increasingly asking for accountability: 'What is the Festival actually giving back? For those outside the inner circle of aftershow parties, what is the benefit?' The magazine *Dani* is very critical, denouncing its many practices, while some local personalities boycott it.[88] After 15 years of the festival, there is no culture of going to the movies among the local young, they feel. A lot of punters attending the festival are from the diaspora. Herzegovina's largest city, Mostar, does not even have a cinema.[89] Dubioza Kolektiv, a local protest rap group, summed up the opposition to the festival with an ironic rhyme (it rhymes in Bosnian): 'Long live the red carpet! Ten days of opulence, 355 days of starvation...'

Reclaiming the Right to Diversity

Dubioza are part of the tiny post-war organic culture. They see themselves primarily as agitators rather than rappers (ie musicians). Their lyrics focus on inciting the development of citizenship values. Their belief is that citizenship action begins at home: you have to care for your immediate environment (rather than destroy communal property, which is common) before you can understand the value of common causes (namely fighting corruption and Big Brother/ *Big Brother*). Though not quite an underground band – they occasionally get mainstream exposure, not least because there is a lot of TV and not much going on – Dubioza do not actively solicit mainstream media attention. It's all about online social networks and word of mouth, which is efficient enough to sell out gigs. Dubioza share their contact network with a small local hip hop scene from the city of Tuzla gathered around the banner FM Jam (a small radio station and publishing house). It also features Bosnia's most prominent rappers, Frenki and Edo Maajka. The latter is enjoying some mainstream success across *Regija* (co-signed by the record company Men Art from Zagreb).

The other alternative networks are Sarajevo's local radio 202 and EFM student radio, though their respective broadcast reaches are tiny (and the radio landscape is competitive; there are hundreds of stations). Interestingly, I discovered the main host from EFM, Zoran Ćatić, via the German-based Internet radio station Funkhaus Evropa. Had Yugoslavia remained one country, this would have been its national network. This feed (in local languages – formerly Serbo-Croat) provides analysis and insight from across *Regija* rather than just serving sensationalist information or nationalist provocation (which still exists). Ćatić's reports could have been on Omladinski Program, I thought when I first heard him. I was not far off. The first thing Zoran said to me when we met for an interview for this book was: 'When I told my mates I was meeting you, they said "Get out of here!" They didn't believe me. We used to bunk off school to listen to Omladinski! You brought us up. Omladinski said "such and such record", [and] we went to buy it.' Zoran is trying to keep that spirit alive on EFM but it is very difficult. 'Young people do not understand satire and irony any more,' he sighs. 'All they know is *"Rat i* Veliki Brat" (war and *Big Brother)*.' This cultural barrier is coupled with a non-existent local music industry. There are only a handful of 'worthy' Bosnian and Herzegovinian alternative bands, such as Sikter (who emerged as a defiance band during the conflict), Skroz, Vunemy and Letu Štuke, but there is no scene. These guys are the first to admit that, as Brano Jakubović from Dubioza put it: 'There is no subculture. Before, rockers and punks used to fight each other for their turf. Now, young people fight each other and kill each other. That's not a subculture... And there is no global connection. Before, we used to stay up just so that we could video *Alternative Nation* on MTV. Now MTV Adria is irrelevant. We went to the opening with Dubioza and we occasionally collaborate, but MTV is an old-fashioned concept. We use YouTube now.'

As ever in times of need, when I contemplate my native culture (now alien to me), I turn to Boro Kontić. He spent the war years in Sarajevo, promoting the voice of reason, and is now the director of Media Centre, a production-cum-research resource. I ask him how come there is no new generation, like we were?

And why are there no new Omladinski Program-style movements? Boro is quiet for a moment. He takes a deep breath and says, 'There's been a total collapse of every system of values here. There is a new system in place that is completely different to what we knew. Rock 'n' roll is no longer the leader. [Pause.] You know, maybe back then we were living in fairyland, a little bit. Maybe we were unrealistic. The cultural foundation of this region is folk, not rock. The war ruptured the continuity between generations. You had Indeksi, then came Dugme [Bijelo Dugme], then it was Crvena Jabuka and Plavi Orkestar, then Omladinski with a new soundtrack... The war was horrific. It literally forced people out. All the creators and innovators are gone. That's a huge loss.'

His thoughts are echoed in what remains of the independent critical press. An article entitled '*Bilo bi dobro da su tu*' ('It would be better if they were here') has been cited on many blogs. Its original source might have been *Dani*, the magazine owned by one of the Senads from Omladinski. The article speaks of the tremendous cultural vacancy created by the loss of trend leaders, which is coupled with the 'brain drain' phenomenon (incidentally, a problem across former Eastern Bloc states unable to offer work/life conditions that match Western opportunities).[90] The article then listed the opinion formers that the country 'needs' back. I was one of them.

My good friend Boris Šiber (Šibi), a former *Nadrealista* and now the head of youth programming on FTV, one of the state networks, has the same explanation for the lack of organic youth cultures: 'First, for me, being young is a state of mind. Audience research forces me to put a cap on 29 but I don't pay much attention to focus groups and demographics. If you want to know what young people do, hang out with them. Do the same things. If you go to Exit music festival [Novi Sad, Serbia], you'll be doing as they do, but you'll also realise that not everyone there is under 29. Still, 90 per cent of young people in Bosnia and Herzegovina do not use their brain. It's turbo-folk and *Big Brother*, dumb it down and especially do not let them think. These kids grew up with no electricity and the post-war decade has been tough in another way. The climate is such that cities have become villages. We [urbanites] are in the minority. There is no Lida Hujić. She's gone to London.'

Here we go again. Šibi is speaking metaphorically but that sense of responsibility to do something collectively good is still the mentality of our breed. In terms of relationship to the dominant culture – that is not just individualistic ('I could be a star!') but also reproducing the grab-what-I-can economy – there is no common link. The chasm appears unbridgeable. I genuinely could not think in what way 'all my connections' might be useful. If anything, people like me are *persona non grata*. The set of skills that afford me a decent lifestyle appear to be of no relevance in Bosnia, even as a guest lecturer to media students. I guess I should mention that in the late 1990s, it was fashionable to interview 'our successful people abroad', something that I always declined to participate in. When I got my PhD, my proud mother was talked into giving a graduation photo to a journalist, which led to a few articles. Unapologetically sensationalist (apparently, I regularly drink coffee with Madonna), the articles were never used to suggest that the education system might benefit from my input. The only opportunity that emerged of genuine interest was a consultant's position at the BBC (advertised circa 2001) to rebuild Bosnia's public service broadcasting (the institution where I'd left a legacy and where some of my former colleagues/friends were still working). However, I did not even get an interview. Only when I complained did I get an apology for the 'obvious' omission. I then went through the charade of being interviewed for a vacancy that had obviously already been filled (the BBC has to advertise vacancies by law). From my experience, it was not about recruiting the most competent person for the job. The Bosnian brief was just a drop in the ocean for the BBC where a bunch of professionals dealing with 'difficult zones' are tenured before moving on. That consulting project would prove to be one among a series of failed initiatives when it came to Bosnia's broadcasting reform, as we shall see. If you have the misfortune of coming from a region that needs 'charity' or help from an 'international public fund' to get back on its feet, you realise that 'individual causes' are primarily addressed as generic (to which models are applied). If it doesn't work, there is no accountability. At the same time, the fact that it hasn't worked usually panders to those locally who favour the status quo. The one losing out is the local good guy, the one you wanted to help in the first place.

I finally succumbed to the idea of 'doing something' to counter to the mass-culture trend in the midst of discussions with various friends about a cultural lift, as things were getting worse. Retaliating against *Big Brother* propaganda with hip propaganda was my thinking. In true DIY style, I decided to film a TV series in London that would break all boundaries and thus open new horizons. With hindsight, it was a crazy idea but I did it anyway. It was called *VIZA* (a backstage pass, but also a pass to see the wider world). You might have thought that the TV networks would have jumped at the opportunity to show to their audiences a brand new project as well as sell it to advertisers. Think again. The story of *VIZA* is that of hip's struggle. It is a prime example of how challenging the status quo, particularly if it hits right where it needs to, involves overcoming many barriers. It also goes some way to proving that innovation (a counter-trend to the homogenising, lowest-common-denominator drive) is the only way forward for diversity, not just in Bosnia but anywhere else in the world.

VIZA: the 'Exclusive' TV Programme that No One Wanted

VIZA should have been dumb-proof. It was anything but. I can shed light on some sabotage, while other factors that acted against it will forever remain perplexing. The only explanation here is the local Bosnian saying: 'Where Bosnia starts, that's where all logic ends.' For starters, I had all the right contacts locally that would ensure *VIZA*'s placement (local production company to offer the product, local agency to attach revenue and TV network to host it and adequately promote it). The product should have been gold to the local market. There was nothing like it. In any case, I didn't care about the money. The main thing was to offer an alternative for audiences.

I had one condition, but it was not set in stone: my preferred TV network was BHT, which is where my former head of programming at TV Sa3, Haris Kulenović, and the production director, Ivan Stojanović, still worked. Under the post-war partition of Bosnia and Herzegovina, public service broadcasting was divided into three feeds: BHT is the state TV channel that covers the whole of Bosnia and Herzegovina and the two other TV channels are FTV for Federacija, which is one part of Bosnia, and RTRS, the channel for Republika Srpska, a post-conflict entity created for Bosnian Serbs (very contentious issues still, but beyond the scope of this book). Any viewer in Bosnia and Herzegovina has access to all these terrestrial channels. With cable, the whole of *Regija* can watch each other's TV channels, including a number of commercial channels (TV Pink, Hayat and OBN being the main ones in Bosnia and Herzegovina).

VIZA was to be a six-part series based around an interview format. Its USP was that it was a local production with international scope. Always a winning formula, getting the balance between local and global right is what had made MTV so successful. The idea was to mobilise A-list stars and brands with a bit of top-notch Hoxtonite stuff to be ahead of trends, but to clearly gear the interviews towards *Regija*. The crew was also international – and therefore 'Western' – but again, working for a local programme. For the most part, the crew generously donated their time. I – someone with 'pedigree' and someone from near the top of the local journalistic hierarchy back in the day – was hosting it. Even though the interviews had to be in English, I was obviously addressing a local audience while doing so. Ashish let me have all the wildest outfits from the catwalk. Of course, it was the next season's collection, in order to be current for the show's premiere. I also purposely left the option for the local network to tag their staff names on to the end credits, even though they had had nothing to do with the series (so that it came across as a home production).

In a world where corporate networks compete for stars (at times even paying them), you can see how Bosnian television stood no chance. With no money or status, I relied on connections and *savoir faire*. Altruism was my motivation and a group of tremendous guests decided to support what they thought was a worthwhile project (Pink Floyd's Nick Mason, Alex Kapranos and Nick McCarthy from Franz Ferdinand, David Suchet (of Hercule Poirot fame) and Agatha Christie's only grandson Mathew Pritchard, Toni Mascolo and his son-in-law James Tarbuck from Toni & Guy, MTV's head honcho Brent Hansen and Hoxtonites Mei Hui Liu and Sasha from Kokon To Zai). Everyone did something special for us. I didn't want generic interviews in hotel rooms. So we went to Toni & Guy's glitzy product-launch party at London's Sketch and filmed at their Hair Academy and headquarters. We filmed Franz Ferdinand at their only solo gig in London (2006 tour), Brent Hansen in his home, and so on.

VIZA was ready to go in December 2006 but for a whole year left in the hands of my local partners, the project got absolutely nowhere. First thing I learnt is that in Bosnia and Herzegovina, the state television networks mostly do not pay directly for programmes but do so via sponsorship. Strangely there were no takers (Coca-Cola, Wrigley's or any cosmetic brands) though I was never given a straight answer as to where the block came from on this front (connections were not what I lacked). Drop the asking price or give it for free, I suggested. Still getting nowhere, I took the matter into my own hands in December 2007. BHT agreed to take it on straight away and paid there and then. All my friends working within the public service institution and those running media agencies were gobsmacked. The second lesson I learnt is that the state television networks owed money to their suppliers (it could be a year's worth of costs for an outside production series) as well as wages for their workers. For example, on FTV, someone who started their job in February would get their first wage in June, if they were lucky (the situation started to improve, which people put down to a new competent marketing manager working on generating sponsorship). In *VIZA*'s case, the head of BHT would not have it unless they paid for it (albeit at a discounted fee). That was a precedent. It became a local joke to 'ask Lida' for monies owed. This is not to sing my own praises but to give an insight into the state of the media, and by extension, the challenges that face any creative project (never mind mine).

The third lesson I learnt was that the cash-flow problem was related to what can only be described as a moronic set-up, namely the legacy of the BBC's consulting mission. At least, that is where local staff laid the blame. Neven Kulenović, who owns the most powerful local media agency in Bosnia, rates the calibre of those consultants at zero per cent. He equally rates BHT's senior management, referring to them as '*gomila ignoranata*' (a pile of ignorants), a feeling shared by the local media community. Under the new strategy, Bosnia's public service functioned as a 'corporation'. Good in theory, non-workable in practice; the first contentious issue became the distribution of the technical assets. They belonged to BHT while FTV hired from them (their offices as well as the studio and editing facilities are in the same building). RTRS was allocated its own from the communal equipment. Consequently, FTV piled up debts by not paying what they owed to BHT, though the debts only really existed on paper. This nevertheless created open antagonism between BHT and FTV. BHT demanded payment. Instead of collaborating, they fought with each other. What's worse is that under the corporation set-up, the future scenario of advertising revenue share stipulated that 50 per cent of advertising must go to BHT while FTV and RTSR got 25 per cent each. However, FTV generated almost four times the revenue of BHT and almost five times more than RTRS. It was an impossible scenario. Public service broadcasting remains in tatters.

VIZA premiered in February 2008. Having actually acquired it, it would have been logical for BHT to give it a good slot and promote it on the channel, but that did not happen. What was more important, it seemed, were petty internal rivalries. Being multifaceted, *VIZA* fell under the remit of different divisions. It eventually went to one and created a row as different people battled to put their names on the credits. The guy who eventually got the credit also had the responsibility of ensuring cross-promotion, to introduce my past work to new audiences as well as updating it with my current interests (footage from Hoxtonite events, London Fashion Week, up-to-date trends and so on). BHT had a show dedicated to fashion and another to lifestyles and trends, so it should have gone there. Nada. My idea was to fashion *VIZA* as a brand that would stand for curiosity and gradually expand the concept into something useful for the young (Toni & Guy were willing to give special treatment should someone from Bosnia show interest, having seen *VIZA*, and Kokon To Zai would offer work placements etc). None of that footage or accompanying promotional interviews was ever shown, so that potential opportunity for the viewer was lost. There was no trailer promotion of *VIZA* on the network either (though we had one prepared, made by Justin Eade, late of MTV, so BHT did not have to invest resources). The few guest-in-the-studio-based entertainment shows hosted by young journalists never requested an interview (in these shows any Bosnian who lives abroad doing anything vaguely public is welcome, because otherwise it is all the same local people interviewed over and over again). Unlike Zoran Ćatić from EFM, who jumped at the opportunity to see me, these guys it seemed had nothing to learn. (The 'proud to be ignorant syndrome' raising its head again.) Even *VIZA*'s so-called 'primetime' slot, at 11.15pm after Monday's sport, made no sense to me.

The perceived mishandling of *VIZA* became a source of ridicule among FTV staff. They put it down to jealousy (among those at BHT who saw it as 'competition') and ignorance (some people simply did not understand the value). Jasmin Duraković, then Head of FTV, regretted not taking on the project. His excuse is that he got entangled with internal politics that eventually led to his decision to resign and pursue his passion (making films) and 'the future' (an infotainment portal). Jasmin had one word for *VIZA*: '*eksluziva*' (exclusive). This is something that all the opinion-formers agreed with. *VIZA* was in a league of its own. Its perceived value was not just in the calibre of guests and in the fact that it was from London but also in the way the interviews were handled. Research, general knowledge and an erudite sense of humour – all are concepts that have disappeared from mainstream entertainment. *VIZA* was a journey into people's lives and careers, which never delved into sex or sleaze and yet it drew the viewer in, I was told. There was no sensationalism. When I was myself interviewed by a bestselling glossy magazine (BHT has a press department who sent a press release), the fashion editor asked me: 'Lida, you always go to Fashion Week, is it true that there are lots of drugs and homosexuals?' I was shocked. But then I realised that she wasn't bigoted – just ignorant. That type of journalism had become the norm, which *VIZA* unwittingly countered. (I knew that *VIZA* was going to be different but hadn't realised the extent to which knowledge had been eroded until I undertook the project.) It was a far cry from the last days of communism when knowledge was power and headlines uncovered things such as 'bugged personal phones'. (It had, in fact, been Jasmin who compiled the list of those who'd been bugged. Then journalist at a youth magazine, he thought it'd be a good provocation, but the Ministry never reacted. I didn't know him back then.)

For all these reasons, *VIZA* had to be primetime (on FTV that would have been on Sunday evening after the highly-rated local sitcom slot) with relentless promotion on the channel. Amel Baftić, my former mate from Omladinski and TV co-host, now a British university graduate and a broadcaster as well as former head of scheduling at FTV said: 'Already, that they paid you is a miracle unheard of on TV but then they put it [on] at 11.15 and don't promote it. That is either jealousy or ignorance. My feeling is that it's a combination of both. That is seriously exclusive material that no one [local] has ever brought to us, not just in Bosnia but in the whole of the Balkans. That is primetime, not just for the key 16 to 35 demographic target but that material should have been a must for anyone to watch.'

What *VIZA* did was to upset the status quo by offering a truly alternative way of treating 'celebrity'. Money was not an issue. The networks could have had it for free so that was not the barrier. The market – and by this I mean the industry, including my own friends who are opinion leaders – was not ready to cope with *VIZA*'s attitude. In an imaginary television world, rock 'n' roll would still be the guiding culture. In a reality in which the commercial industry has settled into functioning in a certain way, *VIZA* was just too much disruption. Even if your mate is the guy who is running FTV and your other mate is in charge of scheduling and they put *VIZA* primetime on a Sunday, the reality is that the programme would be cannibalising the main source of revenue. I think that is the reason it was not taken by FTV rather than that the channel's boss, Jasmin, was busy. If I am to trust Jasmin, his claim that his 'baby', the Sunday sitcom *Lud, Zbunjen, Normalan* generates 60 per cent of the viewing share, then for *VIZA* to follow that show would have been too much of a clash. For all this sitcom's success, the storyline is thin, corrupted by advertorial. When the phone rings, the main character dances to the ringtone before picking up and saying out loud the website address of the network provider while it simultaneously flashes at the bottom of the screen. As for the dialogue, I could not sit and watch that series in the presence of my parents because of the amount of swearing that constitutes the humour and more generally the vulgarity of the rest of its content.

When the main character, a grandfather, is not swearing, he is looking down his pants to see if the Viagra is taking its course. In a previous life, the actor playing him appeared in Emir Kusturica's 1985 Palme d'Or film (*When Father was Away on Business*). Today, the market for film (as brilliant as it is in Bosnia) on its own is too small. Television is where the money is, if you want to live off your talent as an actor. Here, the demands are different. Once, the New Primitivs' humour had been based on irony and satire. Now television is funny because of the stupid Bosnian guy. That perception of the Bosnian is what sells across *Regija*. To put *VIZA* on after that series, hosted by effectively a mutant Bosnian, would have been too much of a jump. *VIZA* was too ahead of its time.

In negotiation stage, I had a similar experience with B92, Omladinski's former sister radio station, now a national radio and television network in Serbia. Its boss, Veran Matić, a true rock 'n' roller, enthusiastically jumped on the opportunity to be the first network to have *VIZA* (before even Bosnia) and open that kind of territory for B92, only to later retract his offer. After 'a lot of thought' and with a 'heavy heart', he came to the conclusion that Serbia, dominated by folk, was too narrow-minded a market for 'foreign' programmes such as *VIZA*. I got a similar reaction from a former colleague of mine who runs a local TV network in Zagreb. This is a network that plays repeats of *The Benny Hill Show* and *Voice of America*, a free news programme, as the network's programming budgets are meagre. After his initial enthusiasm, he did not go into details as to why he did not take *VIZA* but he did mention in our email exchange that the general public's interest when it comes to England is limited to Croatian footballers playing in English clubs. It was a chapter closed for me but at the end of 2009, BHT sent an email requesting permission to submit *VIZA* as their flagship programme for an exchange between BHT and B92. I accepted, though I don't know how far they got with their exchange. The truth is, it doesn't matter any more. The momentum is gone. I still don't believe that *no one* in Zagreb or Belgrade would want to watch *VIZA*. That there were not *enough* people interested is more likely (but whether that was reason enough not to show it, I doubt).[91]

However, once it was finally put on late on a weekday, of course people watched. Some even stayed up specifically to watch. The series has been shown six times so far on BHT. Interestingly, the summer 2009 run got biggest reaction among the public (the first wave of reaction was from the opinion formers for obvious reasons, as they have to be the first to know). Word of mouth had done its bit. Those who missed it before but heard about this 'new thing' caught up.

What's also interesting is that *VIZA* emerged as a small challenger to the status quo at a time when general apathy was being shaken up a little bit. It is almost as if 2007 was the trough of the downward trend, when nationalist politics, corrupt economy and Red Carpet Culture reached their peak and 'real culture' bottomed out. From there, the only way was up, albeit slowly. The catalyst was a symbolic tragic event, which occurred in February 2008 and outraged the public: the unprovoked stabbing of a Sarajevan teenager, who later died from his wounds. Young-on-young murders were regular occurrences, but people just had enough. For the first time in a long time, they spontaneously took to the streets to protest against the lethargy among the authorities. It was a public display of anger on a scale unseen for years.

Orlando's Coming to Sarajevo! ('Orlando who?' 'Bloom!')
In 2008 there were a number of small initiatives challenging the status quo. They came in the guise of small citizen gatherings demanding political accountability, and focused on various issues. This might be the wrongdoing of an individual or a bigger cause, such as teenage delinquency. For example, I picked up a pamphlet called 'The Citizen' signed by six different small organisations protesting against a series of topical issues and calling upon other citizens to join in forming pressure groups. Another initiative was 'With a shoe into the new year', a pastiche of the journalist who threw his shoes at George Bush in protest. Citizens were called upon to join in by bringing a shoe and throwing it at the photos of the party leaders they thought were not doing their jobs properly. A network of civic youth mobilisation also appears to be forming. In 2009, Sarajevo's urban population protested when another 'brilliant' decision came from the public service network to close down the legendary local radio Sarajevo 202. It was saved by this action (at least temporarily). Perhaps the most prolific new initiative from this new wave is Naša Stranka (formed 2008), a new political party 'for change', endorsed by high-profile cultural figures including Danis Tanović and Dino Mustafić. The influence of this party is yet to be seen.

At the tail end of 2007, Mustafić's *Nakaze* premiered, signalling the beginning of a new wave of organic protest culture versus the spectacle culture of *Big Brother*. In 2008, Dubioza Kolektiv released its album *Firma Ilegal*, a fierce critique of corruption and its correlation with the *Big Brother* syndrome. It is a first-rate record of protest rap, reminiscent of Public Enemy (in terms of the power of the lyrics) when rap was still perceived as a threat to upwardly mobile society. Chuck

D famously said that rap was 'CNN for black people'. I'd say that Dubioza is the equivalent to the Bosnian cosmopolitan fight for the right to diversity. When *Firma Ilegal* got exposure on the news, Dubioza considered that as a victory for their cause, as it resonated far beyond the group's fan-base. At the Edinburgh Fringe Festival that summer, Haris Pašović's adaptation of Nigel Williams' *Class Enemy* (Klasni Neprijatelj), which deals with social problems, notably teenage delinquency, created a huge buzz.

In that same week, I was having a break at the Adriatic seaside when I got a text from Ado, a Sarajevan friend who is the greatest connector. (Ado always knows anything there is to know before anyone else.) It said: 'Bill is coming to Sarajevo.'

That would be Bill Carter, the ZOOROPA project guy from the MTV chapter. I hadn't seen Bill for ages. It would be great to catch up.

Ado texted again: 'Orlando's coming, too.'

'Orlando who?!' I replied.

'Bloom!'"

Silly me, how could I not think that Orlando Bloom would decide to come to Sarajevo of all places? But he did. He came over with Bill and a bunch of Hollywood people to explore Sarajevo as the location for a film for which Bill wrote the script; an adaptation of his autobiography. The Bosnian conflict was a big chunk of the story. Orlando would not technically be the lead (he won't be playing Bill). For Orlando, this film would be an opportunity to get involved with something different. He wanted to expand his acting ability beyond the requirements of Hollywood blockbusters. Bill still cannot tell me who the lead is but apparently it is a great young actor. He couldn't get Jennifer Aniston to play the Bosnian girl who picks up the phone in London (my brilliant idea). In fact, on closer inspection of the script, that scene was never there. (Damn!)

After a few days spent in Sarajevo, the crew, just like Bill all those years ago, fell in love with this city. They hung out with my friends in the bars, who all keep Sarajevo's spirit alive in the face of all-out 'primitivism', and it was very low key. Sarajevan humour did not bypass anyone, including Orlando. When he managed to lose his ring, he was immediately teased ('So much for lord of the rings!'). It would be a great boost for Sarajevo's morale if the film is made on location – still the plan, but it's a bumpy ride. Elliott (Ellie) Lewitt, the main producer, is doing everything he can to bring the plan to fruition. We'll do anything (the friends in Sarajevo and some of us scattered around the world) we can, too. Fingers crossed.

The accumulation of tiny citizen movements in cultural opposition could be the tentative beginning of a new chapter for hip's rebirth. Perhaps the incubation phase for something new has started in Bosnia. What is certain is that this is the end of this chapter and also nearly the end of this book. At the end of the decade where hip went chic but clashed with bling, how will it now reinvent itself? We could predict a backlash against bling. I already note (with a cheeky smile on my face) that book clubs and 'literary evenings' are becoming all the rage in Hoxton. In any case, by the time you're reading this, the 'current' cool thing may now be nothing more than last season's fad. Instead of pegging futurology and cool hunting as the next big thing, I want to focus on certainties. In order for hip to flourish, it needs the right fertile ground – a resource for hip that I would like to reclaim.

Conclusion

We've looked at two decades of kinship between the underground scenes that define themselves as an alternative to the mainstream, and maverick businesses seeking to make a quantum leap. At times when the market is in need of innovation and the means of identity expression is in need of diversity, the collision of the two is what challenges the status quo and shapes the zeitgeist. By being at the intersection between economics and culture at a particular stage of technological development, grassroots movements – and by extension the mavericks that share their ideals and aesthetic sensibilities – are the precursors of future trends. They trigger change in established business models and influence the mainstream style and communication industries. At the same time, with every subcultural coming-of-age moment, there is a further step towards positive change in the guise of facilitating liberties.

By the nature of their being a cycle ahead of mainstream consumption behaviours, grassroots movements are attractive to marketers. I have discussed their trajectory from the underground into the mainstream in terms of crossover and sell-out. This is the language of rock 'n' roll, invented in the 1960s, the 'homeland of hip', when hip and rock 'n' roll (an attitude rather than a musical genre) became synonymous. Hip was rebellious. It was about rejecting conformity in favour of individual expression. Paradoxically, this refusal to conform made hip the perfect vehicle for the constant reinvention of new consumption cycles. By rebelling against what it had previously patronised, hip became the lifeblood of consumer society.

Rather than reinventing the wheel, I applied the 1960s blueprint for hip consumerism to the 1990s and the noughties in order to examine how the notion of hip cyclically evolved to cause a paradigm shift in each of these decades. What this approach revealed is a generational precedent. With hip traditionally the domain of youth – or so the marketing myth went – it now appears that we have a case of the 'previous' generation (Generation X, who spawned new consumption trends in the 1990s) being a cycle ahead of the next (Generation Y), in that Generation X reinvented itself to create another new consumption cycle in the noughties. That parents are cooler than kids for the first time in marketing history makes a good sensationalist headline. However, when put in historical context, this claim is not that radical. Marketers have only ever been interested in the rebellious faction of the population, no matter how young or old. It is just that the youth market became all the rage in the 1960s, and then again in the 1990s when cool marketing ruled. The industry at large and even politics went with the cool hype, even though the originators of that hype knew only too well that being youthful was more important for their 'edge' than being young.

In the noughties, that was still the case; what changed was that the mainstream youth market, traditionally the first to accept new trends in the crossover cycle, was pushed a cycle behind. It followed (from the new hip that was not the domain of youth culture) rather than led the way into the mass market. What also changed was the context. The population as a whole is getting older while the youth demographic is shrinking in size. The population may be getting older in age, but not in spirit, and this is reflected in its consumption patterns. The older consumers are the ones with the cash, but the communications industry is only very slowly accepting this fact (for example, 'mature' stars are now being used to advertise skincare). In contrast, the purchasing power of the young demographic has deteriorated significantly compared to their predecessors' and the recession has only worsened this situation. Outside the economic argument (the morality of which I am not addressing here simply because the aim of marketing is to sell), ideologically, a plethora of studies corroborate that Generation Y is more conservative and lacks the ethical framework of previous generations. And yet, the brand and communication industries still invest significant resources into cool hunting in the 'youth market'; particularly the media industry, whose effectiveness is still predominantly judged by its ability to reach the youth demographic.

If you work in the brand communication industry, ask yourself the question: why do you need to know what the kids are doing? If it is to get insight into this demographic, then fine. If it is to project into the future based on their consumption patterns, then broaden your horizons. What kids do may be the next big thing, but equally it may not be. Do not confuse a demographic category with an attitudinal one. Hip moves in mysterious ways – be open-minded. (As someone who works in the industry myself, I know that is tricky.) The fact that there are limitations as to how open-minded the brand industry can be is not a bad thing for hip. This is where I disagree with a lot of critical literature about marketing practice. The marketing industry is homogenising consumption patterns, especially the youth market; this is what the industry is actually meant to do. By doing so, it does not necessarily hinder innovation, because the corporate industry is limited by its own reluctance to take risks. This leaves a recurring gap in the market for new things to develop.

Or at least, this was the case until recently, with the advent of a new technological milestone – Web 2.0. In the race to be the first to know, this instantaneous ability to report will start putting new kinds of pressures on the ability to experiment away from the spotlight, something that was already felt among Hoxtonites as the scene matured into its third generation. This brings new ideological challenges: just as television was indifferent to rock's elitism and rendered its ideology ineffective (which made it possible for MTV to reconcile the two and be ironically cool), Web 2.0 with its power to access anything in real time further degrades established ideological hierarchies. Its impact is yet to be seen but if, say, catwalk collections for the next season are available on blogs even before magazines' websites (let alone their printed versions) and if the high street is able to produce garments very quickly, how will that impact on the high end of fashion (which builds its cachet on exclusivity)? If the wannabes appear to be fascinated by one person more than the 'celebrities' they worship – themselves – and the technology allows them to be the stars of their own networks, how will that impact on the 'celebrity' communication medium? Many more questions arise, prompted by Web 2.0… It could be that the new hip will be judged on its ability to circumvent the predicaments of fast 'outsider' access to fresh ideas. Finding ruses to deflect attention could be the next thing, as a reaction against the attention seeking of nouveau hip and hereditary hip.

Speed of technology has equally caught up the marketing and communication industry. A fundamental shake-up is required to cope with the challenges brought about by real-time content production and dissemination to (global) audiences super-fragmented across social networks. In our story, bloggers and online networks emanating from the Hoxtonite clique were an example of how brands sought to capitalise on hip by using new media to build their image. In other words, this was about advertising on select websites/blogs with relatively small numbers of visitors compared to say, a news channel portal (not to mention search engines), in the belief that those are either gateways to the early majority or simply cooler places to be seen than the universes of the traditional cool brands (in fact, as we've seen, many cool brands also resorted to Hoxtonites to nurture their image). More often than not, advertising on such blogs was coupled with a collaboration of some kind and the all-important launch event (otherwise, where would the equally important photographs to be posted on blogs witnessing this 'exclusive' event come from?). That budgets were initially released from PR and communication agencies rather than the tandem advertising and media agencies (and yet it was technically about buying space to advertise) was a sign of how the established industry structures are changing. (From tentative beginnings, orchestrating hip collaborations has become a sector in its own right.) Beyond these examples, the full impact of the relationship between digital technology and community and how that will affect our understanding of hip is yet to be seen.

The degree of risk-taking was another big theme in my story; not a new theme but just another method of exploring hip's crossover. Here, applying Malcolm Gladwell's idea of the 'tipping point', I talked of hip's trajectory in terms of social epidemics. In this framework, the hipster bug spreads outwards in concentric circles from the nucleus of non-conformists until the outré becomes the ordinary, whereupon hip retreats inwards once more to seek out a new identity. In this model, hipness is measured on a continuum with risk-taking at one end, and risk elimination at the other. Risk-taking is the domain of grassroots movements and businesses seeking to make a quantum leap, whereas the other end is the domain of the corporations and mainstream politics. We followed this trajectory in phases from incubation, via maturity, through to commercialisation.

The focus of this book on select subcultures that went on to provide hip cues for the mainstream – and by extension the new businesses that first adopted the ideals and aesthetic sensibilities of those subcultures to carve out a space for themselves in the commercial landscape – also demonstrated a time pattern for innovation and change. This is a tentative theory, which stipulates that an innovation cycle leading to a paradigm shift in consumption takes a decade, from the seventh year in any decade onwards. This would mean that the next hip cycle is incubating right now. It is emerging somehow, somewhere. It is starting to take shape. It will mature in the period 2014–2016 and peak in 2017. Yes, the technology is there to speed up the process, but whether the process of development of an embryonic movement that will give rise to a new, larger trend can match the speed of technology is another matter (I'd say probably not). In any case, this is all speculation... Let's all meet up in the year 2017, to paraphrase Britpop alumnus Jarvis Cocker.

Meanwhile, the Hoxtonites are in full bloom. They are very much in demand by brands in capacities that mirror commercial trends (namely collaborations, limited editions, events). The next big fad – the thing that is currently current – is the product of the Hoxtonite 'dandy scene'. As we know, the dandies are part of the same network of Hoxtonites that brought to the fore things such as cool knitting or nu rave. With a distinct look and soundtrack, it is now their turn to provide cool cues for the style and communication industries. (I am not saying that the Hoxtonites invented the movement but what I am saying is that they have been influential in making it fashionable. This includes a revival of burlesque in Paris, its original home, which led to the set-up of a burlesque festival in 2009, because for a while the London scene was more developed than the Parisian one and the Parisians were fishing in London for anything to do with that 'theme'. At the same time, Berlin is seeing the revival of cabaret. I am also aware that New York has pockets of dandies. Once again, there is a global web of connections rather than a series of local scenes.)

Indeed it is widely manifested (in the UK), from swing classes to cabaret evenings, from pole dancing to Blitz-themed parties, from Paloma Faith and VV Brown in the charts through to burlesque-influenced style cues in shop-window displays and advertising, such as Virgin holidays' mainstream campaign for their January 2010 sales. A new dress style is also beginning to dominate the high street, involving a crossbreed of (1950s and early 1960s) rockabilly with 1940s elements. This mood is also reflected in the arts world, be it photographic exhibitions or performance art. Interestingly, and on a more personal note, Paloma Faith, as an exponent of this style in the mainstream, has worn in public a lot of clothes from my friend Ashish, whose background is not at all the 'dandy scene' – but as I keep saying, the marketing drive to compartmentalisation does not reflect the underground's refusal to be pigeonholed. (As for VV Brown, I actually discovered her at Ashish's catwalk show last year for this winter's season. I'd not seen her on the underground scene before.)

Whatever the new hip incarnation will be, it is impossible not to take into account the ideological shift wrought by the rise of the famous-for-being famous phenomenon. The conflict between the culture of curiosity that harbours hip, and the culture of voyeurism that promotes fame with no apparent merit, poses some real challenges for hip's potential to reinvent itself. In commercial terms, if the wannabe market is built on the idea of 'celebrity' with little care as to how and why someone got that accolade, then necessarily the idea of paying your dues is under threat. (I am not saying that this is good or bad – it is a fact.) The hierarchy of distinctions in the mainstream is indifferent to the aspect of merit upon which the hip crown was traditionally worn. We're at a stage right now where the difference between nouveau hip, hereditary hip and hip that results from the sell-out (ie the authentic route) no longer matters in mainstream representations. That hip would sell out was inevitable. We knew that at the start of the story; but what we didn't have historically, but appear to have now, following a decade of breeding the famous-for-being-famous, is a lack of sympathy for, or understanding of, the authentic route among the new generation. Before, everyone knew what it meant to be a face. Nowadays, the aspiration is to be a 'celebrity', with all its crass materialist connotations, which (potentially) renders hip's ideology ineffective.

One way of dealing with this scenario is to lament the 'vanilla generation'. Another way is to criticise the media for over-exposing the famous-for-being-famous, who are in turn prepared to go to the most disgraceful extremes of kiss and tell to sell their stories to the press. In Britain, there is a lot of public resentment towards this kind of journalism, but there is also a sense of resignation. Perhaps most alarmingly, there is a sense of loss of direction. Bedding a footballer can lead to a 'better' life than studying at university (accumulating debts and striving to find a job afterwards). Appearing on reality TV and nurturing the cult of fame for no apparent merit can earn you more money than your nine-to-five. At the same time, within the creative industries, this tendency is eroding the distinction between 'real' (actors, fashion designers, musicians) and those who access those opportunities through the 'celebrity' route. Traditionally, you required some form of training to become an actor, a designer or a musician, but now the fame route has devalued that path to achievement. In many cases, 'celebrities' get paid more money to make a record, design a clothing collection, or act in a film or on stage than those who have dedicated their lives to their profession. This poses a real dilemma, in general and in hip's territory in particular. What we're faced with here is a moral issue but morality has never been high on the consumerist agenda (in the boardroom, you think only of the bottom line).

The alternative then is to turn to politics (the supposed guardians of society's moral values) and it seems to me that this is where the problem lies. I'll use the case of Britain but the lessons apply globally. We pay taxes and trust in politicians to preserve our citizenship values but what has happened over the past two decades (so far as my analysis went) has been a systematic erosion of these values in favour of the market values. We've reached a critical point in the crisis of mainstream politics. The recession at the end of the noughties is not just a case of bankruptcy in the literal sense of the word (ie financial meltdown) but it is also revealing a case of moral bankruptcy. 'Bankers' greed' and 'MPs' expenses scandal' are twin symbols of widespread political disillusionment among the general public. In 2009, the public trust in MPs has sunk to the lowest level ever since polls began.[1] That has to be factored in when considering the possibility for hip to reinvent itself. I've addressed hipness in rock 'n' roll terms of crossing over and selling out as well as in commercial terms of reaching the 'tipping point' but it seems to me that a major part of the answer to the burning question 'what's the next cool thing?' lies in the possibility to be alternative, and that is not a market issue but a political one.

I am very much aware that the reader is now expecting some trend forecasting. I thought long and hard as to how best to answer that without falling into the trap of cool hunting – which would mean that by the time this book comes out, my prediction would be last season's. In debates about hip's sell-out, the corporate sector gets the blame. A lot of focus is on gentrification and the way the arrival of brands (resident symbols of negative effect being Starbucks or McDonald's) negatively impacts on the underground communities. Certainly, that has been a leitmotiv in this story, but then the premise that the sell-out is inevitable has been too. We can't have it both ways. Or can we? I realised that we could (a co-existence scenario between independent retailers and chainstores) but that we don't have the resources to do so. Here the culprit is not the market but policy as the supposed guardian of citizenship values. The right to operate on the margins is a right to diversity and that right currently does not seem to be protected by any legislation. Here, I'll make my case by speaking (writing!) from the heart. I have tried to be analytical and as dispassionate as I could throughout this book but this is something I feel strongly about. The right to diversity is also fundamental for hip's possibility to reinvent itself. My premise is that Cool Britannia, rather than the symbol of youthful Britain on the grounds of which New Labour achieved a landslide victory, proved to be the biggest sell-out of them all.

Where is the next cool coming from? This 'sixty-thousand-dollar question' is an easy one. Wherever there is cheap rent and cheap beer, watch out. Hip might be about. For all that Cool Britannia vowed to support creativity (and it owes at least some of its cool campaign to the first-generation Hoxtonites), the next wave of Hoxton hip in the decade 1997–2007 came, once again, from the margins and not as a result of some government-funded initiative. That is not a bad thing, because independence cannot be sponsored. This issue cannot be solved through public funding for arts and creative industries, though each type of incentive is important and should be available. If anything, as I said before, the support for London's fashion community was long overdue. However, being able to create on the margins involves simple questions related to the basic economic survival of a small business as well as purely existential stuff (banal things such the price of rent or price of a pint of beer). This is less to do with Starbucks taking over the high street and more to do with fostering the wellbeing of small businesses. Without preserving the resources for independence, hip will struggle to reinvent itself.

For the second-generation Hoxtonites in London, the ability to survive from the moment you upgrade from a market stall has been a greater challenge than the perceived onslaught of chainstores. The noughties have seen bias towards developers at the expense of independents, which has led to the merciless destruction of small local trade networks. In this context, I have tried to exercise my voice as a citizen, to no avail. In the past year, I was involved in the campaign to save the famous Islington Antiques Market (having lost the battle of saving Spitalfields Market from redevelopment, where I merely signed a petition but other campaigners were fiercely opposing it). Located in Camden Passage (in Angel, Islington, not Camden), this used to be a vibrant patch of land with street market stalls. Three large antique malls were the focal point. It was an antiques dealer's delight on market days. People came from as far as Japan to get their bargains. In the second half of the noughties, a systematic destruction of this network began. The first two malls were converted into a chainstore and estate agent, respectively, killing off the surrounding small shops in the process.[2] A fierce campaign by residents to save the last bastion – the third antique mall – began, but in vain. In spite of the huge public outcry and unanimous rejection by the local councillors of the developers' planning application to convert the mall into a chain retail outlet, somehow it happened. Residents were never given an explanation.

For small independent hip businesses that manage to avoid developers, the struggle is great. Local councils treat the independents and the chainstores with a one-rule-fits-all approach. It is patently obvious that a street boutique or a small café does not have the same financial resources as a chainstore, even though it has the same, if not greater, customer pulling power. High rents (unless the owners are clement), no havens for like-minded stores (as soon as you create a 'hip' community, developers move in), parking restrictions, incongruous recycling policies and, more generally, a lack of understanding of how the creative communities operate at the raw level (the embryo of a trend, if you wish) are all detrimental to the potential of hip reinventing itself.

Most of all, the real killer is something called the business rate. This is an archaic form of taxation that suffocates the independents, and the single most quoted reason as to why a small shop is forced to close down following the gentrification of a neighbourhood. Many Hoxtonites have struggled with this rate and a more sinister facet of the hip trend in London of opening pop-up stores is the gloomy reality of the previous occupant having been forced to close. If I understand correctly, for it is complicated (and frankly boring), the business rate is set by the government and implemented by local councils. A valuation agency assesses the rateable value of a property based on its location. The business rate reflects the rental market potential of a neighbourhood. Needless to say, gentrification pushes the rate up. The prospect of a new shopping mall, the moment the planning application goes ahead, already puts the 'valuation' of the business rate up because of the anticipated desirability of the area (ie rents will go up as chains would want to move in). However, if it weren't for the hipsters (who create a community that also draws in curious outsiders who enjoy what hipsters have to offer), there wouldn't be interested developers.

What 'valuation' does not take into account at all is the human factor, or the nature of the business that it is rating. Neither exists in the equation. Consequently, independent businesses (happily operational before) have to close down, as their profit margins are not high enough to cover the increased costs of rental and the business rate. In my own neighbourhood of Islington, the year 2010 is likely to lead to the massacre of what is left of the independents. A friend who owned a café in Camden Passage had already closed down in January (he also closed his café in Hoxton Square, the profits of which subsidised the newer, Islington-based one – the idea had been to do so until 'Islington' became self-sufficient, but instead its never-ending cost increases led to the closure of both). The rest of the community is very worried about their livelihoods. Another friend who owns an art gallery supporting new artists will have to pay a 72 per cent higher business rate. The average year-on-year increase among traders in Camden Passage is 60 per cent. Remember, we are (at the time of writing) in the greatest recession in living memory. Dear reader, you do the calculation. (So much for Cool Britannia.)[3]

Some of London's greatest tourist attractions, such as Carnaby Street and the Camden Markets, or more recently Spitalfields Market and the Brick Lane area, owe their popularity to London's street-culture heritage. In fact, in each case, the hipsters were the 'advance troops' of the gentrification process. Independent trade is the lifeblood of such networks. The independent network is the source of the type of raw inspiration that ultimately helps consumerism to reinvent itself and is also the fabric of local communities (whether or not they have hip potential). As a tourist, if you read the websites that promote the likes of the Camden Markets, they will tell you that it is the place where fashionistas get inspiration. That was indeed the case in the past when Camden was a 'street market'. Nowadays, it is more of a myth. I do not know a single person who goes to Camden to style scout and I know many style hunters, including the most respected in this field. Already, many are saying that interesting movements are beginning to happen elsewhere. Unless the trend of 're-development' of every single area that has a buzz is reversed, London runs the danger of losing the treasured reputation for eccentricity and experimentation for which it is globally renowned.

The right to operate on the margins without fear of developers is the right of every citizen, not just the style communities. If, in terms of identity politics, the legacy of the 1990s cool was the facilitation of 'minority' liberties, in the noughties the ability to operate outside the corporate sector has become a minority right. The governing political parties, as citizens' tax beneficiaries, owe us that protection. Focus on changing taxation policy for small businesses would be more productive than primarily putting the blame on corporations for wanting their piece of the action (and their ability to pay higher rents for prime locations). Independents will never be able to compete with corporations and will only survive if they are protected in some way. This is common sense but it doesn't exist in legislation (beyond business-rate relief for rateable value below a certain threshold, which cannot apply in hip areas as they are by definition on the up, and desirable). By preserving independent networks, we are preserving resources for diversity and ultimately freedom of expression and democracy.

As for the mainstream 'celebrity' trend, the bubble will eventually burst, as it always does when there is excess (not least because there is less money around). At the end of 2009, *The X Factor*'s winner did not manage to reach the treasured Christmas number one spot in the UK chart for which it was bred. Ironically, a Facebook campaign to drive 'Killing in the Name' by Rage Against the Machine to beat *X Factor* in the singles chart race succeeded. 'Killing in the Name' was not even released as a single. People paid to download it in support of this campaign, which goes some way to showing that for all the millions watching *The X Factor*, there are as many people (or more) who are not interested.

We end the book with another symbolic ending. *Big Brother* the final series is upon us. TV trailers – a pastiche of a burial with former housemates in 'mourning' attending the send-off – are on heavy rotation. I won't be watching but I did try to gaze at the screen in the name of research when the final *Celebrity Big Brother* was aired earlier on in the year. A contestant, a footballer's (or some other sportsman's) wife I have never heard of is in tears. She earned a prize (a photo of her toddler and husband) for completing a task (posing in a skimpy bikini for the other contestants to paint her). She misses her child and I am supposed to have sympathy, which is the last thing I can give someone who, faced with the choice between money and five minutes of fame by entering the *Big Brother* house and her toddler, chose the former. I *cannot* be bothered with this. I flick over. For ten years I tried to find something redeeming in this show and couldn't. But it is all right, everything will be all right, the struggle will soon be over. I will win the victory over myself, as *Big Brother* will be history. *Big Brother*, I can't help it. I don't love you.

The Pimpette signing off,
London, June 2010

Endnotes

PART ONE

1 Dragičević-Šesić (1994)

2 Kundera (1984)

3 Dragičević-Šesić (1994)

4 The official rites of passage in communist Yugoslavia involved: becoming *pionir* when starting primary school, maturing into *omladinac* (*omladina* in the plural) in secondary school, after which you became an 'adult' and could join the Communist Party.

5 Gordy (1999)

6 Bajramović, Dino (2008) quotes the historian Nihad Kreševljaković for the history of the café in Europe (following the Turkish model of coffee houses in Istanbul).

7 Denisoff (1986; 1991 reprint)

8 From now on in this book, MTV refers to MTV Europe. Where MTV USA is mentioned, it will be stated explicitly.

9 Quoted in Denisoff (1986; 1991 reprint)

10 As I implied in the Introduction – I will go on to show how Brick Lane became fashionable. A prime example of how the 'trendiness' of Brick Lane has become a given is the BBC television series called *Material Girl,* first screened in January 2010, which attempts to emulate east London fashion and lifestyle (as 'edgy' – which is how it used to be before it was commercialised). Effectively, east London fashion has become so prominent that producers thought it could make it to primetime TV.

11 Molyneux (1998)

12 Muir (2009), pp 6, 7

13 Goldsmiths College is in New Cross (south London) but many of my art student friends lived in east London where studios were cheap (or they simply squatted). Specifically my connection to YBAs is via Dinos Chapman and his wife who lived in New Cross before moving to east London.

14 The rise and fall of Britpop and its contribution to Cool Britannia is well documented by John Harris in *The Last Party.*

15 Leland (2004), p 288

16 Leland (2004), p 11

17 Williams (1963), p 289

18 From a review of John Leland's *Hip: the History* by Gerry Donaghy, whom I am paraphrasing, posted on: http://www.powells.com/review/2004_11_20.html.

19 Frank (1997), p 7

20 Idem

21 Abbie Hoffman (1971), *Steal This Book* (New York: Pirate Editions), quoted in Frank (1997), p 229

22 See *Altered State* by Matthew Collin.

23 A point made by Frank in *The Conquest of Cool*, which corroborates my own positioning of Generation X as a continuation of baby boomers' legacy but expressed through different idioms.

24 Andrew Ross, *No Respect: Intellectuals and Popular Culture* (New York: Routledge, 1989) quoted in Frank (1997), p 30

25 As implied by Leland (2004).

26 The first words ever to be spoken on MTV in 1981, followed by the video for 'Video Killed the Radio Star' by The Buggles.

Part Two

1 Quoted in *Vanity Fair*, the Music Issue, November 2000. The actual story of MTV and Ogilvy & Mather can be found in *Inside MTV* by R. Serge Denisoff, which describes the early days of MTV USA. Ogilvy and Mather won the pitch to first promote MTV when the channel was launched, a choice that was surrounded by controversy as several insiders suggested that this agency did not actually understand the concept of MTV, but won the pitch because of their American Express connection. The latter was this agency's client, which was a delicate matter as MTV had turned to American Express for initial funding at their outset.

2 Clarke (1992)

3 Banks (1996), pp 113, 114

4 Banks (1996), as before

5 Kuhn (1995), p 167

6 Hicketier (1996)

7 Frith (1993)

8 Thornton (1995)

9 Hesmondhalgh (1996)

10 Source: MTV

11 Gitlin (1983)

12 Andrew Goodwin's *Dancing in the Distraction Factory* is not only an excellent critique of postmodern readings but it also offers an acute analysis of the development of MTV in the USA over different phases of the channel, which is often neglected. This book was fundamental reading and it inspired a lot of my own thinking when I did my PhD about MTV Europe.

13 Frank (1997), p 28

14 Klein (2000), pp 120, 121

15 Frank (1997), p 120

16 Frank (1997), p 30

17 Mort (1990)

18 Ethnic minorities, for example British Asians, were also a keen satellite-TV audience, as they could find relevant programmes not available on terrestrial television.

19 Frith (1993)

20 Denisoff (1988; 1991 reprint)

21 Source: Médiamétrie

22 Frith (1988)

23 My supervisor David Morley wrote an essay about the 1980s programme *Nationwide* and I used that very conventional terrestrial television programme as an analogy for MTV, see Brunsdon, Charlotte and Morley, David (1978).

24 Grant (1999)

25 Other than the song by Dire Straits, there was a campaign called 'I Want My MTV' – when some cable networks in the USA took MTV off in the early days, viewers petitioned and succeeded in getting MTV back on air. The campaign was led by MTV but viewers picked up on it and carried on campaigning off air – MTV was their ringleader, which was another testament to MTV's relevance.

26 To be more precise, it is the 'rock and soul' ideology of authenticity, but it is commonly referred to as rock ideology for brevity.

27 As argued by the communications professor Larry Grossberg (1993).

28 Goodwin (1993)

29 Matthew Collin's *Altered State* is a key text in the story of the evolution of house music in Britain, which grew out of a combination of Chicago house, Detroit techno and the sounds of New York's Paradise Garage. Building on the Anglo-American genealogy of the genre, Hillegonda (Gonnie) Rietveld's book *This Is Our House* provides a good first-hand insight into the early manifestations of house in select countries on the continent.

30 Collin (1997; 2009) in the foreword, p vii

31 Thornton (1995)

32 Pareles (1990)

33 Grossberg (1993), p 206; also see Grossberg (1987) – he published many articles in the late 1980s and early 1990s looking at the shift of rock, if you are interested in that topic.

34 Leland (2004), p 301

35 Negus (1999)

36 I would like to take this opportunity to remember Tony Wilson, who helped me clarify my thoughts here (when I was doing my PhD). The legendary founder of Factory Records, he left us too soon, in 2007.

37 See, for example, Thornton (1995).

38 I make a distinction between 'stereotypes' and 'cultural metaphors' in my PhD, if you are interested in following that line of argument.

39 London Music Week, 26 April to 2 May (sponsored by BBC Radio 1, MTV/VH-1 and *Music Week*)

40 Matthew Collin used this expression in *Altered State* (p 334) – I like it.

41 Klein (2000), pp 120, 121

42 *The Rebel Sell* explores the contradiction between the popularity of the literature at the turn of the noughties, providing a tide of resistance to the corporate-dominated world, and the fact that they actually do not offer a real political alternative. Just like the 'conquest of cool' in the 1960s, the 1990s counterculture became consumer culture. The concept of 'adbusting' comes from Kalle Lasn, see his book *Culture Jam*.

43 Mercer (1990), p 43

44 A point very well made by Mattelart et al. (1984).

45 Martín-Barbero (1988)

46 Webster (1989), p 74

47 Stated in Billig (1995), pp 46, 47

48 Schlesinger (1987)

49 There is a huge amount of literature on this subject. If you want to get deeper, Chapter 4 in my PhD could be a start and you will find various references (by no means exhaustive).

50 Goodwin (1993)

51 An argument propounded by my supervisor, Professor David Morley, who was not left indifferent because of having a student from the war zone, and Kevin Robbins in the book *Spaces of Identity*.

52 This type of reporting, which made Bosnians 'the other', was consistent in Western news coverage except for Sweden, according to a study by an international panel of researchers that corroborates the arguments in *Spaces of Identity*. See, in bibliography, Robertson and Hellman (1997).

53 Paraphrasing Wark (1994)

54 Bell (1995), p 277

55 Gunić (1994), pp 170, 225

56 Gunić (1994), pp 45, 151

57 Hujić (1996), pp 65, 66

58 Eric Gordy's paper delivered at the Popular Music Conference, Ljubljana 1996.

59 For more on B92 and *Otpor*, see Collin (2001; 2004) and (2007).

60 This is taken from Coupland's *Generation X* (though he wasn't writing about Bosnia, it felt relevant).

61 Lešić (ed.) (1995), p 64

62 Quoted in Frank (1997), p 15

63 Typically, in this period, average figures indicated that an hour-long drama production cost $1.5m, compared to $200,000 for reality TV.

PART THREE

1 And performance artist Amy Plant, who was involved with Cast Off at its inception, but less so later.

2 A threefold (volume) fall compared to the 1980s and a turnover of €42 million in 2000, compared to €37 million in 2007, as stated in *Les Echos*, see Peters (2007), p 12.

3 Björk had starred in Lars Von Trier's *Dancer in the Dark*, released in 2000 (Von Trier also composed the soundtrack). The dress was auctioned for charity in 2005.

4 Strange describes his experiences in his autobiography *Blitzed*. Boy George, one of the greatest icons to emerge from the Blitz scene and gain huge international success with Culture Club, and Steve's partner in Blitz crime, called his memoirs *Take It Like a Man*. Robert Elms's *The Way We Wore* is another must-read for anyone interested in the new romantics and more generally an insider's testimony to the development of London's subcultures.

5 Alice Cicolini's book *The New English Dandy* assembles some of the relevant characters, especially in the 'East-end Flâneur' and 'Neo-Modernist' sections.

6 I am not including the 'casuals' or 'scallies' of the 1980s here because that youth trend did not offer the type of cues or anti-establishment idioms that the fashion and communication industries could co-opt. These subcultures embraced select designer labels, on their own terms (rather than as a result of a marketing exercise), which opened a new a market for those things, but in terms of raw inspiration for starting new one-cycle-ahead trends, these were not as fertile for marketing as the elitist club cultures. In this respect, casuals would become more relevant when they triggered a sartorial reaction, resulting in purposefully dressing down or looking scruffy, particularly in the north of England. This would give rise to the baggy look around acid house, first spotted in underground clubs (especially in Manchester and Nottingham). This look would ultimately shape style in the 1990s. Robert Elms's *The Way We Wore* and Matthew Collin's *Altered State* are great reads, for those interested in exploring further.

7 Vogel (2007)

8 Elms (2005; 2006 reprint), p 250

9 The London-based Added Value. Its founder Mark Sherrington (who has since left this agency) shares his experience in *Added Value: The Alchemy of Brand-Led Growth*.

10 See the interviews with streetwear/culture 'fathers' (including Jake Burton, Hiroshi Fujiwara, Obey), Nike's Fraser Cooke or else Jörg Haas (founder of Internet magazine *being hunted*) in Vogel (2007).

11 Elms (2005; 2006 reprint), pp 237, 238

12 Frankel (2002)

13 Weisberger (2003), p 185

14 Sagnard (2008), p 164

15 Simmons (2007)

16 'The New Face Of British Prosperity – Bling Is Dead, Stealth Wealth Is In', press release by Mastercard (London 27 September 2007) – a study in partnership with Future Laboratory. The latter's study 'The Futures Report: Luxury 2008' also identifies this segment.

17 For example 'Beyond Bling', a report by Euromonitor (27 August 2007)

18 In Western societies.

19 Statistical Bulletin: 2008-based national population projections by the Office for National Statistics (21 October 2009).

20 I took this quote from his website www.the50plusmarket.com promoting his book of the same name. A fresher study points to a generational imbalance between the baby boomers and their children and calls for policy change accordingly. In this set-up, the generational divide is deeper rooted. Here, the children of baby boomers (or Generation X) are already at a disadvantage (longer working hours for less money, less social mobility) compared to the parents' generation (something that we took for granted and worked within the system but there comes a burn-out point) and the question is then of what the next generation (Generation Y) is going to be faced with. See Willetts (2010).

21 From the now-defunct *Brand Strategy*, June 2005 Issue 193, the section 'Marketing to Youth'.

22 This looks like a print-on-demand publication: Conception and édition par Ayot.

23 *Paris Chic and Trendy*, 2006 (édition Parigramme)

24 Ungoed-Thomas and Newell (2007)

25 Datamonitor report 'Capitalising on Natural and Fresh Food and Drink Trends (2005)', quoted in Fletcher (2006)

26 AC Nielsen figures quoted in Fletcher (2006)

27 Vyse (2005)

28 See article by Schäuble (2007) and press releases by berlinpaper.com (2007) and *The Associated Press* (2008)

29 Bainbridge (2005); also see Lee (2004)

30 Environmentalists may argue that transportation pollutes the environment, and rightly so. However, this must be weighed against the fact that the bottling of water provides livelihood for a poor community where there is no demand for bottled water unless it is exported to wealthier countries. BBC 1's investigative television programme *Panorama* has challenged Fiji and this was the response (18 February 2008, source: bbc.co.uk):

Panorama: Transport is responsible for a sizable chunk of Fiji water's environmental impact.

Fiji Water: Transportation is just one part of our overall carbon footprint, which we have committed to reducing along with actual carbon emissions by 25 per cent by 2010, and offsetting by 120 per cent this year. Over 99 per cent of the distance travelled by our product en route to accounts in the UK takes place on large, efficient ocean vessels that were scheduled to make that voyage with or without us on board. Packaging is usually a larger contributor to emissions than shipping, and any European (including UK) water bottled in glass will have a higher carbon footprint than Fiji Water in the UK.

31 Wyatt (2004)

32 Dates from around 2006 and reported on various blogs. The original source of information was credited to the now-defunct trend-spotting blog www.reluct.com. Information with an image, dated 09/04/07, can be found on the following link: http://www.thefashionspot.com/forums/f45/papabubble-comme-des-garcons-55541.html.

33 I first took notice as I was on the same trail – watching *Net Plus Ultra*, the programme on the French satellite channel TV5, where I saw the interview with the owner quoted. The trend was later confirmed by some (unofficial) figures from the Mairie de Paris (an increase from 300 to around 1,000 between 2005 and 2007); also see Visseyrias (2009).

34 Ruiz (2008)

35 For comparison purposes, in 2009, this branch took 300 issues of *Vogue*; 40 issues of *i-D*; 80 of *Wallpaper** and 100 of *Dazed & Confused* (often returning 15 to 20 unsold). Unfortunately figures for 2000 are no longer kept. I am grateful to Ellie R from WH Smith Victoria for her help.

36 Association nationale pour le développement des arts de la mode (National association for the development of fashion arts), a competition open to French and international designers founded by Nathalie Dufour in 1989 and hosted annually (www.andam.fr).

37 Conversation between JCDC and Carri Mundane in *IQONS* magazine, distributed on the scene. IQONS is an online fashion community launched to coincide with the 'fashion season' in February 2007. Its launch manifesto was entitled 'Fashion Meets Web 2.0' stating that, as a free promotional resource, its aim was to become for fashion what MySpace already was for music.

38 Zara is a Spanish retail chain owned by Inditex Group. Zara's founder, Amancio Ortega, is Inditex's chairman. H&M (Hennes & Mauritz) is a private Swedish clothing chain, run by a board of directors and CEO (from 1 July 2009) Karl-Johan Persson, who is part of the Persson family that founded the company.

39 To borrow an expression from the book *Trading Up* by Michael Silverstein and Neil Fiske about why consumers want new luxury goods and how companies create them.

40 A book of The Sartorialist's photographs was published in 2009 for readers interested beyond checking out his blog, followed by Facehunter's book in 2010 (see bibliography).

41 He has dropped the 'ć'; though his name originates from the former Yugoslavia, he grew up in Switzerland.

42 Anita's Vintage Fashion Fair, formerly Battersea Vintage Fashion, established in 2004. This is not to be confused with The Vintage Fashion Textiles & Accessories Fair established in 2000. I would say that the latter vintage fair is at least partly behind the new hip etymology of the word 'vintage'. Its founder wanted to convey the sense of connoisseurship and pleasure associated with vintage wine in relation to period clothing and called it 'vintage fashion' thus connoting something exclusive rather than worn out.

43 Roberts (2009)

44 The origin of the concept remains unclear to me. *Vous êtes sur la liste?* by Arnaud Sagnard (2008), p 184 attributes the first to the chain Target, who opened a temporary space at the Rockefeller Center in New York in 2003 to sell Isaac Mizrahi's collection of womenswear. The trend itself is most associated with Comme des Garçons' guerrilla stores, but it is unclear what inspired Kawakubo beyond what I mentioned, which is based on a chat with my friend Rafael Jiminez who worked for Comme des Garçons and was 'in charge' of the guerrilla stores.

45 26 October 2008, Channel 4.

46 I refer strictly to what was reported in the public domain, see for example: Richard Simpson and Simon Cable, 'Peaches Geldof Accused of Leaving Boutique with £500 Dress Without Paying', the *Daily Mail*, 19/04/08 available online: http://www.dailymail.co.uk/tvshowbiz/article-560622/Peaches-Geldof-accused-leaving-boutique-500-dress-paying.html

47 http://www.bbc.co.uk/celebdaq/

48 From a biography on Storm Models website, May 2009.

49 Jean Belot, 'L'homme objet', *Le Figaro* no. 17,699, 6 July 2001, quoted in Segré (2008), p 58

50 Cespedes (2001), p 34

51 Alain Schifres, '*Approchez y a rien à voir*', *L'Express*, no. 2601, 10 May 2001, quoted in Segré (2008), p 42

52 Sparks (2007)

53 Peter Bazalgette (2005), *Billion Dollar Game: How Three Men Risked it all and Changed the Face of Television* (London: Little, Brown), p 101, quoted in Sparks (2007)

54 TLC 'No Scrubs', 1999

55 Tony Salame, CEO of Aïshti, quoted in Chabbott (2009)

56 Cited in Hollingsworth and Lansley (2009), p 123

57 Young (2007)

58 Frith (2004)

59 Idem

60 I've gone for a humorous reference here, quoting Lee Bok ('not the author's real name'), see Bok (2004; updated 2005).

61 If interested in following this line of argument further and if you read French, Segré (2008) provides a literature review in chapter five.

62 Sparks (2007)

63 Hollingsworth and Lansley (2009), p 16

64 I have taken this from Hollingsworth and Lansley (2009), but there is plenty of evidence for the great divide. Just as I was reading through my own chapter, the BBC's *Andrew Marr Show* picked up on the latest statistics, according to which the richest ten per cent of the UK population are a hundred times better of than the poorest ten per cent (31 January 2010).

65 Reported losses were in the region of £36 billion according to a news bulletin on BBC London Radio, *The Vanessa Show*, 24 June 2009, but there were plenty of headlines as the bankers' greed dominated the public agenda.

66 Channel 4 News report in April 2009

67 Woods (2008)

68 Leigh (2006)

69 *Londongrad* is corroborated with a series of press articles, TV documentaries and other books. I will point out the documentary first shown on Channel 4's *Dispatches* on 30 November 2009, 'Lords, Billionaires and the Russian Connections' by Anthony Barrett and a team of investigators which unravelled dubious politics and abuse of power.

70 Wolton (2008)

71 Idem

72 Datamonitor stated in Prosser (2006); other sources are Capell (2007) and *New York Times*' press release (2008), 'Britain is most-indebted rich nation in world'

73 Quoted in Hollingsworth and Lansley (2009), p 192

74 Pook and Fletcher (2006)

75 http://temple3.wordpress.com/2007/10/19/the-fashion-industry-iii-exploitation-by-the-numbers/

76 'Citizens Advice launches online debt management campaign for young people', 12 June 2009, source: CAB press release; research by the Reform and Chartered Insurance Institute cited by *creditaction.org* (December 2008)

77 Quoted in Vogel (2007)

78 'Generation Y: Graduates who dare to demand more', press release for 'Generation Theory' (2009), study by Paul Redmond, Liverpool University

79 MTV Generation v.2 (2009)

80 I mean Comic Relief or Sports Relief and equivalents rather than spontaneous money-raising initiatives when natural disaster hits and money is needed immediately. Celebrities can do great, here, when they pick up phones and people donate. Here, it is about people being compelled to give rather than centred on the 'celebrity' 'doing something for charity' (aren't they good people?).

81 In Vogel (2007)

82 Orwell (1949; 1989 reprint), p 311

83 'Well classy' is chav language, appropriate here to describe someone with money and no class.

84 Interview on *Red Carpet*, NOVA TV, 23 December 2007

85 MacDonald (2007)

86 I must put a personal footnote as my friend Senad Zaimović got some decent equipment for hire as I was finishing off this book, but one example does not negate the rule.

87 Interview with Aida Begić by Durkalić (2008)

88 The world of 'aftershow parties' has been a central theme in this book and so it would be somewhat hypocritical to criticise such a practice in relation to SFF without adding in the footnote that: It is impossible to hold a film festival of any stature anywhere in the world without also providing the opportunity for the inner circle to mingle and network. Sarajevo is no different – the international and local festival attendees from the film and related worlds and the guests of honour is what makes SFF special and I'd say the most prestigious festival in the Balkan region. The reason for the mounting criticism of SFF is to do with the perceived lack of collective benefit compared to the amount of public funding it receives, coupled with other perks.

89 At the end of 2009, Sarajevo opened its first multiplex cinema (there is also one in Banja Luka, the capital city of Republika Srpska, which is the part of Bosnia 'belonging' to the Bosnian Serbs under the Dayton Peace Accord). It shows Hollywood blockbusters. Whether a multiplex could nurture a love of film remains to be seen.

90 Preda (2007)

91 In the name of rock 'n' roll, I would have given the series for free so 'cost of acquisition' was not the barrier.

CONCLUSION

1 Ben Page, CEO of Ipsos Mori UK and Ireland, speaking on BBC London Radio, 4 February 2010.

2 The estate agent, Foxton's, looks like a bar from outside with a huge plasma TV screen, which is left on overnight along with the lights, with no regard for energy-saving at a time when ecology is such a pressing global issue.

3 I went to a meeting about 'business rates' (3 February 2010) at Islington Town Hall. It was very frustrating, as independent traders were there to get some answers and help but none of the clerks were able to offer any because there was no government representative. What's more, they all fit into their box, meaning they don't have the power to influence the business rate let alone the initiative to do something to help independent traders. Yet the publicity material for Islington's tourist potential features snapshots of smiling independent traders. I spoke to, among others, newly appointed staff for local commerce, who simply did not have a clue that there was a problem. This begs the question, on what competency do these people get their jobs? The week after the meeting, said person was spinning their image in the local press as the partisan of small traders ('something needs to be done about business rate'). I am cynical (as the job description has no such box to tick) but can only hope that a public servant will start thinking outside the box, as that's the only way towards a solution.

BIBLIOGRAPHY

Books and Journals

Ali, Monica (2003), *Brick Lane* (New York: Scribner)

Anderson, Benedict (1983), *Imagined Communities* (London: Verso)

Banks, Jack (1996), *Monopoly Television: MTV's Quest to Control the Music* (Oxford: Westview Press)

Bell, Martin (1995; 1996 reprint), *In Harm's Way: Reflections of a War-zone Thug* (London: Penguin)

Billig, Michael (1995), *Banal Nationalism* (London: Sage)

Boorman, Neil (2007), *Bonfire of the Brands* (Edinburgh: Canongate)

Boorman, Neil and Pemberton, Daniel (2005), *Devil's Dandruff: Guide to Nightlife* (London: Duckworth)

Boy George and Bright, Spencer (1995), *Take It Like a Man: The Autobiography of Boy George* (London: Panbooks)

Brunsdon, Charlotte and Morley, David (1978), *Everyday Television: 'Nationwide'* (London: BFI)

Carter, Bill (2004), *Fools Rush In* (London: Doubleday)

Cespedes, Vincent (2001), *I Loft You* (Éditions Mille et une nuits)

Cicolini, Alice (2005), *The New English Dandy* (London: Thames and Hudson)

Collin, Matthew (1997; 2009 reprint), *Altered State* (London: Serpent's Tail)

Collin, Matthew (2001; 2004 reprint), *This is Serbia Calling* (London: Serpent's Tail)

Collin, Matthew (2007), *Time of the Rebels* (London: Serpent's Tail)

Coupland, Douglas (1991), *Generation X: Tales for an Accelerated Culture* (London: Abacus)

Dragičević-Šešić, Milena (1994), *Neofolk Kultura: Publika i Njene zvezde* (Novi Sad: Biblioteka Elementi)

Denisoff, Serge (1988; 1991 reprint), *Inside MTV* (New Brunswick: Transaction Publishers)

Elms, Robert (2005; 2006 reprint), *The Way We Wore: A Life in Threads* (London: Picador)

Feineman, Neil (2005), *Geek Chic* (London: Thames and Hudson)

Frank, Thomas (1997), *The Conquest of Cool: Business Culture, Counterculture, and the Rise of Hip Consumerism* (London: University of Chicago Press)

Frith, Simon (1988), *Music for Pleasure* (Cambridge: Polity Press)

Frith, Simon (1993), 'Youth/Music/Television', in S. Frith, A. Goodwin and L. Grossberg (eds) *Sound and Vision: The Music Video Reader* (London: Routledge)

Gitlin, Todd (1983), *Inside Prime Time* (New York: Pantheon Books)

Gordy, Eric (1999), *The Culture of Power in Serbia: Nationalism and the Destruction of Alternatives* (Pennsylvania University Park: Penn State University Press)

Gladwell, Malcolm (2000; 2007 reprint), *The Tipping Point* (London: Abacus)

Goodwin, Andrew (1993), *Dancing in the Distraction Factory: Music Television and Popular Culture* (London: Routledge)

Grant, John (1999), *The New Marketing Manifesto: The 12 Rules for Building Successful Brands in the 21ˢᵗ Century* (London: Orion)

Grossberg, Lawrence (1987), 'The in-difference of television', *Screen*, 28(2): 28-45

Grossberg, Lawrence (1993), 'The media economy of rock culture: cinema, postmodernity and authenticity', in S. Frith, A. Goodwin and L. Grossberg (eds) *Sound and Vision: The Music Video Reader* (London: Routledge)

Gunić, Vehid (1994), *Evropo, Stidi Se* (Oslo: Micro Trykk Offset)

Hadžifejzović, Senad (2002), *Rat Uživo/ War: Live on Air* (Sarajevo: Senad Hadžifejzović)

Harris, John (2003), *The Last Party: Britpop, Blair and the Demise of English Rock* (London: Fourth Estate)

Heath, Joseph and Potter, Andrew (2005), *The Rebel Sell: How the Counter Culture Became Consumer Culture* (Chichester: Capstone Publishing Ltd, a Wiley Company)

Hebdige, Dick (1979), *Subculture: The Meaning of Style* (London: Methuen)

Hermé, Pierre (2008), *Macaron* (éditions Agnès Viérot)

Hesmondhalgh, David (1996), Independent record companies and the democratisation in the popular music industry, PhD thesis, University of London (Goldsmiths' College)

Hicketier, Knut (1996), 'The Media in Germany' in T. Weymouth and B. Lamizet (ed) *Markets and Myths: Forces for Change in the European Media* (New York: Addison Wesely Longman Ltd)

Hobsbawm, Eric (1994), *Age of Extremes* (London: Michael Joseph)

Hollingsworth, Mark and Lansley, Stewart (2009), *Londongrad, From Russia with Cash: The Inside Story of the Oligarchs* (London: Fourth Estate)

Hujić, Alida (Lida) (1999), MTV Europe: an analysis of the channel's attempt to design a programming strategy for a pan-European youth audience, PhD thesis, University of London (Goldsmiths College)

Hujić, Mersija (1996), *Alipašino in Francuski Bataljon* (Sarajevo: Svjetlost)

Keen, Andrew (2007), *The Cult of the Amateur: How Today's Internet is Killing Our Culture and Assaulting Our Economy* (London, Boston: Nicholas Brealey)

Klein, Naomi (2000; reprint 2001), *No Logo* (London: Flamingo)

Kuhn, Raymond (1995), *The Media in France* (London: Routledge)

Kundera, Milan (1984), 'A kidnapped West or culture bows out', *Granta*, 11:93 – 118

Lasn, Kalle (2000), *Culture Jam: How to Reverse America's Suicidal Consumer Binge – And Why We Must* (New York: HarperCollins)

Leland, John (2004), *Hip: The History* (New York: HarperCollins)

Lešić, Zdenko (ed.) (1995), *Children of Atlantis* (Budapest: Central European University Press)

Maffesoli, Michel (1996), *The Time of the Tribes: The Decline of Individualism in Mass Society* (London: Sage Publications)

Martín-Barbero, Jesus (1988), 'Communication from culture: the crisis of the national and the emergence of the popular', *Media, Culture and Society*, 10(4): 447–65

Mattelart, Armand et al. (1984), *International Image Markets: In Search of an Alternative Perspective* (London: Comedia Publishing Group)

Mercer, Kobena (1990), 'Welcome to the jungle: identity and diversity in postmodern politics' in J. Rutherford (ed.), *Identity: Community, Culture, Difference* (London: Lawrence & Wishart Limited)

Melucci, Alberto (1992), 'Youth silence and voice: selfhood and commitment in the everyday experience of adolescents' in J. Fornas and G. Bolin (eds.) *Moves in Modernity* (Stockholm: Almqvist & Wiksell International)

Molyneux, John (1998), 'State of the Art', Issue 79, *International Socialism*, quarterly journal of the Socialist Workers Party (Britain), July

Morey, David (1981), 'The spaces between the programmes: TV continuity' (London: Comedia)

Morley, David and Robbins, Kevin (1995), *Spaces of Identity: Global Media, Electronic Landscapes and Cultural Boundaries* (London: Routledge)

Mort, Frank (1990), 'The politics of consumption' in S. Hall and M. Jacques (eds) *New Times: The Changing Face of Politics in the 1990s* (London: Lawrence & Wishart Limited)

Muir, Greg (2009), *Lucky Kunst: The Rise and Fall of Young British Art* (London: Aurum)

Negus, Keith (1999), *Music Genres and Corporate Cultures* (London and New York: Routledge)

Orwell, George (1946; reprint 2008), *Animal Farm* (London: Penguin)

Orwell, George (1949; reprint 1989), *Nineteen Eighty-Four* (London: Penguin)

Penn, Mark J. (2008), *Microtrends* (London: Penguin)

Rietveld, Hillegonda (1988), *This is Our House: House Music, Cultural Spaces and Technologies* (Aldershot: Ashgate Publishing Limited)

Robertson, A. and Hellman, M. (1997), Identity in the News of Europe: Looking for Traces of Identification in British, French, German and Swedish Television News, New Europe workshop in Bern, 27 February to 4 March

Rodic, Yvan (2010), *Facehunter* (London: Thames and Hudson)

Sagnard, Arnaud (2008), *"Vous êtes sur LA LISTE?": Enquête sur la tyrannie des branchés* (Paris: Éditions du Moment)

Said, Edward (1978), *Orientalism* (Harmondsworth: Penguin)

Sanders, Annika and Seager, Kerry (2009), *Junky Styling: Wardrobe Surgery* (London: A & C Black Publishers Limited)

Schlesinger, Philip (1987), 'On national identity: some conceptions and misconceptions criticized', *Social Science Information*, 26(2): 219–64

Schwartz, Barry (2005), *The Paradox of Choice: Why More is Less* (New York: Perennial HarperCollins)

Segré, Gabriel (2008), *Loft Story ou la Télévision de la Honte: la téléréalité exposée aux rejets* (Paris: L'Harmattan)

Sherrington, Mark (2003), *Added Value: The Alchemy of Brand-Led Growth* (Houndsmill, Basingstoke: Palgrave Macmillan)

Schuman, Scott (2009), *The Sartorialist* (London: Penguin Books Ltd)

Silverstein, Michael and Fiske, Neil (2003), *Trading Up: Why Consumers Want New Luxury Goods and How Companies Create Them* (New York: Portfolio, Penguin Group)

Sparks, Colin (2007), 'Reality TV: the *Big Brother* Phenomenon', *International Socialism* (Issue 114), 9 April

Strange, Steve (2002), *Blitzed* (London: Orion)

Stroud, Dick (2005), *The 50 Plus Market: Why the Future is Age-Neutral When it Comes to Marketing and Branding Strategies* (London: Kogan Page)

Thornton, Sarah (1995), *Club Cultures: Music, Media and Subcultural Capital* (Cambridge: Polity Press)

Vogel, Steven (2007), *Streetwear* (London: Thames and Hudson)

Wark, McKenzie (1994), *Virtual Geography: Living with Global Media Events* (Bloomington: Indiana University Press)

Watters, Ethan (2004), *Urban Tribes: Are friends the New Family?* (London: Bloomsbury)

Webster, Duncan (1989), 'Coca-colonisation and national cultures', *Overhere*, 9(2):64-75

Weisberger, Lauren (2003), *The Devil Wears Prada* (London: HarperCollins)

Willetts, David (2010), *The Pinch: How the Baby Boomers Took Their Children's Future – And Why They Should Give it Back* (London: Atlantic Books)

Williams, Raymond (1963), *Culture and Society 1780-1950* (Harmondsworth: Penguin)

Wolton, Thierry (2008), *Le KGB au pouvoir: le système Poutine* (Paris: Buchet/Chastel)

Press and Market Studies

Bajramović, Dino (2008), 'Alternativna historija Sarajeva se pisala u kafićima', *Slobodna Bosna*, ('Alternative history was written in caffe bars'), 14 August

Bainbridge, Jane (2005), 'Sector Insight: Bottled water – Clear growth: Bottled water manufacturers are innovating to fully exploit the potential of the UK market', Marketing (reproduced on brandrepublic.com), 3 August

'Bling Is Dead, Stealth Wealth Is In' (2007), press release by Mastercard, 27 September

Bok, Lee (2004; updated 2005), *The Little Book of Chavs: The Branded Guide to Britain's New Elite* (Crombie Jardine Publishing)

Boumphrey, Sarah (2007), 'Beyond Bling', *Euromonitor*, 27 August

'Britain is most-indebted rich nation in world', press release, New York Times 23 March 2008

Capell, Kerry (2007), 'Britain's coming credit crisis', *Spiegel International* online, 9 July

Chabbott, Sophia (2009), 'Saying Bye Bye to Bling Bling: How fashion execs will cope now that "luxury" is a dirty word ', portfolio.com, 17 March

Clarke, Steve (1992), 'Rock Conquers Continent', *Variety*, 16 November

Dennen, Richard (2009), 'Frockn Rolla', *Tatler*, January

Durkalić, Masha (2008), 'Ne možemo živjeti u laži i iluziji i očekivati da imamo zdravu budućnost' ('We cannot live a lie and an illusion and expect a healthy future') *Dani*, 15 August

Fletcher, Anthony (2006), 'UK organic food boom driven by health, says report', foodnavigator.com, 3 November

Frankel, Susannah (2002) 'Fashion & Style: Britannia has its Idiosyncratic Way, Always', *Independent*, 12 September

Frith, Maxine (2004), 'Bling kerching: how going downmarket has transformed the luxury goods industry', *Independent*, 29 September

'Germany: New report says organic food sales soaring' (2007), berlinpaper.com, 12 January

'Germany sees organic food boom, even as world food prices soar' (2008), *Associated Press*, 14 June

Lee, Hope (2004), 'A sparkling performance: bottled water in Italy', *Euromonitor*, 13 August

Leigh, David (2006), 'The tax haven that today's super rich City commuters call home', The Guardian, 10 July

MacDonald, Neil 'Locations, Locations, Locations', *Financial Times*, 30 May 2007

(The) Music Issue (2000), *Vanity Fair*, November

Pareles, Jon (1990), 'An Album is Judged Obscene; Rap: Slick, Violent, Nasty and, Maybe Hopeful', New York Times, 17 June

Peters, Sophie (2007), 'Bergère de France tricote finement son avenir', *Les Echos* (*compétences*/marketing), 26 November

Pook, Sally and Fletcher, Richard (2006), 'Did Topshop lose its head over Kate Moss?', *Telegraph*, 6 October

Preda, Gabriela (2007), 'Jugoistočna Evropa pretvara "odliv mozgova" u "priliv"', *Southeast European Times*, 25 June

Prosser, David (2006), 'Britain becomes "never, never land" as personal debt runs out of control', *Independent* online, 28 September

Roberts, Jo (2009), 'Peroni's Fashion Venture Aims to Raise the Brand's Stylish Profile', *Marketing Week*, 12 February

Ruiz, Genevieve (2008), 'Le Bed and Breakfast séduit aussi la clientèle d'affaires', largeur.com, 3 November

Schäuble, Juliane (2007), 'Organic supermarkets boom in Berlin', *Der Tagesspiegel*, 16 January

Simmons, John (2007), 'These Men Are Innocent', *Observer*, 18 February

Simpson, Richard and Cable, Simon (2008), 'Peaches Geldof Accused of Leaving Boutique with £500 Dress Without Paying', *Daily Mail*, 19 April

Ungoed-Thomas, Jonathan and Newell, Claire (2007), 'Focus: Farmers' markets sell "supermarket" foods', *The Times*, 8 April

Visseyrias, Mathilde (2009), 'Une solution bien adaptée aux propriétaires de chambres d'hôtes', *Le Figaro*, 5 January

Vyse, Leah (2005), 'Supermarkets lose out to independent retailers in growing organic market', foodanddrinkeurope.com, 17 November

Woods, Richard (2008), 'Rich list reveals wealthy reap profits under Labour', *Sunday Times*, 27 April

Wyatt, Caroline (2004), 'French rediscover the art of baguettes', news.bbc.co.uk, 18 July

Young, Robb (2007), 'Luxury no longer means loud in Russia', *International Herald Tribune*, 23 November

Index of Protagonists

About the Author

Based in London, operating globally, Dr Lida Hujić is a brand strategist. Best described as a 'chasm translator' between the corporate world and the underground, her expertise involves tapping into alpha trend-setters' networks of which she has insider knowledge to service clients: either at the very beginning of a strategic challenge for market leader brands (new product development; brand positioning or more generally innovation) or at the very end (communication via innovative tactics). She works for blue chip companies and private companies across industries. Equally, she supports hipsters and start-ups in harnessing their creativity. *The First to Know*, which goes some way to shedding a light on this rare combination, is her first book.

For more information about the book and its author, a series of funky films that bring the stories across the two decades to life (in the phases of hip's cross-over from incubation to maturity and commercialisation) as well as regular updates on what's worth knowing and opportunities to get involved, go to: **www.thefirsttoknow.info**.